The Danger Zone Is Everywhere

AMERICAN CROSSROADS

Edited by Earl Lewis, George Lipsitz, George Sánchez, Dana Takagi, Laura Briggs, and Nikhil Pal Singh

The Danger Zone Is Everywhere

How Housing Discrimination Harms
Health and Steals Wealth

George Lipsitz

With a Foreword by Robin D. G. Kelley

UNIVERSITY OF CALIFORNIA PRESS

The publisher and the University of California Press
Foundation gratefully acknowledge the generous support
of the Lawrence Grauman, Jr. Fund.

The publisher and the University of California Press
Foundation also gratefully acknowledge the generous support
of the Constance and William Withey Endowment Fund in
History and Music.

University of California Press
Oakland, California

© 2024 by George Lipsitz

Library of Congress Cataloging-in-Publication Data

Names: Lipsitz, George, author.
Title: The danger zone is everywhere : how housing
    discrimination harms health and steals wealth / George
    Lipsitz.
Other titles: American crossroads ; 73.
Description: Oakland, California : University of
    California Press, [2024] | Series: American Crossroads;
    [vol 73] | Includes bibliographical references and index.
Identifiers: LCCN 2024007933 (print) | LCCN 2024007934
    (ebook) | ISBN 9780520404397 (cloth) | ISBN
    9780520404403 (paperback) | ISBN 9780520404410
    (ebook)
Subjects: LCSH: Discrimination in housing—United
    States. | Racial justice—United States. | Housing and
    health—United States.
Classification: LCC HD7288.76.U5 L57 2024 (print) |
    LCC HD7288.76.U5 (ebook) | DDC 363.5/10973—dc23
    /eng/20240316
LC record available at https://lccn.loc.gov/2024007933
LC ebook record available at https://lccn.loc.gov
    /2024007934

Manufactured in the United States of America

33 32 31 30 29 28 27 26 25 24
10 9 8 7 6 5 4 3 2 1

Contents

Foreword

George Lipsitz is that rare intellectual who genuinely walks the talk *and* talks the walk. Actually, he doesn't walk. He runs, straight into the danger zone, alert—eyes, ears, and heart wide open. He navigates the danger zone with a surveyor's intentionality and a guerrilla's audacity but always in rhythm with the people. The danger zone is anywhere aggrieved people are struggling: for their lives, livelihood, safety, justice, freedom, and the power to determine their own future. The danger zone, as George continually shows us, is also a place of learning. He has spent the better part of half a century developing and practicing a philosophy of "situated" scholarship, an engaged intellectual practice involving the production and application of new knowledge to social movements. All of his writings exemplify situated scholarship at its best, whether he is interrogating the enduring impact of racism, the weapon of popular culture, the making of an organizer, the crisis in the academy, or the vagaries of neoliberalism. And he understands better than anyone that to be "situated" means to be committed to transforming the world while always remaining embedded in community and movement. This is the definition of "organic intellectual," and it is a perfect description of George Lipsitz. In fact, from the moment I first met George thirty-five years ago, I thought of him as the US version of Stuart Hall, the radical Black British intellectual who cofounded the Centre for Contemporary Cultural Studies at Birmingham University as a response to social crises in England.

George walks the talk but is prone to erasing his own footprints. He refuses to toot his own horn, never seeks credit or appreciation for his contributions, and rarely mentions his movement history. The brief bit of personal history he discloses in this book doesn't scratch the surface. He has had a long relationship with the progressive wing of the labor movement (in Wisconsin, St. Louis, Minneapolis, San Diego, and elsewhere); worked tirelessly on behalf of migrant and excluded workers; played a leading role in antiracist struggles in California and across the country; worked in and with community-based alternative education spaces; and offered solidarity and service to frontline organizers in the danger zones here and abroad—from New Orleans to Okinawa, East LA to Greater St. Louis, and many points in between. And, as is reflected in this extraordinary book, he has dedicated his life to the struggle for fair, affordable, safe housing for all.

The Danger Zone Is Everywhere reveals the hidden relationship among housing, residential segregation, and health—a relationship created and structured by gendered racial capitalism. In the simplest terms, for most white folks homes mean more wealth; for Black, Brown, and Indigenous folks housing means poor health. De facto segregation not only determines property values but also creates food deserts and severely limits access to health care, transportation, libraries, green space, and clean air. Instead, residents get dilapidated housing, housing insecurity, vermin, lead paint, respiratory illnesses, gun violence, trauma, surveillance, trigger-happy police, poor schools, and prison. They are fleeced by landlords, insurance companies, grocers, liquor stores, check-cashing joints, utility and water companies, and the state—in the form of excessive fees, fines, and regressive sales taxes accompanied by little to no services. They are subject to landfills, toxic fumes, lead poisoning, "heat islands," and the worst effects of the climate catastrophe. And high rates of unemployment, the diminution of the welfare state, overpolicing, and what sociologists call the "spatial mismatch" between decent jobs and low-income communities add to the endemic problem of housing insecurity.

George has been thinking and writing about these issues for most of his adult life. Growing directly from his activism, books such as *The Possessive Investment in Whiteness* and *How Racism Takes Place* laid the foundations for *Danger Zone*. In them, he exposed how so-called "color-blind" social policy not only delegitimizes race-based explanations for inequality but also camouflages its deleterious effects on aggrieved communities of color while perpetually rewarding white property owners with equity and a publicly funded criminal legal system to protect its boundaries. But unlike his previous work, *Danger Zone* takes on the health care system directly. He proves that health care policy is as consequential as housing policy in determining the life chances of poor and working-class Black, Brown, and Indigenous communities. He reveals how inequities in access to health care have been deepened by neoliberalization, from welfare state–backed care in the form of Medicare and Medicaid programs to so-called "managed care," or market-based corporate models that emphasize reducing costs, privatizing medicine, and limiting treatment for the underinsured and those who cannot pay.

So what is to be done? The answer, George insists, can be found in the danger zone, where people are already in motion, creating solutions and fighting the forces bent on turning suffering and precarity into profit. The danger zone is where we all must run, where George exhorts all self-proclaimed activist-scholars to be "propositional as well as oppositional." He has always been propositional, always sought answers not only in his exhaustive research but from deliberative democratic practice, from past mistakes and lessons learned, from a critical analysis of crisis and the expectation of a just future. The movements featured at the end of the book all treat health care and housing as collective public resources and human rights rather than as commodities to be sold to the highest bidder. The lesson is clear: health and housing justice is indivisible, and the absence of justice is harming and killing too many of our people. Enter *Danger Zone,* read carefully, and prepare for the struggle ahead. This book can save lives.

Robin D. G. Kelley
Los Angeles
February 25, 2024

Acknowledgments

The path we travel on the journey to social justice is long and the way is hard. But the people we meet along the way—those whom we accompany and who accompany us—make it all worthwhile. I have been fortunate to speak with, work with, and learn from a wide array of readers and interlocutors as I developed this book, and I wish to express my deep gratitude to them here.

Early drafts of the book were shaped by conversations with Tricia Rose, Sarah Rios, Anna Chatillon, Raphaëlle Rabanes, Jordan Camp, Christina Heatherton, Johari Jabir, Lundy Braun, Nan Enstad, Annie Hikido, Jasmine Kelekay, Danielle Purifoy, Ingrid Waldron, Lawrence Brown, Louise Seamster, Andrew W. Kahrl, John Robinson III, and Shanna Smith. Sections of individual chapters benefited greatly the advice of Elizabeth Korver-Glenn, Juana María Rodríguez, and Bernadette Atuahene. Representatives of activist groups whose work is described in the book from East Los Angeles, Halifax, New Orleans, Grand Rapids, Oakland, and San Diego vetted those sections for accuracy. Discussions with Omar G. Ramirez helped me begin to comprehend the generative possibilities of restorative cultural arts practice/praxis. Part of my readiness to learn from these mobilizations originated in my previous work with Asian Immigrant Women Advocates in Oakland, Project Row Houses in Houston, and Students at the Center in New Orleans.

As I confront the danger zones that are everywhere I treasure the accompaniment of freedom-loving friends, allies, and teachers. These include representatives of the Black resistance tradition of New Orleans: Kalamu ya Salaam, Sunni Patterson, Jerome Morgan, Shana M. griffin, Jim Randels, Ashley Jones, Dave Cash, Robert Jones, and Daniel Rideau; the artivistas of East L.A.—Martha Gonzalez, Quetzal Flores, Juana Mena Ochoa, Amy Kitchener, and Betty Marin; and activist engaged scholars Diane Fujino, Jesus Hernandez, Daniel HoSang, Lorgia Garcia-Peña, John-Carlos Perea, Jessica Perea, Walter Johnson, Rachel Buff, Celeste-Marie Bernier, and Jonathan Gomez.

Through my work as board chair of the African American Policy Forum I have had the honor of working with Kimberlé Crenshaw and Luke Harris as they honed and refined the theory and practice of intersectionality and critical race theory. Parts of chapter 5 in this book originated in the article "In an Avalanche Every Snowflake Pleads Not Guilty: The Collateral Consequences of Mass Incarceration and Impediments to Women's Fair Housing Rights," which appeared in volume 59, number 6 of the *UCLA Law Review* in August 2012 and was based on my presentation at a symposium on women, race, and criminalization that Crenshaw organized.

I have great respect, admiration, and gratitude for the fighters for fair housing that I have encountered over the years, whose activism informs and inspires the arguments in this book. Amy Nelson and Caroline Peattie offered valuable feedback on the sections in this book on litigation relating to appraisal discrimination. The book's broader arguments about fair housing owe an enormous debt to Mary Scott Knoll, who introduced me to the struggle and to her colleagues Sharon Kinlaw and Michelle White. Service on the board of directors of the National Fair Housing Alliance gave me the privilege and pleasure of learning from and working with Shanna Smith, Lisa Rice, Jim McCarthy, Vince Curry, John Petruszak, Keenya Robertson, Wayne Dawson, Lila Hackett, Anne Houghtaling, Erin Kemple, and Nancy Haynes. The attention I devote in chapter 1 of this book to the particular injuries that children experience from housing discrimination originated in my work with my friend and colleague Vince Larkins on a fair housing case that revolved around those injuries. Opportunities to attend and present research at fair housing laws and litigations conferences have enabled me to savor and draw from the profound wisdom of Michael Seng, F. Willis Caruso, Chris Brancart, Chancela Al-Mansour, Nadine Cohen, and many others. Being a co-presenter with Scott Chang at many of those meetings gave me opportunities to learn from and be inspired by his profound understanding of both the limits and the possibilities of the law.

I am deeply grateful to UC Press executive editor Niels Hooper for our many years of work together and for his support of this book. Anonymous reviewers of the manuscript provided valuable comments and criticisms of its ideas and arguments, while the sharp eyes and astute critical judgment of copyeditor Elisabeth Magnus greatly enhanced the clarity and precision of the final version. I thank my artist friends, mentors, and interlocutors Omar G. Ramirez and Shana M. griffin for allowing me to use their creative works to illustrate my arguments.

Everything I think, say, write, and do is informed and inspired by the presence in my life of Barbara Tomlinson. I treasure her intelligence, integrity, character, and courage, and thank her for all that has been made possible by her accompaniment.

Introduction

Housing, Health, and Proximity to Toxicity

Housing discrimination harms health and steals wealth. Residential racial segregation is an economic injustice but also a public health menace. Denying people access to safe, sound, and secure housing imposes artificial impediments to acquiring assets that can appreciate in value and be inherited by future generations. It compels many members of aggrieved racialized groups to live their lives in what Tricia Rose describes as "proximity to toxicity,"[1] dwelling in polluted and under-resourced places where life spans are shorter and the burdens of illness are higher. Even relatively high-income and wealthy nonwhite property owners suffer from housing discrimination. They are confined to an artificially limited segment of the market where dwellings are less likely to appreciate in value and more likely to be close to toxic hazards. Moreover, municipal, state, and federal governments have consistently designed, funded, and implemented policies that destroy once-stable neighborhoods inhabited by members of racialized groups in order to replace them with taxpayer-subsidized convention centers, sports arenas, civic centers, office buildings, and luxury housing, and with highways designed to increase home values in areas reserved largely for white residency.[2] Whether their incomes or wealth holdings are high or low, members of aggrieved groups targeted for housing discrimination endure arbitrary, irrational, and unnecessary incidents of discrimination, displacement, and dispossession that combine to undermine their individual and collective health, wealth, and well-being.

1

The Danger Zone Is Everywhere focuses on the factors that make housing insecurity and poor health key components of an unjust, destructive, and even deadly racial order. Residential segregation and group health disparities are usually addressed separately in medical and legal practice, public policy, and academic inquiry. They are treated as discrete and unrelated processes. This book argues that they are mutually constitutive, that health is as much social as it is biological, and that race is a political construction, not a biological entity. The injuries inflicted by housing discrimination have serious medical consequences that produce additional obstacles to accessing education and employment. Unfair access to housing subjects people from aggrieved groups to endless cycles of dispossession, displacement, disinvestment, and debt; to predatory and punitive policing; and to illness, addiction, and incarceration.

EXAMINING HOUSING AND HEALTH CARE TOGETHER

Shortly after the passage of the Fair Housing Act in 1968, Lester Breslow, president of the American Public Health Association, touted the ways in which improving access to safe, stable, and affordable housing could affect the health of the public. "In the long run," he declared, "housing may be more important to health than hospitals."[3] Breslow's acknowledgment of housing as a key social determinant of health marked a clear departure from the long and ignoble history of practices in public health—premised on assumptions that poverty is an inheritable trait and that poor health among racialized groups is caused by their allegedly inferior biological makeup or their dysfunctional behaviors.[4]

Contemporary research documents the continuing salience of Breslow's formulation. Despite the gradual and continuing expansion of the coverage and remedies enabled by the Fair Housing Act, a collective national failure to implement fully its clear mandate to "affirmatively further fair housing" continues to damage the physical and mental health of the nation. David Williams and Chiquita Collins established nearly two decades ago that residential segregation is the single most important cause of the disproportionate exposure to health hazards among people of color in the United States.[5] In 2019, Williams and other colleagues emphasized segregation's continuing effects, especially its impediments to education and employment opportunities and its disproportionate exposure of people to physical and emotional stressors, as well as its association with low birth weights and preterm births, higher risk of myocardial infarction, early onset of sickness, rapid progression of disease, and lower rates of surviving illnesses.[6]

Examining health in relation to housing reveals the importance of what researchers call the social and structural determinants of health.[7] Racial disparities in health are caused by disproportionate exposure to toxic air, water, and land; by residency in places with limited access to fresh food, pharmacies, and physicians; by few opportunities for healthful exercise and recreation; and by the physical and psychic stressors produced by race-based discrimination. These social and structural determinants of poor health do not occur in a vacuum: they are a consequence of racialized subordination structured inside a variety of institutions, some of which at first glance might appear to have little to do with health or housing. This book connects the distribution of determinants of health to discriminatory practices in mortgage lending, insurance risk algorithms, home value appraisals, tax assessments, municipal fines and fees, policing, incarceration, transportation, and urban planning. These structural processes emerge from histories of slavery, Indigenous dispossession, coloniality, labor exploitation, sexism, and misogyny that reproduce and reinforce racism every day in the present. Working together they make up the system of structural racism.

Medical and legal professionals and the public at large generally underestimate the importance of social and structural determinants of health. They most often attribute racially disparate health outcomes to the conduct of individuals in managing personal health care regimes or to immutable genetic characteristics. Both of these attributions underestimate the importance of social and structural factors. In 2011 the Centers for Disease Control, discussing the variables that shape ill and good health, concluded that the elements that most people assume to be decisive in producing physical well-being—such as personal choices about diet, exercise, and use or avoidance of damaging substances—account for only 20 percent of individual health outcomes. The quality and frequency of professional health care shape an additional 20 percent. A mere 5 percent can be traced to genetic inheritance. Significantly, most of the remaining 55 percent comes from the factors most closely related to housing discrimination and the racial wealth gap: from the social determinants of health shaped by racism. An emphasis in medical research and practice on the genetic codes of individuals obscures the significance of the zip codes in which members of aggrieved racialized groups live, work, and play.[8]

Overemphasis on the genetic makeup or health regimes of individuals directs excess attention to the roles played by medicines and medical

VARIABLES THAT SHAPE ILL AND GOOD HEALTH OF AGGRIEVED RACIALIZED GROUPS

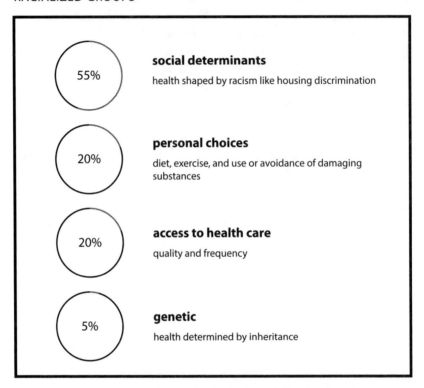

FIGURE 1. Variables that shape health. Graphic by Omar G. Ramirez, based on Centers for Disease Prevention, "Social Determinants of Health: Frequently Asked Questions," 2011, no longer accessible online but cited in Kathryn Strother Ratcliff, *The Social Determinants of Health: Looking Upstream* (Cambridge: Polity Press, 2017), 2, 12.

technologies in improving collective well-being while diverting attention away from advances enabled by adjustments to social and structural forces such as safe and affordable housing. Epidemiologists and historians of health generally agree that most of the reasons for increased life expectancy during the past two centuries emerged out of nonmedical advances in public health, advances achieved through measures such as improved sewage management and garbage collection procedures, cleaner air created by the elimination of coal-burning furnaces, removal of lead from gasoline, safer and more abundant foods, improved housing conditions, and more equitable distributions of wealth. Yet responses to surveys indicate that respondents think that 80 percent of the improvements in life expectancy should be attributed to "modern medicine," virtually ignoring how changes in social and structural determinants of health have led to longer lives. As Gordon Lindsay and colleagues conclude, these beliefs contribute to overfunding the sector of the economy that treats health problems medically while underfunding many of the practices that are most effective in preventing illness. Nearly 20 percent of the Gross Domestic Product in the United States goes to technology-dominated health care interventions while proven and cost-effective public health and housing programs remain starved for funds.[9] Misguided beliefs contribute to the underestimation of the importance to health of available, affordable, accessible, safe, and secure housing.

THE BIOMEDICAL MODEL OF RACE AND DISEASE

Medical and scientific literature past and present overwhelmingly presents race as a biological category. It also tends to present genetic differences as the most plausible hypothesis for observed racial differences in outcomes. This biomedical model of health combines with the tort model of injury in law to offer single-axis solutions to what are almost always multiple-axis problems.

The biomedical model that dominates health care is an individual model. It posits a healthy body that has been temporarily injured and can be restored to a previous state of good health by treatment. It imagines a specific discrete cause for every illness and treats the body as a machine made up of parts that can be fixed or replaced.[10] In attending largely to health at the scale of individual bodies, the biomedical approach treats symptoms of racial health disparities but does not challenge the causal spatial and racial ecologies that relegate people of different races to different places that are marked by grossly unequal and unjust health hazards. For example, the incursion of COVID-19 has been described as a "pandemic" for the nation as a whole, but for Black and Latinx people it should properly be considered a "syndemic": a medical crisis that is shaped and exacerbated by a complex confluence of place-based racialized health and housing vulnerabilities.[11]

The biomedical model of disease treats race wrongly and inaccurately as a biological category rather than a political construction and for that reason leads to ineffective, inefficient, and even counterproductive medical practices. People in the United States spend more on health care than people in any other country in the world, yet the health care system produces declining life expectancies, high rates of maternal childbirth mortality, and stark racial health disparities.[12] Compared to their peers in Japan, Germany, France, and other well-resourced nations, young people in the United States are twice as likely to die between the ages of fifteen and twenty-four. The infant mortality rate in the United States is three times higher than the rate in similar nations.[13]

THE TORT MODEL OF INJURY IN LAW

The struggle for racial justice is impeded by overemphasis on the individualized biomedical approach to illness and infirmity in medicine, but it is equally undermined by the dominance of the tort model of injury in law. Both of these frameworks privilege individual and domain-specific solutions to social problems. They deny medical and legal practitioners the tools needed to address and redress racist injuries. The tort model focuses on harm done to individuals caused by malevolence, carelessness, or neglect: actions that are presumed to disrupt the normal workings of society. It imagines that the injured party can be "made whole"—that is, restored to the previous state before the injury—by personal punishment of perpetrators or personal compensation awarded to plaintiffs. This premise encourages attorneys to view housing discrimination as largely individual, intentional, and aberrant. Yet the perpetration of discrimination in housing comes not only from individuals but from forces and actors who are dispersed, not acting consciously in concert, and grounded in a fully linked and mutually constitutive network of racist subordination that is systemic, structural, collective, cumulative, and continuing.

The biomedical model of disease and the tort model of injury in law are destructively confined to the level of the individual. They encourage medical providers and attorneys to assume that their fields are not connected to each other, that racial disparities in one sphere do not shape or reflect disparities in others. This one-at-a-time approach occludes the larger system in which racial disparities are located, a system that Barbara Reskin accurately describes as "über" or "meta discrimination." In this case, the whole is greater than the sum of its parts because injustices that appear in different institutions are mutually reinforcing, As Reskin argues, racism in multiple domains produces effects that none of them in isolation can produce on their own, effects that "implant *über* discrimination into our minds, culture, and institutions."[14]

Systemic and structural problems require systemic and structural solutions. But efforts to litigate and legislate for fair housing generally ignore the health costs of discrimination, while physicians, clinicians, and public health officials rarely reckon with the ways in which unjust and illegal housing discrimination creates and exacerbates illness and infirmity. This book identifies and endorses ways of seeing and acting upon health and housing intersectionally, structurally, and systemically. Good health and good housing are connected; efforts to promote access to each must attend to the other.

THE DANGER ZONE IS EVERYWHERE

Housing and health care—like nearly every other major social, economic, and educational practice and institution—work as parts of an interconnected network that perpetuates structural and systemic racism. The resulting condition is captured by the title of a Percy Mayfield song recorded by Ray Charles in 1961. The lyrics of that song assert: "The danger zone is everywhere." Racist danger does reside in the medical clinic and the fair housing courtroom obviously, but it festers as well in places that initially might seem to have little to do with race: in patterns of home value appraisal and tax assessment, in rubrics of risk in property and auto insurance, in predatory policing and mass incarceration, and in practices of urban planning. The economic and social injuries inflicted on members of targeted groups because of racial discrimination in these spheres have deadly medical and economic consequences for them and for society at large.

Yet precisely because the danger zone is everywhere, there is opportunity everywhere to join with others to forge new tactics and strategies for racial justice. Systems and structures created by humans can be dismantled by humans and replaced with better ways of knowing, thinking, and living. This book describes a wide range of work under way where people from many different backgrounds in many different realms of life join together to promote health justice and housing justice in response to the conjunctural crises of our times. Their work evidences the urgency people feel to resist unlivable destinies.

The evidence, ideas, and arguments that I present in this book reflect things that I have learned from my nearly sixty years of participation in organized movements for social change, as well from my forty-five years as an academic researcher, teacher, and writer focused on the forces that skew life chances and opportunities along racial lines. I have participated in struggles for housing and health justice as a member of the board of directors of the National Fair Housing Alliance and the Fair Housing Council of San Diego, as a speaker at fair housing laws and litigations conferences and continuing legal education courses, and as a researcher and expert witness in court cases. For ten years I served as chair of the board of directors of the African American Policy Forum. I became aware of the importance of arts-based collaborative campaigns for health and housing justice through my work with Latinx activists in the Building Healthy Communities in Boyle Heights project in East Los Angeles staged by the Alliance for California Traditional Arts and the California Endowment, as well as with Black activists in the Free-Dem Foundations and Students at the Center initiatives in New Orleans contesting the effects of mass criminalization and incarceration in that city. Conducting equity-oriented collaborative community-based research and accompanying activist groups in struggles have led me to conversations and collaborations with grassroots activists in Ferguson and Flint, Milwaukee and Memphis, East Austin in Texas and West Palm Beaches in Florida, the inner-ring suburbs of north St. Louis County, and the southern suburbs of Chicago. Much of what appears in this book originated in those activist meetings and mobilizations.

I identify myself and am identified by others as a white, cisgender, heterosexual male. I attempt, however, to situate my ideas and actions inside the generative political and intellectual traditions of Black feminist intersectionality and the Black Radical Tradition. I am not claiming to be an expert on Black feminist theory, but rather see myself as someone who has been educated by it profoundly through my work with Kimberlé Crenshaw and the African American Policy Forum, by a long history of learning from and with Tricia Rose, and by the occasions where I have shared spaces and been in dialogue with Black womanist cultural workers Sunni Patterson and Shana M. griffin. My ideas and analyses have also been shaped by Black men committed to Black feminism, including Robin D. G. Kelley, Luke Harris, Devon Carbado, and Kalamu ya Salaam. My commitment to the Black Radical Tradition emanates from being a colleague, admirer, and dedicated reader of writings by Cedric Robinson, learning from him that the collective consciousness and ontological totality of Black struggles for freedom and justice are generative points of entry into critiquing and contesting all of the forms of dehumanization that turn difference into domination. Robinson's framework condensed and crystallized intellectually much of what I had previously learned experientially from interactions with my friend and teacher Ivory Perry, an organic intellectual whose years of dedicated direct action protests and community organization in St. Louis produced my earliest education on matters of race and justice.

Nearly everything I think, say, and write about social justice draws on the profound wisdom that I have observed in accompaniment with activists from aggrieved racialized groups. The restorative cultural arts practice/praxis projects of East Los Angeles *artivistas*, especially Rosanna Esparza Ahrens, Ofelia Esparza, Quetzal Flores, Martha Gonzales, and Omar G. Ramirez, guide the arguments and analyses I make throughout this book, but especially in chapter 7. My work with Asian Immigrant Women Advocates in Oakland opened my eyes to the importance of intersectionality as a social movement strategy and to the value of democratic discussions and deliberations for cultivating capacities for solidarity and self-activity among working people.

As a white person drawing on the profound wisdom of activists from aggrieved racialized communities, I inhabit a particularly perilous danger zone. Being ascribed and treated as white can create intellectual enfeeblement because it relies on living with evil and being taught to lie about it. The privileges and preferences allocated to me because of my whiteness no doubt lead me to miss particular practices and ramifications of white supremacy that are important to understand. This makes it likely that any foray I make into writing about race or acting against racism runs the risks of replicating and reinforcing rather than reducing the calculated cruelties of white supremacy. But mistakes can be corrected, while silence about injustice is inexcusable.

Meaningful change cannot be formulated abstractly or forecast prophetically by me or anyone else. Instead it must be forged collectively inside social movement mobilizations: in the work of fair housing councils and public health collectives, in alternative learning circles and arts-based community-building projects, in community gardens and community land trusts, and in all the other diverse and dispersed circles of mutual respect, accountability, and accompaniment that are emerging from many different but interconnected crises.

Struggles for housing and health justice have the potential to revitalize civil society, to replace isolation and atomization with a rich, interactive, responsible, and accountable public life. The radical revolution in values and practices that is emerging is not the province of any one profession, discipline, or social group. It requires the full participation of the greatest possible number of people from the broadest possible range of social positions. This book is aimed at physicians, clinicians, and other health care professionals, at attorneys, advocates, and academic legal researchers, at social workers and urban planners. Yet the changes that are needed cannot emanate exclusively from people credentialed by social institutions as specialists and experts. This book highlights the actions of neighborhood community-building and development activists, environmental justice advocates, campaigners for livable wages, prison abolitionists, and activists insisting on the dignity and democratic rights of people deemed disabled. It shows how health and housing justice alike are impeded by hate crimes, police violence, and draconian immigration surveillance, incarceration, and deportation policies.

FAIR HOUSING ADVOCACY AND ACTIVISM

The people who perpetrate and benefit most from racial housing discrimination reap unearned gains and unfair material rewards that enable them to accumulate wealth and to hoard for themselves a wide range of resources, opportunities, amenities, and advantages. The Fair Housing Act of 1968 was structured to solve this problem by mandating all entities receiving government funds to take steps "to affirmatively further fair housing" and to provide individuals and groups with access to forms of litigation set up to secure justice and to compensate victims. As amended in 1988 and expanded by creative litigation, this law provides an indispensable mechanism for promoting housing and health justice. Its existence has enabled the creation of local nonprofit fair housing agencies mobilized together through the National Fair Housing Alliance. Fair housing advocacy has helped millions of people to acquire assets that appreciate in value and can be passed down across generations, and to secure better living conditions in the present.

Yet despite decades of litigation, legislation, administration, organization, mobilization, education, and agitation, most instances of housing discrimination remain unchallenged and unimpeded. Even when fair housing litigation is successful, judgments and settlements generally secure relief that is inadequate for rectifying the devastating damages to health and wealth caused by discrimination. There is an urgent need for those who see themselves as bystanders—disconnected from struggles for meaningful change—to become upstanders, to become educated and impelled to take action. Full enforcement of existing municipal, state, and federal fair housing laws would help, as would new forms of creative litigation and legislation to increase damage awards and expand the range of protected categories.

This legal realm is important for fair housing. Law sets the rules by which society operates. Racial subordination in the United States has long been constructed, supported, and maintained by laws with overt and covert racist effects. As Dayna Bowen Matthew asserts, law in the United States has been and continues to be "the primary mechanism by which structural racism prevails."[15] The full potential of the movement for fair housing, however, extends far beyond the law. It resides in the potential of struggles for fair housing to revitalize civil society and mobilize active and engaged communities. Fair housing advocacy and activism can create counterpublics working for policies capable of advancing housing and health justice in many different spheres of life.

The groups who suffer from the fatal couplings of housing discrimination and damaged health because of racism are often described passively as "disadvantaged," a term that obscures the intentions, agency, and consequences of those who actively "take advantage" of them. Their experiences of poverty, hunger, and housing insecurity are treated as merely unfortunate consequences of what are assumed to be their inadequate individual behaviors or their deficient collective culture. Their disproportionate health problems are attributed—wrongly—either to genetic properties presumed to be racially determined or to their alleged failures to follow recommended health, diet, and exercise regimens. By individualizing what are in fact collective social conditions, and by ignoring the ways in which legal practice and precedent perpetuate inequity, the designation of "disadvantage" directs attention away from the actual causes of racial economic and health disparities. These practices occlude the ways in which housing discrimination concentrates poverty, compelling its targets to live in polluted areas that have insufficient access to fresh food, physicians, and pharmacies; that are isolated from employment opportunities and access to transportation; that host underfunded and poorly equipped schools; that experience high levels of transience and predatory policing; and that face perpetual impediments to asset accumulation and wealth building.

Even when members of aggrieved racialized groups have high incomes and own their own homes, they find that racist practices compel them to make higher down payments, contend with inflated interest and insurance rates, pay higher taxes, and secure less appreciation in the value of their homes than whites who own comparable dwellings. Class injuries are experienced and exacerbated because of racism. Study after study has documented that middle- and high-income people in aggrieved racialized groups are more likely to live near toxic hazards than their white counterparts; that government agencies impose much higher penalties on polluters of white neighborhoods than on polluters of neighborhoods inhabited by members of aggrieved racial groups; and that exposure to polluted air, toxic dirt and dust, and contaminated water depends more on race than class.[16] At the other end of the class continuum, impoverished white people find it easier to access housing in resource-rich neighborhoods than low-income Black shelter seekers, who are routinely limited to living in dilapidated, unsafe, and health-damaging areas. Even in federally funded and subsidized low-income rental housing, impoverished white residents disproportionately secure units that are less expensive but of higher quality that those available to their Black counterparts.[17]

HEALTH AND WEALTH DISPARITIES

This book highlights racial disparities in health and wealth. Measurements of these disparities vary depending upon the design and execution of the research, the year in which the research is conducted, and the range of populations and health and wealth indicators studied. None of these variables, however, change the evident, clear, and consistent patterns demonstrating the skewing of opportunities and life chances in the United States and around the world along racial lines. Members of aggrieved racialized communities suffer from artificial and arbitrary exclusions from opportunities to rent or own housing, and those exclusions have racially disparate impacts on their physical and economic well-being.

Disparities need to be treated carefully and fully contextualized. Emphasis on racial disparities can lead people to think erroneously that the problem is only the skewed distribution of injuries, rather than the injuries themselves. The health and wealth injuries that are distributed disproportionately by racism should not exist at all. Overemphasis on disparity can wrongly lead people to presume that the terrible suffering caused by housing insecurity and inadequate health care would be fine if only it affected all racialized groups equally. It is, however, precisely the racist sorting that society relies on that makes poor health and poor housing persist because it makes them seem like natural, necessary, and inevitable consequences of racial difference, hiding the ways in which the housing and health care systems are innately unjust, inefficient, and predatory.

Focusing only on racial disparities rather than the injustices built into the health care and housing systems can lead to focusing attention wrongly on *race* rather than on *racism*, to assuming that biological or behavioral factors make members of aggrieved racialized groups unfit for access to health and wealth. This produces policies that focus on fixing the victims of health and housing injustice rather than fixing the structures and institutions that systematically harm them. In addition, emphasis on racial disparities often leads researchers to fail to come to grips with the ways in which racism is not experienced as a stand-alone variable, but always takes place in conjunction with other social identities (class, gender, sexuality) and is attached to a wide range of asymmetrical power relations.

A singular focus on health disparities can make it seem as if white people receive optimal care and that the only remedy members of aggrieved racialized groups should receive is to be brought up to the status of their white peers. Yet racial disparities are symptoms of an entire failed system, one that privileges profits over people and tethers medical decisions to the pursuit of maximal profits by a wide range of actors including insurance firms, medical supply companies, and pharmaceutical marketers. All seekers of medical care are harmed by practices that portray good health as a solely a commodity to be purchased by individuals rather than a public resource that needs to be nurtured collectively and cooperatively. Public health is grievously harmed rather than helped by the biomedical-consumer model based on what Ruha Benjamin astutely describes as "a kind of pathological self-interest that masquerades as independence."[18]

It is far easier to study health and housing injustices than to do something about them. What Benjamin describes as the "datafication" of injustice acknowledges unjust differences between races but evades dealing with how to solve them.[19] Studies of health, housing, and race rarely connect readers to active and ongoing social movements in the process of creating active and engaged publics committed to health, wealth, and housing justice. These connections appear repeatedly throughout this book.

BECOMING AGGRIEVED

Housing discrimination and health disparities are caused, not by the race of their targets, but rather by the racism deployed against them. We do not know anything meaningful about individuals by attaching racial descriptors to them, except for their connection to histories of negative ascription and domination on the one hand, and of resistance and affirmation on the other. For that reason, when I write about the injustices facing Black, Indigenous, Latinx, Asian American, and other groups, I refer to them in the aggregate as "aggrieved racialized populations." This term emphasizes that people are not racialized by biology but rather by social and political practices, processes, institutions, structures, and systems. There are no races; but because people believe race exists, racism persists. Race is a biological fiction, but racialization and racism are social facts. It is the actions of people that make race come into being as a category and that give race its determinate social power. A secondary definition of the word *aggrieved* focuses on it as an expression of grief or injury, but this is not the sense in which it is used in this book. The primary definition of what it means to be aggrieved is suffering from infringements and denials of rights, being treated wrongly and unjustly, and experiencing affliction and distress.

Anthropologist Laurence Ralph identifies becoming aggrieved not as a mere misfortune but rather as an achievement. For him, becoming aggrieved entails recognition of injustice and an intention to take action in response to it.[20] The term *misfortune* applies accurately to the hatred and the structural and systemic discrimination that dole out degrees of mistreatment, disrespect, distress, suffering, stress, and subordination. Ralph argues, however, that becoming aggrieved entails something more. In his formulation, it involves understanding that these conditions are unfair and unjust, that they are experienced collectively rather than simply individually, and that they are caused by racism.

Ralph's ethnography of a Black neighborhood in Chicago reveals how the pervasive presence of premature death haunts the community. Police killings and intragroup violence along with high rates of maternal and infant mortality—as well as deaths from cancer, heart attacks, and other medical conditions—make grief an ever-present element in local life. Police power, economic exploitation, and medical neglect treat Black lives as disposable, render Black suffering illegible, and portray lost Black lives as not worthy of mourning. Being forced to repress or mask grief produces levels of rage and resentment that become misrepresented by people in power as evidence of irresponsibility or mental illness.

Ralph cites Jonathan Metzl's historical study of how the medical profession in the 1850s embraced Samuel Cartwright's diagnosis of rebellion in the era when slavery was legal. Cartwright argued that enslaved people who damaged slaveholder property or who ran away from the plantations evidenced a mental illness that he named drapetomania—a condition to be cured only by whipping. Metzl shows that more than a century later, in 1968, one of the most prestigious psychiatry journals featured an article that attributed militant opposition to white racism by Black people as a sign of schizophrenia and a manifestation of what the authors called the "protest psychosis." Thus more than a century after the end of legal slavery, peer-reviewed publications authored and vetted by distinguished and expert medical professionals interpreted Black resentment of racism as a sign of mental illness rather than as a reasoned, logical, and appropriate response to mistreatment.[21] Anger provoked by unjust conditions can often actually make positive contributions to mental health when it equips people with motivation and resolve to fight back against the social problems that produce and exacerbate grief.[22]

A medicalized understanding of racism and racial disparities persists today, imposing an individualized model of social behavior and mental health on communities whose linked fate demands a collective response. The dominant psychological model holds that when a community is faced with premature death a liminal period of mourning should lead to eventual acceptance and moving on. The community that Ralph studies takes a different path. Its members refuse to repress or mask their grief and instead channel it into acts of collective caretaking. They embrace a woman who seems to have been driven quite mad by her son's murder, accepting her anguished shrieks and cries, and accommodating her seemingly irrational demands. Rather than shunning her or sending her off for treatment by outsiders, they develop a communal framework for care, a framework aimed not just at coping with death but at developing a resolute and collectively enabling affirmation of the value of the lives of members of their group. Ralph describes becoming aggrieved as a way of attempting to make productive and positive use of sorrow, anger, grief, and pain. The solidarity of becoming aggrieved is thus both therapeutic and subversive, extending care and accompaniment to those who share a linked fate while foreshadowing the possibility of an alternative public sphere where Black aspirations and affirmations will be understood and valued rather than feared and repressed.

The disadvantages that flow from many forms of housing discrimination and medical racism can also be seen as provocations that can enable communities to become aggrieved by identifying and contesting the structures and systems that oppress them, and that impel them to generate new approaches to housing and health capable of benefiting everyone. This book argues for the importance of learning from, and being in dialogue and accompaniment with, the oppositional and propositional actions of aggrieved groups. The term *aggrieved racialized groups* offers a way of viewing the fights against housing discrimination and medical racism as harbingers of new social relations, structures, and systems.

CORE ARGUMENTS AND IDEAS

Part I delineates links between the racial health gap and the racial wealth gap, and explains the necessity of understanding and addressing them as parts of a mutually constitutive totality, rather than as independent entities. Chapter 1 starts with a focus on the harm done to children's health and their families' wealth by housing discrimination. It argues that the precautionary principle of pediatric care that requires physicians to attend to all factors that impede healthful early development should make fair housing a primary concern within medical practice. Precautionary principles deployed in pediatric medicine and environmental protection can and should also be applied to assessing damages and developing strategies for fair housing litigation and mobilization. Chapter 2 demonstrates how health problems are housing problems and vice versa, while chapter 3 delineates the terms, tools, premises, and principles that pervade the chapters that follow.

Part II is shaped by recognition that traditional tools and mechanisms to combat racism in medical practice and housing provision are increasingly revealing themselves to be inadequate. The legacy of the biomedical model of disease and the tort model of injury in law leads social justice advocates to propose individual and domain-specific solutions to collective and cross-sector problems. Moreover, the rise of corporatization, fiscalization, and securitization throughout society increasingly shapes key contours of health and housing injustice, including the practices of medicine, medical research, rental housing provision, and tax delinquency collection. This leaves many of the mechanisms that produce injustice in housing and health beyond the scope of traditional health care and housing remedies. Chapter 4 describes and analyzes how the racial health and wealth gaps are perpetuated and exacerbated by low-ball evaluations in the home appraisal industry, artificially inflated tax assessments, tax foreclosure auctions, and municipal policies relating to fines, fees, and debts. Chapter 5 reveals how mass incarceration is both a response to and a generator of a public health crisis—caused in no small measure by housing discrimination and the racial wealth gap. Chapter 6 examines the long history and continuing practices in the insurance industry that associate risk with race through actuarial tables and algorithms that now are utilized outside of insurance to shape risk assessments that lead to predictive policing, biased credit scoring, and tracking in schools.

Part III revolves around a central contention of this book: that it is not enough to have things to think, to feel, or to know. Instead, the current contours of housing and health injustice require us to explore things *to do.* Chapter 7 illuminates the emergence of an active engaged public sphere to promote housing and health justice as exemplified in collaborative and convivial campaigns waged by a wide range of activists. Chapter 8 lays out short-run, middle-run, and long-run changes necessary for health care and housing to be recognized as collective resources and human rights rather than merely commodities to be purchased and hoarded. Chapter 9 concludes with a focus on the historical moment we are in, one characterized by both grave peril and great possibility.

This book is one of many responses to the mass demonstrations and moments of racial reckoning across communities, institutions, and professions in 2020 provoked by the killings of George Floyd and Breonna Taylor and many others. These deaths dramatized in visible and compact form the existence of larger social structures and policies that treat Black people as disposable and Black deaths as not worthy of grief. The Movement for Black Lives called attention to racism's systemic and structural dimensions. It showed how seemingly unconnected and diffuse institutional practices function together in concert to equate Blackness with risk and to exclude Black people from the category of the human.[23] The racism that leaves law enforcement officers and civilian vigilantes largely unaccountable for taking Black lives emerges organically and systematically from a society that does not enforce fair housing and fair employment laws, a society where medical and environmental racism lead to premature mass death among Black people and diminished and prematurely curtailed lives among members of other aggrieved racialized populations.

HOW RACISM HARMS HEALTH AND STEALS WEALTH

Racial health disparities cause more than eighty thousand Black people to die prematurely every year.[24] If the authorities filled a large football stadium with Black people on New Year's Day and gunned them down one by one, they would be doing in one fell swoop what proximity to toxicity, medical racism, and housing discrimination perpetrate systematically each year. Researchers estimate that 886,202 deaths could have been avoided between 1991 and 2000 if the health hazards facing Black people and the health care extended to them had been equal to those of white people.[25] Between four and five million African Americans died prematurely between 1945 and 1999 compared to their white counterparts.[26] A study of excess mortality among African Americans between 1999 and 2020 estimated 1.63 million excess deaths costing the Black community collectively eighty million years of life lost.[27] These premature deaths rob families of loved ones, remove builders and mentors from community life, and deplete the economy of Black America by robbing it of productive earning years.

The racial health gap occurs in part because of the racial wealth gap. One study found that the net worth of the median Black family is $11,000, while the net worth of the median white family is $144,200.[28] Another investigation estimated the median wealth of Latinx families at $36,100 compared to $188,200 for the median wealth of white families.[29] Preferential access to homeownership and other forms of asset accumulation enables one out of every two white families to pass on wealth to the next generation though a large inheritance, while only one out of every ten Black families passes on bequests to succeeding generations. According to sociologist Thomas Shapiro, white people who inherit family money receive on average $102,167 more than Black inheritors do.[30] Only around four out of every one hundred Latinx families and six out of every one hundred Black families expect to receive an inheritance.[31] These disparities do not disappear when accounting for education and family form. Half of white college-educated heads of households receive inheritances greater than $55,000, while half of Black college-educated heads of households receive less than $36,000. Parents in the median two-parent white household have ten times more wealth than the median two-parent Black family. Because of inherited property and the tax breaks that come with it, a Black family earning $60,000 per year has less than 30 percent of the wealth of white families with exactly the same income.[32]

The racial wealth gap is constitutive of—not merely coincidental with—the racial health gap. Starting in the nineteenth century, racial segregation confined Black residents in Baltimore to polluted, poorly maintained, and overcrowded neighborhoods that led to high incidences of tuberculosis. At the same time, similar forms of segregation relegated Chinese residents of San Francisco to dilapidated and overcrowded housing stock located near garbage dumps and stagnant ponds that led to cholera epidemics. In both cities, municipal officials conspired with landlords and developers to subsidize the installation of sewers and other sanitary aids in white neighborhoods that were kept white through restrictive covenants and redlining. These actions protected white people and property from the health crises that segregation produced in the places where Chinese and Black people resided. They produced the very health problems they purported to prevent, creating concentrated zones of disease in nonwhite neighborhoods in order to enable the hoarding of both wealth and health by people designated as white.[33]

The racial wealth gap and the racial health gap have long exerted determinate impacts by mobilizing both private capital and public laws to produce and protect a possessive investment in whiteness. Prejudiced individuals do learn to take advantage of and enjoy the unfair gains, unearned enrichments, and privileges and preferences that this system produces, but the system draws its full determinate force and power not from the accumulation of separate individual acts but from things like the ways in which federal housing and tax policies have codified and augmented the exclusionary practices of professional networks and associations of bankers, real estate sellers, and developers.[34]

HIGHER EDUCATION AS A DANGER ZONE

I occupy a position at work as a professional expert, yet I grapple every day with the vexing problems caused by the ways in which expertise and professional status are deployed destructively in this society, with how they are used to silence the voices and suppress the experiences, aspirations, and needs of disrespected and disregarded social groups. Universities, including the one that employs me, exploit their nonprofit statuses and attendant tax exemptions to shape cities and manage medical care in ways that make both housing and health care more expensive and less accessible. I am employed within the University of California system, an entity that has decided to invest some $7 billion in the Blackstone private equity firm, a company that is the nation's largest landlord of rental properties and whose massive profits flow in part from exploiting scarcities of affordable housing. A United Nations study found that Blackstone engages in predatory practices of inflating rents, imposing onerous fees on tenants, and even charging residents for ordinary repairs.[35]

When Blackstone evicts tenants from any of its three hundred thousand rental units in order to charge the new occupants significantly higher rent, children's health and well-being suffers. Renter families with children are three times more likely to experience eviction than families without children. Evictions disrupt young people's school attendance and damage family health. Women who are evicted while pregnant are more likely than other mothers to experience premature and low-weight births and to have babies in need of extended hospitalization and time in intensive care. These burdens are disproportionately shouldered by members of aggrieved racialized groups. On average, Blackstone-owned property is located in neighborhoods where 58 percent of the residents are not white.[36] These attacks on health are enabled and exacerbated by the centrality of housing discrimination to the racial wealth gap.

Many of my faculty colleagues are architects of—and apologists for—the legal, medical, economic, and social practices that produce racialized disparities in housing, health, wealth, and nearly every other arena of social life. The top administrators of the university system in which I work, like their counterparts around the world, minimize and marginalize research that promotes the structural changes needed to address the needs of aggrieved communities. They make investments in and partner with private profit-making corporations that harm public health, widen the gaps between rich and poor, and perpetuate housing discrimination. They manage their real estate holdings in ways that exacerbate racial injustice and inequality.[37]

BEING PROPOSITIONAL AS WELL AS OPPOSITIONAL

It is not enough to know what we oppose; we have to be clear about what we propose. Seeking to end the many specific forms of medical and housing racism that skew opportunities and life chances along racial lines is a worthy goal. But racism never exists in isolation. It is a crucible in which other cruelties are learned and legitimated, a practice that in its broadest meaning teaches people that hierarchy, exploitation, and injustice are natural, necessary, and inevitable. Racist injustice compounds the injuries people experience from discrimination against other identity categories such as gender, age, sexuality, class position, citizenship status, perceived disability, and language use. We should not seek to build a world in which unfair treatment and suffering continue, just not on a racialized basis. Our argument with racism should not revolve around the identity of its victims but around the fact of victimization itself.

This book coalesces around attempts to

1. show that racism is structural and systemic,
2. redefine the generally understood meanings of what good health is and how it is to be achieved,

3. advance precautionary principles in medicine and law,
4. promote the ideal of a medical and social home for all,
5. call attention to and support grassroots community projects that are building health equity and creating an active engaged public sphere dedicated to health and housing justice through convivial collaboration,
6. demonstrate the importance of treating health care and housing as collective public resources and human rights rather than as commodities to be purchased and hoarded by individuals.

KEY CONCEPTS

Racism

The conventional wisdom that guides public policy and personal behavior most often portrays racism as a matter of personal prejudice rather than of political power. It imagines that racist subordination is the result of many unconnected individual racist acts, and that while a few people are guilty of racist enmity most people remain innocent. But in a society where racism is structural and systemic, seeking to assess individual guilt or to establish personal innocence is a distraction from the greater need to forge collective accountability.[38] To be sure, good intentions are better than bad ones, and attempting to be personally responsible is worthy work. But antiracism cannot proceed on purely personal terms in a society where difference is almost always treated as an excuse for domination, where for centuries racism has been the key modality in which inequality, injustice, and exploitation of vulnerability have been deployed. This book identifies structures and systems of racial subordination, but it does not charge the individuals working in those fields with harboring personal racist animus or taking conscious racist actions—although there are some specific cases where that is indeed the case. The book is not accusing individuals of being racists, nor does it presume that its author is innocent or unaccountable for the perpetuation of racist injustices. I know that many principled and dedicated people are working every day in their jobs and neighborhoods to try to promote a more just world, but they do so, in my judgment, within structures and systems riddled with features that undermine their good intentions. Normal medical uncertainties can lead well-intentioned professionals to turn to uninterrogated cultural stories riddled with nonscientific assumptions about race, class, gender, and sexuality to fill in missing scientific information. Legal professionals relying on limited precedents and faced with attitudes ingrained in the minds of judges and juries can succumb to treating racial subordination as episodic and aberrant rather than structural and systemic. This book is concerned with demonstrating the need for collective responsibility and accountability rather than attempting to accuse or absolve individuals.[39]

Foreseeable Harm, Health Care, and Precautionary Principles

The World Health Organization proclaimed in 1946 that good health is not merely the absence of disease and infirmity; it is a condition of complete well-being—physically, mentally, and socially. Its existence depends on a just, humane, and healthful environment. Drawing on the core principles of pediatric medicine, I argue that health care necessitates addressing and correcting all factors that impede healthy development. This means providing care for individual bodies, but it also requires cultivating and preserving healthful environments, ensuring access to adequate nourishment and shelter, promoting social inclusion and cohesion, and addressing the racial wealth gap that the racial health gap both shapes and reflects.

The routine practices of pediatric care revolve around precautionary principles. They require medical professionals to anticipate and preclude in advance the foreseeable harm that emanates from disruptions of healthy child development rather than merely attempting to treat their consequences after the fact. In instances where the likelihood of serious damage is in dispute, the precautionary principle in medical practice and environmental justice work alike tips the scales in favor of prevention.[40] As repeated policy statements by the American Academy of Pediatrics make clear, providing children with quality health care entails recognizing the structural forces that do harm and taking steps to counter them. Housing justice concerns should be front and center in that work.

Children's health is harmed by schools and neighborhoods that are segregated, by employment discrimination and transit racism, by heat islands and hazardous waste dumps, by food and pharmacy apartheid, and by the effects of poverty, prisons, and predatory policing. Children from aggrieved racialized groups reside in places filled with perils, in areas where absence of continuous well-maintained sidewalks and disproportionate presence of arterial roads make them vulnerable to injuries from traffic accidents, in neighborhoods replete with abandoned dwellings used for criminal activity that increase susceptibility to deaths by fire and firearm-related homicides, and in rural and urban sites devoid of hospitals and trauma centers, leading to long travel times for medical care. Injuries from traffic accidents, fires, firearms, and distance from critical care account for 3.6 times as many deaths among people under the age of forty-four years as the combined mortality toll from cancer and heart disease. Black, Indigenous, low-income, and rural communities carry a disproportionate burden of these injuries.[41] Attending to the needs of these children would make life better for everybody.

Anticipating how health is damaged by many different kinds of interruptions in healthy development requires responding to the health injuries that occur when immigration control officers detain and separate families and keep children in cages in detention centers; when the threat of deportation makes children and their parents afraid to seek medical care; when monolingual English-speaking medical professionals do not make use of adequate translators; and when physicians and clinicians treat bodily ailments without looking for signs of trauma or inquiring about family stress, housing conditions, access to or impediments to consuming healthful foods, and experiences with neighborhood sources of pollution. Extending the precautionary principle of pediatric medicine to all medicine and to legal civil rights advocacy and activism would help counter these unjust conditions. Anticipating and precluding injustices in advance is more just and even more cost-effective than attempting to remedy them one at a time after they have done their damage.

A Medical and Social Home

Pediatric researchers and physicians have long championed the provision of a "medical home" for children as a goal of their practice by making sure that health care is accessible, continuous, comprehensive, coordinated, compassionate, culturally effective, and family centered. This model imagines the "home" as a prized locus of affection, protection, safety, and security. Yet not everyone has access to this idealized version of "home." The existence of artificial, arbitrary, and irrational racist impediments to inhabiting physical homes that are safe, sound, healthful, and accessible places this ideal of a medical home out of reach for millions of children. Moreover, among people who are not wealthy, are not white, are not male, are not cis-gendered or heterosexual, or are perceived to have disabilities, the actual homes in which they dwell may provide none of the qualities encapsulated in the ideal of the medical home. In a society where homes are considered primarily private investments rather than public resources, and where property values increase for some homeowners because other home seekers are excluded from fair housing opportunities, the home can serve primarily as a locus of wealth accumulation and opportunity hoarding, as a social formation suffused with hostile privatism and defensive localism, as a place that has value to the extent that other places become devalued.

This definition of home as a private commodity rather than a public resource is a product of the specific historical and social perspectives produced by the long and continuing history of racial discrimination in housing in the United States. It conflicts directly with Article 25 of the Universal Declaration of Human Rights, which proclaims that everyone has the right to adequate clothing, food, and housing.[42] It betrays the promise articulated (albeit insincerely) by the 1949 Taft-Ellender-Wagner Housing Act, in which the US Congress set a goal of "a decent home and a suitable living environment" for every person under its jurisdiction.[43]

The ideal of a medical home can become reality only when children have equal opportunities to inhabit actual physical homes that enable care to be successful. Yet these physical homes also need to be connected to new kinds of social homes committed to children's health, homes where new kinds of caretaking relations treat medical patients with dignity and respect and where community members are recruited to create their own networks of healing and health. One starting point for meaningful change is emerging from creative practices that mobilize entire communities to work together on issues of housing and health: for example, through arrangements that enable nonclinicians to engage in screening, assessment, and communications with children and parents; practices through which medical professionals develop respectful and reciprocal relationships with people in need of health care; and projects where the profound and relevant medical and health care knowledge possessed by members of aggrieved racialized groups is acknowledged and utilized. We need to promote the creation of a medical and social home that resonates with what Toni Morrison indicated as one of the aims of her writing: to turn the racist house of our society into a race-recognizing, yet nonracist home, through places that acknowledge race specificity without being race bound to racialist and racist prerogatives.[44]

WHERE DO WE GO FROM HERE?

Anthropologist Katherine Verdery described the time in 1989 when the Cold War seemed to have ended as a time when "everything we know is up for grabs, and 'what comes next' is anyone's guess."[45] We are in a moment today that resembles that time, a moment that produces zones filled with danger. In times like these, bright promises are often unrealized and fond hopes cruelly dashed. When new understandings emerge and new energies are unleashed, progress is made unevenly and uncertainly at best through many diverse, diffuse, and sometimes contradictory acts of improvisation and experimentation. Yet the loss of certainty can open the door to new possibilities. As its citations indicate, this book emerges at a time when an enormously wide range of differently situated thinkers, writers, artists, and activists are trying to respond to the current crisis with assessments, analyses, and arguments that might imbue the world with the potential for right things to come to pass. At the same historical moment when the forces of revanchist racist reaction have engaged in violent, vile, open, and unapologetic performances of the immunity and impunity of white racism and white racists, principled people from the entire wide range of social identities are setting forth new policies, programs, and projects rife with possibilities. It is important to learn from and contribute to the knowledge emerging from the evidence, analyses, ideas, and arguments that pervade these broadly dispersed struggles. This knowledge appears in statements, blog posts, tweets, testimonies, pamphlets, broadsides, articles, books, and works of expressive culture. At this moment, everyone counts and everyone can contribute. The only certainty we can have is that no one will do for us what we fail to do for ourselves. No one is coming to save us: no new law, no charismatic politician, no celebrity influencer, no new technology, and no organic generational change. If things are to get better, it is up to us to make them better.

We find ourselves at a moment of great danger, but one where faint glimmers of meaningful change are also visible. Engaging with a similar situation more than a half century ago, Martin Luther King Jr. concluded that in a crisis of this magnitude only full participation by large numbers of people could bring about the changes that needed to be made. King noted then that people around the world were waiting and watching for Americans' responses to racism, militarism, and class oppression. He wondered if we would succumb simply to excuses, to complaints that the odds of success were too small and that the requirements of struggle were too harsh. He counseled another path instead. Although we might wish it otherwise, King advised, we needed to rededicate ourselves to "the long and bitter—but beautiful—struggle" for a new and better world.[46] This book seeks to answer this long-deferred but still relevant call. The danger zone is everywhere, and that is a daunting challenge. But that also means that in every place that exists, we have meaningful work to do.

PART I

Who Hurts?

1

Save the Children

Precautionary Principles for Housing
and Health Justice

In his 1971 song "Save the Children," Marvin Gaye sang about the sorrow of knowing the degree to which the children of today will suffer
tomorrow. He pleaded with his listeners to take actions to help them.
Fifty years later, the life prospects of babies, children, and young adults
are even worse than they were when Gaye issued his plea. Climate
change, gun violence, the stagnation of real wages, growing inequality,
plunder of the public sector by privatization, the high costs of medical
care, housing insecurity, and the reemergence of the most violent and
vile forms of white racism paint a foreboding picture of the life prospects for all young people. Children from aggrieved racialized groups
suffer especially deleterious injuries from racialized housing and health
injustice. This chapter delineates the ways in which housing discrimination damages those children and argues that an embrace of precautionary principles in medicine and law can bring a modicum of healthy
development, well-being, safety, and justice to them.

PROXIMITY TO TOXICITY: DETROIT

The dangers that lead poses to children in the United States made
national headlines in 2016 following the disastrous consequences of
Michigan state officials' earlier decision (in 2014) to change the city of
Flint's source of water to the Flint River over the objections of community members. The documented elevated blood lead levels of children

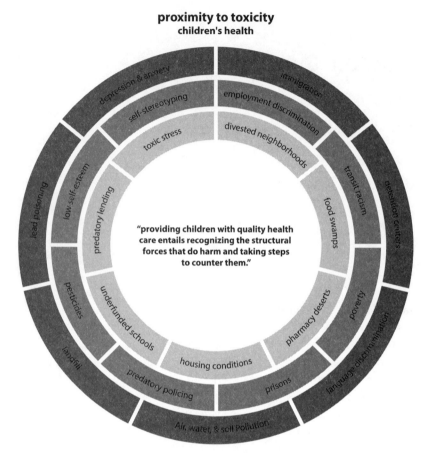

proximity to toxicity
children's health

depression & anxiety
immigration
self-stereotyping
employment discrimination
toxic stress
divested neighborhoods
low-self-esteem
lead poisoning
predatory lending
transit racism
detention centers
food swamps

"providing children with quality health care entails recognizing the structural forces that do harm and taking steps to counter them."

pesticides
underfunded schools
pharmacy deserts
poverty
landfill
housing conditions
language discrimination
predatory policing
prisons
Air, water, & soil Pollution

FIGURE 2. Proximity to toxicity and children's health. Graphic by Omar G. Ramirez.

under the age of five increased from 2.4 percent in 2013 to 4.9 percent in 2015, sparking public outrage.[1] Lead exposure in childhood produces permanent changes in the human body that are associated with poor health and reduced social and economic well-being later in life. No amount of lead is safe, but high concentrations can result in brain and kidney damage, bone loss, asthma, and premature death. Exposure to lead during pregnancy is associated with gestational hypertension, spontaneous abortion, low birth weights, and impairment of infant neurodevelopment.[2]

The calculated cruelty that poisoned the water in Flint understandably attracted widespread attention and condemnation. But the health hazards from lead that Black children faced in Flint are more the rule than the exception. In Baltimore alone since 1993, more than sixty-five thousand children (most of whom are Black) have registered blood lead levels higher than 10 milligrams per deciliter.[3] The Centers for Disease Control identifies 3.5 milligrams per deciliter as a level of concern. The levels of lead exposure in Flint's children during its 2015 disastrous turn were actually safer levels than prevail in Detroit. In one zip code in Detroit, 22 percent of children under the age of six were found to have what is considered toxic levels of lead in their bodies, and in the city at large the figure for blood lead levels of concern is one out of every ten.[4] A 2016 study found that one out of every two children in grades K–12 in Detroit public schools had dangerously elevated blood lead levels.[5] Michigan data from 2016 showed that while 8.5 percent of Michigan's children reside in Detroit, the city accounts for 36 percent of the state's cases of elevated blood lead levels in children.[6]

Children absorb lead via both the digestive tract (by eating chips of lead-based paint or drinking contaminated water) and the lungs (by breathing in lead-contaminated particles).[7] Black children in Detroit and cities across the nation encounter lead-based paint on the inside walls and windowsills of their dwellings and even in the paint on playground swings, slides, and jungle gyms. More than three million children under the age of six in the United States inhabit dwellings contaminated by lead-based paint.[8] Relative to their body size, the gastrointestinal systems of children are larger than those of adults. Children have been found to absorb lead from the GI tract more efficiently than adults (40 percent vs. 5–15 percent),[9] which means that exposure to toxic lead paint inside their homes leads them to absorb five hundred times more lead per exposure than adults.[10] Children are also exposed to lead in the pipes that carry water to their homes. The air they breathe may contain lead from the fumes of nearby waste incinerators, refineries, and smelters. If they live near heavily trafficked roads or runways, or abandoned industrial sites, or demolished buildings, the ground is contaminated with lead that is stirred up in dust and dirt, and children carry it into their homes on their clothes and shoes after playing outside. Largely because of dust from the demolitions of abandoned and foreclosed properties, the percentage of lead-poisoned children in Detroit rose from 6.9 percent to 8.7 percent between 2015 and 2016 alone.[11] Researchers have found a positive correlation between lead concentrations in the air and the percentage of Black children under the age of sixteen in neighborhoods. The same research reveals an inverse relationship between the amount of air lead concentration and the percentage of white children in neighborhoods.[12]

Lead poisoning is a condition directly related to housing discrimination. Long histories of restrictive covenants, mortgage and insurance redlining, blockbusting, and real estate agent steering have combined to confine the 80 percent of the city of Detroit's population that is Black to an artificially small and dangerously inferior sector of the regional housing market. Lax enforcement of building codes and other public health and safety laws leaves large numbers of Black children under the age of six residing in older, lower-quality dwellings. Almost all these children reside in rental properties that are poorly maintained by property managers who work either for individual landlords or for the large-scale investment corporations that recently have started to purchase vast numbers of these buildings. Many of the new investor-speculators are from outside the state of Michigan. Emergency city managers appointed by the state government encouraged speculators to take advantage of the crisis in Detroit by promoting what Rebeca Kinney calls "dereliction by design."[13] Foreclosures and tax forfeiture sales enabled bulk buyers to scoop up large quantities of real estate at bargain prices. At one point, some seventeen thousand dwellings had their water service shut off and were deemed blighted and therefore available for municipal seizure and auction. It was not just buildings that were susceptible to seizure. Children residing in these dwellings could also be removed from their families and sent to foster homes by Child Protective Services officials. The state thus treated parents' inability to pay water bills as individual moral failings that justified taking their children from them. In the first two decades of the twenty-first century some twenty-eight thousand dwellings in Detroit that housed one hundred thousand people went up for auction in tax foreclosure sales.[14]

By 2010, Detroit transitioned from a city where the majority of homes were owner occupied to a majority-renter city.[15] The children whose families rent foreclosed homes experience higher blood lead levels than children living in other properties.[16] The dearth of affordable housing gives owners of rental properties the upper hand when dealing with their tenants. Landlords use the threat of eviction to coerce residents of their buildings to pay high monthly rents for dwellings that have lead-based paint on inside walls, exposed pipes, sewage that backs up into the home, electrical connections that are faulty, fire hazards, heating systems that do not work, and mold and pest residues that pollute the air.[17]

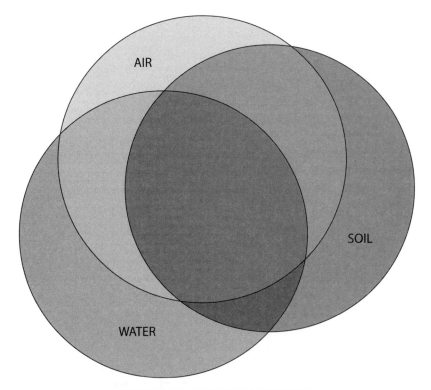

DANGER ZONES HEALTH REDLINING

FIGURE 3. Danger zones to health in redlined areas: polluted air, water, and soil. Graphic by Omar G. Ramirez.

Researchers have found a high correlation between the numbers of children under the age of six with elevated blood lead levels and residency in a dwelling within four hundred feet of a demolished building. The houses that large investors purchase through tax foreclosure auctions are almost twice as likely to be torn down as are independently owned buildings. In Detroit and other places in Michigan, a legal loophole exempts landlords who obtain dwellings through tax foreclosure auctions from obligations to reveal lead hazards to potential renters or buyers.[18] If tenants complain about hazardous lead in their homes, landlords can threaten them with eviction, knowing full well that housing discrimination in the rental market leaves the tenants with severely limited options to move elsewhere.

The children living in polluted environments in Detroit need enforcement of fair housing laws. They need to see an end to the practices of economic predatory extraction that poison the places where they live, work, and play. But public policy combines with private greed to produce housing-related health hazards for them. State policies depicted as innocent cost-saving measures invariably shift risks and costs to the most vulnerable populations. In 2002, for example, Michigan governor John Engler curtailed environmental regulations and eliminated community health programs. The governor terminated a policy that enabled state agencies to help poverty-stricken parents pay utility bills and prevent service shutoffs. A law passed by the state legislature relieves owners of contaminated sites purchased after 1996 from responsibility to clean up, contain, and accept liability for the pollution from which they profit. Cuts in federal funds available to cities and states in 2012 led Detroit to cease its lead abatement program.[19]

Children in Detroit also face danger from the ways in which privatization produces poverty and from the attendant criminalization of poverty that exposes them to a wide range of health hazards. Privatization has led to utility bills in Detroit doubling over the past decade, skyrocketing to levels three times higher than the affordability threshold. As a result, nearly 250,000 residents of Detroit have had water and sewer service disconnected because of inability to pay utility bills.[20] These actions forced a quarter of a million people to choose between paying high costs for bottled water that they could not afford or going without water entirely, damaging their health and that of their neighbors. A study by a local hospital discovered that patients residing on blocks where water service had been terminated displayed a significantly greater likelihood of waterborne illnesses, even if their own house's water supply remained intact.[21]

The air children breathe in Detroit is filled with pollutants. Every year the city's poisoned air causes 3,400 asthma-related doctor's visits, 1,800 hospitalizations, and 690 more deaths than would be expected under normal conditions. Of the nation's eighteen largest cities, Detroit has the highest rate of childhood asthma.[22] The city contains 755 abandoned "brownfield" sites, with battery acid and other pollutants in the ground because of their previous use as manufacturing sites. These places expose children and their parents to toxic levels of pollution, increasing their chances of contracting asthma, heart disease, cancer, and obstructive pulmonary disease.[23]

Rapidly declining property values in Detroit coupled with deliberately inflated property tax assessments leading to wave after wave of foreclosed and abandoned homes are part of a broader pattern of Black dispossession and external wealth extraction.[24] City tax assessors in Detroit brazenly violated state laws by illegally inflating the assessed value of residential properties by more than $600 million, causing more than one hundred thousand residents to lose their homes because of underpaid or unpaid property taxes. Tax foreclosure auctions enabled primarily white investors to purchase at deeply discounted prices large volumes of property previously owned by Black people. These outside investors pursued short-term profits by raising rents, neglecting maintenance, and selling homes through exploitative contract buying and rent-to-own schemes.[25] Black people were forced to leave their homes in Detroit when they could not pay taxes on properties that were illegally overassessed, when they could not afford the exorbitant costs charged for water service, and when they could not meet the expanded costs of deceptive and predatory home mortgage loans and rent-to-own contracts.

Michigan's emergency managers voided pensions owed to city employees and cut back on water and sewer service, while funneling millions of dollars in subsidies to sports teams, arena operators, and developers. The same officials who mandated seventeen thousand homes to go completely without water service provided water for free to the Little Caesar's Arena, which hosts profitable professional basketball and hockey teams owned by rich people who do not need financial subsidies.[26] While Black property owners lost vast amounts of assets because of mortgage and tax foreclosures and tax auctions, Detroit's wealthy owner of Quicken Loans, Dan Gilbert, increased his holdings from $4.5 billion to $49.6 billion during the city's financial crisis, a crisis that Quicken Loans both helped cause and exacerbated. Gilbert's company had more homes in foreclosure after 2005 than any other lender. The Department of Justice charged the firm with making hundreds of fraudulent subprime loans between 2007 and 2011.[27]

PROXIMITY TO TOXICITY: EARLIMART

Twenty-three hundred miles from Detroit, Latinx children who attend elementary and middle schools in the rural California Central Valley town of Earlimart experience dangers daily. Their school day may begin when they place their hands over their hearts and pledge allegiance to the red, white, and blue flag of the United States. Before entering school, however, they have already encountered another flag, one of five that may fly on top of the school's flagpole. A green flag indicates that the air they will breathe that day is of good quality, yellow designates the air quality as moderate, orange shows that the air is unhealthy for students with sensitive conditions, red means that the air is unhealthy and outdoor activities should be limited, and purple proclaims that the air is very unhealthy and requires that all activities be conducted indoors.[28]

The flags flying in Earlimart are part of a system that tells the students they must adjust on their own to the pollutants that pervade the places where they live. This system demands no action from those who create the pollution: the bad air the children breathe, the polluted water they drink, and the contaminated dirt underneath their feet. Because these young people reside in homes located near sites of oil extraction, close to agricultural fields that contain pesticide residues that get dispersed in nearby supplies of air and water, and in proximity to highways where trucks spew exhaust fumes into the environment incessantly, they must spend many days a year indoors. They cannot go outside for the exercise and play that their developing bodies need. One mother whose daughter has to stay inside frequently because of her body's sensitivity to pollutants complains of the injustice that keeps her child from playing outside: her daughter, she says, is cooped up at home "while polluters keep doing their business as usual."[29] Those who choose to defy the flags and play outside can suffer dire consequences. One study of young people in Southern California, for example, found that those who exercised outdoors in areas with high concentrations of ozone had a three times greater chance of contracting asthma than those who exercised in healthier environments.[30]

Pollution in the air outside the school building in Earlimart, as well as in many other places where Latinx children live in economic and environmental sacrifice zones, harms the classroom performance of students inside it. Exposure to respiratory risks has a statistically significant negative impact on student test scores. These risks are not randomly distributed across racial lines but are concentrated in places where large numbers of children are Black and/or Latinx. The greater the percentage of children who are Black and/or Latinx in a school, the greater the likelihood that cancer and respiratory illnesses are present at high levels.[31] These children breathe poisoned air because who they are makes powerful people compel them to live in places where high levels of pollution cause health problems that will harm them their entire lives.

A NATIONAL PROBLEM

Children in Detroit and Earlimart experience blatantly visible versions of the consequences of poor health caused by destructive and predatory housing policies that prevail elsewhere. Twenty-three million dwellings in the United States have one or more hazards caused by lead-based paint.[32] The recycling of lead-based batteries and processes of smelting that remove lead from iron ore pollute both soil and water. They harm communities on the front lines of environmental pollution and the ecosystems that surround them, poisoning people, animals, birds, and plant life. Estimated lifelong earnings lost by people exposed to toxic lead in childhood amount to between $8 and $11 billion in California alone.[33] Among children being treated at asthma-related emergency clinics in San Diego County in California there are five times as many Black children and two times as many Latinx children as white children.[34] Residents of Bayview Hunters Point, a predominantly Black, Latinx, and Asian Pacific Islander neighborhood in San Francisco, experience a hospitalization rate from asthma that is four times higher than the area average. In communities inhabited by members of aggrieved racialized groups in New York City, rates of childhood asthma approach 25 percent, which is four times higher than the city average.[35] Nationally the asthma death rate among children who are Black is seven times greater than the rate among non-Hispanic white children.[36] Children who are houseless have high blood lead levels and high rates of asthma, obesity, malnutrition, dental and visual issues, mental health difficulties, and behavioral problems.[37]

The racial wealth gap perpetuates and exacerbates the racial health gap. A study of five urban medical health centers found that more than a quarter of the patients they treated were behind in rent payments, that one in twelve had experienced multiple recent moves, and that 12 percent had been houseless.[38] People identified as Black make up a little more than 12 percent of the national population but account for 48 percent of the families with children living in shelters because they are unhoused. Half of the nation's houseless children are Black.[39] African Americans make up 24 percent of the population in Oakland, California, but 70 percent of those experiencing houselessness.[40]

Racialized shelter insecurity is a chronic pediatric illness that requires sustained medical attention. A "housing first" approach to medicine would enable all children to reside in safe, healthful, and affordable dwellings. Moving houseless people into secure dwellings is more effective than stand-alone medical treatment in improving mental health and in decreasing rates of hospitalization and emergency room visits.[41] Yet in cities across the nations, politicians, pundits, and professional organizations promote moral panics about what to do about people who are

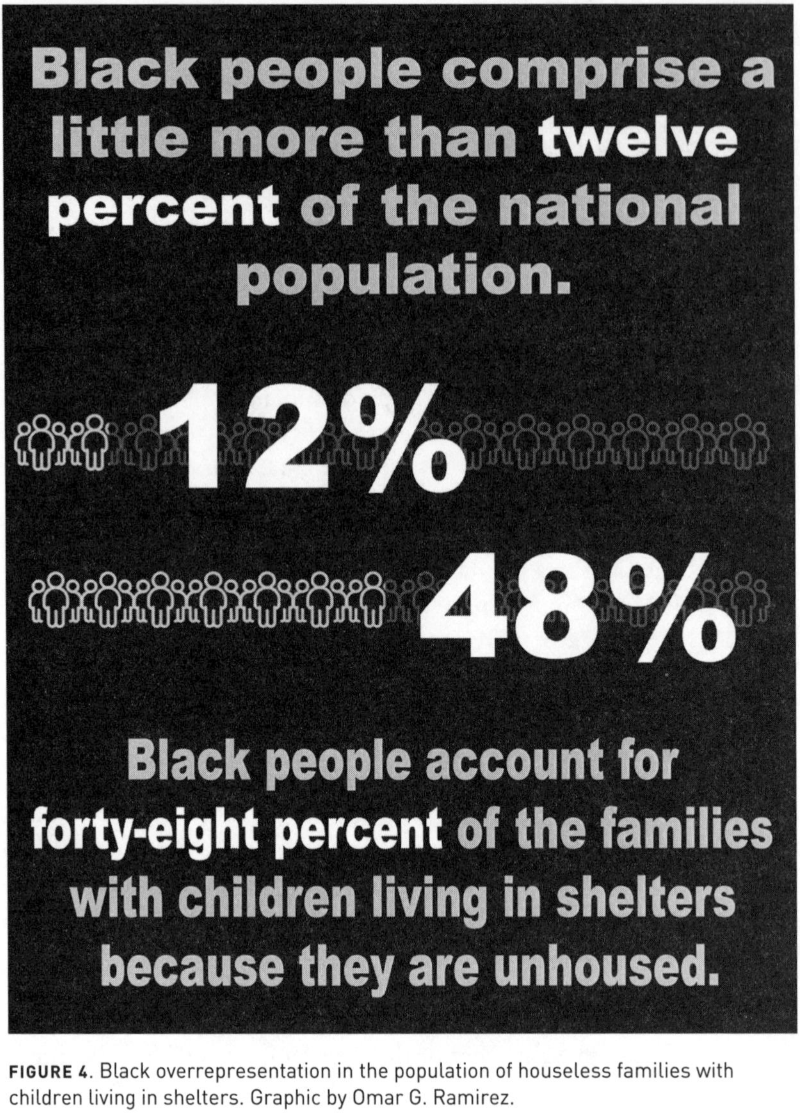

FIGURE 4. Black overrepresentation in the population of houseless families with children living in shelters. Graphic by Omar G. Ramirez.

houseless rather than what to do about a housing system that has too few affordable, accessible, and racially nonrestrictive dwellings. The streets to which the houseless have been relegated and the inadequate shelters provided for them are disabling sites that make people fear being attacked or arrested, places where they suffer from excessive cold or heat, noise, lack of privacy, and inadequate sanitary facilities.[42]

HEALTH AND ADVERSE EARLY LIFE EXPERIENCES

Discrimination against children is especially damaging because young people are in the process of developing physical and social defenses against disease and social disapproval that they will need to rely on as adults. The National Institutes of Health have judged adolescence to be an inherently vulnerable life stage. Young people are less able than adults to defend themselves, to act effectively to change their conditions, and to understand when they are not to blame for their problems. External stigmas and internal self-stereotyping deplete psychological resources and self-esteem that can be important in preventing stress-related obesity and other negative health conditions.[43] Black adolescents between the ages of sixteen and eighteen reporting significant experiences with discrimination develop dangerously elevated levels of blood pressure, inflammation, and stress hormones including cortisol, epinephrine, and norepinephrine by the time they have reached the age of twenty.[44] Stress levels that children from aggrieved racialized groups experience because of racism can disrupt brain development and lead to subsequent negative behavioral, health, economic, and educational outcomes.[45] Exposure to dangerous amounts of lead, arsenic, and magnesium can cause neurodevelopmental disabilities, especially in undernourished bodies lacking the nutrients that can reduce the absorption of these poisons.

Among children living in aggrieved racialized communities, the stress caused by poverty, pollution, and illness becomes exacerbated by what is known as "status-based recognition sensitivity," which is "the tendency to anxiously expect, readily perceive, and intensely react to discrimination and prejudice based on membership in a stigmatized social category or status group."[46] Nancy Krieger explains that being on the receiving end of racist insults and injuries makes people expect to experience them again in the future. These experiences activate what Krieger describes as "the physiology of fear," a mobilization of lipids and glucose that increases energy resources and activates sensory vigilance in ways that elevate blood pressure and can lead to sustained hypertension.[47] Anne Fausto-Sterling observes that "hypertension is an orchestrated response to a predicted need to remain vigilant to a variety of insults and dangers—be they racial hostility, enraging acts of discrimination, or living in the shadow of violence. Over time, all of the components that regulate blood pressure adapt to life under stress."[48] Indeed, experimental studies have found that among people who have been subject to discrimination, any act of experiencing, recalling, or even viewing an incident of discrimination against someone else provokes a stronger cardiac reaction with a slower recovery profile than the reaction that appears in people not exposed to discrimination.[49]

When children discern stark differences between the opportunities available to them and to others and as a result perceive a lack of freedom and opportunity in their own lives, they are likely to develop feelings of hopelessness, helplessness, demoralization, and diminished self-efficacy. As they observe directly or hear indirectly accounts of discrimination experienced by friends and family members, they see that they are part of a devalued social group that is treated unjustly. Especially for children between the ages of ten and twelve, a stage of life when children become more aware of their social status and position, such experiences can produce self-consciousness, anxiety, depression, and anger.[50]

Status-based rejection and recognition sensitivity are conditions that paradoxically increase risks of two diametrically opposed but equally dangerous responses: (1) an excessive introversion that entails a retreat inward to avoid engaging with a world perceived as unremittingly hostile and unfair; or (2) an excessive extroversion expressed through a penchant for recklessness, disobedience, and taking chances, out of the belief that the deck is stacked in favor of failure no matter how much care an individual may exercise.[51] Adverse early life experiences caused by intersections of age, racism, and poverty damage the physical development of children, influencing everything from brain architecture to lung structure, increasing later life vulnerabilities to hypertension, cardiovascular disease, obesity, and cancer, while producing a psychological susceptibility to self-destructive behavior.

The ticking time bomb of adverse early life experiences can lead to physical and mental problems later in life, increasing lifetime risks of depression, alcoholism, suicide, and other factors that shorten life expectancy.[52] Lead poisoning in childhood creates higher risks in adulthood for heart disease, anemia, kidney damage, dementia, and diminished capacity for resisting subsequent environmental injuries.[53] Lung cancer, mesothelioma, and other pollution-related illnesses may not become evident until decades after they have been contracted. Because racist conduct in itself is a health hazard, adverse early life experiences with discrimination can plant seeds of dysfunction in adult life. The effects of discrimination endure long after the discriminatory act seems to have ended. High levels of stress in resource-poor environments produce disease risks that last for generations. Social deprivation and stress can disrupt the workings of the body's immune system.[54] Among older adults, histories of everyday experiences with discrimination are associated with elevated levels of C-reactive protein, which is a marker of inflammation.[55]

For children in aggrieved racialized groups, health problems are almost always also housing problems. Like adults, children need strong relationships inside nurturing places where each person's sense of belonging is affirmed. But waves of gentrification and evictions cause frequent moves that fragment and even dissolve the social support networks needed for mutual respect and recognition. Young children who change residences twice a year or more because of housing insecurity have a high risk of developmental difficulties and ill health, while for older children these moves increase the likelihood of mental health and behavioral issues.[56] In addition, aggressive predatory policing in impoverished neighborhoods can make young people feel like interlopers where they live and create preconditions for psychological disorders.[57] For Black adolescents in such neighborhoods, repeated encounters with law enforcement officers increase levels of stress levels, anxiety, stigma, and fear in ways that over time erode health.[58] Finally, the stress and fear associated with being behind in rent payments increase the likelihood of poor parental and caregiver health, maternal depression, and child lifetime hospitalizations.[59]

PEDIATRIC MEDICINE AND PRECAUTIONARY PRINCIPLES

It should not be surprising that specialists in pediatric medicine have been among the first to recognize that racism is a public health menace. Pediatricians likely perceive the changing demographics of the nation sooner than other physicians. Nearly half of newborn babies in 2019 were nonwhite. In 2020, the number of Latinx children increased by 9 percent while the population of children of Asian descent grew by 23 percent. Children from aggrieved racialized groups are projected to be 60 percent of the child population by 2050.[60] When pediatricians treat these patients, they have to assess and take precautions to counter the role that racism will play in damaging their health and life prospects. In many cases, these effects of racism are already present. For example, during the measles epidemic of 1989–91, children from aggrieved racialized groups had illness rates between four and seven times higher than the rates among white youths.[61]

Access to safe and secure shelter is an antidote to short-term and long-term illness. Early life intervention can be especially valuable. Research shows that each year spent in a better environment during childhood improves long-term health outcomes.[62] When families receive housing vouchers and other assistance that enables them to move from high-poverty to high-opportunity areas of residence, children's school performance and later life earnings improve markedly while bringing significant declines in asthma morbidity.[63] Children in families able to acquire housing subsidies gain greater access to nutritious foods and benefit from leaving polluted places. They are more likely than children in families stranded on waiting lists for housing assistance to experience healthy development, maintain healthy weight, and have their health classified as good or excellent.[64] When low-income individuals and families move to neighborhoods that are safer, cleaner, and filled with amenities, they experience reduced rates of diabetes, obesity, and depression.[65]

Every year some three million households in the United States experience eviction.[66] Among low-income mothers, evictions exacerbate economic hardships and caregiver stress, increase the likelihood of depression, and lead to poorer health for themselves and their children.[67] The injuries that housing instability imposes on children harm all of society. Researchers affiliated with Children's Health Watch note that the unstable housing conditions that children face will cost the nation as a whole some $111 billion in excess (and completely avoidable) health and education expenditures over the next decade.[68] Yet safe, secure, stable, and healthful housing is not merely an economic benefit, it also enhances public health. Societies with high levels of inequality generate worse disease outcomes, while more egalitarian societies are healthier. Inequality is associated with higher rates of mental illness and infant mortality, more low-birth-weight babies, lower life expectancy, and increased incidences of depression and AIDS.[69]

The practice of pediatrics entails taking precautionary measures to prevent foreseeable future harm. In matters of collective public health, deploying preventive and precautionary practices has historically led to major health improvements. Adding iodine to salt succeeded in decreasing nutritional deficiency diseases.[70] Governments used chlorination to disinfect drinking water, which led to drastic declines in cholera and typhoid fever. Similar measures attending to water quality, sewage treatment, garbage collection, and food inspection drastically reduced cases of cholera, dysentery, and typhoid. Occupational safety regulations and engineering changes reduced deaths at work, while improved nutrition and less crowded housing greatly reduced cases of tuberculosis.[71] National, state, and local authorities worked together to promote vaccinations for malaria, diphtheria, smallpox, measles, mumps, rubella, meningitis, and polio.[72] A provision of the Clean Air Act of 1970 that required removal of tetraethyl lead from gasoline reduced amounts of lead in soil and in children's bloodstreams.[73] Mandating seat belts and child restraint seats has reduced automobile accident fatalities and injuries. Educational campaigns and legal prohibitions against smoking and drunk driving have contributed meaningfully to longer life expectancies. Smoke alarms have reduced fatalities from fires. Vaccines have made some once-prevalent diseases now rare.

The commitment by pediatricians to anticipate disruptions in child development and seek to prevent them before they happen rather than belatedly treating them after the fact contains generative potential for solving a wide range of social as well as medical problems. Precautionary principles have played particularly prominent roles in campaigns for environmental justice. Faced with the difficulty of proving definitively that particular pollutants produce specific diseases in specific individuals, environmental activists argue for holistic approaches that attempt to identify and preempt the processes that cumulatively harm the earth and its inhabitants.[74] They urge regulatory agencies to be attentive to practices that may cause future harm, to shift the burden of proof away from relatively powerless people and toward polluters, to insist that chemicals be proved safe before being used, and to require industries that profit from polluting air, water, and land to submit racism impact statements as well as environmental impact statements before beginning new projects. This enables environmentalists to expand the sphere of ecological concern from remedying harm to preventing it.

PRECAUTIONARY PRINCIPLES AND FAIR HOUSING LAW

The precautionary practices that guide pediatric medicine and inform environmental justice campaigns could be of great value if applied to fair housing advocacy and litigation. Precaution is not unknown in the law. Antitrust law requires authorities to assess the potential damage inflicted on market competition by mergers and acquisitions. Before it was undermined by the Supreme Court's execrable 2013 decision in the case of *Shelby v. Holder*, the preclearance provision of the 1965 Voting Rights Act required government bodies in states with histories of racist voter suppression to secure approval in advance of any changes in electoral procedures and district lines, rather than requiring citizens to file suit after the injuries already happened. In the context of voting rights, shifting the burden of proof from victims to perpetrators recognized that even temporary violations of rights and reallocations of racial power would have long-term effects. Once any single voting arrangement was declared invalid, the perpetrators could simply turn to other second-generation methods of voter suppression and underrepresentation, enabling them to enjoy the unfair gains they secured as a result until a long process of litigation provided a delayed day of reckoning. The precautionary principles of environmental activism, pediatric medicine, and voting rights law have the potential to improve medical practice and civil rights law more generally by anticipating and addressing harm before its full effects become visible.

Under the leadership of Chief Justice John Roberts, the Supreme Court has deployed precautionary principles enthusiastically, but only when they have utility for preserving the privilege and power of segregationists and bigots. In its 2007 *Parents Involved in Community Schools* decision, the court overturned decisions by lower courts, abandoned decades of legal precedent, and used the power of the federal government to terminate popular voluntary desegregation programs in the Louisville and Seattle school districts. In the Louisville component of the case, the legal guardian of one white kindergarten student claimed her child had been harmed because the school board rejected his application to transfer to a school of his choice. In fact, as the court acknowledged, he had missed the transfer application deadline, but the school district allowed him to transfer anyway to the school he wished to attend. The Court ruled that even though he had not been harmed, the child still had standing to sue because the desegregation policy of the board *might* one day in the future prevent him from transferring to the school he wished to attend if that transfer upset the racial balance of the student body.[75] In 2023, the Roberts Court overturned Colorado state law and findings by lower courts in order to grant a pre-enforcement order to a web designer who had not yet started her business but feared that sometime in the future state antidiscrimination law might compel her to violate her religious beliefs by designing a website for a same-sex wedding. As with the injury alleged to have been suffered by the kindergarten student in Louisville, the Court engaged in an act of prestidigitation to protect the web designer from potential future harm. If that potential future harm justifies Supreme Court intervention in these cases, children and adults living in places shaped by decades and centuries of actual harmful discrimination in housing that exposes them to current and future health risks should logically (albeit unrealistically) expect the Roberts Court to grant them the same protections the Court has been eager to provide on behalf of white supremacist racial segregation and homophobic religious bigotry.

Although fair housing litigation has most often been grounded in the tort model of injury, the Fair Housing Act itself contains provisions that enable deployment of precautionary principles. In a brilliantly conceived and persuasively argued law review article, Heather R. Abraham points out that the Fair Housing Act makes reducing residential segregation a statutory duty of all government agencies. What Abraham describes as the law's often "overlooked and under-enforced" mandate to every federal agency to affirmatively further fair housing opens the door to recognizing the many ways in which government bodies could use precautionary principles to open up a wide array of fair housing opportunities.[76]

The Fair Housing Act declares: "All executive departments and agencies shall administer their programs and activities relating to housing and urban development (including any Federal agency having regulatory or supervisory authority over financial institutions) in a manner affirmatively to further the purposes of this subchapter."[77] Abraham argues that this mandate requires government bodies to assess the impact of proposed new actions in addition to combating the racial residential segregation that has already taken place. A long history of court cases and settlements has established that the Fair Housing Act applies not only to intentional acts of discrimination but also to the failure by governments and government-funded bodies to consider alternative courses of action that would promote integration. In the case of *Thompson v. HUD*,[78] for example, the court found that the Department of Housing and Urban Development violated the Fair Housing Act by building public housing units only inside the majority-Black city of Baltimore rather than extending them to the surrounding areas of Baltimore County where white people were the majority, noting accurately that the department should have anticipated that its actions would reinforce rather than reduce residential segregation in the area.

Abraham emphasizes that housing discrimination has been not merely a series of individual transactions between buyers and sellers but also the product of a long, ugly, and ignoble history of government action and inaction. Responsibility for patterns and practices that segregate housing resides properly and organically with the agencies charged specifically with responsibilities for shelter and finance, such as the Department of Housing and Urban Development, the Federal Housing Finance Agency, and the Federal Home Bank Loan System. Abraham demonstrates, however, that federal agencies *not* normally thought of as involved in housing actually fund and administer a wide range of housing-related initiatives that should be governed by the mandate to affirmatively further fair housing. These involve policies enacted by the Departments of Transportation, Treasury, Defense, Agriculture, Environmental Protection, and Veterans Affairs, the Federal Emergency Management Agency, the Federal Reserve Board, and the Comptroller of the Currency.

Abraham points out that the Department of Transportation funds highways that destroy the already-scarce supply of housing for members of aggrieved racialized groups, that add to the value of homes in municipalities that use exclusionary zoning to prevent desegregation, and that give priority to the transit needs of the historically white populations of suburban commuters rather than to public transit projects that could augment housing and employment mobility and promote desegregation. Agency block grant initiatives by the Department of Transportation routinely augment the value of past discrimination by funding renewals of a transportation infrastructure purposely designed to segregate neighborhoods by race.

Transit racism harms health even as it undermines the acquisition of wealth. Increased access to affordable or free public transportation would help narrow the racial wealth and racial health gaps. One study found that in 2017 nearly six million people in the United States delayed seeking medical treatment because public transit was too expensive, unreliable, or inconvenient or because they lacked access to a private vehicle. Housing segregation routinely leaves members of aggrieved racialized groups physically distant from medical providers, which results in missed or postponed appointments, delayed treatments, and poor communication between health care providers and patients. Neighborhoods with low levels of private ownership of motor vehicles have disproportionately high rates of breast cancer fatalities and myocardial infarction mortality.[79]

Racial discrimination by automobile dealers contributes to health precarity. Black and Latinx customers pay higher financing costs when purchasing automobiles than white buyers, even when their incomes and credit scores are equal to those of white purchasers who receive more favorable terms. An investigation by the National Consumer Law Center discovered that in forty-four states Latinx automobile buyers were saddled with service contracts that contained higher percentage markups than the contracts offered to non-Latinx customers.[80] These practices siphon off funds that could be used for medical care and make it harder for their targets to be transported to clinics and hospitals.

Abraham identifies the Department of the Treasury as another federal agency derelict in meeting the mandate to affirmatively further fair housing. It administers the Low Income Housing Tax Credit program, designed purportedly to address the dire shortage of affordable housing. Yet the program encourages placement of dwelling units in low-opportunity areas already plagued by the cumulative effects of historic segregation. Through its tax policy the Treasury Department privileges the construction of expensive single-family dwellings and places impediments in the path of developers seeking to build affordable rental units. While subsidizing the kinds of housing least accessible to victims of housing discrimination, the Treasury Department all but ignores its potential to use existing programs and create new ones to fund acquisition of land and credit by community land trusts and other local shared-equity housing organizations attempting to make housing affordable in perpetuity by resisting speculation and promoting stable home values.

Abraham argues that the Environmental Protection Agency could and should add racial impact considerations to its deliberations about environmental impacts and to its oversight of state policy decisions that have ramifications for discrimination and segregation. The Department of Agriculture finances home renovations and repairs, provides support for down payments on homes in rural areas, and administers forms of rental assistance that have significant implications for fair housing. The Department of Defense has at times in the past been the largest landlord in the nation, and today it engages in public-private partnerships that provide not only housing for military personnel but units that are available to be rented by civilians. Enforcing fair housing in those rentals and placing the units in high-opportunity neighborhoods would meaningfully promote desegregation, augment asset assimilation among aggrieved racialized groups, and narrow the racial health gap.

CHILDREN IN DANGER ZONES: WHAT CAN BE DONE FOR THEM AND WHAT CAN BE LEARNED FROM THEM

Medical and legal practices need to change. The biomedical model of disease and the tort model of injury in law impede justice. Wider application of precautionary principles would help make fundamental changes in a wide range of major social institutions. Much needs to be done *for* the children and adults who dwell in danger zones. Yet much can also be learned *from* them, from the ways in which their survival strategies point the way toward new conceptions of housing and health care. Despite all that is stacked against them, these children and those who love and nurture them still find ways to survive and sometimes thrive. They cannot afford to wait for the bureaucratic implementation of reforms that might help them; they have to take action in the present with the tools that are available to them to make better lives and futures possible.

People lacking resources often have to become resourceful, to craft ways to resist and transcend unlivable destinies meted out to them by structural and systemic forces. Out of necessity, community-based mobilizations are developing understandings of health care and housing as human rights to be guaranteed collectively rather than private commodities to be purchased individually. They are devising approaches to justice designed to prevent harm in advance rather than merely punishing its perpetrators after the fact. They are embracing the accountability and responsibility of collective caretaking and collegial community building. In a society guided by neoliberal principles that encourage people to move out of disrespected places plagued by disinvestment and to find housing in places where property values are protected by hostile privatism and defensive localism, these groups ask their neighbors to *lead* where they live rather than to *leave* it. They reject the premise that neighborhood development requires attracting polluting industries or creating opportunities for gentrification projects that will displace current residents. Instead, they pin their hopes for community development on increasing the value of the undervalued places where they dwell by building their own community land trusts, food and housing cooperatives, urban gardens, and restorative justice circles: all practices that proceed by burrowing in, building up, and branching out.

The Building Healthy Communities in Boyle Heights initiative in East Los Angeles exemplifies the potential of community-based mobilization for health and housing justice. The story of how Juana Mena Ochoa used her position as an Artist Fellow with this group to create new forms of convivial collaboration among disregarded and disrespected people demonstrates the extraordinary potential of this kind of work.

Ochoa was born in Guadalajara, Mexico, and moved to Los Angeles in her twenties out of dire economic necessity. In Los Angeles she found jobs as a housekeeper and caretaker for people too ill to care for themselves. Mena Ochoa worked hard and regularly sent more than half of her earnings back home to Mexico to support her younger siblings. She gave birth to two daughters in Los Angeles, one of whom died in infancy. As she attempted to support herself and her daughter by working at low-wage jobs, Mena experienced depression and a series of serious health crises.

In the midst of illness, Mena Ochoa found a creative outlet for herself designing and sewing quilts. This interest led her to attend meetings organized by art activists affiliated with the Alliance for California Traditional Arts (ACTA) and its Building Healthy Communities in Boyle Heights initiative.[81] The Boyle Heights neighborhood is a place where few residents possess health insurance, where poverty too often prevents the purchase of prescribed medicines, where language discrimination and fears of deportation impede access to medical care, and where nearly a third of adult residents describe their health as only fair or poor.[82] Mena Ochoa's skills as an artist attracted the attention and admiration of ACTA staff members, but they were even more impressed by her ability to place her personal problems and practices in a collective community context. "She had voice," recalls ACTA's Omar G. Ramirez. "She was interested not just in her health, but in the health of the community."[83] Intrigued by discovering people who recognized potential in her, Mena Ochoa became active in the group as a member of the steering committee and soon found herself designated as an Artist Fellow with responsibility for coordinating community engagement— an assignment she carried out by organizing women to participate in quilting circles.

Mena Ochoa recognized that the artistic space that quilting enables also creates a social space for laughter, tears, and stories about experiences women share as mothers, wives, daughters, sisters, low-wage workers, and immigrants. Participants talk about their lives not only as laborers and caretakers but also as people left without access to adequate medical care, relegated to residence in neighborhoods rife with pollution, and constantly fending off illness and depression. As an artistic practice, quilting entails finding value in devalued and discarded pieces of cloth and imbuing them with new meaning by suturing them together into blankets that protect the body from the cold and display designs that tell stories, register experiences, and express imagination. Mena Ochoa recognized that quilting fulfills a parallel social function in providing undervalued women with a welcoming space for convivial conversations about the challenges they face. Just as quilts brought new life to abandoned pieces of cloth, the quilting circle revealed new perspectives and possibilities to undervalued women. "This art has helped us to listen," Mena Ochoa relates, "to break those chains, and release some things we have been carrying for a long time."[84]

One of the projects Mena Ochoa initiated convened mothers of students at Roosevelt High School to form a restorative justice quilting circle.[85] Two teachers from that school (Nicolette Tiberio and Omar G. Ramirez) assisted her and the group's members as they discussed their struggles with personal harm and hurt while they sewed quilts together. In quilting sessions, painful topics could be raised tentatively, be dropped discreetly if they became too painful to discuss, but then be picked up again when it appeared safe to do so. The shared practical tasks involved in quilting helped put people at ease. They gave everyone something important to do and allowed conversation to flow back and forth, oscillating between friendly *platicando* (chit-chatting) and somber discussions of serious personal and public issues. Just as the quilting group participants put together pieces of cloth with different colors and textures, they also put together a collective identity among different people grounded in empathetic understandings and connections. Participants' everyday identities receded into the background as they explored what it meant to be cocreators of new craft objects as well as new social relations.

Women in the restorative justice quilting group developed a strong sense of personal and collective efficacy that they carried to other endeavors. Addressing their needs as women became an important impetus for addressing the needs of children, not just their own offspring but all of the children in the community. Some of the members of Mena Ochoa's quilting groups organized a Health Happens in Schools group to assist their student children campaigning for healthier food options on campus. Others joined neighborhood mobilizations designed to get the city to invest in after-school enrichment programs while working with student activists in successful campaigns to get the school district to approve a School Climate Bill of Rights that replaced detentions, suspensions, and expulsions with restorative justice circles promoting collective accountability and reconciliation. The Bill of Rights called for reining in the powers of school police and probation officers and establishing a districtwide Positive Behavior Intervention and Support Task Force made up of students, teachers, administrators, parents, and adult community members working together to build safe and secure environments for young people.

Understanding illness solely as the product of individual actions and as an arena for biomedical intervention fails in dramatic ways to address the needs of women like Mena Ochoa and the children they raise. Vulnerable people do need access to affordable and culturally sensitive medical care. They deserve to receive the most medically recommended treatments for the ailments they feel in their bodies, not just the second-rate remedies to which their limited insurance or absence of insurance restricts them. But they also need spaces where they can feel that their experiences, aspirations, and needs are recognized and taken seriously, where their health and well-being matter, and where they can see themselves as more than mere victims of low-wage labor, immigrant exploitation, predatory policing, sexism, social exclusion, environmental racism, and housing discrimination and insecurity.

The Boyle Heights quilting circles and the activism that emerged from them positioned women participants as cocreators of craft objects that were both functional and beautiful, but also as coauthors of new social relations, possibilities, and practices. The conviviality and confidence nurtured in the quilting circles led their members to participate in projects designed to address the roles that housing insecurity and discrimination play in their neighborhood. Some of them, aware of the effects of the pervasive presence in East Los Angeles of waste dumps and incinerators, metal plating shops, and emissions from car, truck, and bus engines, joined social movement campaigns for expanding access to health care and insurance. They worked to expand the neighborhood's supply of physicians, clinics, fresh fruits and vegetables, parks, and playgrounds. One of their initiatives helped lead to the formation of the Fideicomiso Comunitario Tierra Libra (FCTL), a community land trust dedicated to collective ownership of affordable and accessible housing, to the creation of community gardens and green spaces, and to the development of locally owned and managed socially responsible and culturally sensitive businesses. The community land trust model removes speculation from the housing market, creates new housing that will be affordable in perpetuity, and brings people together to make important decisions that determine their collective destiny. It can be an important tool for economic and physical well-being and improvement that infuses the community with means for working collaboratively for better lives rather than engaging in invidious competition for scarce resources. Arts education and cultural practice can thus sow seeds for political projects that perform a kind of social alchemy that turns the toxic qualities of linked exposures to disease and poverty into a remedial tonic. In these activities, mutual respect and responsibility promote social cohesion and improve prospects for health, healing, and economic self-sufficiency.

Violations of fair housing laws and the absence of medical insurance coverage are important problems to be remedied. Remedial measures, however, need to be undertaken with full recognition that access to wealth and good health does not exist in isolation but rather emerges from the complex interplay of people's social positions and their relationships to power. Like the women organized by Mena Ochoa, all children residing in proximity to toxicity and other danger zones need access to better health care and secure and affordable housing, but they also need changes in the social relations and political practices that leave them subject to the injuries resulting from life in places where poverty and pollution are concentrated. They need places and practices that imbue the future with the potential to create both health and housing justice through the creation of an active and engaged public committed to linking the two.

2

"Livin' in the Red"

Housing as a Health Problem and Health as a
Housing Problem

The funk, soul, and rock music group War recorded their song "Livin' in the Red" in 1986. Its title and lyrics revolve around the practice in personal and business ledgers of using the color red to signify being in debt. The song's infectious rhythms contrast sharply with lyrics that bemoan lacking the funds needed to pay bills and expenses, being besieged by credit investigators and bill collectors, having to rely on welfare checks to pay rent, and depending on food stamps to get something to eat. Its final rhyme pairs life in the USA with not having enough money to pay.

As it played on record players and boom boxes and was aired on radio and television broadcasts, "Livin' in the Red" registered the dire economic and political crises facing Black and Latinx people in the United States at the time. The presidential administration of Ronald Reagan repudiated the aims of civil rights laws and refused to enforce them. Government subsidies helped investors and owners shut down factories at home and move production to low-wage regions overseas. New forms of automation eliminated millions of highly paid blue-collar production jobs, while a variety of measures that restructured the economy channeled wealth to finance, insurance, and real estate owners and investors whose augmented wealth led to the expansion of low-paying nonunion jobs in consumer and producer services. The war on drugs made predatory policing a daily reality in aggrieved communities while the mass incarceration attendant to it disrupted family and social networks, interrupted work histories, and saddled people with criminal records whose collateral conditions barred them from employment and voting.[1] The narrative voice of "Livin' in the Red" describes the problems of one individual speaking in the first person, but the condition of living in the red expressed a collective condition and experience.

Today housing discrimination and its collateral consequences leave millions of members of aggrieved racialized groups living in the red, largely because the places where they live have been redlined. *Redlining* as originally defined narrowly refers to the policy orchestrated by private lenders and the federal government between 1934 and 1968 to deny mortgage loans to neighborhoods inhabited by members of aggrieved racialized groups. Since then, however, *redlining* has come to connote the subsequent broader denial of services and amenities in those areas because of the actions of urban planners, insurance agents, medical providers, and municipal police, fire, and sanitation departments.[2] In concert with the past and enduring injuries suffered by the specific neighborhoods that were redlined by the home loan policies of private sector and government actors in the 1930s, redlining functions today as one element in a circuit of policies and practices that equate aggrieved racialized communities with risk and make racist theories of value central to place making and place taking.[3]

Redlining did not inaugurate an entirely new regime of relegating different races to different and starkly unequal places. The slave plantation, the Native reservation, the Black ghetto, and the Latinx barrio all racialized space and spatialized race long before the housing policies of the 1930s New Deal. Federal policies in that era built on this history to designate dwellings inhabited by members of aggrieved racialized groups as threats to the unearned material gains and hoarded health amenities that accrued to people because of their whiteness. Redlining by the federal government augmented and codified previous policies long embedded in public order and public nuisance policing, racial zoning regulations, restrictive covenants, and government support for the deployment of racial segregation as a means of artificially inflating the property values of private developers of suburbs.[4] The New Deal era not only exacerbated the inequitable distribution of assets and opportunities but made segregated neighborhoods a newly augmented form of financial value for those given preferential access to them. It created an extensive and profitable new housing market by putting the full faith and credit of the federal treasury (built from tax dollars paid by members of all racial groups) at the disposal of lenders and borrowers adhering to the expressly racist exclusionary policies embedded in the property development, real estate sales, and banking sectors of the economy. Along with many other practices that made housing availability contingent on racial valuation, redlining helped solidify the logic of racial risk that today continues to inform and justify school segregation, neighborhood displacement and dispossession, environmental racism, home appraisal and property tax discrimination, the racialization of medical and property tax insurance, and mass incarceration.[5]

Redlining and related forms of housing discrimination produce concentrated disadvantages and fractured social relations. Areas redlined by the Home Owners' Loan Corporation (HOLC) and the Federal Housing Administration (FHA) between 1934 and 1968 today have high levels of detrimental physical and mental health conditions and outcomes, higher rates of subprime mortgages and subsequent foreclosures, high rates of evictions and food insecurity, and large numbers of residents incarcerated.[6] Redlined areas in Cleveland experience infant mortality rates 800 percent higher than the rates in nonredlined neighborhoods.[7] Researchers in Detroit have discovered that redlined areas have high numbers of foreclosures and slower foreclosure recovery rates. In these places large percentages of residents self-report their health as poor.[8] A study of residential segregation in nine US cities revealed that residents of historically redlined areas were twice as likely as residents of nonredlined neighborhoods to have poor health conditions.[9] Residents of Milwaukee neighborhoods suffering from redlining and its attendant and subsequent forms of disinvestment were found to have worse health outcomes than those dwelling in areas that were not redlined.[10]

The places that were formally redlined by bankers and government officials and those that have been effectively medically redlined by the health care system are areas that lack access to physicians, clinics, and hospitals. Lack of sources of fresh food often leads them to be described as "food deserts," but as Ashanté M. Reese argues it makes more sense to describe them as suffering from "food apartheid" caused by supermarket redlining and the concomitant proliferation in their neighborhoods of convenience stores, liquor stores, and fast food outlets as the only sources of food. Reese's research found that the 150,000 residents living in the Black neighborhoods east of the Anacostia River in Washington, D.C., have access to only three grocery stores.[11] Food deserts can also be "pharmacy deserts," where the nearest pharmacy is more than a mile away. That distance may not matter in affluent neighborhoods where people have adequate access to private automobiles, but it can be telling in densely populated Black and Latinx areas where many residents have incomes below the poverty level and lack access to reliable and efficient transit.[12]

Economic redlining in the housing market produces preconditions for medical redlining. High degrees of indebtedness caused by asset poverty and transience increase physical and psychological stressors that can produce hopelessness, despair, and resignation.[13] The concentrated disadvantages caused by legal redlining between 1934 and 1968 and de facto redlining ever since relegate people of subordinated races to residency in places with the highest levels of pollution, poverty, transience, disinvestment, and crime. While urban renewal and gentrification have transformed a few previously redlined neighborhoods into places replete with luxury apartments and profitable businesses, few of these have retained their previous residents, and most of the others remain sites of concentrated disadvantage. Residents of these neighborhoods cannot access the kinds of health insurance that would give them regular and effective professional care. As a result, their medical treatment takes place largely in emergency rooms and clinics in what are known as "safety net hospitals," that is, medical providers of last resort and least resources.

A mere 5 percent of hospitals treat nearly half of the Black patients who use Medicare. In these 574 institutions an average of 43.7 percent of the Medicare patients are Black compared with the 5.2 percent of Black Medicare patients at the 5,166 hospitals whose clientele is primarily white.[14] Twenty-five percent of hospitals account for 75 percent of Black infants born in the United States. Nearly 90 percent of elderly Black people seen in hospitals are served by only 25 percent of medical institutions, most of which are poorly resourced.[15] The hospitals most prominent in treating Black patients have older buildings, have less efficient equipment, and rarely offer high-tech services.[16]

Lack of adequate health insurance often results from the ways in which privatized health care makes medical insurance dependent on employment and thus susceptible to the effects of racist discrimination in hiring. The rate of unemployment among African Americans over the past seventy years has been twice as high as the rate of white unemployment. In fact, the *worst* peaks of white joblessness have been 2.4 percent better than the *average* amount of unemployment among Black workers.[17] Making health care dependent on private sector employment thus reserves the highest-quality care to those who have profited most from past and present racial discrimination in employment, especially those who have professional or high-paying blue-collar jobs. People with recurrent experiences of unemployment, irregular employment, or employment in low-wage jobs receive low-quality medical care or no care at all. These patients are viewed by medical providers and insurers as an economic drain on the health care system specifically and on society more generally because they cannot personally pay for their care. While they cannot pay, they are still charged, however, and wind up with unpayable medical debts that lead to evictions, job losses, and family dissolution.

The intersections of health and housing discrimination are zones of deadly danger. The pervasive presence of housing discrimination creates collective, cumulative, and continuing health hazards for members of aggrieved racialized groups, but those hazards ultimately also pose dangers to everyone.

RESIDING IN THE RED

Residential segregation and housing insecurities are the most important factors skewing economic opportunities and health care along racial lines in the United States. Every year more than four million violations of fair housing laws deny members of targeted racialized groups equal opportunities to acquire assets that can appreciate in value and be passed down to future generations.[18] The artificially constrained housing market produced by discrimination compels its targets to pay inflated costs for shelter, food, insurance, and transportation; to live in places that have polluted air, water, and land; and to develop survival strategies on their own in neighborhoods that host inferior schools and lack access to food, physicians, and pharmacists. For members of aggrieved racialized groups, housing discrimination suppresses wealth building and creates physical and mental stress through artificial, arbitrary, unnecessary, and irrational impediments to dignity and self-determination.

Places shaped by exclusion are rife with exploitation. They offer limited opportunities for employment and entrepreneurship but provide fertile ground for a wide range of wealth extractors who profit from poverty by charging exorbitant rents for inferior dwellings that they do not maintain, who run predatory check-cashing and payday lending businesses, who channel borrowers with good credit into subprime loans and adjustable-rate mortgages, and who purchase and securitize tax debts in order to obtain ownership of many parcels of real estate at bargain prices. Housing discrimination hurts its direct victims, but it harms all of society as well. The direct and collateral consequences of unfair housing misallocate resources, undermine social cohesion, lower productivity, increase crime, and raise the costs of medical care and medical insurance for everyone.

Unhampered and in fact aided by this discrimination, almost all white people seeking to buy homes have access to 100 percent of the houses they can afford to purchase. Homeownership almost always brings them increases in wealth because the property they purchase is likely to appreciate in value over time. Black prospective home buyers from all income groups, in contrast, are limited to an artificially small and inferior housing market. They receive a nearly 20 percent smaller return on their housing investments than their white counterparts. Black people purchasing homes have to contend with unfavorable loan terms, artificially high down payments and fees, reduced home value appraisals, an unfair and disproportionate share of local tax obligations, and inflated rates for homeowner, mortgage, property, and auto insurance. When homes owned by Black people do appreciate in value, they do so more slowly than comparable homes owned by whites. Moreover, the combined effects of discrimination, mortgage redlining, real estate agent steering, and decisions about zoning can make their homes actually *depreciate* in value, giving homeownership among many Black people a relationship to wealth building opposite to that among white people.[19] Wealth holdings for the typical Black household in 2019 amounted to $24,100, far less than the $188,200 possessed by the typical white household. Dwellings owned by white people in 2021 had an average equity of $216,000, while homes owned by Black people had an average equity of only $96,000.[20]

It is not just prospective home buyers and owners who suffer from housing discrimination. Renters also experience racially structured barriers to securing shelter. A 2012 audit of some eight thousand instances in twenty-eight US cities showed that rental agents consistently steer Black shelter seekers to a smaller sector of the market than white would-be renters.[21] Even short-term rentals have racial disparities. A field experiment in 2016 found that people with Black-sounding names were rejected for Airbnb rentals 16 percent more frequently than applicants who had the exact same credentials but whose names signaled that they were likely to be white.[22]

Racial discrimination against apartment seekers causes particularly egregious harm because public policy and private actions have created an artificial shortage of rental housing. For decades, both the FHA and private insurance companies gave favored treatment to owner-occupied housing while treating rental housing (especially in areas inhabited by members of aggrieved racialized groups) as unworthy investments. The FHA insured more than 6.4 million single-family dwellings between 1934 and 1965 but only 650,000 multifamily rental units.[23] The Section 8 voucher program that replaced the provision of public housing rental units remains chronically underfunded and underused. It serves only about one in four eligible shelter seekers while funneling voucher seekers to wait-lists that take years to open up. Because a significant portion of Section 8 rental payments come from the government, they are good deals for landlords, who get payment in full and on time. Yet landlords and property managers are not required to accept the vouchers, and many of them discriminate against prospective tenants who have Section 8 funds as their source of income. The properties that do accept Section 8 vouchers tend to be located in disinvested and racially segregated areas, frustrating the program's potential to affirmatively further fair housing.[24]

Rising rental costs have far outstripped wage gains. Nearly half of hourly employees—some fifty-three million people—are paid an average of $10.22 per hour.[25] Nearly half of renters in Black and Latinx neighborhoods report spending 30–50 percent of their incomes on rent. Average move-in rents have more than doubled since the year 2000, and there is not a single county in the nation where minimum-wage workers can afford the rental cost of an average two-bedroom apartment.[26] Nearly one-third of all households in the United States now spend 30 percent or more of their income on shelter and utilities, while more than eight million low-income renters pay more than half of what they earn monthly for housing.[27] In 2013, 23 percent of Black families and 25 percent of Latinx families who rented dwellings reported paying at least half of their income every month to their landlords.[28] In the San Francisco Bay Area, costs of shelter for nearly half of renters now exceed 30 percent, while one-quarter of renters pay more than half of their monthly incomes to their landlords. A study by the National Low Income Housing Coalition found that in 2018 there were only thirty-six affordable available dwellings for every one hundred low-income households.[29]

Working- and middle-class people of all races struggle with consumer debt. Yet aggressive forms of debt collection proceed along expressly racialized lines. Although debts owed by residents of Black neighborhoods are typically 20 percent to 25 percent smaller than those owed in white neighborhoods, courts in St. Louis, Chicago, and Newark rendered twice as many judgments for unpaid debts against residents in Black neighborhoods as in white neighborhoods, even when controlling for income disparities. Between 2008 and 2012, agents for banks, hospitals, utilities, and companies collecting on auto and home loans seized more than $34 million from residents of St. Louis Black neighborhoods. In Chicago a subprime auto lending firm secured judgments against residents of Black neighborhoods at a rate eighteen times higher than it did against those in white neighborhoods. Court judgments related to high-cost installment loan defaults in St. Louis were issued in Black communities five times more frequently than in white ones. Bankruptcy often occurs when the sums that debtors owe exceed what they can reasonably be expected to pay. Yet even in bankruptcy racial categories exacerbate inequalities: Black debtors are often steered toward Chapter 13 plans rather than Chapter 7 options, which provide faster relief and are less costly.[30]

Residential racial segregation not only impedes asset accumulation for working-class and middle-class people from aggrieved racialized communities but also produces and concentrates poverty. In the last third of the twentieth century, concentrated poverty in the United States increased by 80 percent. Sociologist Douglas S. Massey observes that housing segregation is "the structural feature of American society most responsible for the geographic concentration of poverty observed during the 1970s and 1980s." Massey notes that the already-enormous challenges posed by individual and familial poverty become exacerbated for Black people because housing discrimination leaves them "uniquely burdened with the disadvantages of very poor neighborhoods, which act independently to constrain socio-economic mobility and undermine well-being."[31] A certain number of impoverished white people can always find low-cost housing in resource-rich neighborhoods, but racial discrimination forecloses that possibility for economically challenged and even working- and middle-class Latinx and Black shelter seekers.

What Massey identifies as this unique burden has concrete and calamitous effects. Nearly one out of every three Black children born between 1985 and 2000 grew up in a high-poverty neighborhood, compared to only one out of every one hundred white children similarly disadvantaged.[32] Nearly two-thirds of young Asian American and white people grew up in neighborhoods with high or very high levels of opportunity, but only 29 percent of Native American, 23 percent of Latinx, and 19 percent of Black young people lived similarly. In contrast, 66 percent of Black children, 58 percent of Latinx children, and 53 percent of Native American children grew up in neighborhoods with low or very low opportunities.[33] Only one out of every ten Black children born between 1985 and 2000 had the opportunity to grow up in a neighborhood with less than 10 percent of its residents impoverished, while 60 percent of white children in that generational cohort grew up amid those favored conditions. In 2013, nearly one-third of Black children resided in areas with a poverty rate greater than 30 percent, while virtually no white children lived similarly.[34]

HOUSING DISCRIMINATION AS A PUBLIC HEALTH HAZARD

High housing costs damage public health. People who are cost burdened in the housing sphere find themselves forced to delay purchasing needed medications and to postpone necessary medical treatments.[35] When rents go up and wages stagnate, people can become houseless, not because of personal failure on their part but because of the failure of the market to produce adequate affordable shelter. Cities with high rental costs, low vacancy rates, and severe income inequality are the ones most likely to have high levels of houselessness. When housing is scarce, already-vulnerable groups are the most likely to be excluded: Black people account for nearly 40 percent of houseless people, even though they make up only around 13 percent of the general population. Racial identities exacerbate class injuries: the percentages of Native American, Alaska Native, and Black people who are houseless are greater than the percentages of those groups living in dire poverty.[36]

Nearly a quarter of the people living without shelter are younger than twenty-four years of age. Houseless children are four times more likely to be treated for medical issues in emergency departments than children who are housed. The more than one hundred thousand houseless children in the United States experience disproportionately high levels of diabetes, asthma, urinary tract infections, and mental health problems. A study of houseless children and health in New York City found that among houseless children treated in emergency departments, 38 percent were Latinx, 37 percent Black, 7.5 percent white, and 3 percent Asian American.[37]

Housing discrimination enacts grievous economic injuries, but it also functions as a public health hazard. The stress and stigma of discrimination in the housing market harm the physical and mental health of individuals and undermine the social cohesion needed for secure and healthy communities. Segregation has continuing effects in creating impediments to education and employment opportunities, doling out disproportionate exposure to physical and emotional stressors to members of aggrieved racialized groups, and creating neighborhood conditions that lead to high numbers of preterm and low-weight births, high risks of myocardial infarction, low rates of surviving illnesses, early onset of sickness, and rapid progression of disease.[38] The low-birth-weight and preterm births concentrated in aggrieved racialized communities are associated with high levels of maternal mortality and can cause lifelong cognitive development issues.[39]

Neighborhoods that have suffered in the past and present from mortgage and insurance redlining have disproportionate levels of cancer, tuberculosis, maternal depression, and a wide range of other physical and mental health issues.[40] Medical care is impeded by housing insecurity. Without access to affordable dwellings, for example, cancer patients experience interruptions and discontinuity in treatments because of evictions, frequent moves, and houselessness. The costs of medical care leave them with insufficient funds to pay for safe housing, relegating them to residency in places where they are exposed to radon and other hazards associated with increases in cancer. Studies have shown that housing insecurity is associated with barriers to cancer screening and impediments to treatment. Cancer mortality rates are disproportionately higher in neighborhoods with histories of frequent mortgage denials and foreclosures.[41] A 2022 study found that among cancer patients housing insecurity was the single most significant risk factor for mortality even after adjusting for financial hardship, food insecurity, and impediments to transportation.[42]

Midlife and elderly adults residing in segregated and isolated neighborhoods possess disproportionately higher levels of proinflammatory factors in their bloodstreams, predisposing them to premature heart disease more frequently than their counterparts in more privileged areas.[43] Racially segregated neighborhoods with impoverished residents have the highest percentages of infant mortality, maternal depression, high blood pressure, and heart disease.[44] Women who are Indigenous or Black are three times more likely than white women to die during childbirth.[45]

In pockets of concentrated poverty caused by housing discrimination, residents are exposed to high levels of carcinogens and teratogens, as well as dust, pests, and dampness, all of which increase susceptibility to asthma.[46] Deaths from asthma among African American children are seven times greater than those among white youths.[47] These differentials do not stem from class inequality. Indeed, the racial health gap expands as income rises. Blacks living in poverty are only 8 percent more likely than similarly positioned whites to report ill health, but Blacks with incomes at or higher than 200 percent of the poverty level are

59 percent more likely than equally well-off whites to describe their health as only fair or poor.[48] As their incomes rise, their direct interactions with racist individuals and institutions increase, leading to augmented stress, while housing discrimination continues to exclude them from the neighborhoods with the greatest amenities and advantages. Studies have found that racial identity serves as a predictor independent of class status for the likelihood of disproportionate exposure to polluted air and contaminated fish.[49] The poorest of poor white children face far less exposure to toxic lead than equally and even better economically positioned Black children, a disparity that Sampson and Winter accurately describe as evidence of toxic inequality.[50]

Largely because of housing discrimination and pollution exposure, Asian American and Latinx people suffer from disproportionately high levels of diabetes, tuberculosis, hepatitis B, and cancers of the liver, cervix, uterus, and stomach.[51] Reservations and rural areas inhabited by Native Americans are plagued by the presence of polluted landfills, incinerators, and nuclear waste storage facilities.[52] Indigenous people suffer from an age-adjusted death rate almost 40 percent greater than that of the general population, and they report disproportionately high rates of heart disease, tuberculosis, liver disease, and cirrhosis.[53] The rates of water insecurity are higher among Native Americans than among the rest of the population.[54] One-third of Navajo nation households have no access to running water.[55]

By nearly every indicator, the health of African Americans lags behind more favored groups in the United States. Among African Americans of all classes, residential segregation is associated with high levels of infant mortality, cardiovascular disease, tuberculosis, all-cause mortality, and self-evaluated poor health.[56] The disease and mortality rates for a wide range of illnesses are higher for Black people than for white people, even when controlling for differences in income levels. Being Black means being more likely to die in infancy and to contract heart disease. Black people perish from cancer at a rate higher than any other racial group.[57]

Residential segregation leads to health inequalities. Members of aggrieved racialized groups dwell disproportionately in areas that lack streetlights, fresh food sources, recreational spaces, and health care providers. These neighborhoods are plagued by pesticide drift, floods, and fires. They routinely feature poorly maintained sidewalks adjacent to poorly lit streets designed for high vehicle speeds that cause high numbers of vehicle-pedestrian accidents. Black and Latinx neighborhoods especially suffer from the absence of tree canopies, parks, and gardens. People who live in areas with limited access to parks, trees, and other green spaces have lower life expectancy than residents of areas with those amenities. A study of Los Angeles by public health researchers predicted that if the vegetation index and tree canopies in areas with predominantly Black and Latinx populations were increased to the median levels in the rest of the region, between 570,300 and 908,000 collective years of life expectancy would be gained.[58] In neighborhoods where rooftop tar and concrete streets and pavements trap heat, the paucity of trees, parks, and other green spaces increases temperatures year round. High heat kills people by increasing risks of heart attacks and strokes.[59]

Urban areas that experience higher temperatures than surrounding places are known as "heat islands." These are deadly for the people who reside in and near them; they also raise the earth's temperature in ways that endanger the entire planet.[60] Housing discrimination plays a role in the location of these heat islands. A study of more than one hundred urban areas found that places that had experienced mortgage redlining in the past had dramatically higher land surface temperatures today than neighborhoods that have not been redlined.[61] These areas also have high levels of air pollution. A study examining 1.5 million deaths in California between 2014 and 2020 revealed that the risk of deaths on days of *both* high heat and excessive air pollution was three times greater than on days that experienced *either* high heat or excessive air pollution alone. During the hottest and most polluted days the risk of death increased by 21 percent.[62]

Neighborhoods inhabited primarily by white residents generally have the lowest levels of air pollution. Residents of predominantly and/or exclusively Black neighborhoods, however, experience dangerously high levels of polluted air that can lead to asthma, low birth weights, respiratory illnesses, cancer, and cardiovascular diseases.[63] African Americans from all income groups face exposure to pollution caused by the burning of fossil fuels at a rate 1.54 times greater than the exposures that the population at large experiences.[64] White people are 50 percent less likely than members of aggrieved racialized groups to reside near chemical waste facilities. Moreover, chemical waste facilities located in segregated neighborhoods are almost twice as likely to produce chemical emission incidents as those in white-occupied neighborhoods.[65] Housing discrimination even makes gravity work against the health of Black people when waterborne and airborne pollutants and diseases fester in segregated low-lying areas of flood-prone cities like the Ninth Ward in New Orleans and the Third Ward in Houston. These neighborhoods lack the bioswales, trees, gardens, and permeable street surfaces that protect health and property in advantaged areas predominantly inhabited by white people in those cities.

HEALTH CARE DISCRIMINATION

The communities with the most severe health needs often receive the worst medical care. A 2003 review of more than one hundred studies documented the damage perpetrated by medical bias, stereotyping, and prejudice. It revealed that in 40 percent of quality measures, Black, Indigenous, and Pacific Islander medical patients received poorer care than white patients.[66] Residents of segregated neighborhoods often have to rely on medical care facilities of last resort, such as "safety net" hospital emergency rooms and under-resourced clinics that lack experienced and well-credentialed health care specialists and clinicians. Patients with little or no insurance never know if they will be able to access any medical care at all at any given location, much less secure the optimally recommended medicines and treatments they need. The principles of fiscalized risk management that guide the privatized insurance system deprive these patients routinely of the most medically indicated treatments and medicines. Walk-in clinics offer charity but not justice. They become medical facilities of last resort where doctors in training engage in service learning and provide charity care, but they leave patients waiting in overcrowded rooms for hours in hopes of receiving rationed treatments and medicines in facilities that are under-resourced and inadequate. Yet the providers, primarily trainees and students, receive praise and remuneration for their roles in what Zinzi D. Bailey et al. aptly describe as the "American medical caste system."[67]

Residents of areas rife with concentrated poverty often have urgent immediate need for medical care caused by housing injuries. They live in places where profiteering slumlords neglect building maintenance, leaving residents to contend with pest infestations, broken water pipes, and shutoffs of water, gas, and electricity. Studies show that rental dwellings occupied by Black people are less likely to be properly maintained and repaired than those inhabited by whites. The resulting holes in water-damaged walls and ceilings lead to exposure to allergens caused and exacerbated by mold, dust mites, rats, and roaches. These conditions worsen asthma and other conditions and disorders. In 2012,

Black people nationwide were found 20 percent more likely to have asthma than white people.[68]

Because members of aggrieved racialized groups have historically faced racist obstacles to both rental and owner-occupied housing, they are concentrated in zones of deprivation where transience, disinvestment, and pollution imperil both the acquisition of wealth and the maintenance of health. Municipal zoning codes and public-private development projects contribute to the creation and maintenance of racialized medical sacrifice zones. They concentrate polluting industries and waste disposal facilities in impoverished racially segregated neighborhoods. Municipal authorities routinely provide only sporadic and inadequate garbage collection in these areas while failing to enforce housing codes in them.[69] For several years, city officials in Baltimore gave a wealthy and primarily white neighborhood one extra day of garbage collection each week, while the city's Black neighborhoods were forced to contend with fewer trash pickups and the perils of vacant lots and alleys littered with junk and garbage illegally dumped there by outsiders.[70] People who do not live in the neighborhood discard tires, chemicals, solvents, and other hazardous materials in these sacrifice zones, saving the costs they would incur if they took these items to landfills that charged them fees. The existence of a neighborhood outside municipal jurisdiction where enforcement against littering and dumping is nonexistent provides spaces where people unload trash, garbage, and appliances, breaking the law and profiting from that lawbreaking. When hurricanes, floods, and fires devastate inhabited areas, rebuilding resources are systematically channeled to places where the residents are wealthy and white but are systematically withheld from places populated by members of aggrieved racialized groups.[71]

WORKING IN THE RED

Housing discrimination and medical racism condemn many members of aggrieved racialized groups to be unable to meet rent bills and make mortgage payments, to pay municipal fines and fees, and to manage consumer and medical debts. Yet while their shared condition of "livin' in the red," often leaves them broke, it does not necessarily leave them broken. Living in the red also impels them to develop ways of working in the red that promote solidarity and social cohesion, that cultivate mutual recognition and respect, and that enable them to organize and mobilize for social change.

Despite the grim circumstances they describe, the lyrics of War's song "Livin' in the Red" invite listeners who cannot find jobs that would pay for the costs of car notes, water bills, taxes, and alimony to join the singer in jumping, dancing, singing, living and loving in the red. The song affirms the value of experiencing joy as part of the psychic armor that people need in struggles for survival. At the time that War described the linked fate of Black communities as living in the red, hip-hop producers and musicians described themselves as working in the red, deploying a different association with that same color. For them, the red did not connote debt but rather signified the color used to identify the place on the sound meter that tells recording engineers where distortion begins. In their hands, the red marker designed to warn engineers where *not to go* became a guide to precisely where they wanted *to go*, enabling them to savor creative uses of sounds designated as distorted by the dominant culture and then to use them to augment the music and noise that they produced. They found that the prohibited red area could be worked in creatively and productively, that the heavy dark growling reverberating sounds that set it off could be used to make noise that captured attention, built tension, emphasized rhythm, and resonated inside bodies. Being receptive to dissonance in music and using it creatively provided lessons useful in dealing with dissonance in individual and collective life. Using machines in ways other than they were intended to be used and discovering effective uses for sounds considered beyond the permissible norms of musical composition cultivated abilities to find value in undervalued things and by extension undervalued people.[72] Working in the red in hip-hop displayed the utility of expressive culture for deepening collective capacities for improvisation, invention, inversion, subversion, disguise, and surprise, qualities that are sorely needed by people forced to live in the red in the economy. In keeping with long-standing practices and traditions in the Afro-diasporic world, working in the red encouraged people to recognize that when used in the right ways, poison can be deployed as medicine and something toxic can be made tonic.

In Part II, chapters 4, 5, and 6 delineate the ways in which living in the red for members of aggrieved racialized groups has been shaped structurally and systemically by home value appraisals and tax assessments (chapter 4); by predatory policing and mass incarceration (chapter 5); and by insurance redlining and racialized risk assessment (chapter 6). In Part III, chapter 7 delineates how working in the red convivially and creatively enables people to build an active and engaged public sphere for health and housing justice. Chapter 8 shows how social movement mobilization and grassroots convivial cocreation point toward treating both housing and health care as human rights and collective resources rather than commodities to be purchased privately by individuals. Chapter 9 concludes the book by analyzing what it means to work for housing and health justice at this particular and perilous moment in history.

Before presenting those explorations of living in the red and working in the red, however, chapter 3 explains the importance of identifying and utilizing the right tools for the challenges we face. It argues that making meaningful progress for housing and health justice requires us to be ready, to know the work we want our work to do.

3

If You're Ready

Responding to Health and Housing Emergencies

The lyrics of the 1983 Staple Singers' song "If You're Ready (Come Go with Me)" point the way toward a new and better world, one that is without hatred between the races and freed from economic exploitation and political domination. Lead singer Mavis Staples, backed up by the voices of her sisters Yvonne and Cleotha and accompanied by their father Roebuck, invited listeners to come with her to that world but warned that they had to make themselves ready for the journey. The song asserts that peace, love, and freedom will not simply arrive on their own, that people have to get ready and to be ready to help bring them about.

The theme of being ready resonated with the pulse of aggrieved people at that moment in history. In a time of great danger for the anticolonial and Black freedom movements that he championed in the 1960s, Stokely Carmichael (Kwame Ture) argued that making social change necessitated being ready, being prepared in advance to take effective action when opportunities arise. Echoing a slogan used by Sékou Touré as leader of the newly independent nation of Guinea, Carmichael explained that it is important *to be* ready, so you do not have to *get ready*.

The necessity to be ready is evidenced in the efforts by the leadership of the American Medical Association (AMA) to address and redress the organization's seamy history of complicity with medical racism. In November 2020 the AMA formally acknowledged that "racism negatively impacts and exacerbates health inequities among historically marginalized communities." Its spokespersons warned that "without systemic and structural-level change, health inequities will continue to exist, and the overall health of the nation will suffer."[1] The AMA proclamation announced a noble goal. Yet as with so many of the calls to action prompted by the mass protests in 2020 against the killings of George Floyd and Breonna Taylor, turning proclamations into policies and aspirations into action has proved exceedingly difficult. Long histories of race-based science and medicine leave researchers, physicians, clinicians, and the public at large "not ready" to understand racism's role in damaging collective health. The AMA's own history has contributed significantly to that lack of preparedness.

In the 1900s the AMA allowed local medical societies to exclude Black physicians from membership. It used the designation "colored" in its national physician directory to identify, stigmatize, and marginalize doctors who were not white. Physicians labeled as "colored" by the AMA found that as a result insurance companies canceled their malpractice coverage and banks denied them access to credit. When Congress passed the Hill-Burton Act channeling federal funds to the construction and expansion of hospitals, the Association opposed the campaign by civil rights advocates to deny those funds to medical centers that refused to hire or treat Black people.[2] Taxpayers of all races funded the construction of medical facilities enabled by the Hill-Burton Act, yet racial discrimination in its administration worked to provide white people with special preferences and unfair advantages within the health care system.

The Association worked perniciously and successfully to undermine the 1964 Civil Rights Act by mobilizing its members to defeat a ban against racial discrimination in the employment of medical interns, residents, and admitting staff. It even organized and mobilized its members to oppose a ban against segregating or excluding patients from doctors' offices, clinics, and hospitals on the basis of race. The federal Department of Health, Education, and Welfare (which later became the Department of Health and Human Services) caved in to the pressure campaign launched by the AMA in 1964 that exempted physicians from key provisions of the Civil Rights Act, an exemption that guaranteed the protection and continuation of racist practices in the medical profession. In 1964, Martin Luther King Jr. pointed to the cumulative effects of unimpeded discrimination in federal funding from the Hill-Burton Act, the AMA's endorsement of an exemption for physicians from the 1964 Civil Rights Act, and the substitution of superstition for

science enacted by race-based medicine. King condemned what he called
"the constant use of federal funds to support this most notorious form
of segregation." He called for direct action and creative nonviolence
against medical racism, arguing: "Of all the forms of inequality, injustice in health is the most shocking and the most inhuman because it
often results in physical death."[3]

A half century after Dr. King's condemnation of injustice in health,
the medical profession's views on racism and health may seem to have
progressed substantially. Many researchers, teachers, physicians, and
clinicians now agree with the AMA's 2020 declaration that racism
undermines individual and collective health. They may endorse the part
of the proclamation that affirms that "race is a social construct and is
distinct from ethnicity, genetic ancestry or biology."[4] Yet it is one thing
to state that race is a social construct and quite another to identify,
analyze, and oppose the specific mechanisms by which it is produced
and the specific forms through which it operates. This distinction
became glaringly evident in 2020 when Ed Livingston, deputy editor for
clinical reviews and education at the *Journal of the American Medical
Association*, proclaimed on a podcast that because the civil rights acts
of the 1960s had declared racism illegal, racial disparities in health care
had to be the result exclusively of class stratification rather than racial
inequalities. Livingston seemed to assume that racism had been eradi-
cated because some specific racist practices had been outlawed.

The confidence with which Livingston proclaimed his ignorance
about history and racism testifies to the inadequate education furnished
in medical schools and to the impoverished quality of scholarship in
medical journals.[5] Professional training and distinction did not make
Livingston ready to go where the AMA declared he should go. A similar
level of parochial ignorance pervaded Bruce T. Lahn's erroneous but
widely celebrated attempts in 2005 to use genomic science to revive the
long-discredited notion that studies of brain size "explain" the allegedly
inferior intelligence of Black people. His claims were published and
praised in leading professional journals, despite not being grounded in
empirical evidence. They were, in fact, refuted by subsequent studies
without leading to retraction or even contrition by the journals in which
they were published. Apart from the scientific shortcomings of Lahn's
research, his findings also evidenced the underutilization of interdisci-
plinary methods in medical and scientific training. Lahn's claims rested
on what one perceptive critic accurately describes as "pontifications
about areas of knowledge far outside his areas of expertise" and on

scholarship ignorantly grounded in "loose and sweeping generalizations about human cultural history" that could not stand up to the scrutiny of historians.[6]

Anti-Black sentiment in scientific research and medical practice did not begin with the AMA's historical support for segregation, and just because the AMA now declares itself committed to a new and better course of action, anti-Blackness has not ended. The patterns of the past will continue to shape practices in the present unless people understand their underpinnings and enduring appeal and unless they craft mechanisms that counter their pernicious effects. We cannot go to a better place with the AMA unless, as the Staple Singers advised, we are ready.

This chapter presents terms and tools necessary for becoming ready to meet the challenges delineated throughout the rest of the book. The evidence, ideas, and arguments it presents will be most useful to readers who can make themselves ready: ready to reject the racial science that portrays race as a biological reality rather than a political construction, ready to understand that analyses that are race based need not be race bound, ready to view racism as systemic and structural rather than merely individual and interpersonal, ready to comprehend the ways in which racism in itself poses a hazard to individual and collective health, ready to embrace a multiaxis Black feminist intersectionality, ready to recognize the international dimensions of health and housing injustice, and ready to become equipped fully with the terms and tools needed to bring about meaningful changes.

READINESS TO UNDERSTAND RACE AS A POLITICAL RATHER THAN BIOLOGICAL CATEGORY

In both medicine and law, practitioners frequently err by embracing "commonsense" historically embedded assumptions that races are distinct and that race is a biological reality. Yet race is not a *biological* category: it is a *political* construction that uses small differences in appearance to justify and excuse large differences in status and power. There are no races, only groups of people that are racialized.[7] Race is not a characteristic of individuals; it is a socially produced variable.[8] The genetic traits that people identify as markers of racial identity do not predict any meaningful aspects of biology. Babies birthed by Black women immigrants from Africa in Chicago had birth weights nearly identical to those born to white women, both of which were much better than the birth weights of babies born to US-born Black women. Yet as these immigrant women spent more time in the United States living as people categorized as Black and treated accordingly, the relative health advantages of African-born women and their children began to disappear in a single generation.[9]

Dorothy Roberts has shown how commonly used terms purporting to identify race inaccurately group together people of disparate physical and genetic characteristics. She explains, for example, that a gene variant related to metabolizing some drugs appears in 34 percent of Zimbabweans but in only 3.3 percent of the Luhya in Kenya and in 0 percent of Yorubas in Nigeria.[10] She observes that people from different parts of Africa differ more from one another genetically than they differ from a person from France. A revealing study of hypertension among residents of Chicago found that African Americans had 80 percent higher odds of developing that condition than white people. When researchers adjusted the results to take into account how individual-level factors affected the results, the disparity was only slightly reduced. But when they used neighborhood-level variables, the Black-white disparities disappeared. What appeared to be differences determined by race turned out to be disparities produced by the racism of housing discrimination and its attendant neighborhood race effects. A similar study of hypertension in Puerto Rico disproved previous claims by researchers that high blood pressure was associated with darker skin and therefore evidence of a racial-genetic predisposition. These earlier studies erred by confusing the phenotype of dark skin with its cultural significance. Subsequent research revealed that the most reliable predictor of hypertension was not skin pigment but rather having internalized the experience of being socially categorized as a dark-skinned person and experiencing the social stressors attendant to it.[11] As Roberts concludes, "Race is not a biological category that is politically charged. It is a political category that has been disguised as a biological one."[12]

While race is not a biological category, the racism that people experience can have biological consequences. As Clarence Gravlee argues, race can at times become biology because of racism. Genes and the mechanisms that regulate gene expression interact constantly with the environment. Since racism is one determinant influencing which people experience high levels of social isolation and stress, it should not be particularly surprising that a marginalized racialized group has higher levels of cortisol (mediated by a biologic/gene expression response). This does not demonstrate, however, as too many wrongly assume, that a given racial group is genetically predisposed to have higher cortisol levels. Stress experienced across generations in fetal and early postnatal environments can contribute to heart disease and diabetes later in life, which in turn increase fetal and postnatal stress for the next generation.[13] Studies of the health of aggrieved populations rarely, if ever, take into account the possibility that high levels of stress can lead them to consume sugar-laden and high-fat foods to reduce anxiety. Nor do they consider the impact of ethnically targeted cigarette advertising and the prevalence of fast-food outlets and liquor stores in segregated and disinvested neighborhoods.[14]

The history of medically approved standards of care for babies with too much bilirubin in the blood reveals the pernicious effects of race-based medicine. Hyperbilirubinemia or infant jaundice is a condition of yellow pigment in red blood cells, a condition that is common but when severe may have complications including brain damage. In 2004 the American Academy of Pediatrics guidelines for treating the condition identified East Asian "race" as a significant risk factor for severe cases. These judgments wrongly compressed diverse populations into singular categories that magnified unimportant aspects of their identities while minimizing the importance of individuals' socioeconomic status, migration histories, and access to resources. Carelessly conceived associations produced poor medical practices. Categorization as a high-risk group led newborns of East Asian ancestry to be administered unnecessary excessive treatments with harms that far outweighed their potential benefits because they were associated with increases in phlebotomy and hospitalization. Physicians following race-based guidelines turned to increased use of phototherapy (which can increase some cancers and rates of epilepsy). These overtreatments subjected East Asian parents of newborns to breastfeeding interruptions and increased work-related stressors and general anxiety. Pediatrics researchers conclude correctly that race-based medicine is mired in the fallacy of assuming that general population-level associations are causative at the individual level and in a failure to understand that the concept of race emerges from a sociopolitical system of invidious categorization. "Race is not a risk factor for inequitable disease outcomes," Sharon Ostfield-Johns and colleagues point out, but "racism is—through its explicit and insidious biological effects on human bodies."[15]

Medical policies have long harmed marginalized communities. Examples include the work of the American eugenics movement supporting involuntary sterilization to reduce the Black population, the long and ugly history of unethical medical experimentation on Black bodies, the attendant exploitation of Black patients as captive clinical material, and the Carnegie Foundation–funded Flexner Report of 1910, which closed all but two of the medical schools set up to train Black physicians at a time when racially segregated all-white medical schools dominated the profession. The Flexner Report also recommended that those two remaining schools limit themselves to training public health and hygiene practitioners. Rather than enabling the full range of medical services needed by Black people, the recommendation focused on preventing working-class Black patients in service jobs from contracting diseases that might then be communicated to their white employers.[16]

This history generates underlying assumptions that lead many doctors to treat race as a biological rather than a political category, which then shapes attendant medical research and practice, philanthropic funding, and public policy. It leads medical researchers to direct resources toward isolated biological solutions for what are actually social and political problems. What Dorothy Roberts calls "race-based medicine"— embraced by research foundations, public health agencies, and pharmaceutical companies—allocates grossly disproportionate funds for studies that treat health disparities in genomic terms, not because that approach is the soundest approach to health, but because it is the path most likely to lead to the development of lucrative (even if ineffective) pharmaceutical products to be marketed to members of targeted aggrieved racialized groups.[17] Race-based medicine leads to misdiagnosing social and psychological behaviors such as excessive food consumption or smoking as solely medical problems in need of surgical, pharmaceutical, or genetic treatments. The search for biomedical solutions to social problems fuels the growth of investments in pharmaceutical firms, medical equipment suppliers, and biotechnology companies. Genetic research, however, provides a poor point of entry into studying and treating racial health disparities. Commonsense racial categories are not valid reflections of genetic inheritance, and genetics actually plays a very small role in variations of population health across places and times.[18] Yet the federally funded National Institutes of Health allocates 50 percent more funding for research projects that include the words *gene*, *genome*, and *genetic* than for studies that include the word *prevention*.[19]

Sarah Rios's insightful research on responses to the radical increase in cases of valley fever among farmworkers and incarcerated people in California's Central Valley evidences the harms perpetrated by emphases on genetic causes of disease rather than on the social ecology of health. Rios shows that funders prioritize the development of vaccines imagined to address an alleged genetic propensity among people of Mexican origin to be susceptible to valley fever rather than supporting the more costly, less lucrative, but more effective course of addressing the ways in which poverty, pollution, prisons, and global warming make people employed in outdoor activities such as construction and farmwork or locked up in prisons in polluted places particularly vulnerable to contracting the disease. Hoped-for vaccines are not the only response to the disease grounded in genetic assumptions. When the administrators of prisons in highly endemic counties in California discovered disproportionate numbers of valley fever cases among incarcerated people of Black and Filipino ancestry, they initiated a policy of transferring members of those groups to other prisons. They should have instead protected the health of all prisoners by addressing the ways in which resource extraction, construction, and agricultural cultivation made the spores that transmitted the disease circulate in and around the prisons. Rios observes that this response to valley fever relied on setting an arbitrary "acceptable" level of a debilitating disease and blaming it on the biological makeup of people from the groups that had the most cases, rather than reckoning with the prison system's failure to prevent exposure to valley fever by providing timely and adequate health care, installing air filters, paving over dust-producing dirt, and providing clean water and nutritious food.[20]

Research on responses to type 2 diabetes by James Doucet-Battle demonstrates that pharmaceutical companies and the scientific researchers they fund persist in attributing the prevalence of the disease among African Americans to their biological makeup rather than to the ways that residential segregation, labor exploitation, unemployment, housing insecurity, and the stressors of racism can lead to excessive consumption of unhealthful food products in neighborhoods lacking fresh food options and presenting obstacles to exercise opportunities.[21] In a similar vein, Michael Montoya observes that the time, money, and energy spent collecting personal biological data on people with diabetes diverts attention and resources away from activities such as cleaning up toxic hazards, screening people for disease, attending to the health needs of IV drug users, improving school lunch menus, assisting people to manage caloric ledgers, promoting workplace health and safety, creating opportunities for exercise and securing places where it can occur freely, and combating food and housing insecurity.[22]

It is not that genes do not matter at all, but rather that genes are contextual factors tied to social relations, not independent determining variables. In cases when genetic vulnerability matters, it is almost always in conjunction with risk factors that are primarily social, such as housing segregation and insecurity. As Anne Fausto-Sterling explains, because genes operate inside networks that include social conditions that produce new physiologies, technology and genetic remedies should be aids—but not motors—for solving racial health disparities.[23]

Faulty conceptions of race create a downward spiral in which succumbing to health risks designates people as medical risks but then also positions them as lucrative market opportunities. This impedes their actual access to well-being but creates profitable markets for entrepreneurs purporting to address their illnesses and infirmities. Yet different responses to any particular drug are greater within racialized groups than across them, and simply "knowing" the race of any particular patient is a poor predictor of that person's response to any particular drug.[24] Michelle Smirnova describes how the medicalization and pharmaceutical-ization of social problems reduce complex multiple-axis social problems such as economic inequality, predatory policing, and environmental and medical racism to simple single-axis problems about individual bodies.[25] As Roberts concludes, "Race medicine is bad medicine, it's poor science, and it's a false interpretation of humanity."[26]

READINESS TO BE RACE BASED BUT NOT RACE BOUND

Writing and speaking about racism always runs the risk of leading people to believe that racial differences are real and immutable, that race is a biological reality rather than a socially constructed political category. Some believe that the problems of racism can be overcome through adopting a "color-blind" approach that purports to refuse any recognition of race. This alleged color blindness, however, exacerbates rather than diminishes the power of racism. Because it pervades the practices and processes central to structures and systems, racism cannot be willed away or wished away. It does not disappear if we pretend it does not exist. Color-blind practices will never solve color-bound problems. People who have been racialized cannot ignore what is killing them, and neither should anyone else. Members of aggrieved racialized groups out of necessity often do have to embrace and inhabit tactically and strategically the racialized identities that oppress them, to use their common conditions and linked fates for collective mobilizations that are race based. Yet these struggles do not have to be, and should not be, narrowly race bound.

Antiracism needs to be part of a larger struggle against all of the identity-based practices that use difference as an excuse for domination and render some human lives more valuable than others. This is a lesson bequeathed to us from the long history of Black struggles for freedom in the United States, from what W. E. B. Du Bois identifies as abolition democracy, what Cedric Robinson names the Black Radical Tradition, and what Daniel HoSang calls the struggle for "a wider type of freedom." Beyond being oppositional, these struggles were propositional. To be sure, they called for an end to the expressly racist impediments to Black self-defense, self-definition, and self-determination, but they also entailed envisioning and enacting new democratic practices, processes, structures, and social relations.[27] In these struggles, Blackness was seen as necessary but not sufficient. As Anna Julia Cooper argued in 1892, "The cause of freedom is not the cause of a race or a sect, a party, or a class—it is the cause of human kind, the very birthright of humanity."[28] Antiracism does not have to be merely a way of securing better treatment for victims of racial discrimination; rather, it holds the potential to contest and dissolve all entrenched social structures and their concomitant ways of thinking that turn fellow humans into despised and demonized others.

The practices that use small differences in pigment and phenotype to create large differences in opportunities and life chances do not originate solely or even primarily inside the prejudices, fears, and superstitions of individuals. They flow from long histories of Indigenous dispossession, racialized chattel slavery, and coloniality enacted through conquest, occupation, domination, and exploitation. Recognition of racial ascriptions as linked fates among Indigenous, African, Latinx, Middle Eastern, and Asian peoples and their diasporas leads those peoples to forge reactive racial solidarities in order to resist racism. This is very different from the race consciousness that gives white identity a systemic and structural advantage in political and economic systems around the world and that enshrines whiteness as the unmarked norm against which difference is constructed.

READINESS TO SEE RACISM AS STRUCTURAL AND SYSTEMIC

The dominant understandings of racism focus on acts that are primarily individual, intentional, and interpersonal, treating them as isolated and aberrant deviations from an otherwise just social order. In contrast, a core premise of this book is that racism is a matter more of *power* than of *prejudice*: that it stems from pervasive public and political processes rather than purely private and personal actions. While overt, intentional, and hate-fueled racism indeed appears over and over again through acts of verbal hate speech and violent hate crimes, racism receives its ultimate determinate social impact from its existence in diverse and diffuse social domains and institutions. No racist acts alone. Every individual racist action draws justification and legitimation from a linked chain of practices that make racial disparities and racist domination seem to the actors to be natural, necessary, and inevitable.

READINESS TO SEE RACISM AS A HEALTH HAZARD

Mobilizations for racial justice in the United States have long recognized and responded to white supremacy's production of unjust racist health injuries. Mexican American and Filipino American members of the United Farm Workers union waged strikes and organized consumer boycotts in the 1960s to end the use of poisonous pesticides in the fields of California in hopes of protecting both workers and consumers.[29] Fannie Lou Hamer's visionary leadership of the Black freedom movement in Mississippi included establishment of the Freedom Farm Cooperative, a project that countered Sunflower County's high rates of malnutrition, diabetes, and hypertension by setting up farming cooperatives to produce nutritious food and cash crops; to provide safe, clean, and affordable housing; and to set up small businesses raising catfish, cattle, and pigs.[30] The Serve the People programs of the Black Panther Party revolved around the establishment of People's Free Medical Clinics and campaigns to screen for sickle cell anemia and lead poisoning. Alondra Nelson illuminates the holistic multiaxis nature of the Panther clinics and campaigns as grounded in the concept of "social health," which linked the well-being of individual bodies to broader social transformations.[31] Puerto Rican activists in the Young Lords Party in New York mobilized around demands for regular garbage pickups in East Harlem and pressured physicians at that city's Lincoln Hospital to respond to high levels of tuberculosis, anemia, and lead poisoning by taking steps to provide culturally sensitive competent care.[32] Indigenous activists in Wisconsin in the 1970s and 1980s exercising sovereign rights granted by treaties to fish in the lakes and streams of their territory opposed the development of zinc oxide mining and other extractive industries that threatened to poison their watersheds.[33] In the 1990s, the Asian Pacific Environmental Network organized Laotian and Cambodian immigrants to protest the toxins emitted by the Chevron refinery in Richmond, California. They secured a settlement that required the company to attend to safety hazards and secured funds for a medical center focused on treating the high incidences of breast cancer among immigrant Laotian women in their city.[34]

For these race-based but not race-bound movements, racist danger zones were located where farmworkers labored, where consumers ingested foods, where Black people experienced undiagnosed and therefore untreated instances of sickle cell anemia and lead poisoning, where neighborhoods lacked regular garbage pickups and culturally competent medical care, where zinc oxide mining poisoned traditional fishing sites, and where refinery explosions, fires, and emissions poisoned water, land, and air. The Movement for Black Lives in 2020 walked in the footsteps of these earlier organized struggles by pointing to the deadly presence of racist danger zones on the street where George Floyd was choked to death and in the apartment where Breonna Taylor was shot and killed, underscoring the perils Black people face in all of the places where they live, work, and play.

READINESS TO REPLACE SINGLE-AXIS FRAMES OF ANALYSIS WITH BLACK FEMINIST INTERSECTIONALITY

The single-axis and individualist approaches privileged by the tort model of injury in law and by the biomedical model of health evade and occlude the intersectional causes and consequences of racist health and housing injuries. Reliance on single-axis approaches leads people to address housing discrimination and health separately rather than together. Even worse, it isolates the spheres of health and housing from the long and linked chain of other racializing and racist currents that fuel and flow through them, such as racialized risk assessment in insurance, racist overcharging and oversentencing in criminal cases, race-based predatory policing, racial zoning, and the vicious combination of racially contoured artificially low home value appraisals and artificially high home tax assessments.

Intersectional problems require intersectional solutions. Intersectionality as theorized by Kimberlé Crenshaw in a pair of trail-blazing law review articles in 1989 and 1991 emerged initially as a concept, method, and disposition for discerning and critiquing single-axis categories in employment discrimination law and in feminist campaigns against sexual assault and battering.[35] In these pieces, Crenshaw revealed how single-axis assumptions about a common condition among all women failed to take into account the specific combinations of racism and sexism that Black women experience on the job as both Black people and women, and argued that the domestic violence that threatens all women has different ramifications for women who are immigrants, have precarious citizenship status, or have limited English proficiency. Courts mandated that when filing employment discrimination claims, Black women could claim disadvantage solely as women or solely as Black people, not as who they actually were—namely, Black women whose conditions were some ways similar to those facing Black men and white women but who differed from them significantly as well.

Prior to intersectional arguments, feminist organizations addressing domestic violence followed a single-axis frame similar to the one the courts applied in employment law cases. Shelters set up to shield women from domestic violence adopted policies and rules that presumed that remedies helpful to economically secure white women applied equally and unproblematically to financially and legally vulnerable Black and immigrant women. They called for mandatory reporting of all cases of domestic abuse without recognizing that the courts would treat accused Black men more harshly than white men. They supported mandatory removal of abusers from the home without seeing how that could force women with precarious citizenship status to risk having family members deported. They barred men and boys from domestic shelters, even when those rules made non-English-speaking women lose the language translators in their families that they relied on when communicating with monolingual-English-speaking shelter workers and counselors.

Although very different entities with different intentions and with different degrees of power, both corporate employers and feminist anti-battering organizations shared similar single-axis assumptions about a commonality among all women that failed to take into account the composite and cumulative vulnerabilities of Black women and non-English-speaking undocumented immigrant women of color. These specific cases demonstrated the need for a more dynamic approach to social identities and power, specifically for what Crenshaw described as accounting "for multiple grounds of identity when considering how the social world is constructed."[36]

Intersectionality is often misunderstood and mischaracterized as a theory about the identities of individuals, when in fact it is primarily a tool for understanding the multiple currents of power that flow through institutions, structures, and systems.[37] Paradoxically it is frequently belittled either as only the narrow and parochially exclusive concern of Black women or as an infinitely broad and disembodied universal concept that purportedly renders moot all identity-based mobilization and scholarship. In fact, however, intersectionality as developed by Crenshaw and other feminist and critical race theorists as well as by scholars across the disciplines and by activists in dispersed social locations takes a different stance. On the individual level it asserts that people who belong to more than one group have unique and generative insights about how oppressive power works on many different levels and how it might be defeated. Rather than choosing to identify by either their gender or their race, women from aggrieved racialized groups who deploy intersectional approaches insist on a *both/and* approach. They do not uncritically elevate one identity over others but instead ask *which differences make a difference, when, and where, and why*. On the institutional level, intersectionality demonstrates how single-axis approaches to rights, resources, recognition, and respect place related and linked forms of power in disaggregated silos that render remedies ineffective.

Crenshaw's writing has been especially generative in this effort because it promotes searching for the exclusions embedded in taken-for-granted social categories. Self-defense often does require groups to mobilize collectively around a single identity in response to the consequences of a linked fate. Common conditions and linked fates make collective responses reasonable and necessary. If people catch hell for being Black or women or LGBTQ, it makes sense to respond as a group. As Chela Sandoval and others point out, however, a narrow identity-based mobilization based on race can leave out considerations of gender, while gender-based projects can ignore race.[38] Black women are at the center of Crenshaw's arguments, but she never gives priority to either a narrow gender-first or a narrow race-first stance. Her ultimate concern is not with individual identities but with the ways in which socially constructed differences function to shape injustice and inequality. As Black feminist philosopher Kristie Dotson and critical race theorist Mari Matsuda explain, intersectional thinking entails constant vigilance about the large-scale forces that obscure people's legitimate needs, experiences, and identities most likely to be left out of single-axis approaches.[39] This "disappearing" of relevant factors and multiply aggrieved polities is what is enabled and encouraged by single-axis modes of thinking such as the tort model of injury in law, the biomedical model of health care, and legal and social movement strategies that attend to only one identity at a time or that relegate struggles for fair housing and good health to separate and incommensurable spheres.

Isolating racism from attendant acts of discrimination based on gender, class, sexual identification, language, citizenship status, perceived disability, and many other characteristics and identities is a single-axis approach that is inadequate for acknowledging and acting against the multiaxis and intersectional nature of discrimination as it experienced by people. A racialized or gendered injury is never experienced in isolation. No individual exists solely within one identity category. Every person is in some ways a crowd and as such is affected by multiple identities, identifications, allegiances, and antagonisms.

Women from aggrieved racialized groups face discrimination both as women and as members of racialized groups. Latinx children of undocumented immigrant parents can face stigmatization and endure mistreatment because of their age, race, class position, citizenship status, and language. Extending legal protections to groups aggrieved because of gender or race alone may not reckon with the burdens faced by members of those groups who are multiply disadvantaged because they are also noncitizens, people perceived to have disabilities, or individuals with gender and sexual identities that do not conform to dominant heteronormative categories. Racism, sexism, class oppression, racialized mass incarceration, ableism, homophobia, and transphobia target specific groups for mistreatment, but members of those groups are not equally positioned or equally burdened by their stigmatized identities. Sadly, in their self-defense strategies, leaders of aggrieved groups all too often find it expedient to disavow and abandon the least normative, least respectable, and least powerful members of their own groups. A victory for women is not necessarily a victory for Black women; a victory for Black people is not necessarily a victory for Black people who are women or gender nonconforming; a victory for Black people who are gender nonconforming or women is not necessarily a victory for those members of the group with perceived disabilities, precarious citizenship status, disadvantaged class positions, or limited English language capacity. Single-axis approaches to identity hide these differences within identity groups.

The cumulative force of multiple-axis discrimination comes into clear relief in the ways in which bias against transgender people affects every facet of their lives. It shames and stigmatizes their identities but also consigns them to high levels of unemployment and housing insecurity. One survey found that 30 percent of transgender respondents had experienced houselessness. That injury is compounded by the ways in which they may be turned away from shelters because they are trans-gender or may be forced to reside in shelters based on their assigned sex at birth, which makes them susceptible to additional harassment and violence. Yet gendered identities also interact with racial ascriptions. Transgender people from aggrieved racialized groups have higher levels of unemployment and poverty than their white counterparts.[40] Treating racism as separate from sexism, examining incarceration without addressing shelter insecurity (pre- and postincarceration), or ignoring the health consequences of racism, sexism, and housing discrimination evades the complexity of the conditions that people face. Housing dis-crimination shapes and reflects broader patterns of social stratification and subordination. Individual acts of intentional discrimination func-tion in concert with historically created cumulative vulnerabilities based on identity that amplify and exacerbate each injustice and injury. As former National Fair Housing Alliance president and chief executive officer Shanna L. Smith quips, quoting Polish intellectual Stanislaus Lec, "In an avalanche every snowflake pleads not guilty."[41] The disaggrega-tion of different forms of discrimination into separate and putatively incommensurable spheres occludes the multiple-axis nature of social subordination and impedes efforts to address it.

READINESS TO SEE HEALTH AND HOUSING JUSTICE AS AN INTERNATIONAL CONCERN

This book focuses mainly on the nationally inflected aspects of housing and health injustice inside the United States because that provides the main context where my work has taken place. Yet systemic and struc-tural racism has global causes and consequences. The US nation exists in the world, and increasingly the world makes its presence felt inside the nation. For example, a disproportionate share of the work of caring for those who are ill in the United States falls to poorly paid immigrant women workers who were forced to flee their homelands because of the austerity imposed on those places by multinational corporations and international financiers. A study published in 2020 revealed that 31 percent of home care assistants were immigrants, 28 percent were Black, and 23 percent were Latinx. Pressured by health care corporations seek-ing to pay lower wages, government officials provide immigrant nurses and other health care workers with temporary visas that make them easily exploitable.[42] The precarious economic and political status of these workers enables their US employers to cut costs by paying them

poverty wages. The exploitation of low-wage immigrant women workers who care for the ill and those designated as disabled and who cook,
clean, and provide childcare for high-income and high-consumption
families provides unearned subsidies for their employers and inflated
profits for medical care corporations. The remittances these workers
send back home help support people there who have been deprived of
their former livelihoods on lands seized by agribusiness companies or
who have been paid starvation wages in factories and workshops owned
by multinational corporations.[43] Those displaced by imperialism and
colonial extraction find themselves forced to further subsidize it.

Moreover, the profiteering that dominates the US health care system
causes people all around the world to suffer needlessly from dreadful
and deadly illnesses. They cannot access the medicines they need because
US patent law enables pharmaceutical companies to price medicines far
above what they cost to produce. US corporations promote privatization policies that make access to water too expensive for communities
in need while turning areas of Africa, Asia, the Caribbean, and Latin
America into repositories of toxic waste. Securing rights and resources
for aggrieved groups inside the United States should not come with the
price of exacerbating the abandonment of the health and housing needs
of people around the world. Nor will the world's health problems be
solved by extending the technological and scientific advances of the US
system to more places. Many of these tools for diagnosis and treatment
are indeed inaccessible to the majority of the world's population and
should be made available and affordable. But the fact remains that completely preventable and treatable infectious diseases such as cholera,
malaria, and tuberculosis cause millions of deaths each year because of
the global health and wealth inequality caused by privatization.

In addition, it is not as if the United States has nothing to learn from
the valuable understandings of public health that exist around the
world.[44] Concepts of social medicine grounded in the idea that collective health can best be promoted by access to food, housing, occupational safety, and sanitary infrastructures have a long history and
continuing presence throughout South America.[45] Mobilizations by
activists on behalf of AIDS sufferers in the global South have raised
trenchant critiques of the for-profit biomedical model of health care,
posing in opposition to it an understanding of health care as a human
right and a collective social obligation.[46] Research by Charles Briggs
and Clara Mantini-Briggs reveals how the responses to epidemics of
rabies and cholera by Indigenous community members in Venezuela

enabled aggrieved people to take the lead in devising and implementing public health remedies but also generated new sustainable designs for ecological, social, and political collective life. Their research also reveals how Indigenous residents of the Delta Amacuro region used weeds and plants as sources of pharmaceutical remedies and promoted forms of development freed from fossil fuel extraction by respecting plants and trees as entities vital for human and more-than-human sustainability and survival.[47]

The words and actions of W. E. B. Du Bois and Martin Luther King Jr. point the way toward an inclusive justice that is world traversing and world transcending. Du Bois and King both argued that racist rule in the United States has been an impetus for a global system of domination rooted in fervent allegiance to hierarchies of light skin over dark, wealth over work, exploitation and extraction over collective recognition and accountability. These practices are rooted in the legacy and continuing consequences and practices of Indigenous dispossession, slavery, and coloniality. As Indigenous scholars Jodi Byrd (Chickasaw), Kim Tall-Bear (Sisseton-Wahpeton Oyate), and others remind us, Indigenous dispossession in the United States and around the world is not merely a completed past event but a continuing deadly process. Uncritical acceptance of Indigenous subordination shapes the status and condition of many other aggrieved groups. It is a crucible in which people of many different ascribed and embraced identities whose freedom dreams stand in the way of resource extraction and imperial conquest are "made Indian" by being demonized and dominated.[48] It promotes a way of viewing the world that divides people into hostile camps of groups portrayed as either human or less than human. It creates artificial scarcities in order to foment cruel competition for basic needs such as housing and health care.

Innovative intersectional research by Emma Shaw Crane reveals how ongoing violence against and dispossession of Indigenous communities around the world subsidizes the wealth and life chances of property owners in places in the United States that are shaped by housing discrimination and its attendant spatial imaginaries. In research conducted in principled accompaniment with organizers and activists affiliated with WeCount!, a grassroots organization mobilizing for justice and equality for immigrant workers and their families in Florida, Crane reveals how the lush tropical plants sold to wholesalers and retail customers at Home Depot, Costco, Trader Joe's, Ikea, and Walmart— plants that grace subdivisions and common-interest developments all across the United States—are mostly grown and cultivated in South Florida plant nurseries. The nurseries employ exploited low-wage immigrant Indigenous workers driven out of their countries of origin by state-orchestrated genocidal warfare as well as subsequent neoliberal structures of dispossession and displacement.[49] The Guatemalan state's warfare against Indigenous people—backed by the United States—murdered some two hundred thousand people, enacted the "disappearance" of an additional forty thousand, and destroyed more than six hundred Indigenous communities. Dispossessing and displacing Indigenous people played a central role in the particular form of state building favorable to capital that took on especially brutal dimensions in the 1980s. Warfare aimed at the genocidal disappearance of Indigenous people set the stage for subsequent purportedly peacetime acts of aggression including resource extraction, privatization, plantation monocrop cultivation, predatory policing, and expropriation of small farming units by agribusiness firms. The resulting poverty, hunger, and labor exploitation fueled migration to the United States, including to South Florida, where vulnerable and often undocumented Indigenous refugees from the violence in Guatemala join with similarly displaced migrants from Mexico and El Salvador. As documented in Professor Crane's scholarship and in the report *The Human Landscape* issued by WeCount! in 2018, more than 10 percent of these workers are children, and nearly two-thirds of them are women. Their labor makes suburban front and back yards and common areas beautiful, while the laborers suffer from low wages and wage thefts that leave them unable to pay for medical care and insurance. Their jobs give them constant back and kidney pain, dehydration, inflammation, and urinary tract infections. They labor in tropical heat, often without adequate shade or water breaks, are exposed to poisonous pesticides, are subject to permanent injuries from accidents, and frequently lack access at work to toilets and sinks.

Much of the demand for the plants that they grow is artificially created by homeowner association adherence to advice in underwriting manuals that emphasizes how plants and lawns augment property values. The covenants, conventions, and restrictions that bind members of homeowner associations together in common-interest developments can require a minimum of at least two trees and ten plants at every dwelling. The result is a hidden subsidy to nursery owners and an impetus for exploitation of low-wage Indigenous and immigrant nursery labor. Thus, as Crane astutely concludes, the peaceful and bucolic appearance of owner-occupied subdivisions and common-interest developments that subsidize private property regimes is "transnationally produced through inner and outer wars of U.S. empire."[50]

Crane's exemplary study of how US-backed warfare in Guatemala subsidizes the property values of white suburban homeowners throughout the nation builds on a long history of racial capitalism's international reach and scope. Paige Glotzer's research on the property industry and suburban segregation in the late nineteenth century reveals that the investments that built housing developments in suburban Baltimore originated in England among bankers and individuals looking for profitable returns by investing funds that they secured initially from slavery and colonialism throughout the British Empire. Racial residential segregation in Baltimore offered them surplus profits by creating areas of white opportunity hoarding that contrasted in value with the zones of deprivation imposed on areas where people who were not white resided.[51]

READINESS TO SEE WORDS AS TEMPORARY TOOLS, NOT TIMELESS TRUTHS

When descriptions in this book refer to people as Black, Latinx, Indigenous, Middle Eastern, and Asian, those terms are deployed as markers of political identity. They identify groups with histories of negative ascription by white supremacy and of resistance against it. I use the phrase *aggrieved racialized communities* rather than misleading terms like *racial minorities* to emphasize how difference is used to enact domination and to illuminate how the practices of racialization produce injuries. The term *minorities* can suggesting that exploitation stems solely from anxieties about demographic difference rather than from the opportunities for plunder created by differentiated domination. Moreover, populations that were once minorities and were dismissed as such do not throw off their mistreatment automatically when they become pluralities or new majorities.

Every descriptor of a racialized group contains contradictions. "Latinx" is a pan-ethnic identity forged from negative external ascription but also from internal positive affirmation. In the United States it is treated as a racialized identity, although, as Lorgia Garcia-Peña, Tanya Kateri Hernández, and many others observe, the Latinx population includes people racialized as Black, Indigenous, Asian, and Middle Eastern.[52] In the United States people described uniformly as Indigenous are actually members of many different nations and groups that have become lumped together and racialized by external ascription through acts of discrimination and oppression in social life, popular culture, and law. This process often treats what should properly be seen as relations between nations as relations between races. Yet sometimes the survival and self-defense strategies of Indigenous people lead to embracing a common collective identity that tactically adopts racial terms as useful for internal political mobilization, collective affirmation, and civil rights litigation.

The uppercase letters used in this book to designate Black, Latinx, Indigenous, Middle Eastern, and Asian Americans identify them as historically created aggrieved political groups. These people are not members of different biological races but rather members of groups thrown together politically because negative racial ascription benefits those who enforce racist rule. They are not identifiers of pigment, phenotype, place of origin, or genetic inheritance. I use the lower case with the word *white* in this book because while whiteness is clearly a historical political creation, it is an identity structured in dominance that functions by never having to say its name. My hope is that white people, and all people, can divest themselves of allegiance to and investment in whiteness.

These word choices are tactical decisions for this book based on current understandings. They are not once-and-for-all designations that can guarantee ethical treatment of aggrieved groups. There is no perfect practice in language; every choice that enables something also inhibits something else. Unjust and upsetting social relations cannot be conquered by giving them new names; banning particular words does not erase the social relations that they connote. Yet word choices matter, and in this book I try to use them in ways that respect the wishes of aggrieved groups and avoid perpetuating their suffering and subordination. Years from now the vocabulary deployed in sections of this book may be judged inadequate, inaccurate, and unwittingly offensive. We can take corrective action then. For now, we have to run the risk of making moves that later prove wrong, because silence on matters and mechanisms of overwhelming importance at this moment of ferment and change is unacceptable and inexcusable.

The hurts inflicted on members of aggrieved racialized groups in law and medicine delineated in this book stem from structures and systems that skew opportunities and life chances along racial lines. They reveal shortcomings within legal and medical education and professional practice. The problems of a fully interconnected system of racial subordination cannot be corrected solely by domain-specific reforms within any single institution such as law or medicine. As chapters 4, 5, and 6 will demonstrate, racial health and housing disparities are also produced and perpetuated by actions in many other arenas, by discrimination in home value appraisals and tax policies, by predatory policing and mass incarceration, and by racialized risk assessment and redlining in insurance provision. These chapters in Part II reveal the enormity of systemic problems, while the chapters in Part III delineate how active and engaged public sphere politics is being used to propose systemic solutions.

What Hurts?

4

Cash in Your Face

Appraisals, Assessments, and Predatory
Extraction

The lyrics of Stevie Wonder's 1980 song "Cash in Your Face" describe the humiliation of experiencing housing discrimination, the frustration of seeking a place to live but being turned away with excuse after excuse by rental agents who don't want "your kind" living among them. The song's narrator complains that despite the law that bans discrimination in housing, he runs into gatekeepers who invent pretexts for refusing to rent to him. The song warns shelter seekers from aggrieved racialized groups that while they might have the necessary cash to rent a home they cannot "cash in" because their faces are the wrong color. Wonder's lyrics highlight the most obvious and visible forms of direct discrimination in housing, but the obstacles to housing justice entail more than just these. This chapter delineates how the pretexts and excuses that Wonder's song describes are sometimes not even needed because they are hidden within a rhizomatic network of exclusion effected through the nature of transactions through which dwellings are bought, sold, and assessed for tax purposes.

As depicted in excellent recent and emerging scholarly research and illustrated in the ABC News television documentary film *Lowballed: Our America*, the appraisal industry systematically evaluates property owned by Black people at far less than its true value, while tax assessors overassess those same properties because of the race of their owners. Lowball appraisals and inflated tax assessments rob their victims of equity, reduce the inheritances they can pass on to future generations,

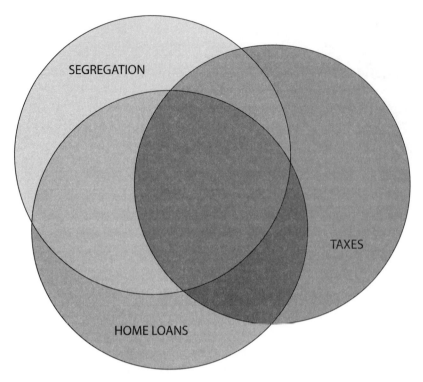

DANGER ZONES HOUSING REDLINING

FIGURE 5. The overlapping injuries of high levels of segregation, denials of mortgage loans, and disproportionately high tax assessments in redlined areas. Graphic by Omar G. Ramirez.

and make them excessively vulnerable to tax liens, foreclosures, and auctions that take their property from them completely.

These practices exacerbate the racial wealth gap, but they also worsen the racial health gap. They damage the ability of members of aggrieved racialized groups to have sufficient assets to purchase adequate medical insurance and treatments, while exposing them disproportionately to residency in communities that sit in proximity to toxicity. Home foreclosures provoke high levels of stress, shame, and anxiety that can cause augmented levels of depression, substance abuse, and suicide.[1] Proximity to—not just actual residence in—foreclosed homes has been found to be strongly associated with mental and physical health crises. In neighborhoods inhabited by low-income Black people, high levels of foreclosure are linked to disproportionate incidences of chronic obstructive pulmonary disease, stroke, and coronary heart disease.[2] The effects of foreclosure extend beyond the particular homes judged in default. Entire neighborhoods suffer from the spread of properties abandoned by the banks and other lending institutions that foreclose on them, making these properties susceptible to fires and to being used for sex work and for drug use and deals. The health impacts of foreclosure are both immediate and long term. One study conducted three years after the peak of the 2008 foreclosure crisis found that neighborhoods affected by it reported even higher levels of health problems at that time than when foreclosures were rampant.[3]

The artificially low home appraisals and artificially high tax assessments imposed on property owned by members of aggrieved racialized groups occur within a broader social ecology of place-based discrimination. Government bodies draw school and legislative district boundaries, establish land use regulations, provide differential kinds of city services to neighborhoods with different racial populations, and collect and administer revenues in ways that create a seemingly endless array of forms of predatory extraction. These actions concentrate hazards, nuisances, and onerous obligations in communities inhabited by members of aggrieved racialized groups while funneling amenities, opportunities, and resources to areas populated mainly by those who administer and profit from discrimination. This chapter explores the ways in which danger zones at the intersections of health and housing are shaped by discrimination in home appraisals, tax assessments, and municipal land use policies.

APPRAISAL DISCRIMINATION

Paul Austin and Tenisha Tate-Austin paid $500,000 to purchase a home in an unincorporated area of Marin County, California, in 2016. The dwelling featured a spectacular view of Richardson Bay, a lushly forested hillside behind it, and ample room for recreation on a property that abutted a hiking trail with an entry to it in the backyard. Living in that location placed the couple and their two children in close proximity to nearby family members in Marin City, where Paul was raised, and to the Miller Creek Middle School in San Rafael, where Tenisha then served as principal. It was also conveniently located near Paul's job as founder and CEO of Play Marin, a nonprofit organization that provides recreational opportunities for children of diverse backgrounds faced with limited recreational opportunities in and around the city of Sausalito.

The Austin family made extensive renovations to their property. They refinished hardwood floors, installed new bathroom fixtures and kitchen appliances, painted the inside walls, and replaced old windows with new ones. They added a new foundation and retaining wall, installed a gas fireplace and a deck, finished the basement, and built an attached unit complete with its own bathroom and kitchen. The changes they made doubled the dwelling's square footage. Seeking to take advantage of lowered interest rates, the couple decided to refinance their mortgage in 2020. The appraiser sent to evaluate the worth of their property provided a figure of $995,000, a sum that seemed decidedly low to the Austins given all the improvements they had made and the significant appreciation in property values of the homes near theirs. They suspected that the lower-than-expected appraisal had something to do with the fact that they were an African American family. So they sought another appraisal. This time they removed all signs of Blackness from the walls and shelves. They took down family pictures and hid African- and African American–themed works of art. Instead of meeting the appraiser themselves, they had a white friend do so after placing pictures of her family inside the dwelling. This time the appraised value of the house was $1.48 million, a difference of almost $500,000.[4]

It pays to be white. The same house with the same features in the same location was judged to have a half million dollars more value when an appraiser believed its owners were white. A similar situation confronted Abena Horton, an African American attorney, and her white artist husband Alex Horton when they sought in 2020 to refinance their home located near the desirable Ortega neighborhood in Jacksonville, Florida. When Abena showed the house to the appraiser, she was treated rudely and was told the house had a value much lower than recently sold nearby dwellings that had fewer bedrooms and bathrooms and significantly less square footage. The Hortons expected a figure around $450,000, based on the structural condition of the home and its proximity to the nearby Ortega River development, a predominantly white area where homes sold for anywhere from $350,000 to $500,000. The appraiser came back with an estimated value of $330,000.

Suspecting that something was amiss, the Hortons arranged for a second appraisal. This time Alex met the appraiser alone after the couple stripped the home of the family's photographs and all signs of Black culture, removing books by Toni Morrison and Zora Neale Hurston from their shelves and replacing them with volumes of Shakespeare plays. The second appraisal came in at $465,000, which was a $135,000 and 40 percent increase over the assessment for the same house when it appeared to be owned and inhabited by Black people.[5]

Angered by encountering one more time the kinds of racism she had faced repeatedly throughout her life, Abena Horton reproached herself for not being more suspicious from the start. "Why did I let myself forget that I live in America as a Black person and that I need to take some extra steps to get a fair result?" she asked. Connecting this incident to its larger context, Horton wrote on her Facebook page, "Racism silently but conspicuously steals wealth. Racism wastes time. Racism raises blood pressure. Racism makes me hate myself for my calm acceptance of what I had to do, and have always had to do to get a fair result. I write this from a place of absolute anguish to sort through my emotions. I want better for my son."[6]

The Austin and Horton families are not the only households injured by appraisal discrimination. In Indianapolis, Indiana, a Black homeowner, Carlette Duffy, received two appraisals on her dwelling in 2021: one for $110,000 and another for $125,000. Suspecting that those figures greatly undervalued the property, Duffy got a white friend to substitute for her during a third appraisal. In advance she removed all family photos and signs of Black culture. With those changes made, the new appraisal came in at $259,000, more than double the figure when the home appeared to be Black owned.[7] Similarly, African American aerospace engineer Stephen Richmond secured a $40,000 increase in the appraisal of his property in Hartford, Connecticut, when he removed all signs of Blackness for its second appraisal.[8] Erica and Aaron Parker received a firm offer in the low $500,000s for their Cincinnati home, but the deal fell through when an appraiser evaluated it at $40,000 below what the prospective buyers offered. The Parkers then sought a new appraisal, but before it took place they removed all family photos and signs of African American identity from the dwelling. This time the appraisal was $92,000 higher than the previous one and was, in fact, nearly $50,000 above the previously agreed-upon sale price.[9]

In Oakland, California, during the summer months of 2020, Cora Robinson sought to refinance the duplex she owned. Her property, purchased for $289,500 in 2006, was portrayed on listing sites as worth close to $1.2 million, which was the median local home sale price in her area. Refinancing would enable Robinson to capitalize on that equity and secure a lower interest rate on her mortgage. The appraisal came in, however, at a mere $800,000, which was $400,000 less than she expected. A second appraisal through a different lender less than three months later (coincidentally assigned to the same appraiser) secured almost the same result at $825,000. These appraisals contained factual errors in their descriptions and made an artificially low estimate of the duplex's value in part because they identified comparable properties only in the largely Black neighborhoods south of Robinson's property rather than in the equally nearby wealthier and whiter Rockridge area. Robinson ultimately succeeded in refinancing her property after a third appraisal compared it with homes in largely white areas and judged it to be worth $1,239,000. That estimate enabled Robinson to pay $769 less per month but did not compensate her for the lower interest rates and reduced payments she would have enjoyed had the first appraisal been done properly.[10]

The differences between the initial and subsequent appraisals received by the Austin, Horton, Duffy, Richmond, and Parker households show how direct racial bias in assessments penalizes Black homeowners. Yet even when intentional bias is absent, the routine practices of assessment contain premises and presumptions that achieve racist ends. In the appraisal industry, where an estimated 97 percent of the professionals are not Black, guesses based on racialized assumptions by industry professionals about the identity and desires of potential buyers substitute for empirical evidence. It has long been the custom among appraisers to assume that the typical buyer is a white person seeking to live in a white neighborhood. Yet in many cities, demand for housing is high among nonwhite shelter seekers in nonwhite areas. When appraisers assume that the potential buyer is white and invested in whiteness, they undervalue property in integrated or majority-minority residential areas.[11] The dominant sales comparison approach favored by the appraisal industry leads appraisers to choose comparisons hinged to the racial composition of neighborhoods in ways that assign high value to homes in areas inhabited by white people but artificially lower values to homes in neighborhoods where residency includes members of aggrieved racialized groups. Appraisers also lower property values in majority-white neighborhoods when people who are not white move in.

As Cora Robinson's experience demonstrates, racialized assumptions held by appraisers play an especially deleterious role in assessing the value of homes in relation to nearby properties that are supposed to be comparable. Comparing sale prices within already-segregated neighborhoods rather than among similar dwellings in different locations simply uses the success of past racist categories as justification for creating new ones. When the Austins sought an appraisal on their dwelling located in proximity to Marin City, which has the only significant Black population in the county except for the San Quentin prison, the appraiser assumed that the comparable units had to be in that municipality. Marin City has a sizable Black population only because restrictive covenants, mortgage redlining, and overt racial discrimination gave white people preferential (and in many cases exclusive) access to residences elsewhere in the county. White supremacy wielded against its residents determined the discriminatory treatment Marin City received over the years from insurers, appraisers, assessors, lenders, and developers. Structural and systemic racism thus accounts for the artificial and arbitrary devaluation of dwellings in and in this case even near Marin City.

Properties owned by people who are not white would shoot up in value if appraisers made comparisons across neighborhoods on the objective basis of the quality and condition of the structure, the availability of amenities, the socioeconomic status of the area, and the actual (rather than merely imagined) demand for the dwelling. In the case of the assessment of the Austin property, comparisons could just have easily been made with comparable houses in nearby areas with wealthy white residents such as Sausalito and Mill Valley. One appraiser stated explicitly that Marin City has a distinct disadvantaged marketability compared to surrounding areas. Yet this was a supposition based only on racial (and racist) assumptions. As the legal complaint filed in the case revealed, the stability of homeownership in Marin City led to very few transactions: three per year in the year of the appraisal and three in the year that preceded it. This supplies no statistically significant or legitimate basis for the appraiser's designation of Marin City as having deficient marketability.[12]

By using Marin City for the location of comparison for a property that was not even technically in Marin City (because it was in an unincorporated area outside it), the appraisers lowered property values and homeowner equity for Black residents of the area and provided a hidden subsidy in the form of inflated home values for historically white neighborhoods that have benefited from redlining and restrictive covenants. This raises the costs of entry into the housing market for people who are not white and undermines the equity- and asset-building capacity of members of aggrieved racialized groups.

Appraisal discrimination undervalues the homes that Black people own and all homes in neighborhoods inhabited by them. Researchers from the Brookings Institution in 2018 estimated that appraisal discrimination undervalued homes owned by African Americans by an aggregate of $156 billion, an average of $48,000 per property.[13] A quantitative 2018 study by Junia Howell and Elizabeth Korver-Glenn found that appraisers judged homes in Houston and the rest of Harris County in Texas differently because of appraisers' racialized assumptions about the identities of neighborhood residents. Appraisers considered dwellings to be worth $162,000 less in Black neighborhoods and $169,000 less in Latinx neighborhoods than homes in an all- or primarily white area. This was the case even though the homes in the areas inhabited by members of aggrieved racialized groups featured housing stock and buyer demand in neighborhoods equal to those in the areas inhabited by white people with respect to rates of homeownership; levels of crime, poverty, and unemployment; commute times; and access to green spaces and recreation areas.[14]

In her pathbreaking book *Race Brokers,* Korver-Glenn outlines some ways in which the appraisal process could be reformed to be less racist. She explains that better outcomes would ensue if appraisers compared homes by cost and structure rather than by neighborhood, and if they evaluated actual demand for housing by people of all races rather than presuming that the typical buyer is a white person committed to living in a white neighborhood. She argues that more fairness would follow if state agencies audited appraisers to see how bias affects their work and if state oversight of developers limited excess concentration of new attractive housing in neighborhoods favored by past histories of white racism and nonwhite exclusion.[15]

Just as new commercial and government projects routinely need to make environmental impact statements about their anticipated effects on air, water, and land quality, developers could also be required to deploy precautionary principles and produce demographic racial demographic and health impact assessments. These measures would address some of the ways in which the routine and ordinary practices of appraisal and property development contain unacknowledged hidden racial biases. They would not, however, attend to the kinds of deliberate and bigoted approaches to appraising emblematized in an overtly racist message sent to sociologist Elizabeth Korver-Glenn about her analysis of appraisal discrimination.

Dave LaVigne learned of Professor Korver-Glenn's work and sent her an email. LaVigne was then owner and president of the LaVigne Appraisals firm in New Bern, North Carolina, a company that conducts commercial and residential appraisals in the Carolinas, Georgia, and Virginia. His message confidently claimed that "racism is not as prevalent as you might think." LaVigne followed this statement, oddly enough, with a series of vile racist stereotypes about people of color as deviant, dependent, and dysfunctional. LaVigne invited Korver to visit him in North Carolina so he could show her a place where "minorities are paid to raise their poorly educated illigitamen [sic] kids. Let's not forget the parents gave the kids obserd [sic] names that most employers immediately refuse to call."[16] LaVigne's rant insinuates that if people of color receive disparate treatment from appraisers it is not because the appraisers *think* they are inferior but because they actually *are* inferior, that they alone have babies out of wedlock and do not value education. Particularly interesting is his complaint that Black people give their children names likely to identify them as Black. He is arguing that white employers therefore refuse to interview them for jobs, even if their résumés indicate they are qualified. Contrary to LaVigne's assertion that racism is less prevalent than sociologists might think, this claim is actually evidence that racism is routinely practiced by employers. Working in a profession that professes to treat people and property objectively, LaVigne makes it clear that he is an appraiser who is deeply invested in treating people not as individuals but as members of racial groups, and that he has decided that these groups are governed by a hierarchy that places white people at the top.

Professor Korver-Glenn posted LaVigne's message on her social media, where it was discovered by Representative Maxine Waters of California, chair of the House Financial Services Committee. Waters pointed to it as evidence of the need to hold the appraisal industry accountable for acts of racial discrimination.[17] A letter posted on real estate listings sites attributed to LaVigne attempted to justify his email to Korver. As might be expected, this effort to address the damage made things even worse. The letter offers a kind of racial (and racist) report card that purportedly accounts for the different outcomes experienced by members of different racial groups. "A person's success is based on several factors," it opines, listing "education, stable family environment, and safe neighborhood" as examples. "While poverty is part of the equation," the letter writer concedes, desired attributes are tied to a person's race and "a person's heritage." Focusing on racial differences, the letter proclaims, "My wife is Japanese, and my lifestyle is heavily influenced as such. Asian families have certain family traits as do Western European as do those of African descent." Without stipulating what these "traits" are that presumably all members of these groups share, the letter's author contends that "marriage and family are Christian concepts for Western Europeans while Asian are none [*sic*] Christian and or Buddhist in some cases." Evidently Jews and Muslims in Europe do not have families in his formulation, and Asians are not Christians (which will come as a surprise to Korean Evangelical Protestants) and must be Buddhists (not followers of Shintoism, Hinduism, Islam, or Zoroastrianism). Concluding this report card on the world's racial groups, the letter proposes that what it describes as "Latin America" has "their sociological baggage as well."[18]

LaVigne's confidence is exceeded only by his lack of comprehension. While he complains about "uneducated" minority children, his mis-spellings and mischaracterizations of entire racialized groups indicate some shortcomings in the education he received at East Carolina University. Rather than refuting any of the evidence, ideas, and arguments that Korver put forth in her two-hundred-page book on the contemporary racialized housing market as it is shaped by housing development, real estate brokerage, mortgage, and appraisal industries, LaVigne defends his profession from allegations of discrimination by citing his own prejudices as authoritative. Readers have every reason to suspect that he deploys these prejudices when deciding on the value of properties that he appraises. In any case, none of the assumptions he makes to deny Korver-Glenn's evidence of widespread discrimination applies to the documented appraisal discrimination reported in this chapter in the cases of Paul and Tanisha Tate-Austin, Abena and Alex Horton, Carlette Duffy, Stephen Richmond, Erica and Aaron Parker, or Cora Robinson. None of these victims of appraisal discrimination is poor or uneducated. They are not deficient in valuing family; in fact they were punished by appraisers precisely when their homes displayed pictures of family members. It may be true that some people with skin colors similar to theirs are poor and have children out of wedlock who do not do well in school, but since the majority of people who are poor and give birth out of wedlock are white, David LaVigne and all of the white people whose property he appraises should expect to be financially penalized for that. As he well knows, they are not. It is not the difference in their skin color or the nature of their culture that leads Black people to be discriminated against, it is the ways in which gatekeepers like LaVigne use that difference as an excuse for and justification of domination and exploitation.

LaVigne's invitation to Professor Korver-Glenn to visit North Carolina so that he could show her unworthy Black people might not include all the sites and history in his city of New Bern that tell a different story.

He does not promise to show her the places where Black men were lynched: John Moore in 1905 and Percy Berry in 1932. His invitation does not include a visit to the forty-city-block area inhabited by thousands of Black people that was destroyed by fire in 1922, an area that the segregationist white supremacist government of the city would not allow to be rebuilt in order to force Black residents to leave town. Expulsion of a large part of the Black population turned New Bern from a majority-Black to a majority-white municipality. LaVigne makes no mention of intending to show Professor Korver-Glenn the four-lane highway built in the 1950s purposely to destroy the Black business district and neighborhood of Five Points. Nor does his proposed tour include perusing more recent material: for example, a report by a city and regional planning expert evaluating the city's plans to rebuild after Hurricane Florence in 2018 and revealing that local officials funneled assistance to downtown businesses and wealthy white neighborhoods while ignoring the dire needs of people in neighborhoods primarily inhabited by Black people.[19]

To their credit, major professional appraisal organizations strongly condemned "the thoughts, language, and tone" of LaVigne's email. "There is no place in our society for the kind of race-based vitriol expressed in this email," they affirmed in a joint statement, adding, "These views are especially troubling coming from an appraiser."[20] Yet merely condemning LaVigne's remarks without auditing his work as an appraiser, without surveying people he worked with and for, and without admitting how the deficiencies in the industry's approach to civil rights enabled LaVigne to inhabit his prejudices so comfortably and publicly simply gestures toward locking the barn door after the horse is gone. A more productive approach by the industry would be to embrace precautionary principles, such as those contained in the analyses and recommendations of the 2022 report of the National Fair Housing Alliance (NFHA) on bias and barriers in appraisal standards and criteria for appraiser qualification.[21] The NFHA report notes that appraisal discrimination violates the 1968 Fair Housing Act and the Equal Credit Opportunity Act of 1974. It details a long history of how appraisal protocols have systematically undervalued homes in communities of color while inflating value in areas inhabited mainly or exclusively by white people. It identifies appraisers' unfounded associations linking race and risk as the operating logic of the appraisal system. It documents improper race-related language in thousands of appraisal reports. Perhaps most important, the study calls attention to the ways in which the procedures and policies of the major appraisal associations marginalize the interests of neighborhoods and consumers victimized by racism while stacking the deck in favor of the interests and viewpoints of those who profiteer within the present system.

Rather than simply seeking to assess the damage already done by appraisal discrimination, the report provided by NFHA puts forth a precautionary agenda designed to prevent discrimination in the future. The NFHA investigation challenges the ways in which the criteria for appraisal credentials and the standard templates for making appraisals create a closed-loop system solely representative of industry perspectives. Qualifications for membership on key boards and for important positions in appraisal professional associations perpetuate the nearly all white demographics of the industry and provide preferences to candidates able and willing to make financial donations to these organizations. The NFHA report argues that the appraisal standards contain vague, confusing, and inaccurate statements about discrimination and about the reach and scope of civil rights laws. The standards never state outright that discrimination is prohibited. The NFHA report points out the racist consequences of the industry's granting broad discretion to appraisers to use the traditional sales comparison approach within rather than across neighborhoods. Precautionary measures recommended by the study include requiring appraisers to undergo comprehensive training in fair housing and to take responsibility for the impact that appraisals have for the skewing of opportunities and life chances along racial lines.[22]

The actions by Black families fighting back against discriminatory appraisals of their homes described earlier in this chapter present visible and vivid evidence of the patterns of devaluation and dispossession caused by racism in appraisals that Korver-Glenn and other scholars have discovered. These actions are generally hidden from public scrutiny and accountability. Appraisal discrimination violates the Fair Housing Act, but it takes place largely unopposed because government bodies do not audit or regulate appraisals and because professional appraisal associations neglect their responsibilities to educate their members and hold them accountable. We can assume that many more instances of appraisal discrimination go unnoticed and therefore uncontested. The fair housing complaints lodged by plaintiffs in this chapter were waged by individuals who had sufficient knowledge to suspect they were being treated unfairly, sufficient resources to seek redress, and sufficient mastery of interior decorating to hide evidence of Black residency and make their dwellings seem to be white occupied. In Marin County and Indianapolis, the families and individuals victimized by appraisal discrimination benefited from resources that enabled them to file lawsuits against the offending appraisers, resources made available to them by the Fair Housing Advocates of Northern California, led by Caroline Peattie, and the Fair Housing Council of Central Indiana, headed by Amy Nelson. Not every victim of discrimination has similar resources.

The Austin family secured a settlement in March 2023 that included an undisclosed monetary amount and a pledge from the appraiser not to discriminate in the future and to attend a training session about real estate discrimination in Marin County. Paul Austin expressed satisfaction with the settlement and voiced his hope that it would encourage people who experience similar discrimination to go to their local fair housing agency for redress. Tenisha Tate-Austin declared that "having to change our identity to get a better appraisal was a wrenching experience.... Neighborhoods of color have been historically undervalued due to deliberate racist housing policies, such as redlining. The ongoing undervaluation of homes in Black neighborhoods perpetuates and exacerbates the racial wealth gap between Black and white families. We hope by bringing attention to our case and lawsuit settlement, we can help change the way the appraisal industry operates, and we can start to see a different trend."[23]

Junia Howell and Elizabeth Korver-Glenn released the results in 2022 of the first major study of appraisal discrimination. Drawing from evidence in the Federal Housing Finance Agency's massive Uniform Appraisal Dataset, which collects information from licensed appraisers, the researchers found that dwellings in white neighborhoods secure appraisals that are twice as high as those in communities inhabited by members of aggrieved racialized groups. Similar homes in similar neighborhoods with the same socioeconomic statuses and comparable amenities are judged by appraisers to be worth more when the neighborhood is inhabited mostly by people who are white. Moreover, the racial appraisal gap is not narrowing but expanding. The researchers found staggering increases in neighborhood racial inequality in appraised values between 2013 and 2021 in some 105 metropolitan areas that had at least five hundred thousand total residents and at least fifty thousand residents from aggrieved racialized groups. Between 2012 and 2022, racial disparities in home value appraisals increased by 75 percent. During the COVID-19 pandemic and syndemic of 2019–22 the average appraised value of homes in mostly white neighborhoods increased by $136,000, while dwellings located in areas inhabited mostly by members of aggrieved racialized groups were judged to be worth only an additional $60,000. Howell and Korver-Glenn discovered that appraisers' valuation of homes judged residences in white neighborhoods to be worth on average $266,000 more than comparable houses in neighborhoods with equal numbers of white and Black residents. Appraisers judged homes in neighborhoods predominantly occupied by white people to be two and a half times more valuable than similar homes in Black neighborhoods.[24]

The evils of appraisal discrimination inflict injuries on innocent individuals, undermine the social cohesion needed for healthy communities, and contribute to the racialization of space and the spatialization of race. Although serious enough by themselves, acts of appraisal discrimination do not take place in isolation. The harms they perpetuate are augmented, extended, and exacerbated by the ways in which artificially low home appraisals take place in concert with systemic practices of artificially high tax assessments on properties owned and inhabited by members of aggrieved racialized groups, as the next section demonstrates.

TAX ASSESSMENT DISCRIMINATION

The artificially lowered home sale values produced by racialized lowball appraisals often take place in a context in which tax assessors artificially inflate the estimated *taxable value* of those same properties despite their artificially low *appraisal value*. These assessments further depreciate the market value of the homes and force their owners to pay higher taxes for inferior living conditions and city services. The assessments leave owners susceptible to tax debts that lead to delinquency sales, enabling white investors to scoop up for pennies on the dollar properties owned by members of aggrieved racial groups.

In his brilliant and indispensable 2024 book *The Black Tax* and in a series of scholarly articles that preceded its publication, Andrew W. Kahrl has proved definitively that the tax system in the United States has always been an engine of racial injustice and inequality. Throughout the nation's history, local tax assessors have consistently overtaxed the lands, homes, and neighborhoods inhabited by Black people. Small debts artificially measured by assessors have been used as pretexts for transferring Black wealth into white hands. Among the copious examples of this that he presents, Kahrl notes that exactly one hundred years before George Floyd was choked to death by a police officer on a Minneapolis street because a store owner suspected him of attempting to pass a counterfeit twenty-dollar bill, Floyd's great-great-grandfather had his property taken from him and his livelihood destroyed because of an alleged tax debt. Floyd's ancestor owned twenty-four acres of land in Harnett County, North Carolina. In 1920, authorities auctioned off that land in a tax sale caused by an alleged debt of $18.83 at a time when land in that county sold for $62 per acre.

While civil rights agitation and mobilization have over time gradually won modest federal government protections for voting, education, and housing, tax administration has remained unrestrained and under control by local tax assessors. Kahrl's research reveals that tax lien investing today has become a multi-billion-dollar industry financed by investment banks, hedge funds, and private equity firms.[25] Throughout the twentieth century tax assessors in Chicago routinely funneled unearned gains to white property owners by underassessing the taxable value of suburban homes, downtown skyscrapers, steel mills, and horse racing tracks, draining millions of dollars from the tax base. At the same time, these assessors overvalued for tax purposes residential property in Black neighborhoods, compelling residents to pay disproportionately higher property taxes. One study of some four thousand properties in Chicago found that levels of overassessment in areas inhabited by African Americans ranged between 35 percent and 100 percent.[26] Homeowners in affluent largely white suburbs with very few impoverished residents enjoyed the lowest effective property tax rates during the 1970s, while property owners in cities with significantly sized impoverished racialized populations paid the highest rates.[27] Residences in Chicago's majority-minority neighborhoods on the South and West Sides paid effective tax rates double those assessed in the wealthy white areas on the North Side.[28]

Development and displacement in Atlanta proceeded along lines similar to Chicago with respect to systematic underassessment of commercial property and to subsidies granted—allegedly to promote development—in areas where massively profitable development was already taking place. Tax increment financing subsidies and the granting of future tax abatements for favored developments ensured that the economic growth these policies made possible would not be fairly taxed in the future.[29]

Protests against the blatant corruption in the tax assessment system in Chicago led county officials to turn to computerized assessment systems that purported to be race neutral. Yet machines are programmed by humans who incorporate their biases into the formulas they devise.[30] Computerized assessment formulas still treated properties on the lowest ends of the market as more highly valued for tax assessment relative to actual value than those properties at the highest end. In a market shaped by decades of overt (and legal) racial discrimination, this meant that properties in Black neighborhoods received higher tax assessments relative to value than those in white neighborhoods.[31]

Inflated tax assessments produce unnecessary vulnerability to tax liens and mortgage foreclosures, which in turn make it easier for assets possessed by people of color to be transferred into white hands. Research by Kahrl reveals how collaboration among developers, tax assessors, and state officials in coastal areas of South Carolina, Florida, New Jersey, and Maryland made properties previously owned by Black people easily available for takeovers by predatory white investors and owners.[32] Dwellings occupied by Black residents of Sapelo Island in Georgia, for example, experienced discriminatory inflated assessments intended to drive them off the land and make it available for speculation and development. The assessed value for tax purposes of one home increased from $10,500 in 2011 to $331,650 in 2012, an advance of some 3,059 percent.[33] When these reassessments led to their intended displacements, sites previously inhabited by impoverished Black people became transformed into luxury developments owned by wealthy white investors. In these situations, tax assessors deliberately ignored the actual current value of the properties in order to tax them on the basis of what they would be worth after development that had not yet taken place.

Properties owned by Black families within a few miles of luxury resorts or golf courses were assessed as if they were the golf course or the resort. Faced with unexpected massive increases in their tax obligations, owners found themselves forced into tax debt and delinquency, conditions that enabled government bodies to foreclose and sell these properties at bargain prices to investors. Once these parcels changed hands, places previously denied even basic services when inhabited by Black people suddenly became sites subsidized by federal flood insurance, enhanced by Army Corps of Engineers projects protecting coastlines from erosion, and made economically viable because of federally funded infrastructure improvements. On lands from which Black people had been evicted, hundreds of millions of government dollars were expended on ecologically unsustainable but economically profitable oceanfront developments owned by white investors. These allocations protected developers and the new owners of the properties from having to pay the costs of the environmental damages caused by the development of luxury housing in ecologically fragile places.[34] Property owners facing increased assessments they judge to be unfair generally have the right to file legal appeals, but the cost of appeals almost always precludes the poorest victims from becoming plaintiffs.

Racially inflated tax assessments enact a process of reverse blockbusting. Blockbusting is the process whereby real estate agents stoke white neighborhood residents' fears of having Black neighbors by promoting panic among property owners that leads them to sell their homes cheaply to the agents, who then sell them at premium prices to desperate nonwhite shelter seekers. Before being declared illegal by the 1968 Fair Housing Act, blockbusting produced rapid turnovers that transformed previously all-white neighborhoods with rising property values into totally segregated areas of Black residency where declining appraisal values deprived homeowners of the equity that they thought they would acquire through homeownership. In contrast, the current deliberate overassessment for tax purposes of property owned by people who are not white does the opposite: it takes land with racialized low appraised values in places ripe for development and drives out residents by jacking up their tax obligations. In an additional insult, once these localities become redeveloped, gentrified, and occupied by new investors and owners, most of them white, the appraised value of their property rises, but tax obligations almost always decrease.[35]

As demonstrated definitively by Kahrl in *The Black Tax*, the system of taxation in the United States has long been an engine of racial inequality.[36] Because of past and present housing discrimination, the home mortgage and local property tax deductions on federal income taxes disproportionately benefit the white people and their descendants who have secured unfair gains and unjust enrichments through preferential access to homeownership. By one estimate in 2018, homeownership among white people stood at 73.6 percent, while the ownership rate for Black people was 42.9 percent.[37] The social policy that assigns low taxes to wealth acquired from capital gains and inheritance artificially inflates the value of income most likely to be in white hands as a result of past and present discrimination. Over the past half century, a relentless series of tax "reforms" that have been portrayed as *tax cutting* have been in fact merely *tax shifting* in ways that advantage people who are white and wealthy at the expense of people who are not. Cuts in personal and corporate income taxes and property taxes have lessened tax obligations tied to the wealth that is disproportionately held by white people. These cuts shift the burden to raise revenues to taxes on consumption such as sales and excise levies, user fees, and fines. As a result, people who are nonwhite must shoulder a tax burden that constitutes a larger percentage of their income than people whose tax obligations come from inherited wealth and capital gains. Moreover, as shown by the fiscal crisis in Detroit delineated in chapter 1, reducing tax obligations for the wealthy deprives governments of revenues for investment in public health, education, and transportation sorely needed by aggrieved communities.

In Detroit between 2010 and 2016 alone, city authorities deliberately violated state law by assessing somewhere between 53 percent and 85 percent of homes in that city at rates far above their market value. These tax assessments violated the provision in the state constitution that forbids property from being assessed at more than half of its true cash market value. If the property is worth $100,000, the assessed value by law can be no higher than $50,000. Yet between 2009 and 2015, large swathes of residential property in Detroit were assessed above the constitutionally permissible level. These assessments cost property owners more than $600 million. As many as one out of every four properties in Detroit is estimated to have experienced property tax foreclosure between 2011 and 2015.[38] One hundred thousand residents of the city lost their homes because of their inability to pay taxes and mortgages. Areas with majority-Black populations in the city of Detroit and the county that surrounds it had dramatically more tax foreclosure auctions than places where the population was primarily white.[39] Discriminatory inflated tax assessments happened most frequently on moderately and inexpensively priced homes: those owned by occupants who were least likely to have the funds, knowledge, and time to challenge erroneous assessments.

The profits made possible because of discriminatory and inflated tax assessments that lead to foreclosure are staggering. By shifting large numbers of houses from owner occupants to speculators and corporate owners, tax foreclosures and auctions in Detroit reduce the amount of available housing, raise rents, and set the stage for the renewal of old forms of exploitation and the invention of new ones. Desperate shelter seekers are lured into contract-for-deed schemes that promise eventual ownership once all payments are made. But these land contracts differ significantly from mortgages. One missed payment can lead to loss of all equity. Land contracts require monthly payments, but unlike rentals they also mandate down payments to the seller, and they absolve the seller of all responsibility for maintenance, repairs, and delinquent tax payments. Contract buyers who make all their payments on time and fulfill all of their obligations can find that they take title to properties that then require them to pay enormous sums in the form of delinquent taxes or face losing their homes to tax foreclosure.[40] One Detroit home purchased for $2,500 was assessed for tax purposes as worth $49,825, was foreclosed on by the county government when the owner could not afford the taxes based on that assessment, and then was sold at auction to an investor for $3,900.[41] Another dwelling was purchased for $20,000 through a land contract company that promised to use the monthly payments made to cover property taxes and water service fees. For tax purposes, the dwelling was assessed illegally at more than twice its sale value at $46,000. The firm that promised to pay the taxes and utility bills did not do so, sticking the contract buyers with a $9,000 bill for overdue taxes. County officials then gained title to the property through foreclosure and sold it to a speculator at auction for $500.[42]

In the 2023 case of *Tyler v. Hennepin County*, the Supreme Court ruled that governments are not entitled to surplus profits from tax fore-closure sales.[43] This litigation was crafted by the libertarian Pacific Legal Foundation in such a way as to have little or no practical effect on the homeowners most vulnerable to tax lien predation. In keeping with the libertarian ideology that seeks to curtail the ability of government bodies to enforce tax collection and generate revenue, the complaint focused on forcing states to handle tax foreclosure proceedings in the same way they treat mortgage foreclosure while leaving in place the ability of private investors to collect excessive fees from tax-delinquent property owners.

THE RACIALIZATION OF MUNICIPAL OPPORTUNITY

Racially disparate tax assessments, liens, and foreclosures play a central role in what Josh Pacewicz and John Robinson III describe as the "racialization of municipal opportunity." Their research reveals that governments and administrative offices in cities and suburbs are architects of a new and decidedly unjust racial order. Looking specifically at majority-white and majority-Black suburbs, Pacewicz and Robinson find that while most municipalities increasingly rely for revenue on traffic tickets, fines, and user fees, the places with the biggest increases in these sources of funds are higher-income Black suburbs. Suburbs with wealthy and middle-class white residents receive significant funds from sales tax revenues generated by big box stores and shopping centers, but developers and investors rarely locate these businesses in places where Black people reside. Black suburban residents with high incomes thus travel to other municipalities to buy goods, consume services, and pay sales taxes. The wealth brought to these majority-white suburbs helps fund their municipal services and decreases their need for income from tickets, fines, and fees. As Pacewicz and Robinson conclude, these "systems of finance constitute a conduit of wealth transfer with broad benefits for many residents of white middle-income suburbia."[44]

These same systems make less wealthy majority-Black municipalities like Ferguson, Pagedale, and surrounding towns in North St. Louis County in Missouri into localities that rely on punitive sources of revenue that subject residents to intense surveillance and harassment, constrained mobility, permanent unpayable debts, and frequent stops, arrests, and periods of incarceration.[45] The pattern that prevails in these suburbs inhabited by Black people also plagues African American residents of large cities. Pacewicz and Robinson found that eight of the ten zip codes with the largest traffic and parking ticket debts in Chicago are majority-Black areas. Chicago traffic monitors issued fifty-four million tickets between 1996 and 2018, bringing more than $2.8 billion in revenue into city coffers. Strategies used to jack up these revenues include giving multiple citations to the same parked vehicle during a day, augmenting fines for moving violations with additional costly citations for failure to display an up-to-date city sticker, and ticketing, towing, and impounding vehicles parked in snow removal zones, even on days where there was no snow.[46]

The tax system makes no overt mention of race. It appears on the surface to be race neutral. Yet in practice it functions as a generator of racist inequalities and injustices. The tax code augments the value of inheritances based on assets acquired initially through expressly racist practices. It offers hidden subsidies to the people who profit most from past and present housing discrimination, and in its present iteration it is structured so that municipalities and states cannot fund the programs for housing, health care, education, and transportation that are most needed by aggrieved communities of color. Like home appraisals, tax assessments and collections are not just inflected with racial disparities; rather, they create a primary site where the disparities are produced, practiced, learned, and legitimated. Tax assessments that lead to foreclosure expose Black property owners to unjust economic and legal penalties, while subjecting municipalities and neighborhoods populated by aggrieved racialized groups to the disappearance of public services, the shredding of the social safety net, higher fees charged by bond sellers on infrastructure improvements, and increased government dependence on revenue from fees and fines. They also contribute significantly to the deterioration of individual and public health because, as Kahrl's research reveals clearly, the fiscal crises caused by racialized tax predation impede funding for water and sewer lines, paved streets, and sidewalks.[47] The next section examines how the ill effects of tax assessment become augmented by other forms of wealth extraction and health injustice.

CREATIVE EXTRACTION, WEALTH, AND HEALTH

In a series of carefully designed and persuasively executed and argued studies, Danielle Purifoy and Louise Seamster have chronicled what they describe as "predatory inclusion" and "creative extraction."[48] They argue that spaces understood to be white take on artificially augmented value through the extraction of resources from places configured as non-white. This plunder is achieved through predatory governance schemes that include annexation, underbounding, racially motivated zoning, and outright land theft.

A white spatial imaginary grounded in an ethos of hostile privatism and defensive localism leads wealthy white communities to hoard resources and opportunities while outsourcing hazards and nuisances to communities of color.[49] The wealthy, primarily white suburban sections of Dallas and Houston in Texas, and of St. Joseph and Grand Blanc in Michigan, profit from their ability to wall themselves off from the toxic burdens, absence of tree canopies, and flood-prone developments in nearby Sandbranch and Tamina in Texas and Benton Harbor and Flint in Michigan.[50] Concentrating hazards and nuisances on land occupied by Black residents artificially increases the value of lands inhabited by whites. Cities annex suburban areas of concentrated white residency and offer them a lavish array of services, while at the same time excluding and underbounding outlying neighborhoods and settlements inhabited by members of aggrieved racialized groups. Residents of outbounded localities outside municipal jurisdictions near Houston and Dallas in Texas, Modesto in California, Moore County in North Carolina, and Tunica, Belzoni, Indianola, and Cleveland in Mississippi have paid sales taxes in the nearby cities where they purchase grocery items, buy gas, deposit money in banks, and pay for health care. But those cities, along with county governments, can exclude them from water and sewer service, from garbage collections, and from protection by police officers and firefighters.[51]

In the mostly Black municipality of Tamina, Texas, unincorporated status undermines property values and opportunities for wealth building, while leaving residents to cope with inadequate infrastructures. Vacant lots become regional dumping grounds while storms make pedestrian paths inaccessible. Pools of water become breeding grounds for mosquitoes. That same unincorporated status, however, has very different effects in the nearby mostly white Woodlands master-planned community. The Woodlands boasts more than one hundred thousand residents, most of whom believe the property values they benefit from stem from their own labor, thrift, and money management. Yet a significant part of the territory of the Woodlands was seized from Tamina against its residents' wishes. Development of the Woodlands was augmented by massive subsidies from the federal government, funds that were unavailable to Tamina. Under the aegis of the National Urban Policy and New Community Development Act, the federal government allocated $8.8 million to build the Woodlands' water infrastructure. Its developers secured nearly $100 million in interest-free loans, loan guarantees, and federal grants. Property taxes are kept low in the Woodlands because county government agencies provide police services and street and road upkeep to the private community corporation that runs the development—all services that county agencies firmly withhold from Tamina.[52]

Tamina suffered from the annexation of its land by the Woodlands. It has tried to contract with the nearby suburb of Shenandoah (which had also been formed by seizing Black-inhabited land and where two-thirds of the population is white) for services, but that city refuses unless it is given the opportunity to annex even more of Tamina's territory and dispossess its inhabitants of their property. The residents of Tamina are blocked from forming their own municipal utility district because doing so requires the approval of county commissioners and officials in the mostly white municipalities that would prefer to use Tamina's land and resources for themselves. The wealth of white spaces in the Woodlands, Shenandoah, and other suburbs does not merely contrast with the deprivation in Tamina—it is *produced* by the power imbalances between them, by the extraction of value from Tamina and by the exclusion of that city's residents from meaningful political participation in the decisions that affect their lives.

Research by Seamster shows that a similar dynamic prevails in the city of Benton Harbor, Michigan, where the population is nearly 90 percent Black. Creative extraction and predatory governance there produce barriers against democratic political participation, making the municipality an exporter of capital to both nearby and distant areas of wealthy white residency.[53] During the first decade of the twenty-first century, long-established historical processes of capital and resource extraction by industries receiving generous tax breaks from Benton Harbor set the stage for actions taken ostensibly in response to the fiscal crisis caused by the economic recession and mortgage foreclosures of 2008. As noted in chapter 1, Michigan's Republican governor and legislature enacted a law that placed "failing" cities in receivership and under state control. This emergency management law targeted the six cities in the state with the largest Black populations and where the elected officials were Black, in effect disenfranchising half of the state's Black voters. Cities with comparable unfavorable fiscal conditions but with majority-white populations escaped review and receivership. The unfairness of this law caused the state's voters to overturn it in a referendum, but the legislature and the governor responded by passing and signing a new law that achieved the same ends while stipulating that this new law could not be overturned by a voter referendum.

In implementing the emergency management law, the state of Michigan blamed the fiscal crisis of the cities on the allegedly incompetent and corrupt management practices of Black elected officials. Yet the financial shortfalls used as evidence for that argument in actuality stemmed from a series of factors that originated outside the city. These include the state's decision to end the redistributive aspects of Michigan's revenue-sharing law, effectively transferring $6.2 billion from struggling cities in order to provide tax breaks to property owners in wealthy white cities and towns. They include the provisions in Michigan law that left local officials unable to respond to the plummet in home prices caused by mortgage fraud in 2008 and immediately afterward. In addition, between 2005 and 2009, federal funding to cities declined by 48 percent.[54]

In Benton Harbor, part of the fiscal crisis stemmed from long-standing subsidies funneled to the Whirlpool Corporation and its production facilities in the city. Whirlpool took some $52 million in tax exemptions, waivers, and credits, while channeling its profits into the construction of a privately owned luxury golf course and lakefront residential development.[55] The emergency managers appointed by the governor of Michigan created a bonanza for wealthy investors and owners by selling off municipal land at bargain rates and privatizing city water systems and other utilities and services. As explained in chapter 1, in Flint this effort at revenue extraction led to a change in the water supply that poisoned local residents with contaminated water, causing immediate and long-term brain damage and developmental disabilities.[56]

Emergency management failed to cure the fiscal ills of Benton Harbor and the other cities where the state took over municipal governance. Under emergency management between 2010 and 2014, Benton Harbor's debt-to-asset ratios did not decline but rather increased. Median property values in Benton Harbor decreased by 20 percent between 2010 and 2016. Yet selling off city assets and reneging on pension commitments in Benton Harbor produced a bonanza of unfair gains and unjust enrichments for wealthy individuals, owners, investors, and corporations. Unlike Benton Harbor, median home values in the nearby wealthy white suburb of St. Joseph actually increased between 2010 and 2016 despite the recession and the regional fiscal crisis.[57]

SYSTEMIC PROBLEMS REQUIRE SYSTEMIC SOLUTIONS

The combination of racially situated lowball appraisals, inflated tax assessments, the racialization of municipal opportunity, and the health and wealth injuries perpetrated by predatory extraction create cumulative and intersectional injustices that allow for no single-axis solution. Obtaining higher home value appraisals and lower tax assessments and ending predatory extraction and the health injuries it produces are necessary measures. But in themselves these changes will not be sufficient. The ever-expanding invention and implementation of new forms of discrimination expose the limits of the tort model of injury in law. The mutually constitutive nature of the racial health and wealth gaps and the role of place in shaping health disparities by race demonstrate the inadequacy of the biomedical model of health care. Taking a domain-specific and one-at-a-time approach to all of the impediments to health and housing justice will never bring adequate damage awards, restore justice to plaintiffs, or provide sufficient healing and well-being to patients. Both housing and health care need to draw on the precautionary principles of pediatrics to anticipate in advance and correct in advance all those forces that harm people and the planet. Individuals need to see themselves as part of groups. Groups need to see themselves as participants in an active and engaged democratic public sphere. Groups need to make practical alliances with each other. Activities that now take place in separate silos, professional practices, and social groups need to be undertaken relationally and together.

Like all professions, the appraisal and tax assessment fields include some people who harbor racial animus and make conscious decisions to discriminate. Yet most of the functionaries who carry out racist policies in home and property valuation do because they have imbibed the common sense of a society structured in crucial ways by the spatialization of race and the racialization of space in nearly every realm of social interaction. Appraisers and assessors do not do their work in isolation; they implement in their professions ideas that have been inculcated in them from living in a society where racial exclusion and subordination are deeply ingrained in the quotidian activities of mortgage lenders, insurance agents, urban planners, police officers, real estate agents, and medical physicians and clinicians. These actors in turn, make the decisions they do in part because of the ways in which racial discrimination by tax assessors and home appraisers imbue spaces with decidedly racialized meanings.

White people who declare themselves to be color-blind, who claim that they do not even see color when looking at others, and who object to race-conscious remedies because they claim they object to treating people as members of groups rather than as individuals behave in ways that diametrically contradict their proclamations. When asked to evaluate the worth of different places, they quickly turn to racial associations and stereotypes. They describe spaces associated with Black people as dirty, dangerous, run down, failing, unpleasant, unsafe, and under-resourced. One experiment by psychologists showed test subjects a picture of a middle-class suburban home and informed them it was up for sale. All of the test subjects viewed photos of the same suburban house with three bedrooms on a quarter-acre lot and all received the same information about its characteristics, features, improvements, and amenities. Those who were told the house was occupied by a Black family gave the dwelling a lower evaluation than those who were told it was occupied by a white family. These researchers found that the sight of even a single Black family in a neighborhood caused viewers to imagine the surrounding area to be less well maintained and less safe. Those who imagined that the neighborhood included other African American households set the value of the home $22,000 lower than those who thought of the neighborhood as exclusively reserved for white residents. Although they were given no actual information about the surrounding neighborhood, when the sellers were identified as Black people the respondents described the nearby area as poorly maintained, isolated from banks and stores, dangerous, and suffering from inferior city services and schools, Moreover, when asked whether a polluting chemical plant should be located near the home even though a school was nearby, the test subjects objected strongly when they thought the neighborhood was occupied by white people but registered lower degrees of opposition when told the area was a locus of residency for Black people.[58]

Home seekers of all racial ascriptions may well recognize how privileges are hoarded in places inhabited largely by white people and may seek to secure those benefits for themselves. Social scientists have found that prospective home buyers across racial lines express preferences for neighborhoods that have no or few Black residents.[59] Yet preference for white neighborhoods is a product of appraisal discrimination, not its cause. Once mortgage lenders, appraisers, real estate agents, and planners equate Blackness with risk and whiteness with safety, they purport to *find* a demand for residency in white areas that in fact they have *created*. Members of aggrieved racialized groups are not immune to the enticements that they imagine flow from property ownership in a mostly white neighborhood, although often they find that their very presence in that area then provokes their white neighbors to move, resulting in devaluation of their property and subsequent neighborhood demographic change.

Appraisers and tax assessors might have no conscious intent of inflicting ill as they evaluate places created and shaped by racially discriminatory mortgage lending, insurance redlining, transit and environmental racism, and predatory policing. Consciously racist people do produce racist places, but racist places can also work on their own systematically to produce people who are both consciously and subconsciously racist. The traditional practices of social science research and political debate encourage us to find the main villains in the story, to determine if appraisers and assessors commit racist acts because of the racist practices of bankers, insurance agents, urban planners, and police officers or if those actors merely follow the pattern established by appraisal and assessment. This is the age-old question of which comes first, the chicken or the egg. Within the complex conjuncture of forces that link race and place, however, asking if the chicken or the egg comes first is irrelevant. What we need, as Ruth Wilson Gilmore quips, is a penetrating analysis of the entire poultry industry.[60]

Discrimination in home appraisals and discrimination in tax assessment are complementary parts of a fully linked system that has no single origin or animating force. The conduct of appraisers and assessors needs to change, but that change needs to be accompanied by broader changes in society. Changing the relationships that link housing discrimination to poor health requires the creative efforts of an active and engaged public committed to fusing health justice with housing justice and to recognizing how and why so many domains of civic life use racial difference as an excuse for political, social, and economic domination. Those spheres include the justice system, where rising mass incarceration has disproportionate detrimental effects on health care and housing opportunities among aggrieved communities. They also include the insurance industry, whose deeply embedded discriminatory practices institutionalize discrimination in many social domains beyond insurance as well. Incarceration and insurance serve as the objects of analysis in the two chapters that follow.

5

If It Ain't One Thing, It's Another

Gender, Housing, Health, and Mass Incarceration

Richard "Dimples" Fields, who billed himself modestly as "Mr. Look So Good," released a best-selling rhythm and blues song in 1982 titled "If It Ain't One Thing, It's Another." The song's lyrics present an inventory of the many things troubling the singer. Some of them recount struggles with personal relationships and health, while others bemoan the pervasive presence of racism in society. The narrator's problems are both private and public, both personal and political. Instead of viewing issues with employment, taxes, addiction, parenting, and romantic and sexual relationships separately, "If It Ain't One Thing, It's Another" recognizes that they occur in concert and cannot be solved in isolation from their mutually constitutive effects.

This book argues that with regard to health and housing discrimination, if it ain't one thing, it's another. This chapter analyzes how seemingly separate conditions are mutually constitutive and intersecting, in this case how health and housing injustices produce, reflect, and shape mass incarceration and augment and exacerbate gender and sexual oppression with disastrous health consequences. The deliberate underenforcement of fair housing laws in neighborhoods inhabited mainly by white people has been accompanied by the deliberate overenforcement of laws against petty crimes in areas inhabited by people who are not white. This disparity creates a self-perpetuating cycle. Members of aggrieved racialized groups are overincarcerated and underhoused. The people suffering most from unfair housing and discriminatory barriers to healthful living are those most frequently sent off to jails and prisons. Incarceration damages their already-imperiled health and undermines the well-being of their communities. While all members of aggrieved racialized groups suffer from these dynamics, they pose particular pain and problems for people who are women, LGBTQ, or gender nonconforming.

Two bills passed by Congress and signed into law by President Lyndon Johnson in 1968 have shaped the relationships that have linked housing to health and wealth ever since. In April of that year the president signed the Fair Housing Act, which banned many forms of residential segregation and obligated all federally funded entities to take steps to affirmatively further fair housing. Two months later, the president affixed his signature to the Omnibus Crime Control and Safe Streets Act, the first in a series of measures that expanded the range of offenses for which people could be prosecuted, increased the length of sentences served by those convicted of crimes, and placed millions of people under new regimes of surveillance and control.[1] Much of the racially skewed opportunity structure of US society ever since has been shaped by the fact that the crime control acts have been continuously, vigorously, and ruthlessly enforced and expanded, while fair housing laws have been consistently, routinely, and openly violated.

During the past half century, while neighborhoods have experienced only minor decreases in racial residential segregation, the numbers of people from aggrieved racialized groups in jails and prisons and on probation and parole have skyrocketed. This is not because this population commits more crimes than members of other groups, but because law enforcement targets them disproportionately for maximum prosecution and punishment.[2] Feverish rhetoric about the need for law and order propelled massive enforcement and expansion of the crime control law, which was designed and implemented to victimize mostly people from aggrieved racialized groups. At the same time, government officials, politicians, and the public at large overtly encouraged and supported defiance of the Fair Housing Act, which, if enforced, would have given racialized people a measure of justice and opportunity. Municipalities, counties, and states routinely continue to ignore their legal obligations to affirmatively further fair housing despite the requirements of the 1968 Fair Housing Act, the 1974 Housing and Community Development Act, and the policies articulated by the Department of Housing and Urban Development.

Both institutional and individual acts of direct discrimination in hiring and housing are crimes. Employers who refuse to hire or promote workers because of their race and/or gender are violating the 1964 Civil Rights Act, as are landlords and property managers who unfairly deny them shelter. Municipal officials who fail to take action to affirmatively further fair housing in their communities, real estate agents who steer home seekers of different races to different neighborhoods, and mortgage lenders and insurance agents who redline communities of color and market inferior financial products to women in them are violating the 1968 Fair Housing Act. These violations of fair employment practices and fair housing laws are hidden crimes that produce visible crimes by creating and exacerbating neighborhood criminogenic conditions such as transience, disinvestment, and unemployment, all of which put people on paths to prison.

Housing discrimination shapes the contours of mass incarceration, and mass incarceration harms public health. Policies that lock up behind bars the very people who have been locked out of access to the housing market cruelly misallocate resources and opportunities. Moreover, injustices in policing and housing provision enact distinct forms of intersectional gender and racial injuries on people from aggrieved groups, especially those who identify or are identified by others as women, lesbian, gay, bisexual, trans, queer, or otherwise gender nonconforming. It is not just that these injustices have disproportionate impacts on aggrieved people: these practices help constitute the experiential meanings of their identities. Created through a plethora of public policies and private actions, they entail more than denials of rights and resources to individuals. They evidence the existence and extent of a concentrated political attack on the health, wealth, and well-being of entire groups of people.

LGTBQ PEOPLE FACE SPECIAL PROBLEMS

While all members of aggrieved racialized groups suffer from links between poor housing, poor health, and mass incarceration, those who are LGBTQ and gender nonconforming face especially daunting and dangerous conditions. Often it is the very intersectional sex and gender identities of people from racialized groups that become criminalized and lead them to be incarcerated. They are more likely than those who are cis, white, and heterosexual to be expelled from school, stopped and arrested by police officers, and sentenced to jail or prison. They experience high rates of bullying and sexual and physical abuse in adolescence and early adult life. They face high risks of developing later-life health problems because of stress, financial instability, housing and food insecurity, and impediments to gender-affirming health care.[3] Young people fleeing hostile homophobic and transphobic home environments and mistreatment in schools find their survival strategies lead them to be charged and incarcerated for running away from home, being truant, or engaging in sex work in order to get money to live. The incarceration rate of all self-identified gay, lesbian, bisexual, trans, and queer individuals is three times greater than the rate of the general adult population. Surveys have found that as many as 30 percent of transgender men and 65 percent of transgender women become incarcerated at some point in their lives. Surveys find that nearly one out of every three Native American transgender respondents and nearly one out of every two Black transgender respondents has been incarcerated.[4]

THE INCARCERATION OF WOMEN AND CHILDREN

The injuries and collateral consequences of mass incarceration function in concert with housing discrimination to enact distinctly gendered and raced injuries on impoverished women from aggrieved groups as well as on their children. At the intersections of race, gender, and class, the health, rights, welfare, and dignity of all women from aggrieved racialized groups—but especially Black women and Latinas—are violated egregiously by the national failure to enforce fair housing and fair employment laws. Women play a central role in mass incarceration because punitive social and carceral policies are almost always enacted through frames that deploy phobic fantasies about the allegedly deviant gender non-normativity of Black women. As Dorothy Roberts observes, punishing Black mothers for the poverty of their children provides this system with its central legitimizing trope.[5] These fabulations function as rationales to explain and justify the intersectional vulnerabilities created by the multiple forms of raced and gendered exploitation that are inscribed inside the routine practices of contemporary capitalism. They are ways to blame and shame the victims and absolve the perpetrators.

The number of women incarcerated in the United States increased by 665 percent between 1980 and 2019.[6] The nation's jails and prisons hold ten times the number of women locked up in all of the nations of western Europe combined. In just two decades the number of women behind bars in the United States increased sixfold, from twelve thousand in 1980 to ninety thousand in 1999.[7] Close to two-thirds of women in prisons and jails in the United States are women from aggrieved racialized groups.[8] One study estimated that the incarceration rate for

Black women was twice the rate of white women.[9] The removal of these women from their families, neighborhoods, and communities has cascading effects because women generally play primary roles in local networks of self-help, social cohesion, and support.

The war on drugs takes a particular toll on Black women and Latinas. The percentage of women prisoners convicted of drug-related offenses was only 10 percent in 1979 but grew to more than one-third by 1998. Drug convictions have accounted for 11 percent of incarcerated white men, 23 percent of incarcerated white women, 24 percent of incarcerated Black men, and 26 percent of Latino men. But these convictions account for 39 percent of Black women and 44 percent of Latinas incarcerated in state prisons.[10]

These disparities do not stem from disproportionate drug use in Black communities. Blacks—who are 13 percent of drug users—make up 37 percent of possession arrests, 56 percent of possession convictions, and 74 percent of those sentenced to prison for drug possession.[11] The results of one national survey released in 2000 found that white youths between the ages of twelve and seventeen were a third more likely to have sold drugs than Black young people the same age. Another study published the same year discovered that white students used heroin seven times more frequently than Black students, used crack cocaine eight times more frequently, and used powdered cocaine seven times more frequently. Yet 75 percent of people nationwide imprisoned because of drug use in those years were Blacks or Latinos.[12] In Los Angeles, Blacks are seventeen times more likely than whites to be incarcerated for drug use.[13] Black people are seven times more likely than white people to be arrested by Chicago police officers for marijuana possession, even though use of the drug by people of these groups is the same.[14]

Poverty and lack of access to medical care can lead suffering people to self-medicate by illegally purchasing pain-killing pills and asthma inhalers, purchases that expose them to risks of criminal prosecution and incarceration. A pill taken in compliance with a physician's prescription is legal, and its consumption is perceived as model patient behavior. The same pill taken by a person too poor to have access to a physician who can prescribe it is perceived as evidence of dangerous refusal of medical advice and even as a criminal act.[15] People convicted of drug-related crimes in affluent white neighborhoods generally receive probation and diversion into rehabilitation programs for the same conduct that leads to incarceration for residents of aggrieved communities.[16]

Most women incarcerated for drug crimes work at low levels of the trade. Minor roles inside drug-dealing networks do not give them better treatment from authorities but instead work to their disadvantage in dealing with the criminal justice system. As low-level operatives they have no information to trade in return for reduced sentences. Their incomes are too low to enable them to pay fines or offer restitution to victims. Even the concessions and amenities sometimes offered to men convicted of crimes do not help them. For example, sentences that entail home detention are nearly always desirable for men, but these sentences may force women to stay in abusive situations. Parole conditions that prohibit drug use do not anticipate users who lack access to medical treatment and turn to drugs as self-medication for the traumas that flow from abuse and poverty. Moreover, the women from aggrieved racialized communities who are deprived of equality in securing employment, housing, and health care are extended a perverse kind of vengeful equity in sentencing. The mandatory sentences attached to drug laws in 1986 prohibit judges from giving women lighter sentences—even if they play lesser roles in crimes, even if they are not likely to offend again in the future, and even if they must shoulder childcare responsibilities. During the first decade that this law was in effect, the numbers of women incarcerated for drug crimes soared by 888 percent.[17]

Children from aggrieved racialized groups make up two-thirds of those sent to adult prisons by judges. The offspring of Black women are more likely than other mothers' children to be arrested and incarcerated. They are more likely to be tried as adults and sent to adult prisons while they are still children, and to be assaulted while locked up.[18] Children incarcerated in adult facilities can have as much as a 30 percent increased risk of subsequent premature mortality between the ages of eighteen and thirty-nine.[19] Placement in lockups designed for adults and populated by them exposes these children to high levels of risk for suicide, rape, and other forms of violence.[20]

In a review of twenty-nine studies involving nearly twenty thousand participants, researchers found that disproportionate contact with and mistreatment by police officers among Black youths is strongly associated with negative health outcomes.[21] Rupa Marya and Raj Patel observe that every police killing affects more than the victim. It creates trauma and stress for relatives, friends, neighbors, and witnesses who inhabit concentric circles of death that erode individual and community health.[22] Eric Garner, suffering from asthma, obesity, and a cardiovascular condition, was choked to death by a police officer in front of witnesses on a Staten Island street in 2014. That killing exposed his family to cruel degrees of stress and sorrow. Three years later, Garner's daughter Erica suffered a heart attack triggered by an asthma episode and died at the age of twenty-seven.[23]

Racial identity looms larger than class identity in these circles of death: Black women with college degrees are as likely to have immediate family members incarcerated as white women high school dropouts. At any given time, 40 percent of African American women have family members who are incarcerated. More than one in four Black women experience a sibling being locked up at some point in their lives. Black children experience a rate of parental incarceration that is five times higher than that for white children. Incarceration of a family member is associated with higher likelihoods of obesity, strokes, and heart attacks as well as with higher rates of behavioral health problems and increased alcohol and drug use.[24]

School authorities single out Black girls for disproportionate disciplinary punishments. A survey by the Southern Poverty Law Center found that Black girls in middle schools received suspensions more than four times as often as white girls.[25] Investigation by the Civil Rights Office of the US Department of Education revealed that schools suspend Black girls at higher rates than young women of any other ethnicity or race and higher than the rate for most boys. It showed that Black children make up 18 percent of youths attending preschool but account for 42 percent of students in those schools suspended once and 48 percent of those who get suspended twice.[26] An important 2015 study sponsored by the African American Policy Forum revealed that young Black women experienced more severe sentences from the juvenile justice system than any other group of girls and that they were the fastest-growing segment of people in the youth detention system.[27]

Many Black women and Latinas first encounter the criminal justice system largely because they are trying to cope with unlivable circumstances. More than 60 percent of women in state prisons reported that they were not employed full time when they were arrested.[28] Girls fleeing homes to avoid physical and sexual abuse are declared delinquent. Once this survival strategy has become criminalized, vulnerability is compounded by the existence of a new criminal record. Research by Veronica Lerma shows how Chicanas are targeted by police and school disciplinary systems, not because of their own behavior, but because of their ties to relatives, peers, and romantic partners who are assumed by the authorities to be criminals. Girls and women in these situations are forced to choose between two negative outcomes: if they maintain ties to family and friends they face the likelihood of being treated as criminals, but if they sever those ties they face the prospect of living cut off from family and neighborhood social support networks.[29]

Education and employment discrimination channel women from aggrieved racialized groups into the carceral system. Latinas and Black women in state prisons are twice as likely as the white women incarcerated there to have failed to complete high school. Raced and gendered barriers to white-collar employment leave women from aggrieved racialized communities overrepresented in low-paying jobs in bars and other entertainment outlets, increasing the likelihood of their vulnerability to participation in sex work and the drug trade. A 2015 study found that unmarried Latinas in the United States had a median wealth of $100, while unmarried Black women had a median wealth of $200. In contrast, unmarried white women had a median wealth of more than $15,000.[30] Another study in 1997 showed that almost 50 percent of Latinas and Black women earned less than $600 per month before incarceration.[31] Their poverty can drive them to turn to shoplifting, petty larceny, and sex work, not as ways to get rich, but as desperate survival strategies. Perhaps most tellingly, studies have found that between 56 percent and 82 percent of incarcerated women report life histories replete with victimization by sexual violence.[32]

WOMEN IN THE CARCERAL COMMUNITY

The combination of domestic centrality and economic marginality leaves women as the members of aggrieved racialized communities with the main responsibility for raising and housing children, as well as increasingly becoming primary caregivers for their ailing and/or disabled parents who lack access to health care because of lifelong impediments to asset accumulation and affordable medical treatments.[33] Women head 71 percent of all single-parent households and 85 percent of single-parent houseless families.[34] Even when they are not the ones incarcerated they shoulder extra unfair burdens in their roles as caretakers and wage earners condemned by housing segregation to dwell in carceral communities—places where large numbers of people are in jail or prison, on parole, or on probation. Mass incarceration shapes every facet of life in these places, routinely damaging health, disrupting family and neighborhood ties, and adding onerous collateral consequences to criminal convictions. One study found that every 1 percent increase in numbers of incarcerated people leads to a 0.4 percent increase in county-level mortality.[35]

Women from aggrieved groups most often have to pay the high costs of legal defense of loved ones, to spend money on trips to visit people locked up in distant prisons, to pay the exorbitantly high costs of commercial bail and the unconscionable fees that telecommunications companies charge for phone calls from and to prisons, and to attend to the health needs and joblessness of formerly incarcerated people returning to their communities of origin and to the needs of children whose parents have been sent away.

The injuries that Black women and Latinas suffer at the crossroads of housing and criminality are intersectional: their race, their gender, and their class position all work together to create a cumulative vulnerability from the impacts of housing discrimination and criminalization that is related to, but also different from, the injuries endured by Black men and Latinos. Employment discrimination against women produces lower incomes. These incomes require female-headed households to spend more of their earnings on shelter than households headed by men or couples. Yet here too racism imposes unequal burdens. Black single-parent households possess only six cents in wealth for every dollar held in households where the sole parent is white.[36] Women from aggrieved racialized groups are the people most likely to receive exploitative predatory subprime loans, while white men are the least likely to get them.[37] Reductions in funding programs designed to assist low-income and no-income people to find housing disproportionately damage women of color.

WHAT HELPS OR HURTS?

Economically vulnerable women and children from aggrieved groups are even punished by policies purportedly designed to protect them. A wide range of state institutions expose impoverished women from aggrieved racialized groups to draconian forms of surveillance and punishment. They prosecute women for exposing a fetus to controlled substances, pressure them to accept sterilization, and threaten them constantly with curtailment of parental rights. Some states simply criminalize poverty—defining a woman's inability to provide adequate shelter for children as child neglect. Sixteen percent of children in foster care were removed from their homes because of physical or sexual abuse, but 84 percent experienced family separation simply because their parents were poor and housing or food insecure or without access to childcare. At least one out of every three children in foster care could have remained at home if only their parents had had access to adequate shelter.[38]

The United States takes children from their parents more frequently than any other nation, and it takes them on a racialized basis. Indigenous and Black children are twice as likely as white children to see their parents' rights terminated. Twelve percent of houseless children end up in foster care, compared to 1 percent of children whose parents are not houseless.[39] More than one out of every ten young people who are Black will experience forced separation from parents and placement in foster care before their eighteenth birthday. This system treats Black children like criminals, forcing them to live in places that lack adequate supervision and protection from the damage done to their psychological and physical health as well as from exposure to physical and sexual abuse. As noted earlier, children who experience houselessness suffer from high rates of asthma, obesity, malnutrition, lead poisoning, behavioral problems, and mental health challenges.[40] Placement in the foster care system early in life significantly increases the likelihood of adult houselessness.[41] According to a statement by the American Academy of Pediatrics in 2018, children taken from their parents can experience a toxic stress that disrupts brain architectures and causes irreparable permanent harm. Children in this condition have increases in cortisol, adrenaline, and other stress hormones that can lead to damage to the physical and psychological structure of the brain.[42]

Housing insecurity makes women from aggrieved groups vulnerable to sexual harassment by landlords and to battering and sexual abuse by family members.[43] Public housing agencies often punish reported acts of domestic violence by evicting the families in which the violence occurs. Seventy-seven percent of households in public housing are headed by women; 45 percent consist of women with children.[44] An increasing proportion of these women are grandmothers compelled to be caretakers for children whose mothers have been incarcerated. Given the shortage of housing available to low-income and no-income people of color, this means that women abused by partners in public housing projects have to choose between reducing the physical dangers they face at home and facing the problems of houselessness.[45]

Section 8 vouchers provide subsidies to private market landlords willing to house very low-income families, the elderly, and the disabled. Eighty-four percent of Section 8 vouchers go to women-headed households, 56 percent to women-headed households that include children.

The women who receive Section 8 subsidies can be evicted from their housing because of violence *against* them.[46] In some cities, ordinances and housing codes empower landlords to evict tenants from dwellings from which at least three phone calls for police assistance have been made, a policy that forces women to choose between being beaten and suffering in silence or experiencing eviction. Some women get evicted from their dwellings because defending themselves against their abuser leads to their arrest.

Section 8 vouchers can expose women to physical or mental pressure from private parties outside the family. These women may be subject to abusive remarks and unwelcome sexual advances by landlords and property managers. Cases adjudicated under the terms of the Fair Housing Act's protections against sexual harassment have involved male landlords touching women's breasts, using pass keys to enter apartments, assaulting tenants, demanding oral sex, exposing their genitals to women residents, and pressuring women tenants to pose for nude photographs. In some cases, landlords have demanded sex from mothers, threatening that if they resist the landlord will lie to child protective services so that their children will be taken from them and put in foster homes.[47] Landlords penalize these women by allowing only one child to live in a two-bedroom apartment when two could live there, by accepting in their dwellings young children but not teenagers, or by refusing to accept vouchers from families with children.

Public housing agencies can deny shelter to entire families if a single member or guest is merely *suspected* of a crime, even if there has been no arrest or conviction.[48] Zero-tolerance policies about crime in public housing mean that a single mother living in public housing whose spouse, romantic partner, or older child may have been charged of drug possession as a juvenile (even if never prosecuted or convicted) has to raise her children alone or move out of one of the few housing units affordable and available to her. A 1996 law passed by Congress instructed local housing agencies to bar people with misdemeanor or felony convictions from publicly supported housing of various kinds for specified periods of time. Human Rights Watch estimates that at least one million people were made ineligible for public housing because of this policy.[49] In Annapolis, Maryland, the public housing authority banned from residence some five hundred people with misdemeanor or felony convictions, many of whom remained on the proscribed list even after completing their sentences and complying with probation terms.[50] In addition, rules that prevent people returning from incarceration from visiting relatives in housing projects inhibit the ability of families to assist the reentry process and disrupt and sometimes even destroy family ties.

HOW MASS INCARCERATION INFLUENCES HEALTH AND HOUSING

Poor public health is a cause as well as a consequence of mass incarceration. People with unaddressed health needs are likely to end up targeted for incarceration in the criminal justice system. Compared to the population at large, people in jails and prisons are three to four times more likely to have speech and hearing impairments, five times more likely to be diagnosed with mental illness, and twice as likely to have a serious disease.[51] Incarceration is itself a disabling process that crowds people into small spaces with poor air and water quality. It often requires hard labor without adequate nutrition or medical care. Jails and prisons are replete with infectious diseases.[52] Instead of allocating funds to treat people with disabilities and illnesses with dignity so that they can be acknowledged and welcomed as worthy humans, this society devotes enormous resources to stigmatizing, mistreating, and incarcerating them, which often leaves their health conditions largely unrecognized, undiagnosed, and untreated.

When houseless people get arrested, charged, fined, and incarcerated, their already poor health gets worse because of the conditions that prevail in jails, such as those that allowed the COVID-19 syndemic to run rampant in those correctional facilities. Jails and prisons have become incubators of disease. Overcrowded carceral institutions have poor sanitation, little ventilation, and inadequate medical care. Unprotected sex and intravenous drug use in jails and prisons make people returning to their families and communities carriers of hepatitis C and sexually transmitted diseases. In California, prisons are placed disproportionately in polluted places, in counties in the state's Central Valley where the disease known as valley fever and other environmentally transmitted illnesses predominate. In Detroit, schemes to gentrify the downtown business district involved moving the county jail away from the central business district and locating it on the city's east side in proximity to a hazardous waste incinerator and waste storage sites. Placing these incarcerated people in a place harmful to their health violated municipal zoning codes in Detroit, but a law passed by the state legislature overrode that prohibition by exempting jails and prisons from mandatory compliance with local code requirements.[53] People who have been caged have higher levels of inflammation than those who have not.[54] The poor health resulting from prison conditions does not remain there. When formerly incarcerated people return home, they bring their ill-nesses with them.

Mass incarceration increases the stress of housing insecurity. Many landlords refuse to rent dwellings to people with criminal records, regardless of how irrelevant their convictions may be to their suitability as tenants. Some even bar residency to prospective renters simply because of arrest records, although many arrested people are innocent and are never charged or convicted of any crime. An investigation by reporters for the *Los Angeles Times* found that nearly fifteen hundred completely innocent people had been incarcerated in the Los Angeles County Jail between 2006 and 2011. These were people wrongly arrested by police officers who were working from incomplete records, who neglected to examine fingerprint evidence, or who were led astray by information on improperly worded warrants.[55] Landlords generally derive information about the arrest records of prospective tenants from computerized databases that are notoriously inaccurate, that have inad-equate controls to distinguish people from others with the same name, that are not consistent about what constitutes an arrest, and that have no safeguards against simple misspellings.[56]

Housing insecurity enacts particular postincarceration injuries on previously incarcerated people and their families. Each time an ex-offender moves after being released from prison, that person's likeli-hood of being arrested or charged with another crime increases by 25 percent.[57] Housing insecurity impedes the healthy development of children, as evidenced by a survey of more than four thousand students in Oregon and California that showed that frequent moves while enrolled in elementary school increased the likelihood of being involved in violent incidents by 20 percent.[58]

Draconian policies produce unpayable debts for incarcerated fathers that further disrupt family life, dissolve family ties, and increase housing insecurity. More than half of people in federal prisons and nearly half of those in state custody are parents, leaving some five million children growing up with a parent in prison. Nearly two-thirds of incarcerated parents have been locked up for nonviolent offenses.[59] Incarceration pre-vents men who owe child support for minor children from meeting their obligations since they have no income. Yet they receive no modification of their support orders. As their debt accumulates, states charge them interest on the unpaid balance. They are also ordered to repay the state the public benefits their partners and children receive while they are locked up. As a result, nearly one-third of men returning from prison have outstanding child support debt. They have debts they cannot pay upon release. An estimated 40 percent of formerly incarcerated men have no or very little income. Unpaid child support can lead to suspension of driver's licenses, which makes securing employment more difficult, while discovery of the unpaid debt can mean re-incarceration.

Punishments for child support debts can include revocation of licenses to work as contractors, while driver's license suspensions prevent debtors from holding jobs as truck, taxi, or Uber or Lyft drivers. If they are caught driving to work or to see and take care of their children while their licenses are suspended, they can be sent back to jail. Nearly one-third of parents ordered to pay child support have annual incomes lower than $13,000, and nearly one in four have no income at all.[60] Parents with incomes lower than $10,000 per year owe an estimated 70 percent of the $115 billion outstanding child support debt.[61]

When children and households of incarcerated fathers receive Temporary Assistance for Needy Families payments from the state, those sums are added to the debts owed by those who are locked up. A study examining data from 2013 found that these parents owed some $30 billion to states and the federal government to reimburse those payments. More than one-quarter of child support debt in the United States is owed to government agencies. Even if they somehow came up with the money to repay those debts, these debtors would discover that the funds would go, not to the children or custodial parent, but to the government. Even when debtors reach the age of sixty-five, governments can garnish large parts of their Social Security benefits, a practice that has distinct racialized consequences because Social Security payments account for 90 percent or more of the annual income for 53 percent of elderly unmarried Black people and 31 percent for married elderly Black couples.[62] Draconian child support collection policies thus lock men returning from incarceration into unbreakable cycles of poverty.

Technical parole violations linked to housing discrimination account for a significant percentage of returns to prison: in California, nearly 40 percent of prison returns stem from minor parole violations. The standards of proof for parole violations are much lower than the standards needed for criminal convictions. Released to ghettos and barrios characterized by racial segregation and concentrated poverty, people who are paroled must live in places where they are more likely to be stopped and frisked by police officers. They are forced to dwell in areas where they are more likely to have casual associations with other people (including relatives) returning from incarceration—associations that in themselves can be technical violations of their parole conditions. Those with disabilities may miss mandatory appointments solely because of impediments to accessible transportation, again, a violation of parole conditions.

While systematic practices of racialized overpolicing, overcharging, and oversentencing send Black women disproportionately to jails and prisons, racialized systems of parole, probation, and policing continue to harm them even after they have completed their sentences and returned to their communities. The collateral consequences of criminal convictions combine with housing and employment discrimination to impose additional obstacles to securing shelter.

The vast majority of arrests, convictions, fines, and incarcerations in the United States are not for robbery, rape, or murder but for misdemeanor offenses. More than ten million times every year, individuals are criminalized because they cannot afford to pay for things like auto license fees or are fined for offenses including jaywalking and loitering. People who are completely innocent of the charges brought against them languish in jail because they cannot post bail. Defendants plead guilty because they cannot afford counsel, cannot afford to spend more time in jail, and are pressured to plead guilty by overburdened public defenders swamped with thousands of cases every year.

BROKEN WINDOWS AND BROKEN PROMISES

Neighborhoods that have been victimized by redlining and the wide range of discriminatory practices attendant to it are designated as appropriate sites for "broken windows" policing. Invented by scholars George Kelling and James Q. Wilson, the metaphor of the broken window conveys the idea that a seemingly trivial eyesore unattended to opens the door to massive misbehavior.[63] In practice it presumes that in neighborhoods shaped by disinvestment and inhabited by members of aggrieved racialized groups minor "quality of life" offenses need to be fully policed and prosecuted. As a result, persons loitering, begging, jaywalking, or sleeping on sidewalks are seen as displaying disrespect for law and disregard for personal responsibility and accountability. Broken windows policing concentrates police stops, searches, arrests, convictions, fines, and sentences in the neighborhoods where people who are most grievously victimized by housing discrimination live. It is not deployed in affluent neighborhoods inhabited primarily by white people. When police departments target neighborhoods inhabited by members of aggrieved racialized groups for nuisance stops and arrests—even when these generally do not lead to convictions—authorities use the number of arrests to justify more stops, arrests, and charges. Broken windows policing enacts a racist double standard. It enacts a racial tax in the form of exorbitant fines, fees, and debts. For example, one out of every two jaywalking tickets handed out by police officers in 2016 in North Sacramento, California, went to Black pedestrians in an area where Black people account for only 15 percent of the population.[64] Poor people who are white rarely reside in places where they are surrounded entirely by other poor people, but the overwhelming majority of impoverished Blacks and Latinos live in areas of uninterrupted concentrated disadvantage.[65]

Misdemeanor prosecutions carried out in the name of broken windows policing enact an onerous and unjust system of regressive taxation. Municipalities collect fines and fees, and in some cases make defendants pay the costs of their prosecution and incarceration. The probation and bail bond systems funnel millions of dollars from poor people to profit-making private corporations. Innocent and guilty defendants alike first enter the criminal justice systems of surveillance, punishment, and control through predatory policing of misdemeanor public order and "quality of life" offenses. As Alexandra Napatoff concludes, these practices work in concert with other forms of racialized subordination to deprive people of "liberty, money, health, jobs, housing, credit, and immigration status and government benefits."[66]

Fines, fees, and other legal financial obligations impose incarceration and often permanent indebtedness on poor people while allowing wealthier people convicted of crimes to simply buy their way out of punishment. These policies help create and grievously exacerbate the racial wealth gap, but they also shape the racial health gap. Having to pay even a small fine can force someone to forgo needed medical treatment, neglect nutrition, and fall behind on rent. Monetary sanctions imposed on people unable to afford the costs of the fines imposed on them disproportionately affect people who are houseless, jobless, or deemed to have physical or mental disabilities. Monetary sanctions do not prevent recidivism; on the contrary, they almost always guarantee cycles of unpayable long-term debt that lead to re-incarceration and impede meaningful reentry.[67]

The American Friends Service Committee estimates that the United States spends $80 billion every year on jails and prisons, while allocating an additional \$123 billion for policing.[68] The social costs of the current system are as deleterious as the economic costs. A decent and democratic society cannot exist when it devotes so much energy and so many resources to producing suffering that leaves so many lives constrained, squandered, and lost. The current regime of mass incarceration is counterproductive; it produces the problems it purports to prevent and exacerbates the harms perpetuated by housing and health injustice.

Moral panics about the perceived lawbreaking of poor people of color fuel the augmented intensity of policing and prosecution in segregated neighborhoods. The resulting disproportionate representation of people of color in the criminal justice system then serves as justification for the continuation of housing discrimination. In neighborhoods inhabited by members of aggrieved racialized groups the problem is not that the windows are broken but rather that promises of freedom and justice have been broken.

IMAGINED CRIMES AND ACTUAL CRIMINALS

Moral panics about crime that focus on punishing individuals evade the real structural and systemic causes of disorder that stem from housing insecurity. David Helps demonstrates that the much-publicized demolition of purported "crack houses" in Los Angeles in the late 1980s and early 1990s did next to nothing to impede the sale and use of cocaine but simply destroyed houses left abandoned because of looting by mortgage lenders that went unprosecuted. Abandoned and poorly maintained dwellings were the product of predatory lending that left residents vulnerable to foreclosure and eviction. Attributing neighborhood blight and crime to these abandoned houses diverted attention away from the fact that they became uninhabited because the predatory lending unleashed by deregulation made foreclosures more profitable to bankers and investors than collecting mortgages paid in full. The money city officials expended on bulldozing empty buildings could have been spent on rehabilitating houses and making them safe and available for occupancy. It could have been used to prevent foreclosures and evictions. Those measures would have given residents a stake in the wellbeing of the neighborhood and would have enabled "eyes on the street" that could make the neighborhood less vulnerable to illicit uses by drug dealers and pimps. Instead, the city demolished scarce housing units, reduced the population of the affected areas, and left them filled with vacant lots that lowered the value of existing standing dwellings and impeded future development.[69] Then they blamed the empty houses for neighborhood crime. Tearing down vacant houses in Los Angeles proved ineffective in reducing crime rates. In Philadelphia, by contrast, repairing and renovating dwellings succeeded in promoting public safety. Philadelphia's Basic Systems Repair Program made funds available to low-income families to repair heating, electrical, and plumbing systems. A study of the effects of that policy between 2006 and 2013 found that the repairs were associated with significant reductions in crime.[70]

It will cost money to fix all that has been broken in health care and housing provision. Building affordable housing units and making them available on a nondiscriminatory basis, providing a decent level of health care for everyone, and turning zones of deprivation into places of opportunity will be expensive. But those steps are actually less expensive and more cost-efficient than the policies in place today that fund prisons and jails while neglecting needs for housing, health centers, and schools. Studies have shown that programs assisting low-income families in obtaining better housing and nutrition actually save several hundred thousand dollars per year through lower Medicaid expenditures, reduced social service and unemployment insurance costs, higher local tax revenues, and reduced funds allocated to the criminal justice system.[71]

The injustices perpetrated by mass incarceration do not exist in isolation. Chapter 4 described ways in which home appraisals, tax assessments, and municipal policies created immediate injuries and cumulative vulnerabilities for members of aggrieved racialized groups. The next chapter demonstrates how racialized risk-based assessments in the insurance industry damage both housing justice and health justice.

Born under a Bad Sign

Race-Based Risk Assessment in Insurance,
Housing, and Health

In his 1967 song "Born under a Bad Sign," Albert King adopts the persona of a man whose life has been filled with hard times and trouble, someone whose only luck has been bad. People who suffer from the cumulative consequences of health and housing racism and their attendant consequences for asset accumulation and family formation might well think of themselves as simply unlucky, as born under a bad sign. In fact, however, what they perceive to be their bad luck is really the logical and inevitable consequence of a fully linked system of racial subordination that makes all of the major institutions of society contributors to unearned and undeserved hard luck and trouble.

Zones of racist danger sometimes come clearly marked. They are plainly visible when a Minneapolis police officer places his knee on the throat of George Floyd for more than eight minutes and chokes him to death; when followers of the president of the United States display swastikas and Confederate flags as they attack the US Capitol, trying to overturn the results of an election their candidate lost; when twenty-one-year-old white man Dylann Roof—proclaiming inspiration from racist manifestos—shoots and kills nine members of a prayer group in a Black church in Charleston; and when twenty-one-year-old white man Patrick Wood Crusius, posting anti-immigrant and white nationalist memes, goes on to open fire and murder twenty-three Latinx shoppers at a Walmart in El Paso. Yet danger zones that are unmarked, that are incorporated in the mundane everyday practices of commerce and urban planning, and that on the surface may appear to have nothing to do with racism can enact even greater damage than these spectacular displays of violent and vile white supremacy. This chapter delineates the many different ways that the routine practices of the insurance industry have played central roles in skewing access to fair housing and good health along racial lines.

INSURANCE DISCRIMINATION LITIGATION

According to a legal complaint filed in 2021 with the US District Court for the Western District of Michigan, the State Farm insurance company terminated the employment of Dr. Carla Campbell-Jackson despite her twenty-eight years of distinguished work for the firm. She had earned BA, MBA, and PhD degrees and had received numerous designations of distinction from her employer as an Insurance Associate and Chartered Property Casualty Underwriter. The company that employed her consistently approved and honored her work in the form of "best in class" job performance reviews that described her as "outstanding" and "superior." Other employees rated her as exceptional and excellent, giving her scores significantly above the company average. In 2005 she received the "Spirit of State Farm Award," the highest honor the company gives to its employees.

As an African American woman, however, Dr. Campbell-Jackson endured repeated racial abuse and harassment on the job. When she received the Chartered Property Casualty Underwriter (CPCU) designation, her white supervisors "joked" that the acronym stood for "Colored People Can't Understand." She informed the company of repeated incidents of racist ridicule and bias among her colleagues, including the circulation among employees of racist messages, hateful graffiti on bathroom stalls, and a letter circulated that ridiculed "Blacks and Hispanish [sic]" people as "welfare recipients," "dumb," and "ugly" and that called for employment discrimination against "minorities and Muslims." She asserted that her coworkers attempted to make her kiss a pig as a form of racist humiliation, frequently used the "N" word in her presence, called for the assassination of President Obama, and bandied about the term DANS to denote "Dumb Ass N*****S." Dr. Campbell-Jackson noted that in 2016 she was among the employees of color who received a letter signed by "the silent majority" that proclaimed that "Hispanish [sic] are lazy and cannot speak English well," that "Blacks are uneducated (maybe one or two exceptions)," that "Muslims are at the bottom of the barrel with Hispanish [*sic*]," and that "the black churches are scams."[1] The lawsuit listed racist incidents Campbell-Jackson experienced at work, including an employee displaying a stick man with a noose around his neck to signify a lynching, pictures of non-white State Farm managers X'd out on a wall, and graffiti that read "No Muslims, Blacks, and Spics."[2]

According to her complaint, in late 2015 and early 2016 Dr. Campbell-Jackson discovered that State Farm was consistently denying claims filed by policyholders from aggrieved racialized groups, a finding that she made known to her supervisors. When asked by company officials to document her complaints, she sent them a large volume of documents. She used her personal email account to send this information, which included one item with confidential claim information. The company responded by firing her for exposing to potential disclosure confidential sensitive information. Campbell-Jackson alleged that her dismissal was retaliation for reporting racist practices. Her complaint contended that company representatives offered Dr. Campbell-Jackson $175,000 in return for a promise that she would remain silent about the racist culture that she had found and contested, an offer that she rejected. The Equal Employment Opportunity Commission ruled in her favor in 2021, finding a determination of reasonable cause that State Farm had engaged in acts of racial discrimination. The commission proposed a settlement in which State Farm would give Campbell-Jackson $474,000 in back pay and compensatory and punitive damages and would provide training sessions for ten specific employees, informing them of their legal responsibilities with regard to harassment, discrimination, and retaliation.

State Farm rejected the EEOC's proposed conciliation agreement, and when Campbell-Jackson filed suit against the company, its representative vowed to contest her claims vigorously in court. In July 2022, US Chief District Judge Hala Y. Jarbou dismissed some of Campbell-Jackson's suit for technical reasons related to the timeliness of her filing the litigation, imprecision about exactly when the racist incidents took place, and failure to exhaust all internal remedies beforehand. The court did not, however, dismiss the remainder of her claim. State Farm declared its innocence and remained committed to opposing the charge of discrimination as the litigation continued.

African American businessman Darryl Williams also filed a lawsuit against State Farm in 2019, contending that the company had rejected his claim for damages caused by a burst pipe in a small apartment building he owned in Chicago. According to the suit, a company claims adjuster told Williams that she disbelieved his claim because of the Black neighborhood in which the building was located, which, she alleged, was the locus of many fraudulent claims. The suit further alleged that State Farm offered the landlord a mere $56,000 for damages that required more than $400,000 in repairs and entailed providing substitute lodging in hotels for displaced tenants. When Williams filed his lawsuit, State Farm denied his account of the conversation with the claims adjuster and then took action to take back the money it had already paid out to him. The costs of litigation and the losses he incurred forced Williams to sell his entire real estate portfolio.[3]

Carla Campbell-Jackson testified on Williams's behalf, delineating what she argued was a racist culture at State Farm. She described a company practice designed to deny as many claims as possible from "inner-city" neighborhoods, on the grounds that those places likely possessed a high risk of fraud. A *New York Times* news story about the Williams case noted that a large number of employees, agents, and customers of color have come forward subsequently to accuse the company of discrimination. In one case, African American agents working for State Farm alleged that they were pressured to work only in Black neighborhoods, then were unfairly accused of writing policies that contained technical violations. Campbell-Jackson's attorney told the *Times* that he was in the process of representing some 150 current and past employees charging the company with racial discrimination.[4]

State Farm asked US District Court Judge Charles P. Kocoras to dismiss the lawsuit filed by Williams on a variety of grounds, including the company's assertion that the claims adjuster had displayed no racial animus in her interactions with Williams. Judge Kocoras ruled that the conversation clearly demonstrated animus because the company's claims adjuster described the South Side of Chicago as "you all's neighborhoods," referred to Williams as "homey," and described him and his tenants and neighbors as "you people."[5]

In keeping with the Federal Rules of Civil Procedure, State Farm's requests for dismissal of these two cases sought to adjudicate the sufficiency of the complaints for trial rather than deciding the merits of the cases. While dismissing some parts of the litigation on technical grounds, Judges Jarbou and Kocoras alike found sufficient factual grounds to allow the cases to proceed. They will be adjudicated eventually by litigation now in progress. The tort model of injury that guides civil rights law may ultimately enable Campbell-Jackson and Williams to secure a small modicum of justice, but it is more likely that the narrow limits of civil rights laws will favor the company. Cases like these are often decided, not on the merits of their claims, but on whether plaintiffs file their complaints on time and exhaust internal remedies. Like the grievance resolution process in employment law, complaints about civil rights violations are handled through an elaborate time-consuming bureaucratic process that enables employers to continue to practice business as usual. Rather than having their grievances heard and resolved directly at the point where the injury happened, plaintiffs enter a realm where attorneys, judges, and hearing officers peruse statements by attorneys and make judgments that mainly decide whether due process is followed, not whether justice is done. The tort model of injury is set up to enable every snowflake to plead not guilty in the midst of an avalanche. Even favorable verdicts that provide relief to individuals do little or nothing to address the broader history that cases like these evidence.

INSURANCE DISCRIMINATION AS A HISTORICAL OUTCOME, NOT AN ABERRATION

The insurance industry is hardly alone in employing people who harbor racist beliefs, and State Farm is not the only firm to be accused of racial discrimination. The treatment and practices exposed by the litigation initiated by Campbell-Jackson and Williams shed light on the entire industry's long culpability in creating and profiting from the unjust racial order in the United States. Insurance companies historically have played major roles in the creation of ghettos and barrios. Their traditional practices of linking risk to race continue today to skew life chances and opportunities along racial lines in significant ways.

During the nineteenth and twentieth centuries, insurers routinely denied coverage outright to people because they were African American. They penalized their agents for soliciting business from Black clients. Even when forced by civil rights laws to offer coverage to African Americans, industry professionals deliberately provided only lower-quality coverage at higher rates.[6] Many insurance companies demanded written guarantees that Black people would be excluded from residence as a non-negotiable precondition for providing coverage on homes, businesses, new residential and commercial developments, and entire neighborhoods. Companies offered substantial subsidies for segregation by offering generous coverage to places where restrictive covenants, mortgage redlining, racial zoning, and real estate agents' steering prevented Black residency, while they denied coverage outright—or offered it at exorbitant rates—to Black and integrated areas.[7] Absentee landlords who owned dwellings in these neighborhoods that were denied insurance coverage often could not sell their properties because of the lack of coverage, so some extracted maximum profits from the buildings they owned (but could not sell) by cutting back on maintenance and safety, creating egregious health hazards for their tenants.[8]

With the capital amassed from payments made by customers, insurance companies financed the construction of massive new housing developments in the 1940s and 1950s. The insurance industry financed developments such as Stuyvesant Town and Parkchester in New York and San Lorenzo Village in California. They demanded that residency be reserved exclusively for white occupancy. Insurance company officials warned builders that racially integrated developments would not qualify for coverage. They even went as far as to deny policies to individual white people seeking to live in integrated neighborhoods.[9]

In addition to the dwellings they directly financed and insured, the industry pursued investment strategies that channeled billions of development dollars toward newly created all-white or nearly all-white suburbs and away from older cities with racially mixed populations.[10] Moreover, the equation of nonwhite races with risk that insurance companies devised for the housing market has subsequently become used as a rationale for similarly exclusionary policies in health care, policing, education, and even credit scoring. This association of Black people with risk achieves racist ends without having to declare racist intent.[11] It judges people by the value ascribed to their perceived race and that of their neighbors with no concern for their personal character or creditworthiness.

State and federal laws have long extended special privileges and immunities to insurance companies, freeing them from much of the accountability and responsibility demanded of other businesses.[12] This process originated during the Great Depression of the 1930s. Almost alone among financial institutions in the United States at that time, the insurance industry had surplus funds to invest precisely because existing government regulations saved it from making the kinds of speculative investments that ruined many banks and investment firms. Possession of liquid assets in the midst of the Great Depression made insurance companies an important potential source of investment capital. They campaigned relentlessly to be free from the very regulatory constraints that had made them wealthy, seeking to be allowed to make potentially more profitable yet speculative investments. Insurance companies may secure less money from premiums than they will have to pay out in benefits, but they can compensate for those losses by reaping rich returns from investing the money they collect. Funds collected from premiums fuel investments in housing developments, shopping centers, and commercial buildings.

Legislation at the state level as early as the 1940s allowed insurance companies to invest in residential and commercial building projects and to secure ten- and twenty-five-year exemptions from taxes for their projects. City agencies used the principle of eminent domain to condemn and seize private properties and turn them over to insurance companies to invest in taxpayer-subsidized developments. These public subsidies enabled the industry quickly to become the nation's largest and most profitable landlord. The McCarran-Ferguson Act of 1945 solidified the status of insurance companies as unique among financial institutions in being exempt from federal regulation and being answerable only to state-level commissions. This exemption from federal supervision enables companies to pit states against each other and to resist regulation by threatening to leave the state entirely. State governments offer massive concessions to the industry to entice firms to continue to do business in their jurisdictions. As a result, opponents of racial discrimination in insurance are compelled to wage campaigns inefficiently state by state. Federal legislation in 1999 further subsidized the industry by smoothing the path for insurance companies to shift their headquarters from state to state, and thereby to search for and secure the least amount of regulation possible.

During the boom years of the 1950s and 1960s, insurance companies required private housing developers to exclude Black residents. They opposed the placement of schools and churches near their new development projects for fear of attracting Black students and parishioners. They designed their new communities as fortresses that inhibited access by nonresidents. Land was cleared for new developments by government bodies using eminent domain to condemn and demolish buildings previously occupied disproportionately by members of aggrieved racialized groups. Demolition forced those residents to move into new locations that quickly became overcrowded. These newly configured neighborhoods could then be targeted as sites for placing hazards and nuisances—such as waste disposal facilities, polluting factories, and diesel-fueled truck traffic—which only increased the comparative advantage of the newly created racially exclusive developments inhabited by white people.

Their initial forays into investing in home loans and housing tracts led insurance companies to pressure states for even greater degrees of deregulation, enabling them to invest in income-producing commercial properties like office and shopping centers, which they located consistently in nearly all-white suburban areas. The racial and spatial politics of insurance company investments thus made white suburbs the locus of amenities and advantages while trapping people of color in declining central cities whose shopping areas could not compete with the suburban stores. Cities faced ascending demands for services but declining tax bases, while properties in suburbs enjoyed increases in market value. People living in cities and barred by housing discrimination from moving to the suburbs enjoyed none of the subsequent returns generated by suburban growth but shouldered the full burdens of the decapitalization of their surroundings caused by waves of capital flight, aided and abetted by state subsidies for highway building and extensions of water and power lines to the suburbs.[13]

A significant yet often overlooked part of the mid-twentieth-century civil rights movement involved opposing the discriminatory practices of insurance companies. While campaigns to desegregate lunch counters, stores, and bus terminals properly loom large in historical accounts of the movement, the story of contestation against the insurance industry remains less well known. The policies of the Metropolitan Life Corporation produced especially intense opposition. In 1963 college students affiliated with the National Association for the Advancement of Colored People (NAACP) accused Metropolitan Life of reinforcing patterns of segregated residency in New York. In 1965 Black mortgage bankers in Chicago demanded that Metropolitan Life begin to make mortgage funds available to Black home seekers on a nondiscriminatory basis. That company's policies provoked a boycott in 1967 orchestrated by twenty national civil rights organizations and supported by Martin Luther King Jr. and the Southern Christian Leadership Conference.[14]

As landlord of the Parkmerced homes, which housed more than eight thousand residents in San Francisco, Metropolitan Life engaged in rental policies deliberately designed to minimize the number of Black tenants in the development. The managers of these dwellings manipulated waiting lists to give priority to white applicants, delayed action on applications by people who were not white, informing them verbally that they would not be welcome tenants, and used discriminatory criteria in judging the worthiness of applicants. An interracial group of Black and white residents sued the company in 1969, charging that these policies deprived

them of the benefits of living in an integrated community, damaged the
reputation of businesses that were owned by the white tenants by making their proprietors seem to be in favor of racial discrimination, and
violated the Fair Housing Act of 1968.[15] Their victory in the verdict
issued by the US Supreme Court in the case of *Trafficante v. Metropolitan Life* established important legal precedents that upheld the law's
intention to support integrated communities and made it clear that not
just individuals but entire communities were harmed by discrimination.
The case established the principle that the weak enforcement mechanisms of the Fair Housing Act left it up to citizens to act as private
"attorneys general" working on behalf of the public at large and to file
suits to enforce it.[16] Winning recognition of the right of citizen enforcement of the Fair Housing Act in the *Trafficante* case was a major victory
for justice, one that led to the expansion of the law's reach and scope in
subsequent years. Yet citizen enforcement relieves the state of much of
its accountability to affirmatively further fair housing by forcing the victims of discrimination to shoulder the financial and legal burdens of
enforcing the law that purports to protect them.[17]

The insurance industry was a key participant in creating the poverty,
disinvestment, and underdevelopment of inner-city neighborhoods
inhabited by Black people in the 1960s. Denials of insurance coverage
killed investments in homes and businesses in these places. The urban
uprisings of the 1960s called attention to insurance redlining as a prime
cause of the urban crises that sparked the rebellions. Fearing greater
regulation by the government and especially worried about the prospect
of nationalization that would make insurance provision become a state
or federal responsibility, the industry embraced a series of "reforms"
that proposed to extend coverage to inner-city areas that had previously
lacked it. Yet the financial resources and concomitant political influence
of the companies enabled them to structure these policies in ways that
only increased their profits, reduced their risks, and exacerbated the
very problems they purported to solve.

The industry's proposed remedy for urban problems came in the
form of public-private partnerships like the Urban Investment Program
of 1967 and the Fair Access to Insurance Requirements initiative of
1968.[18] These programs shifted liability for losses from the companies
to the federal government, while allowing the industry to charge high
prices for premiums that would not be affordable to most ghetto residents but were enticing to people with access to capital, such as absentee landlords and investors. Insuring buildings in areas plagued by bank

and mortgage redlining that were deprived of basic city services by local governments and that were overpoliced but underprotected by law enforcement agencies did not promote neighborhood stability. Nor did it make homeownership a sound investment in these neighborhoods. The insurance industry initiative, however, did succeed in making arson a profitable route for landlords who could make more money by burning their buildings down and collecting the insurance on them than from renting them to tenants. In the 1970s, a wave of suspicious arson fires swept through ghetto neighborhoods, destroying property worth more than $15 billion and directly causing five hundred deaths.[19] A state fire insurance program in Illinois enticed slumlords to take out large policies insuring dilapidated and even uninhabitable properties. Those that burned down, often mysteriously, reaped them hundreds of thousands of dollars.[20]

Investments by insurance companies thus financed the special preferences and enrichments of the possessive investment in whiteness in suburban America, worked to decapitalize racially integrated cities, and developed forms of racialized social governance that produced and reinforced disparities in health, housing, education, employment, and incarceration.

RACIALIZED ZIP CODES: AUTO AND PROPERTY INSURANCE

Despite the existence of civil rights laws, the racially discriminatory policies of insurance companies persist in the present. Using place as a proxy for race, companies use the demographics of zip codes and census tracts to guide agents in setting the rates they charge for automobile and property insurance. Drivers living in neighborhoods populated by large numbers of people from aggrieved racialized groups pay higher rates for insurance, rates that are not a function of their personal driving safety records, miles driven, or years of safe driving experience. Neither the content of their character nor their safe driving records can free them from having to pay the racial premium imposed on them because of the neighborhood race effects of where they reside. Artificially inflated costs of insurance compel Black motorists to spend larger proportions of their incomes on insurance than whites. A study by the Consumer Federation of America revealed that insurers charge drivers in predominantly African American neighborhoods an average of 70 percent more for premiums than residents of other areas.[21] Drivers who reside in Detroit, where 80 percent of the residents are Black, pay higher rates for insurance than the average policyholder in Michigan. Auto insurance premiums in Michigan average $3,100 per year, but premiums in the thirty-seven zip codes with a Black population greater than 50 percent average $5,500. Residents of Detroit find themselves forced to allocate an average of 18 percent of median household income for auto insurance.[22] Similarly, motorists with low and moderate incomes residing in Black and Latinx neighborhoods in the city of Chicago find themselves forced to spend an average of 5 percent of their paychecks on auto insurance compared to the 1 percent paid by residents of nearby white suburbs.[23] This expense leads some people to have to forgo driving altogether, leading them to miss the augmented opportunities for shopping and commuting to work that automobile ownership can provide. It leads others to drive illegally without insurance coverage, which increases their risks of arrests, fines, and costly repairs—ultimately raising costs for all policyholders.

Insurance law in Michigan generates windfall profits for insurance companies and medical providers at the expense of the state's poorest residents. All Michigan drivers are required by law to purchase expensive unlimited personal injury protection, yet the state that makes purchase of these policies mandatory neglects to monitor the insurance industry's physician reimbursements, a practice that undercompensates physicians treating Black patients and discourages use of the health care system by the people who need it most.[24]

Property insurance availability is similarly racialized. The racial makeup of a neighborhood has more influence on the number and nature of policies than other relevant factors including residents' income, building ages and structural conditions, the area's crime rate, population turnover, and frequency of fires.[25] A federal audit conducted in twenty-four cities discovered that more than half of Black insurance seekers experienced some form of racial discrimination in their quest for coverage, while white applicants for insurance were consistently offered and subsequently received superior coverage at lower rates.[26] High premiums charged to residents of predominantly Black neighborhoods sometimes even subsidize lower rates for inhabitants of wealthier white suburbs, even when the worst loss ratios are found outside the areas inhabited by Black people. One study found that residents of the primarily Black neighborhoods in Central Atlanta paid on average $705 in annual premiums compared to the primarily white areas in nearby North Fulton and Northwest DeKalb counties, where policyholders paid on average $349. Yet the loss ratio in DeKalb was some

20 percentage points worse than in Central Atlanta.[27] Another study found that lower-income Black residents in St. Louis paid $6.15 per $1,000 of coverage compared to $4.70 in white neighborhoods, even though the loss ratio was worse in the areas inhabited by whites.[28] Investigators in St. Louis in 1993 found that requests for estimates of insurance costs in high-income white neighborhoods routinely secured immediate quotes, while fewer than half of the requests from inner-city urban zip codes yielded a response. When policies were offered to people in places inhabited by African Americans in St. Louis, they contained inferior coverage, despite claims and loss records comparable to those of white suburban policyholders. Members of aggrieved racialized groups frequently found that filing a claim led to abrupt cancellation of their policies.[29]

The employment and office location practices of insurance companies exacerbate racially targeted underinsurance. Insurers tend to do business where their firms are located, usually within the same or an adjoining zip code.[30] Companies pass up the opportunity to sell profitable policies to worthy customers in Black neighborhoods when they fail to recruit sufficient numbers of African Americans to become agents. Even when they do hire African American employees, they do not generally place offices in the neighborhoods where Black people live. Moreover, African Americans who succeed in securing employment in the industry can experience vicious discrimination and harassment, as the experience of Dr. Carla Campbell-Jackson demonstrates.

INSURANCE REDLINING AS A HEALTH MENACE

The Department of Health and Human Services identifies the inadequate and unequal distribution of insurance coverage as a major cause of health disparities and a major impediment to good public health today. Studies show that low-income members of aggrieved racial groups with poor health have a 65 percent smaller chance of being insured than white people with high incomes and good health. Nearly two-thirds of white workers receive employer-sponsored health insurance, while employment segmentation concentrates Black, Latinx, and Indigenous workers in low-wage jobs that do not provide adequate (or often even any) health insurance. Black and Latinx people are between 1.5 and 2.5 times less likely to have health insurance than white people.[31] Almost half of Latinx people between the ages of eighteen and thirty-four in the United States in 2013 had no health insurance.[32]

Even the existence of insurance coverage, however, is no guarantee of quality care. Workers from aggrieved racialized groups have lower incomes and fewer assets, so even with medical insurance they are often less able to afford required co-payments and deductible costs than white workers.[33] A study of deductibles and co-pays between 2006 and 2017 found that spending on deductibles quadrupled from an average of $121 to $411, while co-payments declined from $227 to $138. Deductibles had accounted for 28.8 percent of health insurance cost sharing in 2006, but they rose to 51.7 percent by 2017. Higher deductibles force seekers of medical care into debt or require them to go without medicines and treatments simply because they cannot afford them.[34] Insurance companies can also be part of conglomerates that profit from the high costs of medicine. The CVS corporation not only controls a large portion of retail pharmacy sales but also sells health insurance through its acquisition of the Aetna managed-care company. Five of the largest insurance companies control more than 50 percent of the Medicaid managed-care market.[35]

Medicaid reimbursements covering health care for impoverished people are too low, discouraging medical care providers from treating those patients. The situation is even worse in many southern and western states where large numbers of Black and Latinx people are concentrated. Although it is gradually starting to change for the better, state governments in these places have consistently rejected the Medicaid expansion option that increases coverage.[36] While improving access to Medicaid coverage is desirable, it will hardly be sufficient. The legislation that established Medicaid as the health care program for the poor deliberately distinguished it from Medicare for the elderly. The impoverished recipients of Medicaid, significant numbers of whom are Black, occupy separate and unequal sectors of health care and insurance that differ dramatically from the coverage enjoyed by the elderly recipients of Medicare, most of whom are white. Medicare supplies coverage modeled on private health insurance plans, while Medicaid is a set of programs modeled along welfare lines administered by state governments, all of whom seek to lower costs and some of which run the program in blatantly racist ways.

The neoliberal audit system that governs medical insurance offers "pay for performance" that provides extra rewards for medical professionals who treat primarily affluent and white patients.[37] The maldistribution of health care insurance means that doctors working in areas inhabited largely by members of aggrieved racialized groups receive lower reimbursements when they treat patients. They find that drugs prescribed to treat diseases more likely to afflict people of color have artificially inflated costs.[38] This system has devastating consequences for the 574 hospitals that treat a disproportionate share of Black patients. They average $283 less in reimbursements per patient per day than other hospitals, have lower dollar values of buildings and equipment, are less likely to feature high-tech services, and are likely to have lower nurse- and staff-to-patient ratios. Their accounts per patient per day range from a paltry $8 in profits to losses of $17. Hospitals with mostly white patients, in contrast, average between $64 and $126 in profits per patient per day.[39] The safety net hospitals that exist are the ones that have been able to survive municipal defunding of medical care and closures caused by expansion of for-profit hospital chains. The proportion of Black residents in an area correlates directly to the likelihood of hospital closures. In St. Louis, eighteen hospitals served Black neighborhoods in 1970, but by 2010 all but one had been closed.[40]

Insurance companies complain that it would be too expensive for them to have to research the financial worthiness or risk of each applicant for coverage, so for the sake of convenience they must group people into categories. But the racial composition of a neighborhood is not a legitimate category of risk, nor is it a predictor of loss. It is only evidence of the workings of racism, a factor that further victimizes people and families for having previously been the victims of redlining, disinvestment, capital flight, racialized zoning, school segregation, transit racism, and employment discrimination. Racialized risk assessment in insurance reflects and reinforces the racial biases built into the tax code that give preferential treatment to the sources of wealth that whites are most likely to possess, such as capital gains and inheritance. A similar dynamic appears in settlements of insurance claims. One adjuster who had previously worked for one of the largest insurance companies confessed that her firm made it a practice to pay smaller settlements to nonwhite claimants than to white policyholders, routinely offering the lowest possible settlements to Latinx claimants. She explained that the company justified lower claims settlements to people from aggrieved racialized groups on the presumption that medical professionals would provide them with inferior—and hence less expensive—care.[41]

ALGORITHMS ARE NOT NEUTRAL

Insurance companies claim that race-neutral actuarial tables and market forces account for the higher insurance costs and lower levels of coverage experienced in communities of color. Yet the algorithms they deploy treat the privileges enjoyed collectively by whites as markers of merit while calculating the effects of racial discrimination against non-whites as evidence of individual moral hazard. As Rashida Richardson observes, "When the impact of racial segregation is ignored, issues of racial inequality appear as naturally occurring phenomena, rather than byproducts of specific policies, practices, social norms, and behaviors."[42]

Insurance provision has never been simply an unregulated market practice. The "market" that these companies claim to be guided by is not the product of free interaction between buyers and sellers but rather a direct and deliberate creation of government subsidies and abdication of government regulatory responsibilities. Actions and inactions by federal, state, and city authorities have played crucial roles in the status and conduct of the insurance industry. Decisions taken by insurance companies to treat nonwhite communities as repositories of risk undermine the goals of the Fair Housing Act. The failure of state legislators and regulators to monitor the harms enacted by these policies displays a clear violation of their obligations to affirmatively further fair housing.

INSURANCE RACISM AS A GENERATOR OF MEDICAL DEBT

Treatment in emergency rooms is expensive. Unpaid bills ruin credit ratings and push people toward bankruptcy. Two million personal bankruptcy filings in 2013 were caused by unpaid medical debts. Money owed for medical care in that year exceeded both credit card and mortgage debt.[43] One study found that more than half of people lacking medical insurance carried unpaid medical debts and that medical debt was connected to two-thirds of all bankruptcies.[44] An article in *Forbes* magazine estimated that as much as half of the nation's population carried medical debts, and more than half of those owed more than $1,000. A study in the *Journal of the American Medical Association* reported $140 billion in direct medical debt, not counting credit card balances and unpaid bills that might bring the total to as much as $1 trillion. One survey found that nearly 40 percent of people surveyed in the United States reported that they or a family member did not seek treatment for a medical matter because of fear about its costs.[45]

A study conducted between 2017 and 2019 found that slightly more than 10 percent of adults carry medical debts, a condition that renders them reluctant and even unable to access needed medical care and lessens their ability to pay for food and shelter. Even insured people face unpayable out-of-pocket costs for medicines and treatments. One in four Medicare recipients spends at least 23 percent of their incomes on out-of-pocket medical costs. Middle-class people are as likely as impoverished people to incur medical debts, while women face higher levels of medical debt than men. Black adults have the highest levels of medical indebtedness of any ascribed racial group, while people of all ascribed identities who face the combination of food and housing insecurity have the highest levels of medical debt.[46] One survey found that nearly half of Black adults reported being unable to pay their outstanding medical debts.[47] Catherine Bliss astutely describes this process as the "medicalization of structural disadvantage," a self-perpetuating process that exacerbates the conditions it purports to cure.[48] Curtailing the processes that produce unpayable medical debts would be more than a measure of economic justice. It would also enhance public health. Pursuing profitable returns on investment leads medical centers and hospitals to give highest priority to patients with private health insurance. Since health insurance is tied to jobs in an economy where employment discrimination remains rampant, this system places Black patients in a separate and decidedly unequal segment of the health care system.

In his splendid research on uninsured Latinx people in Chicago, Robert Vargas shows that emergency room treatment can incur bills of $6,000 per visit. The cost of childbirth in a Chicago hospital is more than $7,000. The charge for a single asthma inhaler can be as much as $250. People who cannot pay these bills are harassed by debt collectors and can have their already low wages garnished, leaving them with no way to pay for the medicines and medical equipment they need. Vargas argues that few choices are open to them: accumulating debt, leaving serious and debilitating medical problems untreated, or committing a crime by buying remedies in the criminalized informal health care economy.[49]

The care that emergency room patients receive is generally cursory and perfunctory, and even that care is strictly rationed. People treated in clinics and emergency rooms are denied the medicines and therapeutic procedures that are most medically indicated. In effect, the health care system treats the people with health problems who need uncompensated care as criminals, as "freeloaders" who should be held responsible for paying personally the costs of the harms that they endure collectively, cumulatively, and continuingly from racial and spatial oppression.[50] As Leslie Hinkson observes, in both the housing and health care systems African Americans are both overcharged and underserved.[51]

INSURANCE, ADDICTION, AND INCARCERATION

Like white middle-class Americans, impoverished Black and Latinx people have been encouraged to use prescription drugs to ease pain. Unlike their more privileged counterparts, however, members of aggrieved racialized groups have greater needs for these drugs because they suffer from disproportionate incidences of workplace injuries, untreated medical conditions, and traumatic stress. When they cannot afford the drugs they seek in order to ease pain, to help them work the long hours their low wages require, to offset the injuries they suffer because they cannot afford medical care, or to increase their odds of surviving, some of them purchase illegally the pills, asthma inhalers, and drugs that they feel they need from underground dealers. They have easier access to illicit prescription drugs than to a living wage, maternal leave, or childcare.[52] When they obtain drugs that have not been prescribed for them, they are criminalized as non-normative, even though they live in a society where drugs are prescribed routinely to promote putatively normative behavior. Impoverished people of color found in possession of nonprescribed drugs find that legal authorities do not make meaningful distinctions between the buying and selling of hard drugs and illicit prescription medicines. They are treated as drug dealers and sent to jail without recognition of the forces that drive them to the underground economy.

After incarceration, the collateral consequences of criminal convictions can prevent people from getting jobs, renting apartments, living in public housing, and acquiring professional licenses, making them even more vulnerable to suffering from poor health and even more likely to feel that they need to commit crimes to secure pain-reducing drugs. Incarceration itself is an additional health hazard for people dependent on opioids because forced withdrawal behind bars creates diminished tolerance after release. Formerly incarcerated people attempting to manage the problems of postrelease housing insecurity and unemployment by medication may take pills their bodies can no longer tolerate. One study found that people newly released from prison are forty times more likely than the general population to die of an opioid overdose within two weeks of release. Overdose rates for these formerly caged people stayed at levels ten to eighteen times higher than those of the general population even as long as a year after reentry.[53]

Vargas notes that providing universal health insurance would help people be healthy, avoid substance abuse, and lessen their involvement in criminal activity. The private profit-centered system that now exists, however, offers only what he calls "hyper-individualized, deficit based, and pathological notions of health literacy."[54] The routine practices of the insurance industry hinder fair housing and public health, while hyperindividualized, deficit-based, and pathological notions also contribute to the detrimental effects on health of mass incarceration, as explained in chapter 5. The arguments that Vargas advances received confirmation in a 2022 study demonstrating that areas that hosted expansion of Medicaid coverage under the Affordable Care Act, as limited as Medicaid is, still experienced significantly lower levels of arrests by police officers for drugs, violence, and low-level "quality of life" offenses than areas that did not expand Medicaid. Increased insurance coverage enabled people to receive the kinds of treatments that prevent involvement with the criminal justice system, while at the same time lessening the demonstrated negative health consequences that follow from hostile engagements with law enforcement officers.[55]

RISK ASSESSMENT AND CREDIT SCORING

Limited access to health and property coverage constitutes only a small part of the insurance industry's culpability in creating and sustaining structural and systemic racism. Risk assessment procedures developed initially by insurance companies serve as the basis for racially discriminatory policies in banking. The lending industry routinely uses credit-scoring systems that magnify the qualities white people are most likely to have and minimize histories of sound money management by members of aggrieved racialized groups. They assign disproportionate weight to past relationships with mainstream financial institutions that are notorious for their histories of discrimination and exclusion. Borrowers who qualify for prime loans but are steered irresponsibly by discriminatory lenders into predatory subprime loans get punished additionally with lower credit scores, not because of their financial mismanagement, but because of the loan categories available to them. In this way, conventional credit scoring mistakes the riskiness of the kinds of credit offered to members of aggrieved racialized groups for the worthiness of the individual borrowers forced to use those products.[56] One study found that adopting fairer credit-scoring models that take the history of discrimination into account and draw on more sources of financial information would increase annual mortgage lending to Latinx and Black borrowers by as much as 16 percent and enable nearly ten million more consumers to be eligible for prime or near- prime loans.[57]

RISK ASSESSMENT AND PREDICTIVE PREDATORY POLICING

Racialized risk assessment in insurance provides the mechanisms used in predictive predatory policing. In both spheres, risk assessment simply codifies past injustices into models that generate the futures they purport to predict. For example, residence in a neighborhood replete with criminogenic conditions marks people convicted of crimes as likely to commit future offenses. Putatively neutral but racially inflected variables include education levels, employment records, and financial histories. Because housing discrimination confines Black people disproportionately to resource-poor neighborhoods, place here serves as a proxy for race. The predictive policing model deployed in Broward County, Florida, in 2013–14, for example, wrongly identified as high risk for reoffending many people who did not reoffend. The people harmed by these incorrect assessments were twice as likely to be Black as to be white. The model also designated as unlikely to reoffend some people who did commit new crimes. Those in that category were twice as likely to be white as Black. The racialized biases built into the model made it useless and even counterproductive for public safety by freeing white people likely to commit crimes while keeping locked up Black people unlikely to do so.[58]

THE LIMITS OF LITIGATION

In August 2023 Judge Jarbou ruled that Dr. Campbell-Jackson had not presented sufficient evidence to support her claims that State Farm had engaged in retaliation and harassment. The judge granted summary judgment to State Farm and dismissed the case. Noting that summary judgment is not a means of resolving factual disputes, Judge Jarbou ruled against Campbell-Jackson largely on procedural grounds, charging that the plaintiff had failed to exhaust all internal remedies inside the company's grievance processes, that only one instance she cited constituted actual harassment, that the company had responded properly to her complaints, and that her firing was justified. Campbell-Jackson and her attorney announced their intention to appeal that ruling. The case brought by Darryl Williams on behalf of his Connectors Realty Group is at this time still unresolved.

Company representatives and supporters and some readers of this book may well conclude that the decision in Dr. Campbell-Jackson's case absolves the company and the broader insurance industry of culpability in the unjust racial order. It is possible, however, to reach a very different conclusion from the same evidence. The procedural obstacles that inhibit successful litigation, the burden of proof that plaintiffs shoulder, and the reluctance of the courts to issue judgments against powerful and wealthy defendants demonstrate the limits of civil rights law specifically and racial liberalism more generally. The courts find virtually every snowflake not guilty, but fail to acknowledge the presence of the avalanche.

The costs of health insurance for policyholders have increased measurably as the quality of care has declined. But the social costs of the insurance system are much greater than what is visible in premiums, deductibles, and co-pays. The direct and overt racism that caused Dr. Carla Campbell-Jackson and Darryl Williams to enter into litigation is only the tip of the iceberg in an industry that creates and exacerbates racial disparities as a routine part of its ways of conducting business. In concert with home appraisal and tax assessment discrimination, the municipalization of racial disadvantage, and the impact of mass incarceration on the racial health gap and the racial wealth gap, risk-based assessment in insurance renders racist subordination structural and systemic. The chapters in Part III that follow next explore how efforts to create an active and engaged public constituency for health and housing justice offer alternatives to the current indecent and unjust racial order.

What Helps?

7

Wade in the Water

An Active Engaged Public Sphere for Health
and Housing Justice

When Martin Luther King Jr. was assassinated in 1968, people in Black ghettos rose up in rebellion. The Poor People's March tried to carry on his work by convening in Washington, D.C., to pressure the US Congress to address economic inequality and injustice. In that same year, rhythm and blues singer Big Mama Thornton recorded a new version of the venerable spiritual "Wade in the Water." Thornton's version of the song issued a roll call of differently situated women and announced that each of them was going to wade in the water. Thornton's recording contained no overt political message, but under the surface it called Black people to action by continuing a long history of hidden communication through song.

In the era of slavery, African people held captive in America sent messages to each other through covert means. The tyrants who held them in bondage forced enslaved people to sing songs to make them work harder, to inculcate inside them rhythms that matched the expected pace of their arduous labor. At times the enslavers compelled their captives to sing hymns that signaled acceptance of the Christian Bible, especially the parts that they thought taught slaves that they should obey their masters and not expect rewards in this life but rather hope to receive them in heaven. People who were chained and bound, who labored under the lash of their overseers' whips, and who could be killed at the whim of their armed oppressors could not rebel openly very often, so they developed covert forms of resistance. They composed songs that focused on the parts of the Bible that held possible alternative meanings, returning again and again to the story told in Exodus of enslaved people escaping to freedom, to the words of prophets who condemned earthly kings, and to the promise in the book of Revelation of a final day of judgment and the coming of a New Jerusalem. They placed messages to be decoded by insiders in the lyrics they sang.

The words of the song "Wade in the Water" seemed to their oppressors to be a celebration of the salvation promised by immersion in water during baptismal ceremonies. To their fellow captives, however, "Wade in the Water" held multiple deep meanings. Harriet Tubman used it to call people held in bondage to escape by stepping into rivers along the route so that the bloodhounds trailing them would lose the runaways' scents. Arthur C. Jones notes how in its forms preserved after emancipation "Wade in the Water" conveyed and sustained a powerful collective general commitment to take action in this world, to engage in deep introspection and be prepared to become a new person, and to work together for freedom and justice. Overt references to the Christian rite of baptism by immersion also contained and communicated covert references to West African cosmologies that treated water as a conduit of connection between the living and their ancestors of past generations.[1]

This chapter explores the work being done by people today who are wading in the water and inviting others to follow them. They do so by cocreating collective and convivial sites that serve as parallel institutions seeking to fill needs for health care and housing. They offer solutions to serious social problems by deepening collective capacities for democratic deliberation and decision-making from the bottom up. They recognize that opening up opportunities for fair housing and enhanced public health requires the creation of mobilized counterpublics, of masses in motion capable of envisioning and enacting new ways of being in the world.[2] Unlike the dominant publics called into being by the state through electoral politics and governance and by capital though investment, employment, entertainment, and advertising, counterpublics assemble voluntarily to advance collective interests that are not served by the state or capital.

This chapter describes a variety of small local initiatives launched by people struggling for public health and fair housing, for environmental and reproductive justice, for economic development without displacement, and for a democratic distribution of resources, rights, and responsibilities. Some of these endeavors fight for the creation of new and better housing units and access to shelter in the areas that discrimination keeps them from inhabiting. Some address needs for community-accountable medical care. Almost all of them seek to augment the use value of the economically devalued places they inhabit as devalued, disrespected, and disregarded people. All of them connect the healing of individual bodies to changes in broader social structures and systems.

Community mobilizations for housing and health justice frequently operate in tandem with collaborative arts and culture projects that serve as sites where an active and engaged public sphere for health justice and housing can come into existence. As Doris Sommer notes, at its best, artistic practice helps people experience empathy, deepen discernment, interrupt habit, resist simple solutions, and envision and enact a creative common existence.[3]

PROYECTO CONTRASIDA POR VIDA

The work that Proyecto ContraSIDA por Vida carried out in San Francisco's Mission District in the 1990s and early 2000s leaves a legacy that clearly illustrates the utility and power of convivial and collective community collaboration in constructing medical and social homes. In the midst of the debilitating illnesses and mass deaths among LGBTQ people caused by the AIDS epidemic in the 1980s, Latinx and Black (including Black Latinx) organizers and their friends, lovers, and allies in the largely Latinx Mission District in San Francisco recognized the ways in which homophobia in medical, legal, and political practice impeded proper medical care. Although Proyecto received funds from the National Task Force on AIDS Prevention, which originated as a project of the National Association of Black & White Men Together, a gay multicultural antiracist organization, from the start Proyecto expanded the meaning of multiracial, multiethnic, and multigendered organizing.

At a time when the medical, legal, and political establishments inflicted terrible and unnecessary harm on people with AIDS—by refusing to conduct screening and testing, withholding research funds, denying care, and blaming the victims—relentless direct action protests and repeated challenges to government agencies and medical professionals were required to get the state and the medical profession to even begin to face up to the crisis responsibly.[4] While fully engaged in these struggles, the creators of Proyecto recognized another dimension of the problem: that LGBTQ Latinx people needed reasons to not give in to despair, to believe that life is worth living, to want to survive. People vulnerable to AIDS judged correctly that the biomedical model of disease treatment offered too little to lesbian, gay, bisexual, transgender, and queer people coping with the intersectional problems caused by race, language, citizenship status, poverty, and gender and sexual identities perceived to be non-normative. Proyecto embraced the mission of providing "a safe space, programs and services that invigorate Latina/o bisexual, lesbian, transgender and gay *gente* [people] in the San Francisco Bay Area with debate and desire, intellectual thought, erotic imagination and heartfelt passion."[5] The group's name indicated that it was both oppositional and propositional, against AIDS (ContraSIDA), but also on behalf of life (por Vida).[6]

The activism of Proyecto illustrates how identity-based social justice activism can cultivate a positive marginality within aggrieved groups by building the shared sense of accountability and responsibility that can emerge from collective action. Organized coordinated resistance to injustice among lesbian, gay, bisexual, transgender, queer, and gender non-conforming young people produces health-enhancing measures that enable stigmatized and mistreated people to view their social marginality as a positive source of critique and action, to make themselves possibility focused rather than problem focused.[7]

In an era when even seemingly enlightened and credentialed medical and public health professionals dealt with AIDS as a discrete disease and an isolated public health concern, the uncredentialed activists affiliated with Proyecto recognized the need to attend to the entire social ecology of the illness: to the economic, racial, legal, social, cultural, and even spiritual elements that shape individual and collective well-being. Proyecto promoted practices designed to enrich its constituency's cultural and political worlds despite the specter of AIDS, viewing harm reduction as the key means for prevention and treatment. The group's activities promoted sex-positive programming as a way of countering shame and tapping erotic energy and desire as a part of healing. Attentive to the ways in which tensions, antagonisms, and rivalries within the community impeded social cohesion, Proyecto committed itself to multigender, antiracist, and difference-affirming organizing. Recognizing the multilingual, multinational, and multiracial demographics of the Mission District's LGBTQ residents, Proyecto deployed interlingual wordplay and humor replete with puns and jokes grounded in different variations of the Spanish language in its posters and proclamations. The project brought people together to participate in arts education, to play together on a soccer team, to join multilingual discussion groups, to attend classes on photography and sculpture, to engage in tai chi exercises, to learn video production, and to secure instruction about makeup, sewing, and drama from skilled drag queens as mechanisms for savoring the life-affirming qualities of belonging in community. The organization hosted a series of community forum discussions and workshops on career planning, developed a transgender support group, and organized retreats. As Juana María Rodríguez argues in her splendid analyses of Proyecto's creation of its social and medical home, by connecting HIV prevention and treatment to cultural programs, sports games, repurposed mass media images, multilingual wordplay, and the creation of neologisms, the group worked successfully to "dismantle external definitions of language, gender, sexuality, and culture," thereby enabling the creation of a collective "community-in-process."[8]

Adela Vázquez brought her experiences as a transgender woman immigrant from Cuba to her job as an outreach worker for Proyecto. She initiated projects that shattered the silences that surrounded trans women, encouraging them to define themselves through collaborative work. Vázquez created opportunities for people having sex with trans women to understand their partners more fully. She encouraged trans participants to become aware of the dangers of the illicit selling of hormones and educated the community at large that being trans is not the same thing as being gay. Yet Vázquez also attended to the intersectional qualities of identity, making special efforts to challenge and change anti-Black racism by confronting the historical repressions and suppressions of Black identities in Cuban and Puerto Rican communities.

Vazquez found great value in projects that enabled previously disrespected people to become more visible to the broader community and to become more involved in defining themselves. She discovered that efforts to prevent HIV took on new, broader, and deeper meanings when enacted through art. Vazquez helped form a theater group that performed a play with a cast in which all the actors were trans, an experience that elevated their consciousness and imbued them with new courage. She recognized as well, however, that education and organizing needed to address the material needs of the community, making sure that the doors at Proyecto were always open and that the people who passed through them could get free clothes and services as well as ideas and inspiration.[9]

Activists affiliated with Proyecto saw that it would not be sufficient simply to make the existing medical treatment system more accessible to previously excluded people. They perceived an imperative to reimagine medicine as a complex social practice. Proyecto portrayed sex-positive playful practices as central to healing through performative practice and witty wordplay. Its organizers created the persona of La Condonera—a fairy distributing condoms to patrons of queer clubs and dance halls. They organized Las Diablitas—a soccer team whose games provided a nurturing queer-positive space for women under the age of twenty-five. The names used in these cases turn negative ascription into positive affirmation. They transform the "fairy" from a term of humiliation into a queer dispenser of lifesaving devices. By celebrating the young women playing soccer as "little devils," they invert a word used by religion to promote fear and use it as a basis for fun. A similar inversion appeared in the lobby of Proyecto's headquarters in the form of a painting of the Catholic Corazón, the sacred heart of Jesus pierced by a lance and surrounded by a crown of thorns. In this painting, an icon of a church that many Proyecto participants had experienced as homophobic and sex-negative became resignified as a locus of queer desire, pain, and agency. Votive paintings known as retablos connected Catholicism to diverse spiritual traditions through images of yin and yang, an ankh, and the moon, as well as the Bible.[10]

Proyecto's convivial arts practice, creative wordplay, and conception of health care as a collective (rather than merely individual) practice gave birth to the process and theory of organizing that the organization named RICCA, after the Spanish word for "rich," which in this case connotes well resourced, desirable, and productive.[11] Deployed as a living theory in action, RICCA coalesced around five central tenets: (1) envisioning the group's work as a lively cultural practice that cultivates subjective beliefs, values, and attitudes in responding to objective oppressive structures and systems; (2) deploying new ways of naming, new forms of visibility, and new concepts of agency as mechanisms for individual transformations; (3) treating community as something that is forged rather than found, that emerges and grows in supportive spaces whose preservation required battles against gentrification, evictions, and rent increases; (4) creating interventions in places where forces that influence queer Latinx intersect, meeting people where they are and respecting who they are, refusing to prescribe or require pure stances or pure identities but instead mobilizing intersectional knowledge to develop and sustain collective recognition and promote collective resistance; and (5) promoting an atmosphere where the dominant institutions controlling immigration law, health insurance, policing, and education are recognized but contested in ways that do not completely determine the group's priorities or occlude the necessity for recognizing participants not as isolated citizens of the nation-state but as people whose opportunities and life chances have been shaped and defined by histories of coloniality, migration, displacement, and oppression.[12]

Proyecto pioneered a new, flexible, and immensely generative approach to identities, grounding them in shared ideas, ideals, affiliations, associations and alignments rather than in static and narrow categories reducible to embodied race, gender, or sexuality.[13] No single identity based on solidarities of sameness could speak to the needs of a neighborhood that included people from at least twenty-three different Western Hemisphere countries, whose residents included men who had sex with men, women who had sex with women, transgender people, and queer youths. Struggles for survival and pathways to self-recognition led Proyecto's constituents to change identities strategically, to identify with different sexual identities in different circumstances, and to chafe against single-axis identity frames that would require them to define their identities solely by the people with whom they had sex, by the nature of the work they did to earn their living, by their country of origin, by the language(s) they spoke, or by their ascribed race. As Ariana Ochoa Camacho et al. explain insightfully, identity for Proyecto was not about an essential allegedly authentic self but rather was a product of a "process of making claims within a contested field of social relations."[14]

The very actions and ideas that made Proyecto innovative and effective, however, made many of its successes illegible to public health administrators and philanthropic institutions. This illegibility had distinctly gendered dimensions. Funders of AIDS projects imagined their constituency largely as gay men and sometimes also as trans women, while Proyecto found ways to serve the whole community, including the queer women who did extraordinary work as caretakers. Moreover, the organization's emphasis on qualitative changes in people and society at large conflicted with audit systems and evaluations used by government and private funders that emphasized quantitative measures of the number of people served and precise calculations of diminished illnesses and deaths. In addition, Proyecto's understandings of identities as flexible, fluid, and always in process confounded funders accustomed to treating disparities in health by focusing on one group at a time. On occasion, funders complained that money they donated to Proyecto intending solely to solve the problems facing gay men was being misused because the group had a wider constituency.

After several years of successful work whose fruits and benefits persist today in the work of many different activists, artists, and organizations,

Proyecto eventually found it impossible to make its complex intersectional mission conform to the narrow single-axis categories favored by funders. The group terminated its existence in 2005. Its ways of working, however, continue to offer valuable guidelines for people who have to live in a neoliberal society yet nonetheless desire to think and act according to values that extend far beyond narrow market calculations. Working with Proyecto equipped participants with something like what performance theorist Diana Taylor in another context calls "repertoires of embodied memory": in this case an inventory of stances, skills, strategies, terms, tools, and dispositions for refusing unlivable destinies and cocreating a rich and rewarding collective social existence.[15]

It was difficult, however, to instantiate those repertoires inside a single institution in a city shaped by neoliberal development. Even more devastating to the vision of Proyecto than the group's illegibility to single-axis funders was the neoliberal combination of gentrification, housing insecurity, and discrimination in mortgage loans and insurance. As Rodríguez notes in her 2020 reflection on the legacy of the organization, the financially challenged working-class and immigrant population of the Mission neighborhood became displaced by mostly white and well-paid workers in the technology industry. The 60 percent of building leases in the city of San Francisco held by technology businesses drove up rental costs beyond what community organizations, art spaces, queer bars, and music clubs could afford. The shortage of affordable and accessible housing destroyed the social ecology of the Mission District that had nurtured and sustained Proyecto. At an informal reunion among Proyecto activists in the summer of 2017, participants discovered that almost none of the group's veterans still lived in the city, having been displaced and scattered all across the region.

Shared access to housing had enabled the congregation of a critical mass of refugees seeking to escape homophobia, transphobia, and anti-immigrant racism, and that had led to the creation of Proyecto. Gentrification of the neighborhood eliminated badly needed affordable dwellings but also shredded the social fabric needed for queer Latinx self-defense, self-definition, and self-determination. Gentrification changed the class nature of the neighborhood, but it also functioned as a racialized process of profit accumulation that destroyed a democratic and culturally responsive antiracist social formation.[16]

The Mission District's relative abandonment by capital enabled it to emerge initially as a site for Proyecto's convivial cocreation among its queer Latinx population. Yet that same location and condition made it ripe for the processes of gentrification that radically transformed its demographics and democratic possibilities. Physical location and place-based development also shaped the emergence and trajectory of an exemplary form of convivial activism in Canada in the early twenty-first century as Indigenous and African Nova Scotian communities discovered families of resemblance and linked fates because of their parallel residency in places located in proximity to toxicity.

THE ENRICH PROJECT

The Environmental Noxiousness, Racial Inequities, and Community Health organization (ENRICH) in Canada works with Indigenous, Black, and other racialized communities as they battle pollution and environmental contamination. ENRICH recognizes and respects the dignity and autonomy of differently situated aggrieved racialized groups. Yet it offers them opportunities to see the ways in which settler colonialism and anti-Black and Anti-Indigenous racism work together to facilitate, justify, and excuse these communities' disproportionate exposures to environmental hazards.[17] Landfills containing garbage and waste materials as well as industries that discharge toxic pollutants into the air, water, and land are located disproportionately near communities of African and Mi'kmaw descent in Nova Scotia and other places of Indigenous and African Canadian residency.[18] The ENRICH Project seeks to support rather than supplant local community-based initiatives grounded in long histories of struggle and forged from collective commitments to active presence, collective continuation, and creativity.

In one of its early campaigns, ENRICH recognized that the pollution produced by a landfill that contaminated the soil and poisoned the drinking water of the African Nova Scotian residents of Lincolnville had causes and consequences both similar to and different from the pollution from effluent wastewater discharged from a treatment facility in the Pictou Landing First Nation Reserve in that Province that caused high rates of cancer and respiratory disease. ENRICH worked with activists in both communities and helped make them aware of each other. The ENRICH Project supported community conversations that were grassroots designed and executed to identify common concerns and generate new strategies for struggle. Separate conversations in African Nova Scotian and Mi'kmaw communities encouraged participants to process how pollution and contamination harmed them personally, damaged their families, and undermined their collective resilience and resolve.

These meetings set the stage for convergence workshops where African Nova Scotian and Mi'kmaw activists joined together and met with academic allies. Workshops foregrounded the need for research assessing the impacts of pollution and contamination and formulating meaningful remedies. Scholars associated with ENRICH worked with community members to design equity-oriented, collaborative, community-based research about the political, socioeconomic, cultural, and health effects of environmental racism. Guided by deep commitments to shared learning and labor, the academics and activists worked together in a spirit of mutual recognition and respect. They formulated new methods of asking and answering questions, collecting data, and disseminating findings. Researchers learned to conduct research *with* and *for* aggrieved racialized communities rather than merely *about* them, while community activists found ways to connect their immediate experiences and aspirations to broader historical currents and power relations. In the process of crafting solutions to public health problems, participants honed and refined their collective ability to see how settler colonialism is a continuing process rather than a completed past event and how anti-Blackness and coloniality in perpetuity relegate African Nova Scotians and other Black communities and Indigenous people across Canada to disproportionate exposure to toxic hazards.

The ongoing ENRICH Project provides opportunities for academics, activists, and environmental organizations to work together. They share the labors of research design, data collection, analysis, and public education. They join together to plan and execute political campaigns and mobilizations. Scholars publish articles in peer-reviewed journals and make presentations at professional meetings. Community members learn to use Geographic Information Systems (GIS) mapping and analysis techniques to illustrate the location of waste sites near African Nova Scotian and Mi'kmaw communities. Academics and activists alike participate in community meetings and public engagement events, and work with legal experts and government officials to craft promising legal and administrative measures. An important part of the organization revolves around empowering community members without academic credentials to engage in citizen science, conducting their own studies to identify and test contaminated drinking water and to participate in building a rural water-monitoring network among Mi'kmaw and African Nova Scotian communities across the province and later across all of Canada grounded in sharing information and devising collective strategies for making water supplies safe.

Urgent health needs require the ENRICH Project to battle for the closures of existing polluted sites and to protest the emergence of new ones, to insist that public agencies and private corporations respect treaty rights, and to resist the processes that place hazardous wastes where historically affected racialized communities reside. Yet ENRICH maintains that merely reforming current practices will not be sufficient for protecting the health and dignity of aggrieved communities. The organization advances a transformative and antiauthoritarian agenda designed to promote and secure a radical revolution in values, not only a realignment of relations between social groups but also a redefinition of the relationships between profits and people and between humans and the other-than-human world. New personalities and polities are called into being by creative projects that entail the posting online of open-source community-created and -focused maps that reveal the location of sources of pollution threatening Mi'kmaw and African Canadian communities. One creative project in 2015 invited young people to envision and inhabit new identities by creating works of expressive culture for an art showcase appropriately named *Time to Clear the Air: Art on Environmental Racism.* These projects connect needs for distributive justice—for a fair allocation of health conditions and opportunities— with desires for procedural justice, for a world where previously disregarded and disrespected people participate in making the key decisions that shape their lives.[19]

A study conducted by the ENRICH Project that included focus groups with community members prompted African Nova Scotians in the town of Shelburne to form the local South End Environmental Injustice Society (SEED). The group created a community map that connected the high rates of cancer among Shelburne's African descent residents to their proximity to contaminated water, air, and soil.[20] Community members noted how injuries to physical health also harmed mental health. SEED founding member activist Louise Delisle noted the stress caused by having to care for sick loved ones and watch them die, dealing with air so polluted that washed garments cannot be placed to dry on outside clotheslines, and enduring relentless social stigma because of who one is and where one lives.[21]

Working with ENRICH enabled SEED activists to learn about water testing by members of the Black community in Lincolnville. That project entailed identifying water flowing toward residences from a toxic landfill, developing tools for residents to use to test the water, and building collective knowledge about contaminants and their effects.[22] Informed

by the project in Lincolnville, activist scholar Ingrid Waldron collabo-
rated with a hydrogeologist and an environmental science researcher to
create the Rural Water Watch Association, designed to build shared
capacities throughout Mi'kmaw and African Nova Scotian communities to test well water and manage the water supply to protect the people's health. Rural Water Watch held workshops in the African Nova
Scotian communities of Shelburne and Lincolnville to train residents on
how to manage their drinking water supply.[23]

ENRICH draws on the generative ways of being and ways of knowing that Indigenous and Black people have developed and defended over
centuries. Social worker, water protector, and community activist
Dorene Bernard explains that she views her fight for clean water as her
responsibility as a Mi'kmaw woman and treaty rights holder but also as
part of her personal healing journey and part of the collective healing
needed by her people. Yet working on research with experts from settler
colonial institutions requires a clear break with the past by insisting that
the research not replicate the asymmetrical power relations that cause
deprivation in the first place. Bernard points to the ugly and ignoble
history of research conducted *on* rather than *with* Indigenous people.
She references the discovery by historian Ian Mosby of unethical medical experiments conducted in the 1940s on malnourished First Nations
children in government-funded and church-administered residential
schools, experiments apparently conducted without the subjects' knowledge or informed consent.[24]

Bernard points to the disgraceful legacy of this kind of scholarship in
order to underscore the need to establish equal and reciprocal relations
today between researchers and the populations they study. But she also
notes that the patterns of the past continue to shape the present. The
very existence of the residential schools harmed health and well-being
in the past and continues to do so today. Through the Indian Residential School system the Canadian government placed Indigenous children
in religious schools where Christian clergy attempted to indoctrinate
them into giving up their cultural identities and assimilating into the
settler colonial society. Bernard notes that while settler society and its
government have offered sporadic apologies and granted limited compensation to a few victims of the residential school system, there has
been no substantive reckoning with the continuing impacts of this mistreatment on survivors and their families and descendants. She situates
the fight for clean water and against environmental contamination in
the present as part of a longer continuing struggle to tell evidence-based

narrative histories, to decolonize the established educational and political systems, and to provide healing from the hurts of history. While the Canadian government professes an interest in reconciliation with Indigenous people, Bernard insists that genuine reconciliation can take place only through positive actions addressing the systemic forms of racism that affect individuals and communities, that enact harm and impede healing.[25] This version of reconciliation would meet the needs of Indigenous people, but it would provide benefits for portions of settler colonial society as well. Settler environmental activist Sadie Beaton points to the important resources contained in Indigenous ontologies and epistemologies, emphasizing how "frontline racialized communities often hold access to the crucial truths that we need to heal and to survive this crisis. They have been speaking these truths all along. These truths are embedded in the stories, languages, and laws of Indigenous nations. The rest of us need to do the work of listening and letting these voices take the lead so we can move toward the transition we need."[26]

PRISON THEATER AND OTHER DRAMAS

In her wide-ranging and generative book *Prison Theatre and the Global Crisis of Incarceration,* Ashley E. Lucas delineates how collaborative work among artists, educators, incarcerated people, and their allies helps build social cohesion and promote health through interactive theater productions in jails and prisons.[27] Prison theater activism builds mutual recognition and support by creating activities that promote trust, break down barriers, augment individual and collective efficacy, and improve the health of participants.

As explained in chapter 5, poor health and rapid transmission of AIDS, COVID-19, valley fever, and other conditions constitute a routine part of life in overcrowded and underfunded jails and prisons. Incarcerated people come disproportionately from neighborhoods with poor health conditions. They have higher degrees of illness and disability than the general population. They receive inadequate medical care behind bars, and they bring their ill health back to their home communities upon reentry. Oppressive, unpredictable, and manifestly unfair prison discipline practices are designed to promote resignation, fatalism, and despair among the incarcerated. They are designed to produce people with broken spirits and broken bodies.

Prison theater productions can convey information and propose remedies for particular health problems such as AIDS and COVID-19. They do so by emphasizing the importance of mutual recognition and respect, sex education for children and adults, and the pursuit of changes in social structures as significant components of securing better health. Sometimes they help provoke direct structural changes. Lucas shows how in the Westville Female Prison in South Africa a play revealed to the public the jailers' practice of leaving the corpses of those who had died next to ill patients in the infirmary. The performance brought about change by itself because it embarrassed the institution's administration sufficiently to make them remove the corpses from among the living.

Lucas emphasizes that theater as a practice innately requires collaboration and reciprocal respect. Working together on a common creative project builds intersubjective investments and friendships. In carceral institutions set up to divide people and isolate them from each other, theater productions can be especially important in building empathy, offering experiences of collaboration and cocreation. They enable participants to express vulnerability and openness. Public performances offer incarcerated people an audience before which they can demonstrate mastery, intelligence, and creativity. They offer an opportunity to reconnect with loved ones visiting from the outside and to be seen and admired by their peers, their captors, and a public that otherwise scarcely knows that they exist. Performances are preceded by script readings, rehearsals, and strategic conversations with other participants, and they are often followed by discussions that take place immediately after shows and then continue in the following days, weeks, and months as new productions get planned, produced, and performed. Lucas assesses the plays themselves to be the least important part of the process, because regardless of the aesthetic success or failure of any performance, the work of theater achieves the much more difficult and more socially important task of promoting group interaction and breaking down the social and institutional barriers responsible for radical divisiveness in the lives of incarcerated people and their families and friends, who are often made to feel ashamed of their connections to people defined as criminals. Perhaps most important, participation in prison theater counters the smallness of incarceration's endless petty indignities and humiliations with the opportunity to be part of a larger world, to ask and answer big questions, and to embrace—if only vicariously—the greatness of possibility. When incarcerated bodies participate in embodied theatrical performances, the caged body—which in the prison functions as an object of control, a locus of pain, and a threat to others—becomes replaced by the affirmed artistic performing body that takes center stage (literally and figuratively). Prison theater reveals value in undervalued people. It responds to invasive oversight with unbridled expressive display and performance, and it counters the humiliations of surveillance cameras, body counts, and guard towers with open presentation of the talent, ability, and creativity that incarceration squanders. Prison theater educates and agitates, organizes and mobilizes—not by lectures, sermons, or manifestos but through embodied social practice where learning depends on doing and where individual survival and success depend upon convivial communication and collaboration.

As Lisa Biggs observes, not all of the drama that takes place behind bars happens on stage.[28] Incarcerated people are compelled by their captors to perform docility, to express contrition, to feel shame, to internalize obedience, and to "do their own time" by remaining detached from and indifferent to those locked up with them. They are told that better treatment and possible parole requires performing those affects and demonstrating constant compliance. On the surface, most prisoners appear to knuckle under, but under the surface many stage counterperformances that resist the institution's intended effects. A powerful example of that process resides in the actions taken by Jerome Morgan, Robert Jones, and Daniel Rideau when they were incarcerated in Louisiana's notorious Angola penitentiary for a combined more than fifty years. The sentences they received, along with the state of Louisiana's draconian parole policies, made it seem certain they would spend the rest of their lives behind bars. They had every reason to give in to despair and resign themselves to their fates as Black men wrongly convicted (Morgan and Jones) and excessively sentenced (Rideau). Yet they waged long struggles for exoneration, which were ultimately successful when the convictions of Morgan and Jones were overturned and they and Rideau were freed from incarceration. The victories they won in the legal system, however, started with the things they had imagined and performed while locked up.[29]

Morgan, Jones, and Rideau developed a practice they named "epping," a term signifying the "episodes" they imagined they would experience when they left the prison.[30] They treated these episodes not as things that *might* happen when they got free but rather always as things that *would* happen. It took powerful mental energy to envision these scenarios, which might seem completely unrealistic given their circumstances. They had no funds to pay attorneys' fees and the costs of legal appeals. They had no outside allies with the willingness or capacity to argue for reopening their cases. They could, however, act as if they would one day be free. They met together in the prison and told each other stories about what they intended to take place in their postprison existence.

Some of the episodes articulated in epping sessions revolved around personal pleasures and acts of consumption. The men described what it would be like when they were reunited with spouses, siblings, children, and parents. They talked about getting fried chicken from Popeye's and owning and driving new cars. Jones even had his contacts smuggle into the prison an operator's manual for the latest-model BMW so he would know how to drive it when he obtained one. The episodes that pervaded the bulk of the epping sessions, however, and which expanded in scope with practically every iteration, were narratives about working together to set up a mentoring project for young Black men in New Orleans that would enable those youths to overcome the conditions that led so many into the clutches of mass incarceration. Rideau, Jones, and Morgan envisioned providing young men with job training and employment, with group housing that would keep them from houselessness, and with instruction from a curriculum designed to develop critical writing skills, learn peaceful forms of conflict resolution, model male social etiquette based on respect for women, and promote opportunities to participate in public life through connection to activist community organizations. Years later, all of these dreams became reality as Rideau, Jones, and Morgan established and administered Free-Dem Foundations, the very youth mentoring and community development program they had conjured up while epping.

Morgan explains how artistic expression and performance aided him in cocreating epping sessions and using them as the basis for his eventual exoneration, release from prison, and after-incarceration success in working with Jones and Rideau to found the Free-Dem Foundations' youth mentoring and community development program. When he was growing up, Morgan was small in stature and had to adjust to the new circumstances he encountered as a foster child moving from foster home to foster home. Creating art enabled him to turn negative circumstances into positive opportunities. He made friends and won admiration by drawing headshots of classmates and famous athletes, by performing in school plays, by selling painted images on jeans, and by organizing a group of friends to participate in and win lip-synching contests. Morgan explains that "my early talent creating art was the primary characteristic that enabled me to deeply imagine a hope and faith" as he mastered the challenges of "growing from an infant in places housed by state-paid parents, with a houseful of nonrelated children, who had no other parent."³¹ The confidence and self-respect Morgan gained from artistic achievement positioned him to reach out and make friends with other children in each foster home and neighborhood that he entered, a history that equipped him to make positive connections with many of the men he later encountered in prison.

While incarcerated, Morgan taught himself how to cut hair using only a small pocket comb and a disposable razor. Cutting and sculpting the hair of other prisoners gave him opportunities to help them feel better about themselves by acquiring a look that enabled them to regain a modicum of the dignity the captors daily tried to take from them. His artistry with the hair of men undergoing the traumas of incarceration led Morgan to engage in relaxed conversations with a wide range of them, to witness their diverse responses to racism and incarceration. Barbering honed his understanding of the need to be patient with people and to withhold premature judgments about them. He increased his skills at listening, discerning what others could teach him and expressing empathy as a means of making connections. Prison classes in graphic design provided Morgan with an opportunity to utilize the skills he had acquired as a child drawing pictures and decorating clothing. Behind bars he turned to writing as a primary form of personal development and social connection. "Writing became my Best Friend," he declares, hailing it as a central mechanism for his maturation as an adult.³²

The Free-Dem Foundations project founded by Rideau, Morgan and Jones provides writing, reading, learning, craft apprenticeship, and business ownership mentoring programs for Black males between the stages of puberty and young adulthood. Youths between the ages of seventeen and twenty-four, who are eligible to be enrolled in one of the various Louisiana apprenticeship programs or trade programs, can participate in this six-month life skills and professional development course and attain a high school diploma or equivalent if this is not already achieved. The course entails collective writing workshops run according to the story circle pedagogy. In these sessions students voice anger and assess the injuries they incur from structural racism, but as noted above they also learn male etiquette and respect for women, social management skills, and methods of peaceful conflict resolution. All participants are also required to observe and participate in public life through engagement with community organizations working to reform the criminal justice system and fighting to rebuild the environments of the Black neighborhoods abandoned by developers and the city that were damaged by the flooding in 2005 attendant to Hurricane Katrina and have been neglected ever since. In the short run the project cannot offer its young students the material resources that they need and deserve, but it does help them see that improvisation, imagination, invention, and art can be their best friends.

BUILDING HEALTH COMMUNITIES IN BOYLE HEIGHTS

The art activism of Juana Mena Ochoa described at the end of chapter 1 exemplifies the possibilities of the Restorative Cultural Arts Practice/ Praxis (RCAP) approach to art, health, and housing. Mena Ochoa and other traditional folk artists connect people to information about affordable and available medical insurance and care. But they also use music, dance, quilting, theatre, and visual art as mechanisms for calling communities into being, solidifying social cohesion, dispensing moral instruction, preserving cultural memory, and generating mutual recognition and respect through acts of cocreation and principles of collective witness. The Building Healthy Communities in Boyle Heights project shifts concerns about health care away from exclusive emphasis on individual behavior and inherited traits to highlight and work on the social determinants of health attendant to poverty, pollution, predatory policing, mass incarceration, hunger, and housing insecurity.

The project involves people from all age groups but offers especially meaningful opportunities to young people through youth-oriented arts programs. Artists, activists, and teachers mobilize students to reject the idea that East Los Angeles is a place without value. Young people write essays mapping the hidden cultural treasures in their neighborhood. They find inspiration in the resolve of working people to survive and thrive. They discern the beauty of murals, yard art, and brightly colored vending carts. They enjoy the sounds that emanate from mariachi bands, boom boxes, and home stereos. They appreciate the generosity and love extended to them by relatives, neighbors, and merchants. High school students produce silkscreen posters that publicize their campaigns to demand more healthful food options in school cafeterias and to replace the school system's punitive detentions, suspensions, and expulsions with dispute resolution inside student-run restorative justice circles. These circles are cultural performances that have social effects. They entail conversations, deliberations, and decisions that imbue students with power and responsibility. They give them the ability to address conflicts without blaming, shaming, or shunning those who have done wrong. Instead they welcome everyone into a collective project of reconciliation, repair, respect, repentance, reparation, and restoration.

Works of expressive culture produced by young people and adults under the aegis of Building Healthy Communities in Boyle Heights disseminate information about the availability of low-cost medical insurance and health care. Community artists assemble altars from found and fabricated objects that serve as focal points for identifying ailments of the body and expressing determination to recover from them. Juana Mena Ochoa's quilt-making circles become informal sites where women openly discuss their problems with food and housing insecurity, with personal and family illnesses, and with incidents and patterns of domestic violence. Building Healthy Communities runs songwriting workshops where children and adults collectively compose and perform melodies and lyrics that voice desires for individual and collective well-being. One group wrote, performed, and placed online the song "El Colas Medical." This piece features lyrics about the difficulties facing people with low income and/or noncitizen status in securing medical care and treatment. The words of the song proclaim that health care should be a right, not a business. Another workshop created songs for use in campaigns to transfer city funds away from expenditures on the police and toward youth recreation, education, and enrichment programs. When people compose a song together, differently situated individuals augment their capacities for cooperation and negotiation. As they run breaths and sounds through their chests and mouths, tap their feet, snap their fingers, clap their hands, and move their bodies, they feel the cumulative power of the group somatically as well as psychically.

Another project carried out in accord with the RCAP practice/praxis was the mural *Interconnected Relations*, painted by the Mutual Workforce Academy. The mural depicts both health issues confronting areas populated by members of aggrieved racialized groups and potential positive interventions to address those issues, such as community gardens and development of renewable energy sources. The project also functions in and of itself as an intervention. The mural was made using organic-based mineral pigments rather than paints with lead or other pollutants in them. These pigments allow vapors to pass through them, lowering the neighborhood heat index and making it possible for the mural to last a long time with no bubbles or peeling that might require touch-ups.

The artists and activists associated with Building Healthy Communities in Boyle Heights connect personal problems to political solutions. They participate in social movement campaigns for expanding access to

FIGURE 6. *Interconnected Relations*—a portable traveling mural created by the Mural Workforce Academy as part of an exhibition for the US Green Building Council. Photo by Omar G. Ramirez, mural by Workforce Academy.

health care and insurance and for recognizing and countering the effects of the pervasive presence in East Los Angeles of waste dumps, metal plating shops, and emissions from car, truck, and bus engines. They work to expand the neighborhood's supply of physicians, clinics, fresh fruits and vegetables, parks, and playgrounds. The Fideicomiso Comunitario Tierra Libra, described in chapter 1, seeks to provide affordable housing in perpetuity safe from speculation and to promote the creation of culturally sensitive and socially responsible small businesses. Arts education and cultural practice sow seeds for political projects performed through a kind of social alchemy that transforms segregation into congregation. Reciprocal respect and responsibility promote social cohesion and improve prospects for health and healing.

Building Healthy Communities in Boyle Heights convenes an alert, active, and engaged constituency for health. It educates participants about the availability of and necessity for low-cost medical care and insurance, the importance of access to fresh and nutritious food, and the need to address environmental hazards in the neighborhood. Yet it also augments collective capacity for a different kind of well-being, that of accompanying one another in facing up to the harsh realities of hunger and housing insecurity, displacement and deportability, predatory policing and poverty, and economic exploitation and political demonization. Through a deft blend of traditional arts practice and political mobilization, Building Health Communities in Boyle Heights recruits previously disrespected and disregarded people to become active creators of a new public sphere.

THE 45907! PROJECT

Fair housing litigation against the Wells Fargo Bank for damages caused by predatory lending, reverse redlining, and the foreclosures that took place because of them during the subprime financial crisis of 2008 secured a substantial settlement paid to fair housing councils throughout the nation. With its part of the settlement, the Fair Housing Center of Western Michigan funds a project that creates new opportunities, amenities, and affiliations in one local zip code that has been especially affected by long histories of redlining and other unfair housing practices. The 45907! Project in Grand Rapids promotes neighborhood improvements and economic development initiatives in a zip code that according to the 2010 US Census had a per capita income $7,000 less than the city at large. The project serves neighborhoods where home sales on average were $27,000 less than those in the rest of Grand Rapids. The area's residential population was 55 percent Black, 29 percent Latinx, 12 percent white, and 4 percent Native American, Asian American, or "other."[33]

In addition to rehabilitating vacant properties and bringing them up to code and supporting business start-ups, the 49507! Project establishes a vibrant public sphere by promoting resident involvement in its planning and administration while offering employment to people returning from incarceration. One key part of the project supports young people's creative artistic expressions and exhibitions. The project revolves around purchasing dilapidated dwellings and rehabilitating them, with some of the construction work carried out by formerly incarcerated people who would otherwise be prohibited from that work because of the stigma of a criminal record, their lack of contacts and connections, and prejudice stoked by decades of moral panics about crime. The project devotes special attention to reducing hazards to children from lead paint on inside walls and playground equipment as well as from insect infestations and mold. It creates a safe walking route to an elementary school and includes efforts to clean up, improve, and expand recreational areas. The initiative features community listening sessions, arts programming for young people, and a mural project identifying the neighborhood as a center of multicultural creativity and collaboration.[34]

The 49507! Project repairs and renovates buildings, but it also focuses on restoring relationships and repairing ruptures among differently situated people in the city. Participants work together to make neighborhood improvements, to plan and enact economic development programs, to deepen resident involvement in deliberation and decision-making about the future of the neighborhood, and to create opportunities for artistic expression and collaboration. New relationships grounded in mutual respect and recognition emerge from the work of demolishing dilapidated houses, rehabilitating and rebuilding dwellings, cleaning up vacant lots and constructing new homes on them, providing down payment assistance to first-time home buyers, improving and cleaning up park areas, and recruiting high school students for training in violence prevention techniques.

HEALTHY KIDS, PROMOTORAS, AND SALUD AMBIENTAL LIDERES TOMANDO ACCION IN SAN DIEGO

The Environmental Health Coalition (EHC) works in San Diego area neighborhoods in municipalities on both sides of the US-Mexico border. It mobilizes a multiracial, multilingual, and multinational constituency on behalf of clean, healthy, environmentally and economically sound conditions. The organization recruits residents to investigate the presence of polluted air, toxic chemicals, and hazardous waste in the places where they live, work, and play. Its Salud Ambiental Lideres Tomando Accion (SALTA) program (Environmental Health Leaders Taking Action) deploys an interactive curriculum that trains people to be community organizers, policy advocates, and neighborhood health teachers and promoters.

Women accustomed to traditional domestic roles as mothers, daughters, sisters, aunts, and grandmothers take on new identities as teachers, guides, organizers, and leaders through the EHC promotora program. Promotoras go door to door and speak with neighbors and strangers about the damage done to the neighborhood (and especially its children) by industrial air pollutants such as metals, paints, toxic wastes, and diesel fumes. They educate parents about lead hazards in the home and direct them to ways to improve household ventilation to lessen the likelihood of respiratory problems caused by mold and carbon monoxide poisoning. They assist residents in applying for lead remediation services and show them how they can reduce their use of pesticides and switch to nontoxic home cleaning products. Promotoras conduct home energy assessments that lead to more efficient, less expensive, and environmentally conscious practices. Although they forge alliances with expert researchers and health care professionals, the activists of the EHC take primary responsibility for improving health care and housing in their region and in the process build the mutual respect and social cohesion that they and their neighbors desire and need.[35]

The EHC views broad social change as fundamental to improving individual and community health. It participates in Let's Go San Diego!, a ballot initiative that proposes establishing a local climate justice–centered transit system. Partnering with other groups, EHC organizers collect signatures to place on the ballot a proposal to fund frequent twenty-four-hour transit service, no-cost passes for seniors, veterans, and people designated as disabled, and fast and environmentally clean rail and bus service from neighborhoods in their area currently plagued by poor transit service and polluting, inefficient, and expensive car-centered development.[36]

As its activities promote self-help and resilience, the EHC also mobilizes politically to pursue substantive changes in public policy and to challenge the private profit–driven practices of polluters that damage the community. EHC's #healthyhoods initiative secured approval for a green land use development plan in the municipality of National City that entails closing polluting businesses, protecting endangered creeks and parkland, building pedestrian paths, opening up green spaces, and constructing affordable housing units in sites near public transit. At a time when city planners, politicians, and prospective investors tell residents of polluted areas that in order to prosper they need to accept any kind of development at all, the activists mobilized by the EHC insist on clean businesses that provide permanent good jobs to neighborhood residents. In an era when almost all infrastructure spending subsidizes the indirect costs of making and transporting products, the EHC has succeeded in winning expenditures on infrastructure projects that promote health and recreation.[37]

CONVIVIAL COCREATION

The community-based activist arts and educational institutions described in this chapter help people feel valued, respected and protected. They help them to name, understand, and contest the ways that racial subordination haunts their existence. They can also generate new knowledge useful for solving long-standing scientific and social problems. Grassroots mobilizations have historically played decisive roles in focusing the attention of researchers, physicians, public health authorities, and housing agencies on the dangers of lead poisoning, air and water pollution, and mass incarceration.[38] In professional and academic circles, healing, political action, and art generally occupy separate and often-incommensurable realms. In community life traditional arts and expressive culture function as devices for building social cohesion, identifying political problems, establishing relations of mutual recognition and respect, and deepening individual and collective capacities for democratic deliberation and decision-making.

In curing the ills of the body politic, community-based centers also help heal individual bodies. Activities promoting collective engagement and social cohesion lead to improved health outcomes. High levels of collective efficacy at the neighborhood level can lower morbidity and mortality, while reducing incidences of depression, obesity, and risky behaviors.[39] Efficacy can flow from the social cohesion forged from activities in civil society; in forums for democratic deliberation and decision-making about neighborhood problems; in the collective creation and maintenance of story circles; in housing rehabilitation; and in community gardens, food cooperatives, community land trusts, and diverse forms of restorative cultural arts practice/praxis.[40]

The efflorescence of arts-based health and housing projects stems from convictions that what are now generally treated as separate and unrelated spheres need to be seen as interdependent and mutually constitutive relationships. What are now portrayed as *technical* problems to be resolved solely by credentialed experts need to be understood as *political* problems that can be addressed by the creation of an informed and energized public committed to health and housing justice. This will require radical changes in the actions of professional practitioners in medical and legal education, in clinical practice, in the structures of public and private health insurance programs, in urban planning policies, in environmental protection laws, and in fair housing systemic investigations, litigation, and legislation. Changes of this magnitude, however, cannot be mandated or implemented from the top down, they must be built from the bottom up. They will not simply be found; they must be forged. They require more than pronouncements and proclamations, instead needing to emerge out of widely dispersed new practices, procedures, and processes that create new social possibilities. Like the epidemiologists who are crafting new perspectives in Latin America in the wake of neoliberal privatization and evisceration of the social wage and public sphere, we need to view the promotion of health equity and improved health as work that includes widespread dispersed mobilizations by nonstate actors working collectively in social movements and community centers.[41]

Everything Is Everything

Health and Housing as Human Rights and
Public Goods

In her 1998 song "Everything Is Everything," Lauryn Hill sang about the
fate meted out to young Black people like herself, people who seem to lose
the game before they start to play, whose dreams are often deferred and
frequently destroyed. Yet while chronicling the obstacles to a new and
better world, Hill nonetheless affirms her faith that eventually change will
come. One source of that change comes from the ability she displays in
the song to look honestly at the "what is" without losing touch with the
"what can be." That capacity to discern liberating potential inside debilitating circumstances, what Cornel West calls "prophetic vision," shapes
the strategies of the activists in law and medicine working for health and
housing justice whose work forms the focal point of this chapter.[1]

Prophetic vision fuels efforts to make a way where there seems to be
no way. It informs initiatives that discover occluded value in undervalued
places and undervalued people. This chapter starts by describing prophetic vision–inspired grassroots place-based projects of convivial cocreation taking place in seemingly abandoned and isolated urban sacrifice
zones. It then demonstrates how these can serve as models for envisioning
and enacting profound changes in law, medicine, and public policy.

LOTS LEFT TO BE VACANT AND LAWS WRITTEN TO BE WEAK

Urban and rural sacrifice zones replete with housing insecurity and
health hazards exhibit the striking scars of abandonment and isolation.

Block after block of boarded-up dwellings, closed businesses, cracked and broken pavements, alleys filled with abandoned cars and discarded appliances, and open spaces without tree cover give the appearance of great peril and very little promise. People who dwell in these places do not generally have the power to prevent the foreclosures that leave houses empty or lead to their demolition. They cannot meaningfully contest the zoning regulations that channel polluting industries into their neighborhoods and inhibit the development of affordable housing. They are trapped by public transit policies that leave them distant from jobs and shopping venues. They cannot stop the patterns of predatory policing that lead them into cycles of unpayable debts and recurrent incarceration.

The collective, cumulative, and continuing effects of housing discrimination prevent residents of sacrifice zones from moving away to better-resourced neighborhoods. They lack the political influence needed to stop city officials and outsiders from treating their community as a place where garbage can be dumped, where rats and roaches are allowed to fester, where grass is uncut, and where weeds and vines are left to spread. The blocks in their neighborhood often contain overgrown, untended, and poorly lit vacant lots filled with trash and debris.

Lots left vacant leave a lot to be desired. Yet in places where most people see only problems, prophetic vision can perceive possibility. Through place-based projects for health and housing justice, vacant lots in sacrifice zones have been transformed into places where community members hold meetings, stage performances, and sponsor dances. They serve as sites that host pop-up businesses, food co-ops, and community gardens. In some cases propelled by exceptional imagination and initiative, previously vacant lots have been envisioned as sources of solar power and as locations for the construction of shared-equity housing.

In an African American neighborhood in Washington, D.C., plagued by the absence of stores selling fresh food, a community gardening initiative appropriates previously unused open space to grow vegetables, stage cooking demonstrations, hold concerts and dances, and host free health screenings conducted by Black medical students. Works of art created by children decorate the back fence of the garden, while a community center next to it displays creatively assembled and arranged painted jugs and water bottles. The garden serves as a school that teaches children lessons about nature, health, and entrepreneurship. It offers parents access to gardening tools and provides them with a place where their children will be protected under the watchful eyes of neighbors. Cultivating the land collectively rather than apportioning plots to individuals promotes a collective consciousness that highlights the ways in which a linked fate requires people to work collaboratively to solve common problems that might otherwise seem solely to be individual concerns.[2]

In the Franklin District in Sacramento, installing solar panels in vacant lots forms part of a broader comprehensive development plan that encompasses renovating dilapidated dwellings, building new affordable units, and connecting the neighborhood to transit-based economic development. Visionary neighborhood activists recognize that lots that appear empty and useless are actually bathed in sustained sunshine that might be captured by solar panels and used to generate electricity. The solar project could provide energy sufficient to lower utility costs in the neighborhood, while generating a surplus to be sold to utility companies and raise funds for further community development.[3]

In Houston's Third Ward, artists formed Project Row Houses to purchase, renovate, and decorate some of the many abandoned small shotgun houses in the neighborhood. They transformed empty buildings into art galleries and made the entire neighborhood adjacent to Emancipation Park into a collective work of social sculpture. Round after round of art installations have called attention to common concerns and served as provocations for collective community discussions and deliberations. In 2017 curator Ryan N. Dennis and artist Simone Leigh coordinated an exhibit in seven art houses by the Black Women Artists for Black Lives Matter Collective. During the fall and winter of 2019–20, artists displayed site-specific installations that addressed the maternal mortality crisis confronting Black women. Their artwork served as provocation and stimulus for public presentations and collective conversations about the high rates of deaths and complications after birth plaguing Black mothers in the Third Ward and elsewhere. Artists were asked to create their work as a response to a local plan for improving maternal health in the Houston area devised by a wide range of people with experience in health care, behavioral health, social services, government, business, and philanthropy. Public forums about the artworks enabled many different points of entry to the issue, enabling participants to share information about support services and to craft strategies for improving maternal health. As Dennis explains, "Art is a conduit for us to communicate and have meaningful conversations. The art houses have always been a beautiful way for us to elevate the conversation around the work happening at a level localized to the Third Ward."[4]

In addition to turning abandoned dwellings into art galleries, Project Row Houses renovated some of the shotgun houses and offered them as rent-free dwellings for single mothers with children attempting to complete college degrees. Several of the mothers who benefited from this housing subsequently returned to the community as credentialed professionals dedicated to uplifting the area and its residents. Parks honoring neighborhood heroes now occupy once-vacant spaces. Playgrounds have appeared in places previously occupied by crack houses. Vegetables grown on vacant lots counter food insecurity and provide young people opportunities to develop skills that can lead to job opportunities in landscaping and food services.[5]

Restoring vacant land in Philadelphia forms the core of a collaborative effort between the National Fair Housing Alliance (NFHA) and the Pennsylvania Horticultural Society. The NFHA sued the Federal National Mortgage Association (known as Fannie Mae) because that agency neglected maintenance of foreclosed properties in neighborhoods inhabited by members of aggrieved racialized groups across the nation.[6] The NFHA secured a $35 million settlement to promote neighborhood stabilization, support access to credit and homeownership, and fund residential development and property rehabilitation. Part of the settlement funds went to the Roots to Reentry and Landcare programs of the Pennsylvania Horticultural Society. These programs recruit men and women returning from incarceration to enter job training programs that lead to employment in landscaping and vacant lot cleanups. Their labors turn abandoned lots into safe clean and green places for community conviviality, in some cases leading to significant reductions in neighborhood burglaries and gun violence along with major decreases in residents reporting feelings of depression. Once green spaces are installed, people living nearby often feel it is safer to venture outside their homes and interact with neighbors.[7]

Seemingly unused land in New Orleans provides a venue for religious fellowship and community education and mobilization focused on healing wounds caused and exacerbated by the criminalization of poverty and attendant mass incarceration. In a city plagued by bitter rivalries and violent competition for scarce resources, a place where homicides occur frequently and large numbers of residents are sent off to jails and prisons, visionary members of African American church congregations take over the grassy neutral grounds that divide traffic on neighborhood streets and turn them into places for congregation, reflection, and repair. They stand together holding signs that call for an end to interpersonal violence and for the initiation of collective community reconciliation. They transform the neutral grounds into public sacred spaces for collective mourning of those killed by gun violence, but also into sites where compassion can be expressed and extended to families with loved ones in jails and prisons. They pray for both the sinner and the sanctified, and for both the perpetrators and their victims, asserting that no person's value should be determined solely by the single worst thing they have ever done. The gatherings proceed from the premise that it is essential to find something left to love in all people, even in those who have harmed others. Church members staging demonstrations and holding ceremonies have turned ordinary streets into sites for popular education, advancing the idea that criminal violence will not be stopped by retaliatory violent policing and punishment. They assert instead that securing the peace requires a collective commitment reaffirming the value of life among people intent on restoring pride, and reclaiming and loving the community's detached and disenfranchised children, families, and neighbors.[8]

The Acta Non Verba Youth Urban Farms Project in Oakland, California, provides a creative and safe outdoor space that is a source of fresh fruits and vegetables in an area plagued by food apartheid—filled with convenience stores and fast-food outlets but very few grocery vendors. The Oakland neighborhoods in the downtown and west areas of the city nearest San Francisco Bay host an average of one store selling groceries for every ninety-three thousand residents.[9] In that place, the Acta Non Verba Project attracts young people who have high levels of risk for diabetes, depression, and heart disease to work with their parents in learning about nature and science, to eat organically grown produce, to participate in drum and dance circles, and to play games. The youths learn about the patience and effort necessary for designing and successfully completing complex tasks. They develop economic survival skills by figuring out how to market and sell the food they have grown. The group's Community Supported Agriculture (CSA) BeetBox Program supports local farmers as well as the young people served by Acta Non Verba. All profits from the CSA initiative go directly into participants' savings accounts.[10]

Projects that reclaim unused land identify and cultivate the hidden value that exists in undervalued places and among undervalued people. They operate somewhat outside the logics and priorities of a market society. They make important interventions on behalf of public physical and mental health by turning physical segregation into an impetus for

ADDRESS

WHAT IS IN NEED OF BEING
ADDRESSED?

REPAIR

HOW DO WE GO ABOUT
REPAIRING SOCIAL AND
INDIVIDUAL WOUNDS?

RESTORE

WHAT STEPS CAN BE TAKEN
TO RESTORE AND HEAL?

TRANSFORM

HOW CAN WE EXPERIENCE
TRANSFORMATION?

FIGURE 7. Interventions to address, repair, restore, and transform undervalued places and their residents. Graphic by Omar G. Ramirez.

social congregation, transforming objects and conditions created by racist subordination into tools for liberation. They demonstrate to themselves and others how oppressive conditions can be subverted, inverted, and overcome.

A LAW MEANT TO BE WEAK HAS BEEN MADE STRONG

The history of fair housing advocacy has exemplified a similar kind of inversion. Through imagination and improvisation, fair housing advocates have discerned and activated latent emancipatory possibilities embedded in a law initially designed to be so weak that it was virtually unenforceable. Relentless activism by fair housing activists, creative litigation, and congressional legislation have expanded the role of citizen enforcement, increased penalties for violations of the law, and extended legal protections to a wider and ever increasing range of groups. Legislation designed to be weak has been made strong by citizen activism. Fair housing councils in cities all across the nation have become parts of a democratic public sphere that brings together people from different classes, races, religions, ascribed abilities, and sexual and gendered identities to work together to forge solutions to common problems.

Fair housing activism faces daunting odds and often falls short of its intended goals, but over time it has made a significant difference in using opposition to discrimination as an incentive to craft new practices and policies.[11] Like lots left to be vacant, laws written to be weak have been transformed by collective community collaboration and cocreation.

HEALTH CARE TOOLS DESIGNED TO BE STRONG
CAN IN PRACTICE BE WEAK

Physicians and clinicians can also learn much from the prophetic vision of activists for health and housing justice, but from almost the opposite direction. Unlike housing justice advocates, who have had to find ways to make strong a law written to be weak, medical practitioners confront the ways in which the biomedical model of disease and the consumer model of health care that are touted to be strong all too often produce weak results. Unlike residents of sacrifice zones, whose lack of resources impels them to invent new ways of being resourceful, medical experts find that all too often abundant resources do not generate resourcefulness in them or their patients. Vast sums are expended on medical treatment and care in the United States, but health indicators lag behind those in other relatively affluent nations. Physicians and clinicians struggle with the ways in which the aspirations for profits among companies that sell insurance, pharmaceuticals, and medical equipment take precedence over the needs of patients. Hospitals routinely require doctors to use software that automatically makes patients pay for unneeded and costly but highly profitable tests and procedures. Only a small part of the costs of emergency room care goes to compensate physicians. The overwhelming majority of medical expenditures flow to hospital administrators, contract management groups, and manufacturers of drugs, medical supplies, laboratory equipment, and imaging devices. Requirements to collect and record patient information sometimes have little to do with medical treatment and are often designed instead to produce data that can be sold to profit-seeking third parties. Medical contract management groups can fire without cause physicians who complain about safety concerns or excessive bills.[12]

As medical centers increasingly become targeted to produce profits for investors, financial pressures provoke them to seek to become generators of profits for themselves. The physical expansion of hospitals and medical schools is touted as a way to augment and improve medical care in disadvantaged neighborhoods. In practice, however, it often entails making medical centers responsible for exacerbating and profiting from housing discrimination. Clearing land for hospital expansion often requires tearing down low-cost housing units in places where they are already scarce. Even worse, offering medical students, staff, and administrative personnel incentives to live nearby raises rental costs for those currently in the neighborhood, leading to the displacement of the previous residents and forcing them to move to newly overcrowded and under-resourced neighborhoods rife with health hazards. Johns Hopkins University in Baltimore offers as much as $36,000 per housing unit for its employees to purchase townhouses near its facilities in East Baltimore, a sum that subsidizes the housing costs of professionals living in dwellings that are too expensive for the institution's low-wage workers and the existing residents of the neighborhood to buy.[13] The University of Rochester aided some 280 faculty and staff members in acquiring mortgages on dwellings near their place of employment at Strong Hospital without addressing at all the ways in which these subsidies compounded the costs of entry into the housing market for the victims of historical housing discrimination.[14] Similar projects displacing vulnerable populations through expansions of university and medical center holdings have taken place in Chicago, New York, Miami, Philadelphia, and Los Angeles.[15]

Despite high costs, the current practices of medical treatment and care are failing. They fail patients who wrestle with both the high costs of good health and the physical prices they pay for a global economic system that encourages unhealthful diets and discourages environmental protections. Medical care and treatment fails dedicated medical professionals, many of whom will leave their practice because of burnout caused by high caseloads, excessive paperwork, and frustrations caused by lack of knowledge and training for dealing with social determinants of health. While the prospect of more resources is always enticing and frequently justified, the medical profession sorely needs to access the kinds of resourcefulness that can emanate from creating new social relations in undervalued places and among undervalued people.

THE WAY WE DO THE THINGS WE DO: PROPHETIC VISION
FOR FAIR HOUSING AND COLLECTIVE HEALTH

In his labors as president of the National Association of Real Estate Brokers (an equal opportunity and civil rights organization for African American real estate professionals, consumers, and communities), Ron Cooper often remarked that working for fair housing often resembles the task of changing the direction of a big ocean liner. A large ship moves slowly. Its direction cannot be altered by one swift action. Changing direction requires many individual crew members to perform a large number of small and tedious tasks that are nearly imperceptible in the short term but that add up to a major shift in the long run.[16] Part of the pursuit of housing justice and health justice conforms to that pattern. It requires relentless dedication to making small moves that can contribute to major shifts in direction in the middle and long run.

We cannot expect the dominant approaches to medicine and law and to health and housing to disappear overnight. We cannot argue them out of existence through our writing and speaking, no matter how passionate or persuasive we try to be. Systems and structures responsible for racism cannot be willed away or wished away; they have to be worked on and worked through by collective action that enables large numbers of people to see for themselves the necessity for radical changes. This chapter highlights actions underway in diverse places attempting to achieve the kinds of short-run and middle-run reforms in health care and housing that can pave the way toward long-run transformations.

Short-Run Remedies

Questionnaires

Expanding the routine practice of asking patients and clients to answer questionnaires can be a useful short-run intervention by both medical and legal professionals. Traditionally questionnaires distributed by doctors have rarely asked about housing, while the questionnaires administered by fair housing lawyers have generally neglected the social determinants of health. In the wake of the mass mobilizations of 2020, this has started to change. Questionnaires surveying medical patients about the ways in which their housing circumstances affect their health and similar queries asking fair housing plaintiffs about the medical consequences of denials of housing opportunities are sowing seeds for intersectional approaches in both of these spheres.

These questionnaires can help patients and clients to be heard more clearly and fully by their physicians and their attorneys. At the same time, questionnaire answers provide credentialed professionals with information about patients and clients that they all too frequently lack and that their professional training often discourages them from seeking. Dr. Margot Kushel, professor of medicine and division chief at the Division of Vulnerable Populations at Zuckerberg San Francisco General Hospital and Trauma Center, observes that some physicians are afraid to face the problems they will encounter if they inquire about a patient's housing status. She argues that this reluctance impedes proper medical practice. "If you don't ask it, you are not knowing one of the most fundamental things that is going to determine your patient's health and well-being," she warns. "Once you know it, you can plan together."[17]

Relevant evidence about the intersections of health problems and housing as well as suggestions for their solutions can emerge from questionnaires that ask about instances of housing denials that may have made victims feel embarrassed, self-conscious, upset, and sad; that threaten family and friendship support networks; and that make respondents fearful of new social occasions and of generally venturing out into the world. Questionnaires can survey respondents about how housing discrimination and insecurity may have led to sleep and appetite disturbance, overeating, smoking, and inappropriate use of medicine and drugs. Medical specialists know well that the stress from discrimination has ramifications for contracting or exacerbating conditions related to hypertension, ulcers, upset stomach, headaches, asthma, arthritis, insomnia, neck and back pain, and intensified allergic reactions. Fair housing advocates and attorneys need to keep these consequences in mind and seek out physicians, psychologists, and psychiatrists willing to see fair housing clients over a period of time and testify as expert witnesses in order to assist litigation that asks courts to calculate the damages that should be paid to victims of discrimination.

Knowing how to respond to information elicited from questionnaires is also important. Kushel points out that inattention to structural and systemic issues can lead clinicians to make moralizing judgments about the behavior of patients without taking into account its structural causes. She urges professionals: "Push back against this individual narrative that blames individuals for . . . basically being on the receiving end of systemic injustice. Push back against the language, the dehumanizing language. Push back against discussions that this problem is caused by substance abuse or mental health problems. I say those are illnesses, problems, complex social constructions, however you want to say it. And they don't scare me. I know how to manage them. I'm not afraid of them. These are not moral failures. These may be, in some cases, precipitates. But these are not the cause."[18]

Questionnaires can pave the way to enhanced and augmented medical and legal practice. Physicians, clinicians, and attorneys alike could make productive use of answers to questions that focus on the connections between illness and spatial constraint and isolation. Young patients and their parents could be asked if the children have been exposed to acts of racial discrimination, if they have often moved residences, if the family feels welcome and respected where they live, if they and their neighbors suffer from suspicion, surveillance, and subordination, and if they experience food insecurity. Survey questions about family histories of place-related and race-related conditions such as housing segregation and the resulting spatial and social distribution of amenities and hazards could illuminate conditions that help produce high levels of low-weight births and infant mortality, high blood pressure, heart disease, and cancer. These would point toward needed changes in both health care and housing provision.[19]

Questionnaires need to be designed to promote maximum and fully informed participation. That means they should be administered orally for patients who cannot read, should be adjusted to the reading level and dominant language of patients, and should take into account the likelihood that long histories of experience with being questioned by social workers, police officers, immigration officials, and employers may make respondents fearful about giving answers that might be used against them. Questionnaires need to be administered in the language of the people being questioned, and translators and clinicians need to be aware of translator shortcomings and disagreements as well as the ways in which idiomatic expressions in different languages can disguise intended meanings.

Small Group Learning Circles about Housing and Health

Distributing, administering, and processing questionnaires among health care patients and fair housing clients could be a first step toward creating small group cross-sectoral conversations that link health care and housing. The results of the questionnaires could be discussed in groups that bring together patients, clients, doctors, lawyers, paraprofessionals, family members, and neighbors to meet on equal terms. Cross-sectoral conversations in which differently situated persons share perceptions, experiences, and aspirations would facilitate efforts to craft tactics and strategies that address the stigmas of both illness and discrimination. Unconventional conversations like these contain the potential to liberate both health care professionals and fair housing advocates from their specialized silos, to fuse together knowledges now held separately by differently situated individuals and groups, and to stake claims for the importance of good health and fair housing for society at large, to articulate a public interest in healing the body politic as well as individual bodies. These measures are mechanisms for bringing back together what has been torn apart by discrimination, professional specialization, and social stratification.

Middle-Run Remedies

Short-run reforms have their limits. None of them can escape the possibility of being co-opted and manipulated for unjust ends. But each of them has the potential to educate and activate an interactive public sphere constituency aware of the structural and systemic relationships that connect housing discrimination and poor health. Perhaps most important, each of them deepens collective capacities for democratic deliberation and decision-making by recruiting people to work collectively to analyze and act upon the conditions that damage them.

Political Alliances and Actions

Short-run reforms can also help point the way toward needed middle-run changes. For example, questionnaires and conversations will expose the ways in which the current "medical home" model for pediatric care has failed to produce equity for Black and Brown families. As Kendra Liljenquist and Trumaini Coker insist, "A structural redesign of preventive care in the pediatric medical home is needed" for children who suffer from both racism and poverty.[20] The redesign they recommend includes changing the structure of health care by waging campaigns to fund Medicaid fully for the economically needy along the lines that now guide funding for Medicare. While acknowledging the enduring value of the key components of the medical home model in pediatrics, they also insist that the effectiveness of the metaphorical medical home of pediatric care depends on guaranteeing the healthfulness, cleanliness, safety, security, and affordability of the actual homes in which people dwell. Allison Bovell-Ammon and colleagues call for alliances among medical professionals, community housing providers, fair housing advocates and attorneys, and officers of financial institutions.[21] Like Liljenquist and Coker, they recognize that major changes need to be made in public policy, pointing particularly to construction of more units of affordable housing and increases in financial assistance to renters and prospective home buyers as ways to improve collective public health.

Qinjin Fan and colleagues advocate providing short-term rental and mortgage assistance as a routine part of treating cancer patients and propose having a housing care coordinator as part of the medical team providing treatment.[22] They call for clinics to contract with attorneys who can help patients address substandard housing conditions and avoid evictions. In addition, they argue that medical care has to take into account patients' housing situations, for example by understanding that houseless people should not be prescribed medicines that require refrigeration or increase urination and by recognizing that the use of infusion pumps powered by electricity will not be useful to people living on the streets or in overcrowded and under-resourced shelters. Starting with the intention of providing the best possible care for cancer patients, Fan and her colleagues wind up arguing for full enforcement of fair housing laws, zoning reforms, and programs that promote employment and community development.

Fair housing advocates and activists have long called for the creation of an independent and well-financed government fair housing agency external to the Department of Housing and Urban Development (HUD). Leaving fair housing work to HUD creates an unworkable conflict of interest because the department's mandate requires it to partner with some of the very entities most responsible for housing discrimination: lenders, builders, property management companies, nonprofits, and local governments. HUD's dependence on funds allocated to it by Congress makes the department susceptible to political pressure from some of the very people and institutions who are most invested in the profits made from housing discrimination. This dependency has left the department's Fair Housing Assistance Program and its Fair Housing Initiative chronically underfunded and lacking continuity and consistency.[23]

Legislation at the federal level could also open up new opportunities and possibilities. New federal laws could require the property insurance industry to make public information about its actions in communities historically plagued by segregation. Legislation should also give the Federal Reserve Boards and the Comptroller of the Currency the power to bring disparate-impact litigation against mortgage brokers and lenders. The establishment of a bank within the postal service would diminish the numbers of people who are unbanked and consequently disadvantaged in demonstrating creditworthiness. Some state laws already embrace principles that have not yet been approved at the federal level such as banning refusal to rent to tenants because their income is supplemented by Section 8 vouchers and prohibiting refusal to rent or sell dwellings to people because of their sexual identity or gender presentation. The American Housing and Economic Mobility Act proposed by Senator Elizabeth Warren that now awaits congressional action would ban housing discrimination based on gender identity and marital status, sexual orientation, and source of income. Expanding these categories of people protected by the Fair Housing Act needs to be accompanied by increasing penalties for those found guilty of discrimination and by authorizing judges to issue cease and desist orders to stop unjust practices immediately.

Senator Warren's proposed legislation calls for the creation of a down payment assistance program for first-time home buyers with low or moderate incomes who reside in low-income historically redlined communities. The bill would extend the requirements of the Community Reinvestment Act to nonbank mortgage lenders and credit unions and would augment the ability of community groups to inform regulators' assessments of the degree to which fair lending mandates are being obeyed. It would address the shortage of affordable rental units by allocating some $45 billion per year for ten years to aid the construction and preservation of housing for working-class people. One estimate predicts that this part of the bill would lower existing rents by 10 percent, create 1.5 million new construction jobs, and bring into existence more than three million new dwellings. An additional $2 billion would be authorized by this bill to make funds available in areas that have been targeted by predatory lending for new loan modifications, principal reductions, purchases and rehabilitations of vacant lots, and loans to owners with negative equity that would allow them to rehabilitate dwellings and maintain ownership of them.[24]

New laws are also needed at the municipal level. Inclusionary zoning ordinances and laws that require just cause for evictions, statutes that limit landlord rent increases over time, and regulations that ban the use of irrelevant arrest histories in considering suitability to occupy dwellings would help bring more fairness, stability, social cohesion, and desegregation to housing while addressing the injustices perpetuated by the racial wealth gap. Studies show that inclusionary zoning enhances health. Municipalities with inclusionary zoning policies in place experience uniformly better cardiovascular outcomes than places where such policies are absent. Researchers have found that inclusionary zoning policies are associated with lower prevalence of high blood pressure, less prevalence of high cholesterol, and lower incidences of people needing blood pressure medication. Higher levels of financial support for inclusionary zoning and/or housing trust funds are similarly associated with lower levels of high blood pressure problems, fewer instances of high cholesterol, and reduced need for blood pressure medication.[25]

Cities and states could address the deleterious consequences of corporate ownership of housing by banning the use of shadow corporations that hide ownership in order to evade accountability and responsibility, by limiting the number of dwellings that can be legally owned by any one entity, and by imposing a tax on absentee landlords in order to raise funds to remedy the nuisances and hazards their neglect causes.

The Transformation of Medical and Legal Education and Practice

The moment of racial reckoning brought on by the mass mobilizations of 2020 called attention to the fact that very few medical schools and law schools present courses that adequately address racial disparities in health and wealth, that cover the history and pervasive presence of intersectional structural and systemic racism, or that face up to the many ways in which medical practice, public health, and civil rights laws and litigation have failed to curtail past and present racist injustices.[26] These flaws need to be corrected. Yet the skewed demographics of medical and law school student bodies and faculties leave members of aggrieved racialized groups egregiously underrepresented, rendering them vulnerable to marginalization and denigration during professional training and in subsequent professional life.[27] A more racially diverse student body in medical education might do more than desegregate demographics: under ideal conditions it could facilitate redefinitions of professional work along the lines pioneered by Ingrid Waldron at the School of Nursing at Dalhousie University, where the curriculum revolved around the concept of nurses as patient advocates and leaders of community health initiatives. Her work corresponds to the long-declared commitment by the American Academy of Pediatrics to train physicians to be advocates for the health of all children, especially those from underserved populations.[28]

Demographic imbalances and the absence of training in cultural and structural competency in professional schools contribute to the large numbers of physicians and lawyers who hold implicit and explicit racial biases that influence their judgments and decisions about their relations with patients and clients.[29] Doctors and lawyers alike have deficient understandings of how fair and affordable housing, environmental regulation, better education, and higher wages could be crucial mechanisms for improving public health. They do not generally know that ill health is one of the main consequences of housing injustice.[30]

The ignorance that follows from deficient professional training is especially harmful in the context of the present neoliberal regime of risk management in medicine, insurance, and banking that shapes how physicians and attorneys carry out their work. Through racialized risk management, people *with* problems are viewed *as* problems. People who control next to nothing are blamed for nearly everything, while people and institutions that control significant resources are absolved of their responsibilities to promote health and protect rights. Excessive focus in medicine on the health of individual bodies and the emphasis in law on individual actions and desires occlude the existence of a rigged and structurally unjust system that creates insurmountable impediments to good health and economic well-being for people from aggrieved racialized groups. In medical and legal practice this means that the very conditions that kill people get a free pass while the people who are being killed find themselves blamed for failing to perform miracles by overcoming the odds against them.[31]

Risk factor models in medical research and practice concentrate almost exclusively on individual and molecular causes of disease, and consequently hide, protect, and excuse the socioeconomic causes of racial disparities. They function as what medical anthropologist Michael Montoya (following James Ferguson) aptly describes as an "anti-politics machine" that reinforces and expands forms of state power while depoliticizing responses to social problems. They position the nexus of race and health as a matter fit for technical administrative management rather than democratic political deliberation and decision-making.[32]

Medical school teaching is riddled with misrepresentations of racism. One study revealed that a shocking 96 percent of preclinical lecture slides at one institution treated race as a biological rather than a political category, and another study revealed that significant numbers of medical trainees believe that Black skin is thicker than white skin and that the nerve endings in Black people make them less susceptible to pain than white people.[33] A 2016 study found that 50 percent of white medical students surveyed held unfounded notions about biological differences among races. As a result, medical professionals recommend inappropriate or inadequate treatment for Black patients based on misguided presumptions, such as the idea that the biological makeup of Black people makes them feel pain less than white people do, that they are prone to exaggerate reports of pain, and that they have innate proclivities for misusing pain-killing drugs. Dorothy Roberts shows how these beliefs lead to Black and Latinx patients being twice as likely as whites to be denied pain-easing medications for conditions such as painful fractures of long bones.[34]

Studies have found consistently that white physicians devote less time to Black patients than to white patients with identical ailments. Black patients receive fewer pain medications than whites with identical conditions, get less frequent recommendations for cardiac diagnosis and therapeutic procedures, receive fewer referrals for renal transplantation, and get less frequent recommendations for curative surgery for non–small cell lung cancer. Black patients routinely confront racialized patterns of care that are inconsistent with generally accepted and recommended treatment guidelines.[35] African Americans and members of other aggrieved racialized groups are less likely than white patients to receive the most medically indicated treatments for the same illnesses, even when they possess the same levels of medical insurance and access to medical care.[36]

Jonathan M. Metzl and Helena Hansen call for the creation of medical education that equips students with structural competency, by which they mean attunement to outcomes beyond individual conditions and interactions and recognition that racial disparities in health are not merely injustices perpetrated against targeted groups but also impediments to improvement in overall population health. Metzl and Hansen focus on preparing medical professionals to recognize the roles played by social systems, structures, organizations, and institutions in producing unequal and inadequate patient care.[37] They view structural competency, not as a diversion from, or an alternative to, education in anatomy, physiology, histology, embryology, and neuroscience, but rather as recognition of the ways in which narrow disciplinary specializations fragment and decontextualize knowledge and prevent effective integrative thinking and medical practice.[38]

Medical journal articles about illnesses such as hypertension that have sharp racial disparities seldom mention inequality or discrimination. Despite the large body of evidence demonstrating that race is a political rather than a biological category, much medical research literature continues to treat *race* rather than *racism* as a risk factor, emphasizing the dynamics of genetics but neglecting the effects of structural and systemic racism. Misguided researchers in physiology and pathology attribute differences in pulmonary kidney function and pain sensation to biological racial differences, even though research has consistently shown that there is no biological basis for categorizing people by race.[39] When professional medical journals deign to publish pieces about structural and systemic racism, they usually confine them to letters, commentaries, and editorials rather than research articles. As Bailey and her colleagues observe, this conveys the impression that interrogations of racism are suitable for discussion but not for discovery.[40] The legacies of racist exclusion in medicine leave these journals with too few peer reviewers and too few editors with firsthand knowledge of the causes and consequences of racism and expertise in studying it.[41]

Predominant practices in medicine not only fail to bring about health justice but actually exacerbate the inequalities responsible for health disparities. Neoliberal policies aimed at making poor people responsible for the costs of uncompensated care lead to rationing treatments in ways that deny effective medicines and cures to some of the people who need them most.[42] Treating ailments like hypertension among Black people as a problem of biological makeup rather than social inequality leads to prescriptions of expensive but ineffective medicines that generate medical debts that patients cannot pay.[43]

Desegregating the demographics of the faculty and student populations in medical and law schools is important work. Ending the underrepresentation and marginalization of aggrieved racialized groups in professional practice can improve the prospects for health and housing justice. Yet while necessary, these changes will not be sufficient by themselves. It is simply not enough to change the demographics of the professions without challenging their premises, practices, and presumptions. There need to be changes in the curricula of the professional schools, in the attitudes and practices of practitioners, and in the interactions between credentialed professionals who possess expert knowledge and the people most affected by racism in housing and health care.

Metzl and Hansen note the importance of making a shift in clinical training in medicine based on the recognition that self-determination and self-management are not merely desired political goals but also positive health practices. There need to be changes in the relations between credentialed professionals who possess expert knowledge and the people most affected by racism in housing and health care.

One encouraging model comes from Pittsburgh, where a consortium of campus researchers and community groups is now working to offer adolescent Black girls classes leading to doula certification. This curriculum honors and draws on the traditions of midwifery in the Black community, deepens collective knowledge about reproductive health, and opens up pathways to health care careers for Black women. In the same city, the Freedom House 2.0 project offers training in first aid, cardiopulmonary resuscitation, and safe driving to people interested in becoming emergency medical technicians and ambulance drivers but also engages them in on-the-job training in skills like intubation and infusion that can lead to health care careers.[44] The 2.0 designation pays tribute to the original Freedom House project in Pittsburgh that pioneered the concept of paramedics providing emergency medical treatment. That initiative deployed previously unemployed or underemployed but subsequently fully trained residents of the traditionally African American Hill neighborhood to provide emergency medical services that had previously been carried out ineffectively by untrained police officers. In 1972 alone, the thirty-five-person Freedom House crew working in the first specially configured ambulances for emergency medicine treated seven thousand patients.[45]

Radical Changes in Legal Education and Practice

Legal education and practice need to make changes as radical as those needed in medicine. With a few distinguished exceptions, law schools do not direct significant resources toward education in civil rights law and critical race theory. This has resulted in the unwillingness and perhaps inability of the profession at large to come to grips with the degree to which the courts have abandoned the principle and practice of equal protection and equal opportunity. The tort model of injury has been used to render invisible large patterns of racial subordination by recognizing as discrimination only specific episodes of intentional discrimination that proclaim animus openly. Over four decades the courts have inverted laws designed to inhibit racist rule into prohibitions against racial recognition and as a result have designated as "racist" school desegregation, affirmative action, voting rights protections, and bans on employment tests and qualifications that systematically discriminate against members of aggrieved racialized groups. At the same time, as Joy Milligan has demonstrated, the courts increasingly contend that it is too late to remedy the ongoing effects of centuries of past discrimination, that repair can be made only in response to discrimination that is "atomized, transient, and easily repaired," and that broad patterns and practices of racist exclusion and subordination produced and maintained by government bodies are the product of amorphous societal processes that make racial injustice no one's fault because it is everyone's fault. Only discrete episodes and events that can be traced to the intentional animus of an individual perpetrator are actionable from this perspective, a commitment that, as Milligan explains, "renders past [and I would add continuing] discrimination invisible, irrelevant, and unrecognizable."[46]

Robert Schwemm, widely acknowledged as the leading expert and theorist of fair housing law, explains how revanchist and reactionary court decisions have made winning fair housing cases increasingly more difficult. Strict new pleading rules now require plaintiffs to produce evidence about disparate treatment and discriminatory intent *before* discovery begins. Rulings that impose severe limits on the ability to file class action suits have been coupled with the willingness of businesses and government agencies to view paying monetary judgments and agreeing to expensive settlements as acceptable costs of doing business, allowing discrimination to continue. Schwemm acknowledges the enduring value of fair housing litigation in identifying patterns and practices of discrimination. He endorses developing more effective means of enforcing the law by city, state, and federal officials and administrators. He recognizes the importance of demonstrating that not just individuals but entire communities and the public at large are served by effective fair housing policies. Yet Schwemm also proposes that the most important results of fair housing litigation may come from the ways in which it educates the public about the range, reach, and scope of discrimination and from fair housing's role in creating the preconditions for an engaged and active political constituency willing to take action on behalf of social justice.[47] Some of that education will take place in courtrooms, but much more will need to emanate from active and engaged public sphere mobilizations for housing justice.

Despite the limits crafted by conservative courts, expanding the reach and scope of fair housing litigation remains an important means of advancing housing and health justice. Law is not merely an assemblage of static texts but rather an ongoing dynamic and dialogic practice. The Fair Housing Act authorizes and enables a broad range of remedies for a wide array of unjust acts. Not every courtroom battle has been lost. Case law, out-of-court settlements, and administrative actions have established clear precedents for treating access to safe and secure housing as a necessary component of economic opportunity, democratic citizenship, and personal dignity. Successful fair housing litigation brings some justice to aggrieved individuals and groups, corrects irrational and destructive distortions of market relations, and promotes the productivity and creativity of people unjustly hindered by discrimination.

Residents of a Black neighborhood near Zanesville, Ohio, and areas of Latinx residency near Modesto, California, won important victories and settlements through litigation focused on the health and environmental consequences of housing discrimination.[48] These can serve as models for others faced with similar exclusions and injuries.[49] Future litigation specifying the damages to health perpetrated by housing discrimination could secure creative remedies. Damage awards could fund health care for individuals and for entire communities. One reasonable approach for cases that entail damages to childhood health would be to create a victims' escrow fund paid for by those doing the discriminating, administered by a fair housing center with court oversight or through a court-appointed trustee. This fund could be tapped later in life for treatments, medicines, and counseling for people harmed as children when the long-term impacts of their mistreatments become visible. There is a precedent for this kind of structure in the law. A settlement reached by the city of Elgin, Illinois, with the US Department of Housing and Urban Development, the Department of Justice, and the Hope Fair Housing Center included a victims' fund to compensate residents for future problems caused by discriminatory enforcement of the local housing code.[50]

A large body of case law and attendant administrative decisions has established definitively that the public at large has a stake in the formulation and implementation of fair housing remedies.[51] The Department of Justice has the power and obligation to monitor potential settlements of court cases precisely because the law holds that the public interest has to be represented in clashes that originate in disputes between plaintiffs and defendants. The pursuit of that public interest does not simply express the needs of an already existing polity; rather, it helps bring into being a new social world grounded in reciprocal recognition and responsibility.

While the field of medicine faces an unprecedented moment of reckoning about racism as a public health issue, fair housing advocates, activists, and attorneys confront new realities. A racist and revanchist backlash against fair housing and other civil rights remedies long predated the mass demonstrations of 2020, but the specter of a mass antiracist constituency lead to even greater defensive retrenchment by the defenders of possessive investments in whiteness. Resistance to racial justice is deeply entrenched in national life. The National Fair Housing Alliance recorded 31,216 complaints filed in 2021, an 8.7 percent increase over the previous year. Private citizen-led fair housing organizations processed nearly three-quarters of the complaints lodged in 2021, a number more than two and a half times greater than the number dealt with by local, state, and federal government agencies. Because the Fair Housing Act has not been fully enforced at any level of government, community-based groups find themselves with enormous amounts of work to do.[52]

Significant changes in both medical and legal education could equip health care workers and fair housing attorneys with augmented capacities for working collaboratively and collegially with plaintiffs, advocates, researchers, religious social justice groups, and members of the general public in fair housing litigation and mobilization. The expertise of specialists remains indispensable: the practice of law and medicine alike require particular knowledges and skills that patients and clients do not generally possess. Yet different kinds of expertise emerge from different experiences. The direct victims of housing and health injustice know much about how harm happens, why remedies fail, and how to survive—and sometimes even thrive—despite the failures of medical and legal practice. Changing society means changing the people we are into the people we need to become, challenging social hierarchies, transforming social relations, and developing new understandings of the connections between housing and health.

Long-Run Remedies

Health and Housing as Collective Resources Rather Than Private Commodities

People suffer needlessly because medical care and shelter are structured to be commodities for sale and mechanisms for profitable returns on investment. Privatization of health care and housing creates and manipulates artificial scarcities that use racial difference (and other differences in social identities) as excuses and justifications for arbitrary and irrational exclusions that make people sick, poor, and politically disenfranchised. In a neoliberal society where single-axis thinking and methodological individualism disaggregate complex and interrelated social processes and reduce them to their discrete parts, practices of privatization come to be seen as natural, necessary, and inevitable. The tort model of injury in law and the biomedical model of health individualize injustice and illness while deflecting attention away from the shared social circumstances that skew access to housing and health along racial lines.

A neoliberal society that reduces all human activity to the pursuit of personal wealth promotes vicious competition among people encouraged to see each other as enemies. While beneficial in the short run for those positioned to profit from it, this zero-sum system ultimately harms everyone. It poisons the well from which we all must drink by exacerbating inequality, spreading diseases, undermining social cohesion, raising costs, suppressing productivity, and squandering talents and abilities that society sorely needs.

Efforts to reform law and medicine in the short and middle run have the potential to promote a radical revolution in values in the long run. Breaking free from the constraints of the individualized tort model of injury in law and the biomedical model of health, and understanding health and housing as public resources and human rights rather than private commodities and investments, hold the potential for ending unnecessary suffering while improving social conditions. Long-run changes can produce a practice of public health that connects the well-being of individual bodies to the health of the entire body politic and a practice of housing provision that offers a decent home and living environment to all.

Denying medical insurance and health care to noncitizens, incarcerated people, and the poor spreads disease and ill health while increasing the monetary and social costs of housing and medical treatment. Viewing health care and housing as market relations rather than social relations exposes children to long-term health damages because of the poverty that their parents have experienced due to racial discrimination in employment, housing, education, and taxation. Placing public resources in private hands has led to poisoned water in Flint and polluted air, water, and land in Detroit and Earlimart, to utility fees that generate unpayable debts that lead to eviction and houselessness, and to corporate profiteering that jacks up the cost of medical care. The insurance industry's practices of racialized risk assessment and the banking industry's racialized biases in credit scoring negatively affect what kinds of medical care people receive, how employers treat job applicants, how landlords view shelter seekers, and why police offers and prosecutors deploy differential levels of surveillance, stops, arrests, and charges in different neighborhoods.

The Universal Declaration of Human Rights

The Universal Declaration of Human Rights adopted by the United Nations in 1948 proclaims that all humans have the right to adequate housing, health care, food, clothing, and support in the event of sickness, disability, unemployment and old age. A subsection of the declaration holds that all children hold the same rights to social protection and that motherhood and childcare deserve special assistance. Committing to the healthy development of children as a primary public policy aim would have important ramifications for fair housing and public health. But it also would enable recognition of the ways in which gun violence, environmental pollution, and punitive immigration policies enact excessive particular harm on young people.

There is no meaningful way to secure the healthy development of children, however, without also protecting the health and well-being of their parents, extended families, caretakers, and neighbors. This could be advanced by adopting a child's bill of rights, funding parental leave and early childhood education, and improving children's health and education outcomes through increased spending on the Supplemental Nutrition Assistance Program and an expanded Child Tax Credit. Paid family leave, subsidized childcare, increases in the minimum wage, and limits on rent hikes position parents to better meet the health needs of their children. Additional Medicaid expansion would produce many benefits for public health and safety. Yet as currently configured, that expansion has proceeded too narrowly, neglecting the ways in which Medicaid policies create an unjust two-tiered system of health care that victimizes impoverished members of aggrieved racialized communities and cruelly limits and even excludes the transition-related health care needs of transgender people.[53]

Redirection of Resources

The adoption of a single-payer system of health insurance providing access for all, as guaranteed in most prosperous nations other than the

United States, would meaningfully and positively improve the quality and availability of health care. Making more housing vouchers available and extending them to higher rents while requiring landlords to treat them equally with other sources of income would promote access to safe and sound shelter. It would also help shelter seekers use vouchers to pay for utility connections and security and cleaning deposits. The American Friends Service Committee in its North Star Vision project calls for a massive redirection of funds toward health and housing and away from mass incarceration. This initiative proposes moving resources away from punishment and retribution and instead investing instead in healing, reconciliation, and the promotion of human dignity and opportunity. The proposal revolves around the goals of embracing healing, reconciliation, and accountability; investing in providing housing, health care, food, and mental health services; welcoming back into community life people returning from incarceration; ending the perpetual punishments that come with long sentences and the collateral consequences of criminal convictions; reducing the number of people locked behind bars; creating meaningful interactions between people in prison and people outside; ending racial profiling in policing; terminating the ability of corporations to reap surplus profits from prison programs; and replacing predatory policing with restorative justice circles and community-centered and orchestrated public safety initiatives.[54]

Convention on the Rights of the Child (CRC)

The United States is the only member state in the United Nations that has not ratified the global Convention on the Rights of the Child (CRC). Although signatories do not always live up to its principles, the CRC commits governments around the world to give priority to policies that protect the best interests of the child, protect children from discrimination, promote young people's survival and development, and offer participation and inclusion in health care practices and decisions to minors.[55] Elizabeth Barnert and her colleagues note accurately that the health care system in place in the United States is concerned more with its own well-being and profitability than with the needs of children and their families. These researchers recognize that the wealth and power of the health care industries make it unlikely that the United States will ratify the CRC any time soon, but they wisely argue that its principles can nonetheless be valuable in pointing the way toward changes in many areas of national life. They explain how honoring the rights of children can be of value to all people, even those who are not young, because it offers a template for broader policies of inclusion. Granting rights to children recognizes that differently situated people require differently conceived and targeted remedies. Paying attention to the particular health needs of people because of their stage in life also makes it possible to attend to the differently situated health and wealth statuses structured by race, gender, sex, socioeconomic status, and perceived disability. Implementing policies designed to promote equitable development for children can author and authorize approaches to health care specifically and public policy more generally that understand that treating differently situated people equally and interchangeably only perpetuates inequality and injustice. Viewing health care intersectionally, however, opens the door to new understandings of social membership and subjectivity that point toward social justice.

International Convention on the Elimination of All Forms of Racial Discrimination (CERD)

Under the aegis of the International Convention on the Elimination of All Forms of Racial Discrimination (CERD), adopted by the United Nations in 1965, all member states commit themselves to promote and encourage universal respect and rights and freedoms for all, regardless of race, sex, language, or religion. In a 2008 progress report on the implementation of that commitment in the United States, international experts noted that efforts to combat racial discrimination in housing, education, health care, and employment remained underfunded, lacked enforcement, and were spread piecemeal throughout agencies with conflicting mandates and goals.[56] Among others, Barbara Reskin identifies residential segregation as a key source of these injustices, making the fight for fair housing a crucial locus of action for a fight against racial discrimination that could span diverse institutional structures.

The Replacement of Cartesian Cause-and-Effect Analyses with Design-Centered Approaches to Wicked Problems

Working for health and housing justice in the long run requires challenges to the single-axis thinking embodied in overemphasis on the tort model of injury in law and the biomedical model of disease and health care. It also exposes some of the single-axis thinking that plagues social science research. Barbara Reskin and Leah Gordon (among others) have noted how scholars in the mid-twentieth century gradually moved away from holistic analyses of racism as an interrelated system to focus instead on single-domain disparities and prejudices.[57] Searching for isolated identifiable causes and positivist, lineal causal correlations between variables within single domains while excluding from study the fully linked systems in which they exist leads to scholarship that is timid in its approach and tentative in its conclusions. This is not to say that factor incidence and causal relations do not matter but rather to recognize that they are rarely the exclusive or decisive elements determining health.[58]

The high analytic standard required for definitively establishing causal connections between isolated variables almost always impels scholars to present their findings as merely suggestive and in need of additional study. They identify race-based disparities and concede that racism might be their cause, but their methods are incapable of revealing and analyzing the multiaxis dimensions of racist structures and systems. They overemphasize what can be quantified and undervalue what cannot. As with the tort model of injury in law and the biomedical model of disease, the emphasis on correlation between variables in social science research is a single-axis approach that looks for anomalous flaws in an otherwise healthy and well-functioning system. As Reskin explains, however, racial disparities are not anomalies in need of mechanistic correction; they are the logical and necessary product of an interconnected system of subordination.[59]

The disparities highlighted by correlations can be useful; they are cited over and over again in this book to illuminate relationships between race and place and wealth and health. Yet the search for simple cause-and-effect relations between discrete variables ultimately does too little to explain the existence and persistence of racial subordination. Single-axis cause-and-effect correlations are most useful in situations where technical solutions are needed to solve clearly identifiable flaws that can be corrected by properly situated actors. These conditions do not apply when analyzing the workings of structural and systemic racism, where the problems are political and interrelated and concern many different actors at many different levels.

It might be possible, for example, to quantify the short-term improvements in wealth and health caused by the arts-based community mobilizations for housing and health justice chronicled in chapter 7. Those calculations, however, would not begin to capture the long-term consequences of those interventions, nor would they in any way meaningfully assess those projects' contributions to deepening capacities for democratic deliberation and decision-making and creating an active and engaged public sphere in civil society committed to health and housing justice. Some injuries and some remedies defy quantified assessment. As T. L. Lewis asks when pressed for evidence showing concrete metrics of successful outcomes in social justice work, "How many people love more deeply? How many communities grow closer? How many families did you keep together in the hundred-year battle to tear apart our families? How many children knew they were loved despite the system— that wires, walls, windows, and bars could not separate them from that which they deserved the most . . . ?"[60]

The ways of calculating injuries within economics are almost always shaped by presumptions about self-interested maximizing of wealth and by calculations that, as Stephen Marglin explains, represent "more an ideological commitment to the superiority of the episteme than a serious attempt to unravel the complexities and mysteries of human motivation and behavior."[61] Peer-validated social science research can be valuable, and it does not do any good to be uncritically or unreflexively antipositivist. But it is important to resist the tendencies in social science research to reduce ungainly, dispersed, and complex social processes to limited cause-and-effect relationships that, while suited for short-term fixes and long-range grand theoretical projections, occlude the political and culturally necessary political work needed to make meaningful change possible.[62]

More complete, albeit less decisive assessments of those projects would come from what design theorists describe as solving "wicked problems." Wicked problems are those that have indeterminate, inherently political, and complex qualities. As Barbara Tomlinson explains, the problems posed by social systems of subordination are also wicked in the other generally understood ramification of the word as "entrenched, reprehensible, iniquitous, heinous, vicious acts of domination and degradation that are nonetheless overlooked, treated as local anomalies, defined out of serious consideration."[63] They require serious attention.

An Active and Engaged Public Constituency for Health and Housing Justice

Effecting meaningful changes in the long run will require the full participation of the greatest possible number of people from many different realms of social life. Substantive change will not be doled out from the top down; it needs to be won from the bottom up. No one is coming to save us. No one will do for us what we fail to do for ourselves. In times like these of crisis, turmoil, upheaval, and uncertainty, there is much at stake. Forces are in motion that can propel the world and its people either forward or backward. The vile, violent, and hate-filled public sphere often makes us wish things were otherwise and tempts us to want to scramble off to some private refuge. But there are no real escapes from the problems we face, only an ever-expanding number of opportunities to respond to them honestly and honorably with clarity, conviction, and courage.

Hard Times (No One Knows Better Than I)

The Bitter but Beautiful Struggle

The "Danger Zone" in the title of this book comes from the lyrics and title of a song released by Ray Charles in 1961. I conclude here with a reference to another one of his recordings from that same year: "Hard Times (No One Knows Better Than I)." The song relates a mother's warning to her child that life will be filled with hard times. It then presents the child's descriptions of the hardships that ensued, proving she was correct. The subtitle of the song in parentheses invokes the authority of experience, asserting that no one knows more about hard times than the people who suffer from them the most.

Continuing injustices in housing and health care mean that hard times are here and that even harder times lie ahead. Housing discrimination steals wealth, harms health, and renders racism structural and systemic. No one suffers from this more than the members of aggrieved racialized groups who live in proximity to toxicity, who are eyewitnesses to the worst predations of racial capitalism, and who suffer injustices because of all the structures and systems that deploy racism to promote domination and capital accumulation. Having suffered much, however, they also know much. The survival strategies of members of aggrieved racialized groups are a rich repository of practices, tactics, and strategies that all of society needs to learn in order to combat structural and systemic racism. While it is hoped that eventually everyone will have a seat at the welcome table of justice, no one knows better what can and should be done to achieve that end than the people who formed the front lines of the mass demonstrations and mobilizations of 2020 and who are waging the wide range of battles for health and housing justice across institutions in many dispersed sites that are analyzed in this book.

In hard times, the historical survival strategies of aggrieved communities of color can be of especially vital importance. They illuminate viable means of struggling, striving, surviving, and sometimes even thriving despite overwhelming obstacles. Precisely because precarious conditions leave them no room for error, these communities have often been the most perceptive opponents of injustice and the most inventive creators of new democratic practices and institutions. Forced by grim realities and inescapable necessities, members of aggrieved racialized groups wage what Dr. King described as "the long and bitter—but beautiful—struggle" for a new and better world.[1] Learning from them and joining with them is both a moral imperative and a practical necessity. The danger zone is everywhere, but that means that everywhere that people are, there is meaningful work to do.

RACISM IS LIKE A CADILLAC; THEY MAKE A NEW MODEL EVERY YEAR

Malcolm X used to tell his followers that racism is like a Cadillac because a new model appears every year. When you are driving a 2024 Escalade, the operator's manual for a 1968 Cadillac De Ville is of limited use. In the same fashion, the mentalities that informed the practices of civil rights mobilization and public health advocacy in 1968 provide insufficient mechanisms for negotiating the health and housing injustices of 2024. Still, a Cadillac remains a Cadillac, and racism remains racism. Both the 1968 and 2024 model Cadillacs are big, costly, dangerous, and death dealing. The same can be said for the racisms of 1968 and 2024. Combating health and housing injustice in 2023 requires an operator's manual that is attuned to the prevailing model of racism today in order to design new solutions to new problems but that also recognizes the long histories undergirding the injustices of today.

Housing and medicine function differently today than they did fifty years ago. Economic concentration, securitization, and fiscalization in housing markets have turned racial capitalism's health care and housing systems into central mechanisms of predatory extraction. When the Fair Housing Act became law in 1968, homeownership constituted a relatively safe investment, one funded by loans from banks with local ties and direct stakes in the health of the local economy. Decades of deregulation of the banking and private equity industries, however, have transformed housing into a globally traded asset, a site where large corporations purchase and make surplus profits from buying and selling mortgage debts, tax liens, and foreclosed dwellings. Corporate investors today own millions of housing units, a concentration of ownership that makes it difficult to enforce fair housing laws and building codes while making it easier for owners to raise rents, evict tenants, and pressure municipalities into supplying them with massive subsidies for luxury development.

Corporate control shapes medical care as well. Inflated health care costs result from the actions of monopolies in the pharmaceutical industry that shape the promotion and sale of prescription drugs, from the profit-first mentality guiding large hospital chains, from corporate protocols that guide physician decision-making, from health insurance programs that keep for themselves revenue diverted from health care and pass on high out-of-pocket costs to patients, and from the large profit margins enjoyed by makers of medical devices, equipment, and tests.[2]

THE NEOLIBERAL CONJUNCTURE

The radical changes that have transformed housing and medicine into corporatized, fiscalized, and securitized entities are part of larger neoliberal economic, political, pedagogical, and social projects that place individualism, competition, and self-interest at the center of the social world. These projects presume that cooperation, mutual support, and community consciousness are oppressive fetters on the free market and impede the development of the aggressive personalities that neoliberalism prioritizes and privileges. Neoliberalism creates a world that coalesces around the insistence that all people are—and all people must be—acquisitive and avaricious, that all institutions must serve as generators of lavish returns on investment, and that the unbridled pursuit of self-interest will "free" people from accountability, responsibility, and obligations to others. Elevation of private profit over the public good and the privileging of market relations over interpersonal relations produce a winner-take-all society in which the winners believe they never have enough.[3]

Yet while neoliberalism promises prosperity, for most people it delivers austerity. It channels massive tax breaks and other subsidies to wealthy investors and owners while saddling the majority of the population with stagnant or declining incomes; rising health care and housing

FIGURE 8. Shana M. griffin, *Spatialized Violence,* 2020. Part of griffin's *Cartographies of Violence* series, which visualizes practices of Black enslavement, confinement, segregation, disposability, erasure, and disappearance spatialized, etched, and inscribed in violent housing and land use policies that have displaced and dispossessed Black people. Acrylic and paper on wood, 24 x 24 inches. Used by permission of the artists.

costs; reductions in environmental protection; increases in fines, fees, and debts; and reduced government expenditures on education and transportation. The structural economic policies enacted through neoliberal principles create a culture filled with hate, hurt, fear, avarice, envy, and hostility. It stokes phobic fantasies about demonized "others" and channels violent rage against them. As Doris Sommer so aptly explains, it produces people who increasingly become "inured to suffering and afraid of love."[4]

In neoliberal society all forms of education, governance, and risk assessment treat racism wrongly—as a merely technical problem to be managed rather than as the inevitable political product of systemic and structural political manipulation and exploitation. Neoliberal premises and presumptions make securing safe and affordable fair housing and promoting public health impossible because these goals cannot be realized by individuals one at a time acting as isolated consumers or competitors. Housing and health justice alike require convivial and collective mobilization for change. Fusing the fight for housing justice with the need for health justice requires new practices, policies, personalities, and polities. It requires providing funds for projects that cultivate the determination and ability to overcome the alienation, isolation, and manufactured powerlessness of a society where people lack the collective efficacy produced by meaningful democratic participation in making the decisions that affect their lives. In a society governed by neoliberal principles there is little that prepares people for such democratic activity. Consequently, in addition to seeking to achieve worthy practical and material changes, mobilizations for health and housing justice can be important in developing and deepening collective capacities for democratic deliberation and decision-making.

HARD TIMES TODAY

Unfair gains and unearned enrichments made possible through structural and systemic racism have become central components of the interests and identities of wealthy people and powerful corporations. They rely on a false sense of psychological superiority and cultural centrality ensconced in the collective identity of whiteness that increasingly seems to be the only thing nonelite white people believe they can possess. It is not that the antiracist mobilizations of 2020 made their opponents more racist, but rather that sustained exposure and criticism of the privileges and preferences attached to whiteness brought into the open the presumptions and premises that were already there. The more that whiteness becomes exposed as a fabricated system of social advantage, the more fervently many of its beneficiaries will cling to it and attempt to use it as a weapon against democratic ideas, actions, policies, and programs. Seeing powerful politicians, pundits, and plutocrats increasingly embrace white supremacy so openly can be discouraging, but it should not be surprising. To mix metaphors (in a characteristically postmodern fashion), it is precisely because the boat is rocking and the table is shaking that the veils are being dropped and the masks are coming off.

The increasingly visible embrace of overt white supremacy proceeds through a politics of contempt and cruelty. People in need of health care and housing are blamed and shamed as individual failures. They are demeaned and demonized as deficient and dysfunctional. At the same time, racism, sexism, homophobia, transphobia, and nativism serve as the core components of hate-filled mobilizations financed lavishly by what seems to be the most brutal, belligerent, surly, and self-pitying group of "haves" in the history of the world. They help bring into being personalities who seek not only to deprive other people of their basic rights to health and housing but—even worse—to punish sadistically those who are in need. In seeking to hurt others, however, they also harm themselves. As Jonathan Metzl demonstrates in *Dying of Whiteness,* resistance to the Affordable Care Act and the insistent refusals by state governments to accept federal subsidies to expand Medicaid have been embraced by many white voters even at the expense of their own health. Because they imagine incorrectly that these policies are designed primarily to help Black and Latinx people, they deny themselves health care that they desperately need.[5]

The 1996 Welfare Reform Act greatly limited immigrants' access to public health insurance. Resident aliens who enter the country legally and hold green card status are nonetheless deemed ineligible for Medicaid and for the Children's Health Insurance program for their first five years of residence in the United States. Even after qualifying for those services, they may find that the state in which they live denies them those benefits.[6] Immigrants are scapegoated as undeserving recipients of taxpayer largesse, but in actuality their presence in the nation and the economy most benefits many of the people who despise them. Having large numbers of immigrants in the workforce actually lowers health costs for citizens because the immigrant population is younger, in better health, and less likely to use health care services than the native-born population. Immigrant laborers contributed more than $100 billion more to the Medicare trust fund than they cost that system between 2002 and 2009. As Patricia Illingworth and Wendy E. Parmet observe, "Without young immigrant workers, the health premiums of citizens would rise."[7]

State and federal laws that deny medical insurance and medical treatment to noncitizens impede cost-effective preventive care while causing and exacerbating medical conditions that end up being treated in emergency rooms, where costs are much higher that the costs of prevention and regular physician visits. Citizens who have insurance and dwell in places where large numbers of people are uninsured do not gain privileged access to good medical care for themselves in that situation.

Instead, the low level of insurance policyholders in their locality leads to fewer medical treatment centers and fewer doctors, consequently imposing higher costs on those who are insured. Similarly, denying insurance and medical care to children of immigrants lowers the rate of vaccinations against infectious diseases, lessening herd immunity and leading to widespread outbreaks of once-rare diseases like measles and pertussis. Among immigrant adults, lack of insurance can mean delays or absence of treatment of sexually transmitted diseases, which may then be transmitted to insured people.[8] We should oppose racial subordination in health care and housing even if it could be proven to be cost-effective and efficient because it is immoral and unfit conduct for human beings. But it is not even economically rational or productive. The fact that so many people cling to their whiteness, however, testifies to its powerful political and cultural appeal among large parts of the populace and its enduring role inside institutions.

Performances of cruelty against vulnerable people succeed politically by stoking sadism in the body politic while damaging the health of individual bodies. These have terrible consequences for public health. Instead of providing safe and sanitary dwellings, preventive health care, and treatments for mental health issues and drug dependency, taxpayers authorize expenditures on policing and punishing the poor in ways that spread and exacerbate illness and disease. Policies that purport to protect public safety in reality increase harm and damage health. Municipalities routinely criminalize housing insecurity by arresting, fining, and jailing houseless people for the "offenses" of jaywalking, lying on sidewalks, littering, or holding open containers of beverages.[9] Politicians, pundits, and their plutocrat funders propose even more draconian measures, such as those deployed by city police and county sheriffs in Lancaster, California, who round up houseless people and transport them to the desert, where they are left to die.[10] On the streets and behind bars, houseless people are denied the medical care they need. As explained in chapter 5, predatory policing also leads to aggressive confrontations between police officers and residents of urban sacrifice zones, confrontations that can easily escalate into tragic loss of life. Sadly, protests against these police killings of unarmed Black people have been met by efforts by both major political parties to allocate even more funds and to provide even more lethal weapons to the very police forces responsible for the killings in the first place, setting in motion a dynamic that can only lead to more violence. Although police departments routinely hide the number of people their officers kill and there is no reliable national database of people killed by the police, the organization Mapping Police Violence reports at least 1,145 deaths at police hands in 2021 and 1,183 in 2022. Nearly two-thirds of these killings emanated from police responses to reports of suspected nonviolent offenses or incidents in which no crime was reported. At least 115 people killed by police officers in 2021 were stopped initially because of an alleged traffic violation.[11]

Racism's central mechanism of turning fear of difference into an excuse for domination provides a crucible in which other cruelties are learned and legitimated. We live in a time when these cruelties are on full display. The Supreme Court's overturning of the settled law established in the *Roe v. Wade* decision has opened the door to state legislation that makes women's bodies into breeding machines owned by the state, to legislation that steals from women the ability to control their own fertility and their futures, and to legislation that forces victims of incest and rape (even those as young as ten years old) to give birth to their abusers' babies while compelling girls and women to carry nonviable pregnancies to term—at the risk of sepsis, loss of the uterus, and death.

State laws and administrative orders banning evidence-based supportive health interventions for transgender and gender-diverse youth and criminalizing conscientious health care providers promote cruel and harmful misrepresentations of transgender youths and adults while denying them access to necessary medical interventions. State laws banning gender-affirming care for youths in need of it compel doctors to violate their sacred oaths to do no harm because they force these physicians to violate the guidelines of all the major medical organizations and withhold necessary treatments. Explicit legal exclusions from Medicaid for transgender people place them in precarious situations. They can often have standing for legal recognition as transgender only when they challenge how nonrecognition exposes them to conditions that place them in dangerous positions in shelters, public space, and carceral institutions. Yet the Medicaid system's insistence on not recognizing the existence of transgender people denies them access to precisely the medical diagnoses of gender dysphoria that they need.[12] Elected officials dismiss the long-established consensus of medical research by cruelly defining gender-affirming care for transgender youths as child abuse, while vigilantes egged on by well-financed media and political campaigns make bomb and death threats to hospitals that provide that care. The governor of Florida supports and signs a law that enables the state to seize transgender children from parents for the "crime" of helping their children get the medical care that is needed for their specific conditions.

The danger zone of today is shaped by a vicious revanchist backlash against racial justice, one that promotes punitive policies against people in need of health care and housing as part of a coordinated strategy to protect and preserve the unfair gains and unjust enrichments funneled to whiteness by public and private policies. At a time when children from aggrieved racialized groups become ill disproportionately and experience premature death because of housing and health injustice, legislatures in at least ten states (with a dozen more pending) ignore the racialized health crisis and instead pass laws that prohibit K-12 and college teachers from informing students about the true history of racism in the United States on the grounds that this knowledge might make white children feel uncomfortable. White supremacist police and vigilante violence is celebrated by right-wing cable television and radio media personalities—egged on by the former president of the United States and supported by his wealthy donors.

Efforts at meaningful change have been thwarted by the abject failure of governments at all levels to enforce civil rights laws. Neither of the two main political parties has faced up to the health care emergency illustrated by the COVID-19 syndemic, or to the dire shortage of affordable housing caused by privatization policies and the transformation of homes and apartments into globally traded financial assets. These failures are related. In its initial phases the COVID-19 syndemic hit hardest in places where housing was overcrowded, where workers interacted directly with the public as cashiers, public transportation users, and health care workers, and where people endured incarceration in cramped jails and prisons.[13] Many of the people contending with housing insecurity during the syndemic also worked in low-paying but high-risk jobs as "essential workers" forced to endanger their health by traveling on crowded public transit systems to jobs as health care personnel, as retail sales people, and as agricultural laborers.[14] As medical anthropologist, ethnographer, and folklore theorist Charles Briggs observes, "Epidemics X-ray society in such a way as to not only reveal deep fractures and inequities but—altogether too frequently—render them lethal."[15]

The mechanisms impeding understanding of structural and systemic racism rely on fables about a past that never happened and fantasies about a future that will never arrive. A fundamentally flawed and decidedly dishonest narrative about history is deployed to relegate racism to the distant past, to claim that white racism no longer exists because the

Civil War ended slavery and civil rights acts outlawed segregation. Yet the patterns of the past continue to shape injustice in the present through inherited wealth, recognized legal precedents, and pervasive social practices established initially during the eras of slavery and segregation. We see present manifestations of this past in the power and privilege emanating from wealth passed down through generations that was initially secured through overtly racist legal and economic preferences for whiteness. Slavery unwilling to die haunts the present in historically created and continued restrictions on popular democracy such as the Electoral College, the gerrymandering of state and congressional legislative districts, felony disenfranchisement, and measures making voting registration dependent on the forms of identification that racialized would-be voters are least likely to possess. Mechanisms of voter suppression that were initially constructed to protect slavery and Jim Crow segregation persist today to protect whiteness's disproportionate power, unfair gains, and unjust enrichments.

When fables about the past being over are shown to be false, the protectors of the privileges of whiteness sometimes turn to fantasies about the future. Even though racism has not completely disappeared, they argue, it soon will disappear because new generations of young people seem less racist than their parents, because each decade brings new visibility to celebrities and entertainers who are not white, and because artificial technologies separate people and their personas from embodied identities. The proponents of these fantasies tell us that change takes time when in fact, as Catherine MacKinnon has argued, it is actually resistance to change that takes time.[16] In response to problems that demand backbone, these fantasies of current or soon-to-arrive postracialism offer only a wishbone.

There is no automatic inbuilt mechanism of progress in history, only the actions of humans that produce both progress and regress. Fantasies of an innocent past and a color-blind present fuel the folly of pretending that a postracial future is on the way—that it can be secured without costs, without struggle, without accountability or responsibility. A false past and a fabricated future distort the workings of time, especially with respect to the links that connect past, present, and future forms of racial discrimination in housing, health care, employment, education, transportation, taxation, debt collection, insurance, and incarceration. These work relentlessly today as they have in the past: they continue to skew opportunities and life chances unjustly along unequal racial lines.

MASSES IN MOTION FOR JUSTICE

Despite pervasive resistance, struggles for health justice and housing justice are emerging every day in widely diverse contexts and places. According to the American Public Health Association, within two years of the killings of George Floyd and Breonna Taylor, statements identifying racism as a public health hazard had been adopted by more than two hundred city and town councils, county agencies, boards of education, and public health departments and associations.[17] The American Association of Medical Colleges announced a commitment to engaging in self-reflection and education about the long and continuing history of racially exclusionary practices in medical training, and to taking steps to promote greater racial diversity in the profession.[18] Inside schools of medicine and in undergraduate premedical school programs, students and faculty members are attempting to build on previous efforts to increase demographic diversity, improve understanding of the social and structural determinants of health, reduce stigmatizing practices and biases, and challenge curricula that acknowledge racial health disparities but wrongly attribute them disproportionately to biological risk factors.[19] As physician and public health specialist Gbenga Ogedegbe recognizes, achieving the emancipatory aims articulated in the Movement for Black Lives in 2020 demands that "all institutions must be accountable, and all must contribute to eliminating the deeply embodied racism that is woven throughout the fabric of U.S. society."[20]

Increased attention to racial justice is encouraging, but the path from aspiration to achievement on these issues can never be smooth or easy. Racism cannot be wished away or willed away simply by proclaiming good intentions. The premises and practices of racial domination are deeply rooted in a vast array of public and private social policies and processes, in powerful and pervasive structures and systems. People who have been taught all their lives by nearly every major social institution to view racism as merely a matter of personal private prejudice are not well positioned to recognize its place as a locus of public power. People accustomed to understanding racism as a series of aberrant individual, interpersonal, intentional, and isolated actions are not well equipped to discern the ways in which racial domination is enacted, not only by hate-filled snarling racists brandishing guns, nooses, flaming torches, and swastikas, but also calmly and quietly through the ordinary practices of smiling functionaries who shape the everyday conduct of business, law, medicine, education, urban planning, and policing. Some of the people and institutions who seem willing to consider reforms often simply hope to make the crisis go away rather than to establish justice. They shrink large political and moral issues that need to be addressed into small technical or public relations problems that need only minor adjustments in administration and that proclaim good intentions but eschew the difficult work of producing good practices.

Reckoning with the full power and deadly consequences of racial subordination requires short-term and middle-term reforms inside law and medicine and many other areas of social practice, but the true value of these reforms will reside, not solely in the changes they produce in the short and middle run, but rather in the ways in which those changes create transformative experiences that equip as many people as possible with deepened capacities and desires in the long run for the kinds of mutual respect and recognition, honesty and accountability, and democratic deliberation and decision-making needed to upend white supremacy. Changes of this magnitude cannot be attained merely through small reforms in existing practices; they require a radical revolution in values and the promotion of active and engaged participation in public life by people from all sectors of society.

WHO CARES?

In her impassioned study of racism and infant mortality, Monica Casper deploys the dual meanings of the query "Who cares?" as an effective rhetorical device. The verb *to care* connotes feeling interest, concern, or anxiety, yet it can also refer to attending to the needs of someone who is sick. Casper asks readers who cares about the shockingly high numbers of Black infant and maternal deaths in the United States. She also asks who will care for the needs of pregnant women and their offspring.[21] A similar two-sided question needs to be asked about housing and health justice. Who is concerned about the suffering and premature death dealt to members of aggrieved racialized groups by the collateral health consequences of housing discrimination? Who will take responsibility for reducing the number of things that kill and increasing the number of things that cure?

These are not new questions. In 1899 W.E.B. Du Bois addressed racial health disparities in his sociological study *The Philadelphia Negro*.[22] He noted how the damages done to the health of Black people in Philadelphia by housing discrimination, environmental pollution, and medical racism provoked no alarm within the dominant white supremacist institutions. Rather than taking responsibility for the racial disparities produced systemically and structurally, white people attributed the poor health of the Black population to innate inherited biological weaknesses and used those alleged weaknesses as an excuse for passive indifference at best and increased discrimination at worst. Du Bois charged that there had been few cases like this in the history of "civilized peoples" where the suffering of fellow humans had provoked such "peculiar indifference."[23]

Domination provokes passivity, which promotes feelings of powerlessness, isolation, alienation, and apathy. Powerful forces in society beckon people to think of themselves as consumers and spectators, as investors and owners, rather than as workers, neighbors, and members of communities with shared opportunities and responsibilities. In the face of the sharp and systemic crises plaguing the environment, the economy, education, and electoral politics, most people feel that the important decisions that shape their lives are made elsewhere and by others. The dreadful dearth of democracy writ large in the plutocracy that is the political system is writ small in the everyday experiences of powerlessness that people confront as they seek to secure good health and decent housing.

The downward spiral of destruction we experience impels us to ask what kind of people we are going to be and what kind of world we wish to build for ourselves and leave to the future. It challenges us to inquire from whom we can and need to learn. In the face of systemic structures and practices of oppression and deprivation, the very survival of people of color has been a miraculous accomplishment in itself. They have created medical and social homes through parallel institutions that promote practices of healing and health maintenance forged from folk remedies, networks of intergenerational instruction, apprenticeship, and membership, and protective relations that promote healthy adaptations to stress. What once seemed to be their partial and parochial experiences are now general conditions. Their survival strategies have much to teach others.

For millions of people, the killings of Taylor and Floyd were not merely isolated events but actions that illustrated, embodied, distilled, and crystallized complex histories of subordination. The official coverups and justifications of these murders exposed in condensed and dramatic form the meanness and mendacity of white supremacist rule. The legal immunity and performative impunity of the killers made it clear that only a massive collective response could fend off a future of relentless social and physical death. This radical conjuncture sent out shock waves that are still reverberating and hold the potential for a better future but provide no guarantee of it. As always, the future is unwritten. It is up to us to write it. What we do and how we do it can make all the difference in the world. We can contest the peculiar indifference to suffering in our world and participate meaningfully in a struggle that is certain to be brutal and bitter but that through our efforts perhaps might also be made beautiful.

Notes

INTRODUCTION

1. Tricia Rose, *Metaracism: How Systemic Racism Devastates Black Lives—and How We Break Free* (New York: Basic Books, 2024).

2. Tanya Maria Golash-Boza, *Before Gentrification: The Creation of DC's Racial Wealth Gap* (Oakland: University of California Press, 2023); Paige Glotzer, *How the Suburbs Were Segregated: Developers and the Business of Exclusionary Housing, 1880–1960* (New York: Columbia University Press, 2020).

3. Caroline Richmond, "Obituary: Lester Breslow," *The Lancet* 380 (July 21, 2012): 212.

4. Nayan Shah, *Contagious Divides: Epidemics and Race in San Francisco's Chinatown* (Berkeley: University of California Press, 2001); Harriet A. Washington, *Medical Apartheid: The Dark History of Medical Experimentation on Black Americans from Colonial Times to the Present* (New York: Anchor Books, 2006); Natalia Molina, *Fit to Be Citizens? Public Health and Race in Los Angeles, 1879–1939* (Berkeley: University of California Press, 2006).

5. David R. Williams and Chiquita Collins, "Racial Segregation: A Fundamental Cause of Racial Disparities in Health," *Public Health Reports* 115, no. 5 (2001): 404–16.

6. David R. Williams, Jourdyn A. Lawrence, and Brigitte Davis, "Racism and Health: Evidence and Needed Research," *Annual Review of Public Health* 40 (2019): 101–25.

7. Kathryn Strother Ratcliff, *The Social Determinants of Health: Looking Upstream* (Cambridge: Polity Press, 2017); Ingrid R. G. Waldron, *There's Something in the Water: Environmental Racism in Indigenous and Black Communities* (Winnipeg: Fernwood, 2018).

8. Centers for Disease Control and Prevention, "Social Determinants of Health: Frequently Asked Questions," 2011, no longer accessible online but cited in Ratcliff, *Social Determinants of Health*.

9. Gordon B. Lindsay, Ray Merrill, and Riley J. Hedin, "The Contribution of Public Health and Improved Social Conditions to Improved Life Expectancy: An Analysis of Public Awareness," *Journal of Community Medicine and Health Education* 4, no. 5 (2014): 1–5.

10. Lisa Strohschein and Rose Weitz, *The Sociology of Health, Illness, and Health Care in Canada* (Toronto: Nelson Education, 2013).

11. Crista E. Johnson-Agbakwu et al., "Racism, COVID-19, and Health Equity in the USA: A Call to Action," *Journal of Racial and Ethnic Health Disparities* 9 (2022): 52–58.

12. Michelle Smirnova, *The Prescription-to-Prison Pipeline: The Medicalization and Criminalization of Pain* (Durham, NC: Duke University Press, 2023).

13. Richard G. Rogers et al., "Dying Young in the United States: What's Driving High Death Rates among Americans under Age 25 and What Can Be Done?," *Population Bulletin* 76, no. 2 (2023): 1–4.

14. Barbara Reskin, "The Race Discrimination System," *Annual Review of Sociology* 38 (2012): 17–35.

15. Dayna Bowen Matthew, *Just Health: Treating Structural Racism to Heal America* (New York: New York University Press, 2022), 24.

16. George Lipsitz, *The Possessive Investment in Whiteness: How White People Profit from Identity Politics*, 20th anniversary ed. (Philadelphia: Temple University Press, 2018).

17. Junia Howell, Ellen Whitehead, and Elizabeth Korver-Glenn, "Still Separate and Unequal: Persistent Racial Segregation and Inequality in Subsidized Housing," *Socius: Sociological Research for a Dynamic World* 9 (2023): 1–16.

18. Ruha Benjamin, *Viral Justice: How We Grow the World We Want* (Princeton, NJ: Princeton University Press, 2022), 11.

19. Benjamin, *Viral Justice*.

20. Laurence Ralph, "Becoming Aggrieved: An Alternative Framework of Care in Black Chicago," *RSF: The Russell Sage Foundation Journal of the Social Sciences* 1, no. 2 (November 2015): 31–41.

21. Jonathan Metzl, *The Protest Psychosis: How Schizophrenia Became a Black Disease* (Boston: Beacon Press, 2009).

22. Ralph, "Becoming Aggrieved"; Mindy Thompson Fullilove, *Urban Alchemy* (New York: New Village Press, 2013).

23. Jodi Rios, *Black Lives and Spatial Matters: Policing Blackness and Practicing Freedom in Suburban St. Louis* (Ithaca, NY: Cornell University Press, 2020).

24. David Satcher et al., "What If We Were Equal? A Comparison of the Black-White Mortality Gap in 1960 and 2000," *Health Affairs* 24, no. 2 (March 2005): 459–64.

25. Steven Woolf et al., "The Health Impact of Resolving Racial Disparities: An Analysis of US Mortality Data," *American Journal of Public Health* 98, suppl. 1 (September 2008): S26-S28.

26. Clarence C. Gravlee, "How Race Becomes Biology: Embodiment of Social Inequality," *American Journal of Physical Anthropology* 139 (2008): 47–57.

27. César Caraballo et al., "Excess Mortality and Years of Potential Life Lost among the Black Population in the US, 1999–2020," *JAMA* 329, no. 19 (May 16, 2023): 1625–1710.

28. Lipsitz, *Possessive Investment in Whiteness.*

29. Tonantzin Carmona, "Understanding Latino Wealth to Address Disparities and Design Better Policies," Brookings, July 13, 2023, www.brookings.edu/articles/understanding-latino-wealth/.

30. Thomas M. Shapiro, *The Hidden Cost of Being African American: How Wealth Perpetuates Inequality* (New York: Oxford University Press, 2004).

31. Carmona, "Understanding Latino Wealth."

32. Lipsitz, *Possessive Investment in Whiteness.*

33. Glotzer, *How the Suburbs Were Segregated*; N. Shah, *Contagious Divides.*

34. Glotzer, *How the Suburbs Were Segregated.*

35. AFSCME 3299, "Letter: Unions & Housing Advocates Continue to Call on UC to Divest from Blackstone and Instead Chart New Course on Affordable Housing," March 15, 2023, https://afscme3299.org/media/news/letter-unions-housing-advocates-continue-to-call-on-uc-to-divest-from-blackstone-and-instead-chart-new-course-on-affordable-housing/.

36. Alliance of Californians for Community Empowerment and Private Equity Stakeholder Project, "Blackstone Comes to Collect: How America's Largest Landlord and Wall Street's Highest Paid CEO Are Jacking Up Rents and Ramping Up Evictions," March 25, 2023, https://pestakeholder.org/reports/blackstone-comes-to-collect-how-americas-largest-landlord-and-wall-streets-highest-paid-ceo-are-jacking-up-rents-and-ramping-up-evictions/#:~:text=The%20Private%20Equity%20Stakeholder%20Project,highlights%20San%20Diego%20County%2C%20where.

37. Davarian Baldwin, *In the Shadow of the Ivory Tower: How Universities Are Plundering Our Cities* (New York: Bold Type Books, 2021); Lawrence T. Brown, *The Black Butterfly: The Harmful Politics of Race and Space in America* (Baltimore: Johns Hopkins University Press, 2021).

38. Anne Pollock, *Medicating Race* (Durham, NC: Duke University Press, 2012).

39. Carolyn Moxley Rouse, *Uncertain Suffering: Racial Health Disparities and Sickle Cell Disease* (Berkeley: University of California Press, 2009).

40. Bernard Goldstein, "The Precautionary Principle Also Applies to Public Health Actions," *American Journal of Public Health* 91, no. 3 (2001): 1358–61.

41. Sadiqa Kendi and Michelle Macy, "The Injury Equity Framework: Establishing a Unified Approach for Addressing Inequalities," *New England Journal of Medicine* 388 (2023): 774–76.

42. Bret Thiele, "The Human Right to Adequate Housing: A Tool for Promoting and Protecting Individual and Community Health," *American Journal of Public Health* 92, no. 5 (May 2002): 712–15.

43. Robert E. Lang and Rebecca H. Sohmer, "Legacy of the Housing Act of 1949: The Past, Present, and Future of Federal Housing and Urban Policy," *Housing Policy Debate* 11, no. 2 (2000): 291–98.

44. Toni Morrison, "Home," in *The House That Race Built: Black Americans, U.S. Terrain,* ed. Wahneema Lubiano (New York: Pantheon Books, 1997), 3–12.

45. Katherine Verdery, *What Was Socialism and What Comes Next?* (Princeton, NJ: Princeton University Press, 1996), 16.

46. Martin Luther King Jr., "A Time to Break Silence," in *A Testament of Hope: The Essential Writings and Speeches of Martin Luther King, Jr.,* ed. James M. Washington (New York: Harper Collins, 1986), 231–34.

CHAPTER 1

1. Mona Hanna-Attisha et al., "Elevated Blood Lead Levels in Children Associated with the Flint Drinking Water Crisis: A Spatial Analysis of Risk and Public Health Response," *American Journal of Public Health* 106, no. 2 (2016): 283–90, https://doi.org/10.2105/AJPH.2015.303003.

2. Committee on Obstetric Practice, "Lead Screening during Pregnancy and Lactation," Committee Opinion No. 533, August 2012, www.acog.org/clinical/clinical-guidance/committee-opinion/articles/2012/08/lead-screening-during-pregnancy-and-lactation#:~:text=Committee%20on%20Obstetric%20Practice&text=Abstract%3A%20Prenatal%20lead%20exposure%20has,in%20both%20children%20and%20adults.

3. L. Brown, *Black Butterfly*.

4. Christine MacDonald, "Detroit Kids' Lead Poisoning Rates Higher Than Flint," *Detroit News,* November 14, 2017, www.detroitnews.com/story/news/local/detroit-city/2017/11/14/lead-poisoning-children-detroit/107683688/; Alexa Eisenberg et al., "Toxic Structures: Speculation and Lead Exposure in Detroit's Single-Family Rental Market," *Health and Place* 64 (2020): 1–10.

5. Heather Moody, Joe T. Darden, and Bruce Wm. Pigozzi, "The Relationship of Neighborhood Socioeconomic Differences and Racial Residential Segregation in Childhood Blood Levels in Metropolitan Detroit," *Journal of Urban Health* 93, no. 5 (2016): 820–39.

6. Childhood Lead Poisoning Prevention Program (CLPPP), "2016 Data Report on Childhood Lead Testing and Elevated Levels: Michigan," Childhood Lead Prevention Program, Division of Environmental Health, Michigan Department of Health and Human Services, May 1, 2018, updated November 26, 2018, www.michigan.gov/-/media/Project/Websites/mileadsafe/Reports/2016_CLPPP_Annual_Report_5-1-18.pdf?rev=607b44316e234a4fbf41375bd80c1882.

7. Jayajit Chakraborty and Paul A. Zandberger, "Children at Risk, Measuring Racial/Ethnic Disparities in Potential Exposure to Air Pollution at School and Home," *Journal of Epidemiology and Community Health* 61, no. 12 (December 2007): 1074–79.

8. Ratcliff, *Social Determinants of Health*.

9. A.R. Abelsohn and M. Sanborn, "Lead and Children: Clinical Management for Family Physicians," *Canadian Family Physician / Medecin de Famille Canadien* 56, no. 6 (2010): 531–35.

10. Harriet Washington, *A Terrible Thing to Waste: Environmental Racism and Its Assault on the American Mind* (New York: Little Brown Spark, 2019).

11. Steve Neavling, "Lead Poisoning Endangers Generations of Detroit Children with No End in Sight," *Metro Times*, November 18, 2020, www.metrotimes .com/news/lead-poisoning-endangers-generations-of-detroit-children-with-no -end-in-sight-25809555.

12. Robert J. Sampson and Alix S. Winter, "The Racial Ecology of Lead Poisoning: Toxic Inequality in Chicago Neighborhoods, 1995–2013," *Du Bois Review* 13, no. 2 (2016): 261–84; Paul B. Stretesky, "The Distribution of Air Lead Levels across U.S. Counties: Implications for the Production of Racial Inequality," *Sociological Spectrum* 23, no. 1 (2003): 91–118.

13. Rebecca Kinney, "America's Great Comeback Story: The White Possessive in Detroit Tourism," *American Quarterly* 70, no. 4 (December 2018): 777–806.

14. Heather A. Moody and Sue C. Grady, "Lead Emissions and Population Vulnerability in the Detroit (Michigan, USA) Metropolitan Area, 2006–2013: A Spatial and Temporal Analysis," *International Journal of Environmental Research and Public Health* 14, no. 12 (2017): 1445, and "Lead Emissions and Population Vulnerability in the Detroit Metropolitan Area, 2006–2013: Impact of Pollution, Housing Age and Neighborhood Racial Isolation and Poverty on Blood Lead in Children," *International Journal of Environmental Research and Public Health* 18, no. 5 (2021): 2747.

15. Eisenberg et al., "Toxic Structures."

16. Eisenberg et al., "Toxic Structures."

17. Moody, Darden, and Pigozzi, "Relationship."

18. Heather Moody, Linda Elaine Easley, and Melissa Sissen, "Water Shutoffs during Covid-19 and Black Lives: Case Study Detroit," *Environmental Justice* 15, no. 5 (2022): 313–18.

19. Alexandra R. Mueller and Utpal Dutta, "Brownfields and Children under 18 in Detroit," *Journal of Civil Engineering and Architecture* 15 (2021): 17–27; Rector, *Toxic Debt.*

20. Josiah Rector, *Toxic Debt: An Environmental Justice History of Detroit* (Chapel Hill: University of North Carolina Press, 2022).

21. Moody, Easley, and Sissen, "Water Shutoffs."

22. Rector, *Toxic Debt.*

23. Eisenberg et al., "Toxic Structures"; A. Mueller and Dutta, "Brownfields"; Moody and Grady, "Lead Emissions" [2021]; Moody, Darden, and Pigozzi, "Relationship."

24. Andrew W. Kahrl, *The Black Tax: 150 Years of Theft, Exploitation, and Dispossession in America* (Chicago: University of Chicago Press, 2024); Danielle Purifoy and Louise Seamster, "Creative Extraction: Black Towns in White Space," *Environment and Planning D: Society and Space* 39, no. 1 (2021):

47–66; Louise Seamster, "When Democracy Disappears: Emergency Management in Benton Harbor," *Du Bois Review* 15, no. 2 (2018): 295–322.

25. Eisenberg et al. "Toxic Structures."

26. Moody, Darden, and Pigozzi, "Relationship"; Moody and Grady, "Lead Emissions" [2021].

27. Rector, *Toxic Debt.*

28. AirNow, "Air Quality Index (AQI) Basics," accessed October 14, 2023, www.airnow.gov/aqi/aqi-basics/.

29. Sarah Rios, "Valley Fever: Environmental Racism and Health Justice" (PhD diss., University of California, Santa Barbara, 2018).

30. Phil Brown et al., "The Health Politics of Asthma: Environmental Justice and Collective Illness Experience," in *Contested Illness: Citizens, Science, and Health Social Movements,* ed. Phil Brown et al. (Berkeley: University of California Press, 2012), 108–22.

31. Rachel Morello-Frosch, Manuel Pastor, and James Sadd, "Environmental Justice and the Precautionary Principle: Air Toxics Exposures and Health Risks among School Children in Los Angeles," in *Contested Illnesses: Citizens, Science, and Health Social Movements,* ed. Phil Brown et al. (Berkeley: University of California Press, 2012), 64–76.

32. Neal J. Wilson, "Building Equity by Eliminating Lead Poisoning: Prospects for a Green New Deal," Working Paper No. 131, Global Institute for Sustainable Prosperity, August 2021, www.global-isp.org/wp-content/uploads/WP-131.pdf.

33. Jill E. Johnston and Andrea Hricko, "Industrial Lead Poisoning in Los Angeles: Anatomy of a Public Health Failure," *Environmental Justice* 10, no. 5 (2017): 162–67.

34. Sydney Leibel et al., "Screening Social Determinants of Health in a Multidisciplinary Severe Asthma Clinic Program," *Pediatric Quality and Safety* 5, no. 5 (2020): 1–6.

35. Lindsay Dillon and Julie Sze, "Police Power and Particulate Matters: Environmental Justice and the Spatialities of In/Securities in U.S. Cities," *English Language Notes* 54, no. 2 (Fall/Winter 2016): 13–23.

36. Julie Sze, *Environmental Justice in a Moment of Danger* (Oakland: University of California Press, 2020).

37. Kiana D. Bess, Alison Miller, and Roshanak Meddipanah, "The Effects of Housing Insecurity on Children's Health: A Scoping Review," *Health Promotion International* 38, no. 3 (2022): 1–11, https://doi.org/10.1093/heapro/daaco06; Jonathan M. Gabbay, Amanda M. Stewart, and Ann Chen Wu, "Housing Instability and Homelessness: An Untreated Pediatric Chronic Condition," *JAMA Pediatrics* 176, no. 11 (November 1, 2022): 1063–64, https://doi.org/10.1001/jamapediatrics.2022.3258. I use the term *houseless* rather than *homeless* because the latter has collected a number of stigmatizing assumptions about lack of shelter as a personal problem caused by personal failings rather than a social problem caused by society's failure to offer access to safe, healthful, and affordable dwellings. It also mistakenly implies that people who lack secure housing do not make homes in the sense of communities. Yet houseless people do make social homes for themselves as they sleep on the streets, in

vacant lots, in parks, under overpasses, or in their cars and trucks. Many of those who are houseless live in encampments where they interact constantly with other similarly situated people and work constructively for mutual survival. Gordon C. C. Douglas, "Reclaiming Placemaking for an Alternative Politics of Legitimacy and Community in Homelessness," *International Journal of Politics, Culture, and Society* 36 (2022): 35–56.

38. Megan Sandel et al., "Unstable Housing and Caregiver and Child Health in Renter Families," *Pediatrics* 141, no. 2 (2018): 1–10.

39. Earl J. Edwards and Pedro Noguera, "Seeing Our Most Vulnerable Homeless Students," in *Systemic Racism in America,* ed. Rashawn Ray and Hoda Mahmoudi (New York: Routledge, 2022), 112–38.

40. Gabbay, Stewart, and Wu, "Housing Instability and Homelessness."

41. Gabbay, Stewart, and Wu, "Housing Instability."

42. Liat Ben-Moshe, *Decarcerating Disability: Deinstitutionalization and Prison Abolition* (Minneapolis: University of Minnesota Press, 2022).

43. Portia Johnson et al., "Association of Perceived Racial Discrimination with Eating Behaviors and Obesity among Participants in the *Sister Talk* Study," *Journal of the National Black Nurses Association* 23, no. 1 (July 2012): 34–40.

44. D. Williams, Lawrence, and Davis, "Racism and Health."

45. Andrew S. Garner and Jack P. Shonkoff, "Early Childhood Adversity, Toxic Stress, and the Role of the Pediatrician: Translating Developmental Science into Lifelong Health," *Pediatrics* 129, no. 1 (2012): e224–e231.

46. Wayne Chan and Rodolfo Mendoza-Denton, "Status Based Recognition Sensitivity among Asian Americans: Implications for Psychological Distress," *Journal of Personality* 76, no. 5 (2008): 1320.

47. Nancy Krieger, "Discrimination and Health Inequities," in *Social Epidemiology,* ed. Lisa F. Berkman and Ichiro Kawaki (New York: Oxford University Press, 2000), 36–75.

48. Anne Fausto-Sterling, "Refashioning Race: DNA and the Politics of Health Care," *differences: A Journal of Feminist Cultural Studies* 15, no. 3 (2004): 27–28.

49. Jeremy P. Jamieson et al., "Experiencing Discrimination Increases Risk Taking," *Psychological Science* 24, no. 2 (2013): 131–39.

50. Kathy Sanders-Phillips et al., "Social Inequality and Racial Discrimination: Risk Factors for Health Disparities in Children of Color," *Pediatrics* 124, no. 3 (2009): S176–S186.

51. W. Chan and Mendoza-Denton, "Status Based Recognition Sensitivity"; John Mirowsky and Catherine Ross, *Social Causes of Psychological Distress* (New Brunswick, NJ: Aldine Transaction, 2012).

52. Carol Koplan and Anna Chard, "Adverse Early Life Experiences as a Social Determinant of Mental Health," *Psychiatric Annals* 44, no. 1 (2014): 39–45.

53. Gerald Markowitz and David Rossner, *Lead Wars: The Politics of Science and the Fate of America's Children* (Berkeley: University of California Press, 2013): Washington, *Terrible Thing to Waste.*

54. James S. House, *Beyond Obamacare: Life, Death, and Social Policy* (New York: Russell Sage Foundation, 2015).

55. Tené T. Lewis et al., "Self-Reported Experiences of Everyday Discrimination Are Associated with Elevated C-Reactive Protein Levels in Older African-American Adults," *Brain, Behavior, and Immunity* 24 (2010): 438–44; Miriam E. Van Dyke et al., "Socioeconomic Status Discrimination and C-Reactive Protein in African-American and White Adults," *Psychoneuroendocrinology* 82 (August 2017): 9–16.

56. Timothy Jellyman and Nicholas Spencer, "Residential Mobility in Childhood and Health Outcomes: A Systematic Review," *Journal of Epidemiology and Community Health* 62, no. 7 (July 2008): 584–92; Sandel et al., "Unstable Housing."

57. Velma McBride Murry et al., "Racial Discrimination as a Moderator of the Links among Stress, Maternal Psychological Functioning and Family Relationships," *Journal of Marriage and Family* 63, no. 4 (2001): 915–26; Fullilove, *Urban Alchemy*; Mindy Thompson Fullilove, *Root Shock: How Tearing Up City Neighborhoods Hurts America and What We Can Do about It* (New York: Ballantine, 2015).

58. Courtney E. Boen, "Criminal Justice Contacts and Psychophysiological Functioning in Early Adulthood: Health Equity in the Carceral State," *Journal of Health and Social Behavior* 61, no. 3 (2020): 290–306.

59. Sandel et al., "Unstable Housing."

60. Nancy McArdle and Delores Acevedo-Garcia, "Consequences of Segregation for Children's Opportunity and Well-Being," in *The Affordable Housing Reader*, 2nd ed., ed. Elizabeth J. Mueller and J. Rosie Tighe (London: Routledge, 2017), 113–22.

61. Johnson-Agbakwu et al., "Racism, COVID-19."

62. Raj Chetty and Nathaniel Hendren, "The Impacts of Neighborhoods on Intergenerational Mobility I: Childhood Exposure Effects," *Quarterly Journal of Economics* 133, no. 3 (2018): 1107–62.

63. Raj Chetty, Nathaniel Hendren, and Lawrence F. Katz, "The Effects of Exposure to Better Neighborhoods on Children: New Evidence from the Moving to Opportunity Experiment," *American Economic Review* 106, no. 4 (2016): 855–902; Craig Evan Pollack et al., "Association of a Housing Mobility Program with Childhood Asthma Symptoms and Exacerbations," *JAMA* 329, no. 19 (May 16, 2023): 1671–81.

64. Antwan Jones, Gregory D. Squires, and Sarah Crump, "The Relationship between Inclusionary Zoning Policies and Population Health," *Housing and Society* 49, no. 1 (2022): 38–57.

65. Jonathan M. Metzl and Helena Hansen, "Structural Competency: Theorizing a New Medical Engagement with Stigma and Inequality," *Social Science Medicine* no. 106 (2014): 126–33.

66. Allison Bovell-Ammon et al., "Housing Is Health: A Renewed Call for Federal Housing Investments in Affordable Housing for Families with Children," *Academic Pediatrics* 21, no. 1 (2021): 19–23.

67. Matthew Desmond and Rachel Tolbert Kimbro, "Eviction's Fallout: Housing, Hardship, and Health," *Social Forces* 94, no. 1 (2015): 295–324.

68. Bovell-Ammon et al., "Housing Is Health."

69. Nancy Krieger, "Embodiment: A Conceptual Glossary for Epidemiology," *Journal for Epidemiology and Community Health* 59 (2005): 350–55; Richard Wilkinson and Kate Pickett, *The Spirit Level: Why More Equal Societies Almost Always Do Better* (London: Allen Lane, 2009).

70. Washington, *Terrible Thing to Waste*.

71. Lindsay, Merrill, and Hedin, "Contribution."

72. Centers for Disease Control and Prevention, "A Century of U.S. Water Chlorination and Treatment: One of the Ten Greatest Public Health Achievements of the Twentieth Century," *Morbidity and Mortality Weekly Report* 48, no. 29 (1999): 621–29.

73. Michael Stein and Sandro Galea, *The Picture of Health* (Washington, DC: APHA Press, 2022).

74. Sarah E. L. Wakefield and Jamie Baxter, "Linking Health Inequality and Environmental Justice: Articulating a Precautionary Framework for Research and Action," *Environmental Justice* 3, no. 3 (September 2010): 95–102.

75. Lipsitz, *Possessive Investment in Whiteness*.

76. Heather R. Abraham, "Segregation Autopilot: How the Government Perpetuates Segregation and How to Stop It," *Iowa Law Review* 107 (2022): 1963–2025.

77. Quoted in Abraham, "Segregation Autopilot," 1971.

78. Thompson v. U.S. Department of Housing and Urban Development, 348 F. Supp. 2d 398 (D. Md. 2005).

79. Muhieddine Labban et al., "Disparities in Travel-Related Barriers to Accessing Health Care from the 2017 National Household Travel Survey," *JAMA Network Open* 6, no. 7 (2023): 1–14.

80. Carmona, "Understanding Latino Wealth."

81. Alliance for California Traditional Arts, *Building Healthy Communities: Approaching Health through Heritage and Culture in Boyle Heights* (Los Angeles: California Endowment, 2014).

82. Opportunity360, *Report for Census Tract: 2042*, Opportunity360 Measurement Report, Enterprise Community Partners, n.d., 24, accessed December 11, 2019, enterprisecommunity.org/opportunity360, no longer accessible at website.

83. George Lipsitz and Alliance for California Traditional Arts, *Saludarte: Building Health Equity on the Bedrock of Traditional Arts and Culture* (Los Angeles: Alliance for California Traditional Arts, 2020), 69.

84. Lipsitz and Alliance, *Saludarte*, 68.

85. Akira Boch, Betty Marin, and Quetzal Flores, "Restorative Justice through Quilting—A Building Healthy Communities Story," YouTube, August 14, 2020, www.youtube.com/watch?v=zrm51DC7S4Y&feature=youtu.be.

CHAPTER 2

1. Tricia Rose, *Black Noise: Rap Music and Black Culture in Contemporary America* (Hanover, NH: Wesleyan/University Press of New England, 1994); Jordan T. Camp, *Incarcerating the Crisis: Freedom Struggles and the Rise of the Neoliberal State* (Oakland: University of California Press, 2016).

2. Richard Powell and Jeremy Porter, "Redlining, Concentrated Disadvantage, and Crime: The Effects of Discriminatory Government Policies on Urban Violent Crime," *American Journal of Criminal Justice* 48 (August 2022): 1132–56, https://doi.org/10.1007/s12103-022-09688-3.

3. Nick Graetz and Michael Esposito, "Historical Redlining and Contemporary Racial Disparities in Neighborhood Life Expectancy," *Social Forces* 102, no. 1 (September 2023): 1–22.

4. Glotzer, *How the Suburbs Were Segregated;* Kelly Lytle Hernández, *City of Inmates: Conquest, Rebellion, and the Rise of Human Caging in Los Angeles, 1771–1965* (Chapel Hill: University of North Carolina Press, 2017); Walter Johnson, *The Broken Heart of America: St. Louis and the Violent History of the United States* (New York: Basic Books, 2020); George Lipsitz, *How Racism Takes Place* (Philadelphia: Temple University Press, 2011).

5. K-Sue Park, "How Did Redlining Make Money?," Just Money, September 25, 2020, https://justmoney.org/k-sue-park-how-did-redlining-make-money/; Glotzer, *How the Suburbs Were Segregated;* Graetz and Esposito, "Historical Redlining."

6. Powell and Porter, "Redlining"; Christopher J. Lyons, Maria B. Velez, and Xuanying Chen, "Inheriting the Grade: HOLC 'Redlining' Maps and Contemporary Neighborhood Crime," *Socius: Sociological Research for a Dynamic World* 9 (2023): 1–19; Sebastian Linde et al., "Historic Residential Redlining and Present Day Social Determinants of Health, Home Evictions, and Food Insecurity within US Neighborhoods," *Journal of General Internal Medicine* 38 (June 2023): 3321–28, https://doi.org/10.1007/s11606-023-08258-5.

7. Jason Reece, "Confronting the Legacy of 'Separate but Equal': Can the History of Race, Real Estate, and Discrimination Engage and Inform Contemporary Policy?," *RSF: The Russell Sage Foundation Journal of the Social Sciences* 7, no. 1 (2021): 110–33.

8. Elizabeth McClure et al., "The Legacy of Redlining in the Effect of Foreclosure on Detroit's Residents' Self-Rated Health," *Health and Place* 55 (2019): 9–19.

9. Anthony Nardone, Joey Chiang, and Jason Coburn, "Historic Redlining and Urban Health Today in U.S. Cities," *Environmental Justice* 13, no. 4 (2020): 109–19.

10. Emile E. Lynch et al, "The Legacy of Structural Racism: Associations between Historic Redlining, Current Mortgage Lending, and Health," *Population Health* 14 (June 2021): 1–10.

11. Ashanté M. Reese, *Black Food Geographies: Race, Self-Reliance, and Food Access in Washington, D.C.* (Chapel Hill: University of North Carolina Press, 2019).

12. M. Stein and Galea, *Picture of Health.*

13. Courtney E. Boen, Lisa A. Keister, and Nick Graetz, "Household Wealth and Child Body Mass Index: Patterns and Mechanisms," *RSF: The Russell Sage Foundation Journal of the Social Sciences* 7, no. 3 (2021): 80–100.

14. Gracie Himmelstein, Joniqua N. Ceasar, and Kathryn E. W. Himmelstein, "Hospitals That Serve Many Black Patients Have Lower Revenues and Profits: Structural Racism in Hospital Financing," *Journal of General Internal Medicine* 38, no. 3 (2023): 586–91.

15. Ashish J. Jha et al., "Concentration and Quality of Hospitals That Care for Elderly Black Patients," *Archives of Internal Medicine* 167, no. 11 (2007): 1177–82.

16. G. Himmelstein et al., "Hospitals That Serve."

17. Moon-kie Jung, *Beneath the Surface of White Supremacy: Denaturalizing U.S. Racisms Past and Present* (Stanford, CA: Stanford University Press, 2015).

18. Shanna Smith and Cathy Cloud, "Welcome to the Neighborhood? The Persistence of Discrimination and Segregation," in *The Integration Debate: Competing Futures for America's Cities,* ed. Chester Hartman and Gregory D. Squires (New York, Routledge, 2010), 9–22.

19. Gregory D. Squires and Charis E. Kubrin, *Privileged Places: Race, Residence, and the Structures of Opportunity* (Boulder, CO: Lynne Rienner, 2006); Chenoa Flippen, "Unequal Returns to Housing Investment: A Study of Real Housing Appreciation among Black, White, and Hispanic Households," *Social Forces* 82, no. 4 (2006): 1523–55; Camille Zubrinsky Charles, *Won't You Be My Neighbor? Race, Class, and Residence in Los Angeles* (New York: Russell Sage Foundation, 2006).

20. Natasha Hicks et al., *Still Running Up the Down Escalator: How Narratives Shape Our Understanding of Racial Wealth Inequality* (Durham, NC: Samuel Dubois Cook Center on Social Equality, 2021).

21. Margery A. Turner et al., *Housing Discrimination against Racial and Ethnic Minorities* (Washington, DC: US Department of Housing and Urban Development, Office of Policy and Development Research, 2013).

22. Benjamin Edelman, Michael Luca, and Dan Svirsky, "Racial Discrimination in the Sharing Economy: Evidence from a Field Experiment," *American Economic Journal: Applied Economics* 9, no. 92 (April 2017): 1–22.

23. John Robinson III, "Making Markets on the Margins: Housing Finance Agencies and the Racial Politics of Credit Expansion," *American Journal of Sociology* 125, no. 4 (2020): 974–1029.

24. Stephen Menendian and Richard Rothstein, "The Kerner Commission and Housing Policy: The Road Not Taken: Housing and Criminal Justice 50 Years after the Kerner Commission Report," with Nirali Beri, in E. Mueller and Tigue, *Affordable Housing Reader,* 41–51.

25. Matthew, *Just Health.*

26. Samuel Stein, *Capital City: Gentrification and the Real Estate State* (New York: Verso, 2019).

27. Antwan Jones, Squires, and Crump, "Relationship."

28. Matthew Desmond, "Unaffordable America: Poverty, Housing, and Eviction," in E. Mueller and Tigue, *Affordable Housing Reader,* 389–95.

29. Ryan Finnegan, "The Growth and Shifting Spatial Distribution of Tent Encampments in Oakland, California," *Annals of the American Academy of Political and Social Science* 693, no. 1 (January 2021): 284–300.

30. Paul Kiel and Annie Waldman, "The Color of Debt: How Collection Suits Squeeze Black Neighborhoods," ProPublica, October 8, 2015, www .propublica.org/article/debt-collection-lawsuits-squeeze-black-neighborhoods.

31. Douglas S. Massey, *Categorically Unequal: The American Stratification System* (New York: Russell Sage Foundation, 2007), 111.

32. Sampson and Winter, "Racial Ecology."

33. Center on the Developing Child, *Moving Upstream: Confronting Racism to Open Up Children's Potential* (Cambridge, MA: Center on the Developing Child, Harvard University, 2021), 1–20.

34. Patrick Sharkey, *Stuck in Place: Urban Neighborhoods and the End of Progress toward Racial Equality* (Chicago: University of Chicago Press, 2013).

35. Antwan Jones, Squires, and Crump, "Relationship."

36. Gregg Colburn and Clayton Page Aldern, *Homelessness Is a Housing Problem: How Structural Factors Explain U.S. Patterns* (Oakland: University of California Press, 2022).

37. Lawrence Chang et al., "Association of Homelessness with Emergency Department Use among Children in New York," *JAMA Pediatrics* 177, no. 6 (2023): 637–40.

38. D. Williams, Lawrence, and Davis, "Racism and Health."

39. Aijaz Farooqi, M. Adamson Fredrik Serenius, and Bruno Hägglöf, "Executive Functioning and Learning Skills of Adolescent Children Born at Fewer Than 26 Weeks of Gestation," *PLoSOne* 11, no. 3 (2016), https:/doi.org/10.1371/journal.pone.0151819.

40. Zinzi D. Bailey, Justin M. Feldman, and Mary T. Bassett, "How Structural Racism Works: Racist Policies as a Root Cause of U.S. Racial Health Inequities," *New England Journal of Medicine* 384, no. 8 (2021): 768–73.

41. Qinjin Fan et al., "Housing Insecurity among Patients with Cancer," *Journal of the National Cancer Institute* 114, no. 12 (September 21, 2022): 1584–92.

42. Nicole Mlynaryk, "Cancer Patients Facing Housing Instability Show Greater Risk of Mortality," *UC San Diego Today*, September 16, 2022, https://today.ucsd.edu/story/cancer-patients-facing-housing-instability-show-greater-risk-of-mortality.

43. David Ansell, *The Death Gap: How Inequality Kills* (Chicago: University of Chicago Press, 2017).

44. Nancy Krieger, "Discrimination and Health Inequities," *International Journal of Health Services* 44, no. 4 (2014): 643–710; D. Williams and Collins, "Racial Segregation"; Sampson and Winter, "Racial Ecology"; Stephanie White and Olutosin Ojugbele, "Addressing Racial Disparities in Medical Education," *Curriculum in Context* 6, no. 2 (July 2019): 1–6.

45. Smirnova, *Prescription-to-Prison Pipeline.*

46. Ratcliff, *Social Determinants of Health;* S. White and Ojugbele, "Addressing Racial Disparities."

47. Dillon and Sze, "Police Power."

48. Cynthia G. Colen, "Addressing Racial Disparities in Health Using Life Course Perspectives: Toward a Constructive Criticism," *Du Bois Review* 8, no. 1 (2011): 79–94.

49. Robert Bullard, "Environmental Racism and the Environmental Justice Movement," in *Global Environmental Politics: From Person to Planet,* ed. Simon Nicholson and Paul Wagner (New York: Routledge, 2014), 238–45.

50. Sampson and Winter, "Racial Ecology."

51. Nadine Ehlers and Leslie R. Hinkson, "Introduction: Race-Based Medicine and the Specter of Debt," in *Subprime Health: Debt and Race in US Medi-*

cine, ed. Nadine Ehlers and Leslie R. Hinkson (Minneapolis: University of Minnesota Press, 2017), vii–xxxi.

52. K. M. Schmit, Z. Wansaula, R. Pratt, and A. J. Langer, "Tuberculosis-United States," *Morbidity and Mortality Weekly Report* no. 66 (2017): 289–94.

53. Ehlers and Hinkson, "Introduction."

54. M. Stein and Galea, *Picture of Health.*

55. Matthew Henry, *Hydronarratives: Water, Environmental Justice and a Just Transition* (Lincoln: University of Nebraska Press, 2022).

56. Dolores Acevedo-Garcia, "Zip Code-Level Risk Factors for Tuberculosis: Neighborhood Environment and Residential Segregation in New Jersey, 1985–1992," *American Journal of Public Health* 91, no. 5 (2001): 734–41; Colen, "Addressing Racial Disparities"; Richard S. Cooper et al., "Relationship between Premature Mortality and Socioeconomic Factors in Black and White Populations of U.S. Metropolitan Areas," *Public Health Reports* 116, no. 5 (2001): 464–73; Sue C. Grady, "Racial Disparities in Low Birthweight and the Contribution of Residential Segregation: A Multilevel Analysis," *Social Science and Medicine* 63, no. 12 (2006): 3013–29; Sharon A. Jackson et al., "The Relation of Residential Segregation to All-Cause Mortality: A Study in Black and White," *American Journal of Public Health* 90, no. 4 (2000): 615–17; Thomas A. La Veist, "Racial Segregation and Longevity among African Americans: An Individual-Level Analysis," *Health Services Research* 38, no. 6, part 2 (2003): 1719–34; S. V. Subramanian, Dolores Acevedo-Garcia, and Theresa Osypuk, "Racial Residential Segregation and Geographic Heterogeneity in Black/White Disparity in Poor Self-Rated Health in the U.S.: A Multilevel Statistical Analysis," *Social Science and Medicine* 60, no. 8 (2005): 1667–79.

57. Ansell, *Death Gap;* Gilbert C. Gee and Chandra L. Ford, "Structural Racism and Health Inequities: Old Issues, New Directions," *Du Bois Review* 8, no. 1 (2011): 115–32; Dorceta E. Taylor, *Toxic Communities: Environmental Racism, Industrial Pollution, and Residential Mobility* (New York: New York University Press, 2014).

58. Rachel Connolly et al., "The Association of Green Space, Tree Canopy and Parks with Life Expectancy in Neighborhoods in Los Angeles," *Environment International* 173 (March 2023): 107785, https://doi.org/10.1016/j.envint.2023.107785.

59. J. Voelkel et al., "Assessing Vulnerability to Urban Heat: A Study of Disproportionate Heat Exposure and Access to Refuge by Socio-Demographic Status in Portland, Oregon," *International Journal of Environmental Research and Public Health* 15 (2018): 640, https://doi.10.3390/ijerph15040640; Eric Klinenberg, *Heat Wave: A Social Autopsy of Disaster in Chicago* (Chicago: University of Chicago Press, 2015).

60. Bev Wilson, "Urban Heat Management and the Legacy of Redlining," *Journal of the American Planning Association* 88, no. 4 (2020): 443–57.

61. Jeremy S. Hoffman, Vivek Shandas, and Nicholas Pendleton, "The Effects of Historical Housing Policies on Resident Exposure to Intra-urban Heat: A Study of 108 US Urban Areas," *Climate* 8, no. 1 (2020), https://doi.10.3390/cli8010012.

62. Md Mostafijur Rahman et al., "The Effects of Coexposure to Extremes of Heat and Particulate Air Pollution on Mortality in California: Implications for Climate Change," *American Journal of Respiratory and Critical Care Medicine* 206, no. 9 (2022): 1117–27.

63. House, *Beyond Obamacare;* Bailey, Feldman, and Bassett, "How Structural Racism Works."

64. Linda Villarosa, *Under the Skin: The Hidden Toll of Racism on American Lives and on the Health of Our Nation* (New York: Doubleday, 2022).

65. Amanda Starbuck and Ronald White, *Living in the Shadow of Danger: Poverty, Race and Unequal Chemical Facility Hazards* (Washington, DC: Center for Effective Government, 2016).

66. Bailey, Feldman, and Bassett, "How Structural Racism Works."

67. Bailey, Feldman, and Bassett, "How Structural Racism Works," 770.

68. Dolores Acevedo-Garcia and Theresa L. Osypuk, "Impacts of Housing and Neighborhoods on Health: Pathways, Racial/Ethnic Disparities, and Policy Directions," in *Segregation: The Rising Costs for America,* ed. James H. Carr and Nandinee K. Kutty (New York: Routledge, 2008), 197–235; Dillon and Sze, "Police Power."

69. Bailey, Feldman, and Bassett, "How Structural Racism Works."

70. L. Brown, *Black Butterfly.*

71. Robert Bullard and Beverly Wright, eds., *Race, Place, and Environmental Justice after Hurricane Katrina* (New York: Routledge, 2009).

72. Rose, *Black Noise.*

CHAPTER 3

1. N. Jamiyla Chisholm, "American Medical Association Declares Racism a Public Health Threat," ColorLines, November 19, 2020, https://colorlines.com/article/american-medical-association-declares-racism-public-health-threat/.

2. Robert Baker and Matthew K. Wynia, "Living Histories of Structural Racism and Organized Medicine," *AMA Journal of Ethics* 23, no. 12 (2021): E995–E1003.

3. Quoted in Charlene Galarneau, "Getting King's Words Right," *Journal of Health Care for the Poor and Underserved* 29 (2018): 5.

4. Chisholm, "American Medical Association."

5. Carolyn Crist and Lindsay Kalter, "JAMA Podcast on Racism in Medicine Generates Backlash," *The Hospitalist,* March 5, 2021, www.the-hospitalist.org/hospitalist/article/236777/diversity-medicine/jama-podcast-racism-medicine-faces-backlash.

6. Sarah Richardson, "Race and IQ in the Postgenomic Age: The Microcephaly Case," *Biosocieties* 6, no. 4 (2011): 429–46.

7. Dorothy Roberts, *Fatal Invention: How Science, Politics, and Big Business Recreate Race in the Twenty-First Century* (New York: New Press, 2012); Dorothy Roberts, "The Problem with Race-Based Medicine," in *Beyond Bioethics: Toward a New Biopolitics,* ed. Osagie K. Obasogie and Marcy Darnovsky (Oakland: University of California Press, 2018), 410–14.

8. Camara Phyllis Jones, "Invited Commentary: 'Race,' Racism and the Practice of Epidemiology," *American Journal of Epidemiology* 154, no. 4 (2001): 299–304.

9. Gravlee, "How Race Becomes Biology."

10. Roberts, *Fatal Invention.*

11. Gravlee, "How Race Becomes Biology"; Ryon J. Cobb et al., "Self-Identified Race, Socially Assigned Skin Tone, and Adult Physiological Dysregulation: Assessing Multiple Dimensions of 'Race' in Health Disparities Research," *SSM—Population Health* 2 (2016): 595–602.

12. Roberts, *Fatal Invention,* 4.

13. Gravlee, "How Race Becomes Biology."

14. Arline T. Geronimus et al., "Do US Black Women Experience Stress-Related Accelerated Biological Aging: A Novel Theory and First Population-Based Test of Black-White Differences in Telomere Length," *Human Nature* 21 (2020): 19–38.

15. Sharon Ostfield-Johns, Elena Aragona, and Louis Hart, "Removing Race from Hyperbilirubinemia Guidelines Is Not Enough," *JAMA Pediatrics* 176, no. 12 (2022): 1163–64.

16. Alexandra Stern, *Eugenic Nation: Faults and Frontiers of Breeding in Modern America* (Berkeley: University of California Press, 2015); Earl H. Harley, "The Forgotten History of Defunct Black Medical Schools in the 19th and 20th Centuries and the Impact of the Flexner Report," *Journal of the National Medical Association* 98, no. 9 (2006): 1425–29; Washington, *Medical Apartheid.*

17. Roberts, *Fatal Invention;* Catherine Bliss, "The Meaning of Health Disparities," in Ehlers and Hinkson, *Subprime Health,* 107–27.

18. House, *Beyond Obamacare.*

19. Ronald Bayor and Sandro Galea, "Public Health in the Precision-Medicine Era," in *Beyond Bioethics: Toward a New Biopolitics,* ed. Osagie K. Obasogie and Marcy Darnovsky (Oakland: University of California Press, 2018), 267–70.

20. S. Rios, "Valley Fever."

21. James Doucet-Battle, *Sweetness in the Blood: Race, Risk, and Type 2 Diabetes* (Minneapolis: University of Minnesota Press, 2021).

22. Michael J. Montoya, *Making the Mexican Diabetic: Race, Science, and the Genetics of Inequality* (Berkeley: University of California Press, 2011).

23. Fausto-Sterling, "Refashioning Race."

24. Pollock, *Medicating Race.*

25. Smirnova, *Prescription-to-Prison Pipeline.*

26. Roberts, "Problem with Race-Based Medicine," 414.

27. W.E.B. Du Bois, *Black Reconstruction in America, 1860–1880* (New York: Free Press, 1998); Cedric J. Robinson, *Black Marxism: The Making of the Black Radical Tradition* (Chapel Hill: University of North Carolina Press, 2000); Daniel Martinez HoSang, *A Wider Type of Freedom: How Struggles for Racial Justice Liberate Everyone* (Oakland: University of California Press, 2021).

28. Anna Julia Cooper, *A Voice from the South: By a Black Woman of the South,* facsimile ed. (New York: Praeger, 1969), 121.

29. Laura Pulido, *Environmentalism and Economic Justice: Two Chicano Struggles in the Southwest* (Tucson: University of Arizona Press, 1996).

30. Monica White, *Freedom Farmers: Agricultural Resistance and the Black Freedom Movement* (Chapel Hill: University of North Carolina Press, 2019).

31. Alondra Nelson, *Body and Soul: The Black Panther Party and the Fight against Medical Discrimination* (Minneapolis: University of Minnesota Press, 2013).

32. Pablo Guzman, "The Party," in *Boricuas: Influential Puerto Rican Writings: An Anthology,* ed. Robert Santiago (New York: Ballantine Books, 1995), 52–59; Iris Morales, "Palante, Siempre Palante," in *The Puerto Rican Movement: Voices from the Diaspora,* ed. Andres Torres and Jose E. Velasquez (Philadelphia: Temple University Press, 1998), 210–27.

33. Larry Nesper, *The Walleye War: The Struggle for Ojibwe Spearfishing and Treaty Rights* (Lincoln: University of Nebraska Press, 2002); Rick Whaley and Walter Bresette, *Walleye Warriors: An Effective Alliance against Racism and for the Earth* (Philadelphia: New Society, 1994).

34. Bindi Shah, *Laotian Daughters: Working toward Community, Belonging, and Environmental Justice* (Philadelphia: Temple University Press, 2011); Josh Parr, "Young Laotian Women Build a Bridge in Richmond," *Shades of Power* 1, no. 4 (1998): 1–4.

35. Kimberlé Crenshaw, "Demarginalizing the Intersection of Race and Sex: A Black Feminist Critique of Antidiscrimination Doctrine, Feminist Theory, and Antiracist Politics," *University of Chicago Legal Forum* 14 (1989): 139–68; Kimberlé Crenshaw, "Mapping the Margins: Intersectionality, Identity Politics, and Violence against Women of Color," *Stanford Law Review* 43, no. 6 (1991): 1241–99.

36. Crenshaw, "Mapping the Margins," 1245.

37. Barbara Tomlinson, *Undermining Intersectionality: The Perils of Powerblind Feminism* (Philadelphia: Temple University Press, 2019).

38. Chela Sandoval, *Methodology of the Oppressed* (Minneapolis: University of Minnesota Press, 2000).

39. Kristie Dotson, "Theorizing Jane Crow, Theorizing Unknowability," *Social Epistemology* 32, no. 5 (2017): 417–30; Mari Matsuda, *Where Is Your Body? And Other Essays on Race, Gender, and the Law* (Boston: Beacon Press, 1997).

40. Jennifer L. Glick et al., "Housing Insecurity and Intersecting Social Determinants of Health among Transgender People in the USA: A Targeted Ethnography," *International Journal of Transgenderism* 21, no. 3 (2020): 337–49.

41. Shanna L. Smith, keynote address, Fair Housing and Public Policy Conference, Santa Barbara, CA, April 5, 2008, author's notes.

42. Akemi Nishida, *Just Care: Messy Entanglements of Disability, Dependency, and Desire* (Philadelphia: Temple University Press, 2022).

43. Neferti Tadiar, "Manila's New Metropolitan Form," *differences* 5, no. 3 (Fall 1993): 154–78; Neferti Tadiar, "Domestic Bodies of the Philippines," *Sojourn* 12, no. 2 (1997): 153–91.

44. Nancy Krieger, *Epidemiology and the People's Health: Theory and Context* (New York: Oxford University Press, 2011).

45. Jaime Breilh, *Critical Epidemiology and the People's Health* (New York: Oxford University Press, 2021); Howard Waitzkin, *Medicine and Public Health at the End of Empire* (New York: Routledge, 2016).

46. João Guilherme Biehl, "The Activist State: Global Pharmaceuticals, AIDS, and Citizenship in Brazil," *Social Text* 22, no. 3 (2004): 105–32.

47. Charles L. Briggs and Clara Mantini-Briggs, *Tell Me Why My Children Died: Rabies, Indigenous Knowledge, and Communicative Justice* (Durham, NC: Duke University Press, 2016); Charles L. Briggs, *Unlearning: Rethinking Poetics, Pandemics, and the Politics of Knowledge* (Louisville: University Press of Colorado, 2021).

48. Jodi A. Byrd, *Transit of Empire: Indigenous Critiques of Colonialism* (Minneapolis: University of Minnesota, 2015).

49. Emma Shaw Crane, "Lush Aftermath: Race, Labor, and Landscape in the Suburb," *Society and Space* 41, no. 2 (2023): 210–30.

50. Crane, "Lush Aftermath," 210; WeCount!, *The Human Landscape: Wages and Working Conditions of Plant Nursery Workers in South Miami-Dade County* (Homestead, FL: WeCount!, 2018), https://drive.google.com/file/d/1G-C_X0FQ7kkg-C9qha95pgz_x8t8sgRv/view?pli=1.

51. Glotzer, "How the Suburbs Were Segregated."

52. Lorgia Garcia-Peña, *Translating Blackness: Latinx Colonialities in Global Perspective* (Durham, NC: Duke University Press, 2022); Tanya Kateri Hernández, *Racial Innocence: Unmasking Latino Anti-Black Bias and the Struggle for Equality* (Boston: Beacon Press, 2022).

CHAPTER 4

1. Sarah A. Burgard, Kristin S. Seefeldt, and Sarah Zellner, "Housing Instability and Health, Findings from the Michigan Recession and Recovery Study," *Social Science and Medicine* 75, no. 12 (December 2012): 2215–24; Kathleen A. Cagney et al., "The Onset of Depression during the Great Recession: Foreclosure and Older Adult Mental Health," *American Journal of Public Health* 104, no. 3 (March 2014): 498–505; Bernadette Atuahene, "'Our Taxes Are Too Damn High': Institutional Racism, Property Tax Assessments, and the Fair Housing Act," *Northwestern University Law Review* 112 (2017–18): 1501–64; Kyungsoon Wang, "Neighborhood Foreclosures and Health Disparities in the U.S. Cities," *Cities* 97 (2020): 1–14.

2. Kyungsoon Wang, "Housing Instability and Socioeconomic Disparities in Health: Evidence from the U.S. Economic Recession," *Journal of Racial and Ethnic Health Disparities* 9, no. 6 (2022): 2461–67.

3. Wang, "Housing Instability."

4. Jonathan Edwards, "A Black Couple Says an Appraiser Lowballed Them. So, They 'Whitewashed' Their Home and Say the Value Shot Up," *Washington Post*, December 6, 2021; Kristin Jones Neff, "How the Austin Family's Historic Marin City Pole Home Became at the Center of a Legal Fight against Discriminatory Housing Practices," *Marin* magazine, January 21, 2022; Stacy M. Brown, "DOJ Intervenes in Black Couple's Home Appraisal Lawsuit," *Minnesota Spokesman Recorder*, February 20, 2022.

5. Debra Kamin, "Black Homeowners Face Discrimination in Appraisals," *New York Times*, August 27, 2020; "Jacksonville Couple Says They Faced Discrimination in Home Appraisal Because of Wife's Race," ABC News, October 14, 2020; Anne Schindler, "Jacksonville Couple Sees Home Appraisal Jump 40 Percent after They Remove All Traces of 'Blackness,'" FirstCoast News, August 25, 2020, www.firstcoastnews.com/article/news/local/jacksonville-couple-sees-home-appraisal-jump-40-percent-after-they-remove-all-traces-of-blackness/77-c3087e8c-0c65-4fb9-8319-da82f5c0ea20#:~.

6. Schindler, "Jacksonville Couple."

7. Alexandra Burris, "Black Homeowner Had a White Friend Stand in for Third Appraisal. Her Home Value Doubled," *Indianapolis Star*, May 13, 2021.

8. Kamin, "Black Homeowners Face Discrimination."

9. Lucy May, "This Black Family's Home Appraisal Grew by $92,000 after They Removed All Signs of Their Race," WCPO Cincinnati, August 19, 2021, www.wcpo.com/news/our-community/this-black-familys-home-appraisal-grew-by-92-000-after-they-removed-all-signs-of-their-race.

10. Laura Hepler, "A Black Couple 'Erased Themselves' from Their Home to See if the Appraised Value Would Go Up. It Did—by Nearly $500,000," *San Francisco Chronicle*, December 5, 2021.

11. Junia Howell and Elizabeth Korver-Glenn, "Neighborhoods, Race, and the Twenty-First Century Housing Appraisal Industry," *Sociology of Race and Ethnicity* 4, no. 4 (2018): 473–90; Maureen Yap et al., *Identifying Bias and Barriers, Promoting Equity: An Analysis of the U.S. PAP Standards and Appraiser Qualifications Criteria* (Washington, DC: National Fair Housing Alliance, 2022).

12. Heather R. Abraham, "Appraisal Discrimination: Five Lessons for Litigators," *SMU Law Review* 76, no. 2 (2023): 205–62.

13. Andre Perry, Jonathan Rothwell, and David Harshbarger, *The Devaluation of Assets in Black Neighborhoods: The Case of Residential Property* (Washington, DC: Metropolitan Policy Program, Brookings Institution, 2018).

14. Howell and Korver-Glenn, "Neighborhoods, Race."

15. Elizabeth Korver-Glenn, *Race Brokers: Housing Markets and Segregation in 21st Century Urban America* (New York: Oxford University Press, 2021).

16. Brentin Mock, "Federal Legislation Could Tackle the Racial Gap in Home Appraisals," Bloomberg.com, March 1, 2022, www.bloomberg.com/news/articles/2022-03-01/bill-would-address-racial-bias-in-appraised-home-values; Andrea Brambila, "Appraisal Ethics Rule under Review after Federal Scrutiny," Inman, March 11, 2022, www.inman.com/2022/03/11/appraisal-ethics-rule-under-review-after-federal-scrutiny/.

17. Mock, "Federal Legislation."

18. Brambila, "Appraisal Ethics Rule."

19. Ranger Ruffins, "The Answer Really Lies in the Community: Exploring Inequity in Resilience Planning through Community Voices: A Study of Post-Florence New Bern, North Carolina" (MA thesis, University of North Carolina, Chapel Hill, 2020); Olivia Paschal, "This Is the Red Cross: Do You Have Food?," *The Atlantic*, October 4, 2018, 1–13; Dr. Erroll L. Royal, *Traces of*

Places and Faces of African Americans from the New Bern Community (Las Vegas, NV: Independently Published, 2022).

20. Mock, "Federal Legislation."

21. Yap et al., *Identifying Bias and Barriers.*

22. Yap et al., *Identifying Bias and Barriers.*

23. Fair Housing Advocates of Northern California, "Lawsuit Alleging Race Discrimination in Home Appraisal Process Settled with Appraiser," press release, March 6, 2023, www.fairhousingnorcal.org/press-releases-and-statements/discrimination-lawsuit-alleging-race-discrimination-in-home-appraisal-process-settled-with-appraiser#:~:text=The%20settlement%20agreement%20included%20an,the%20history%20of%20segregation%20and.

24. Junia Howell and Elizabeth Korver-Glenn, *Appraised: The Persistent Evaluation of White Neighborhoods as More Valuable Than Communities of Color* (St. Louis, MO: Weidenbaum Center on the Economy, Government, and Public Policy, 2022).

25. Kahrl, *Black Tax.*

26. Andrew W. Kahrl, "Capitalizing on the Urban Fiscal Crisis: Predatory Tax Buyers in 1970s Chicago," *Journal of Urban History* 44, no. 3 (2018): 382–401.

27. Andrew W. Kahrl, "Investing in Distress: Tax Delinquency and Predatory Tax Buying in Urban America," *Critical Sociology* 43, no. 3 (2017): 199–219.

28. Bernadette Atuahene and Christopher Berry, "Taxed Out: Illegal Property Tax Assessments and the Epidemic of Tax Foreclosures in Detroit," *UC Irvine Law Review* 9, no. 4 (2019): 847–86.

29. Dan Immergluck, *Red Hot City: Housing, Race, and Exclusion in Twenty-First Century Atlanta* (Oakland: University of California Press, 2022).

30. Ruha Benjamin, *Race after Technology: Abolitionist Tools for the New Jim Code* (Cambridge: Polity Press, 2019); Yarden Katz, *Artificial Whiteness: Politics and Ideology in Artificial Intelligence* (New York: Columbia University Press, 2020).

31. Kahrl, *Black Tax.*

32. Kahrl, "Capitalizing"; Andrew Kahrl, "From Commons to Capital: The Creative Destruction of Coastal Real Estate, Environments, and Communities in the U.S. South," *Transatlantica* 2 (2020): 1–16.

33. Atuahene and Berry, "Taxed Out."

34. Kahrl, "From Commons to Capital."

35. Kahrl, "Capitalizing"; Kahrl, "From Commons to Capital."

36. Kahrl, *Black Tax.*

37. Palma Joy Strand and Nicholas A. Mirkay, "Racialized Tax Inequity: Wealth, Racism, and the U.S. System of Taxation," *Northwestern Journal of Law and Social Policy* 15, no. 3 (Spring 2020): 267–304.

38. Atuahene and Berry, "Taxed Out."

39. Emma Stein, "Detroit Overtaxed Homeowners $600m. Years Later, Advocates Still Seeking Reparations," *Detroit Free Press*, January 22, 2022.

40. Dan Immergluck, "Old Wine in Private Equity Bottles? The Resurgence of Contract-for-Deed Home Sales in US Urban Neighborhoods," *International*

Journal of Urban and Regional Research 42, no. 4 (July 2018): 651–65; Atuahene and Berry, "Taxed Out."

41. Bernadette Atuahene, "Predatory Cities," *California Law Review* 108, no. 1 (2020): 107–82.

42. Atuahene, "'Our Taxes.'"

43. Tyler v. Hennepin County, Minnesota et al., 598 U.S. 631 (2023).

44. Josh Pacewicz and John N. Robinson III, "Pocketbook Policing: How Race Shapes Municipal Reliance on Punitive Fines and Fees in the Chicago Suburbs," *Socio-Economic Review* 19, no. 3 (2021): 975–1003.

45. Walter Johnson, "What Do We Mean When We Say 'Structural Racism'?," *Kalfou* 3, no. 1 (Spring 2016): 36–62; Jodi Rios, "Flesh in the Street," *Kalfou* 3, no. 1 (Spring 2016): 63–78.

46. Pacewicz and Robinson, "Pocketbook Policing"; Kasey Henricks et al., *475,106 Mistakes: When Tickets Are Issued under False Pretenses* (Chicago: University of Illinois Chicago Institute for Research on Race and Public Policy, 2022).

47. Kahrl, *Black Tax.*

48. Purifoy and Seamster, "Creative Extraction."

49. Lipsitz, *How Racism Takes Place.*

50. Purifoy and Seamster, "Creative Extraction"; Seamster, "When Democracy Disappears."

51. Charles S. Aiken, "Race as a Factor in Municipal Underbounding," *Annals of the Association of American Geographers* 77, no. 4 (1987): 564–79.

52. Purifoy and Seamster, "Creative Extraction."

53. Seamster, "When Democracy Disappears."

54. Kahrl, *Black Tax.*

55. Seamster, "When Democracy Disappears."

56. Andrew R. Highsmith, *Demolition Means Progress: Flint, Michigan, and the Fate of the American Metropolis* (Chicago: University of Chicago Press, 2015); Mona Hanna-Attisha et al., "Elevated Blood Lead Levels in Children Associated with the Flint Drinking Water Crisis," *American Journal of Public Health* 106, no. 2 (2016): 283–90.

57. Seamster, "When Democracy Disappears."

58. Courtney M. Bonam, Hilary B. Bergsieker, and Jennifer L. Eberhardt, "Polluting Black Space," *Journal of Experimental Psychology—General* 145, no. 11 (2016): 1561–82; Jennifer L. Eberhardt, *Biased: Uncovering the Hidden Prejudice That Shapes What We See, Think, and Do* (New York: Penguin, 2020); Courtney M. Bonam, Valerie J. Taylor, and Caitlyn Yantis, "Racialized Physical Space as Cultural Product," *Social and Personality Psychological Compass* 11, no. 9 (September 2017): 1–12.

59. Charles, *Won't You Be My Neighbor?*; Michael Emerson, Karen J. Chai, and George Yancey, "Does Race Matter in Residential Segregation? Exploring the Preferences of White Americans," *American Sociological Review* 66, no. 6 (December 2001): 922–35.

60. Gilmore deploys the "chicken-egg conundrum" in her chapter "Forgotten Places and the Seeds of Grassroots Planning," in *Engaging Contradictions: Theory, Politics, and Methods of Activist Scholarship*, ed. Charles Hale (Berke-

ley: University of California Press, 2008), 32. The elaboration about the entire poultry industry came in a presentation I witnessed her make at the Southern California Library in Los Angeles in 2011.

CHAPTER 5

1. Naomi Murakawa, "The Origins of the Carceral Crisis: Racial Order as 'Law and Order' in Postwar American Politics," in *Race and American Political Development,* ed. Joseph Lowndes, Julie Novkov, and Dorian T. Warren (New York: Routledge, 2008), chap. 10; Ruth Wilson Gilmore, *Golden Gulag: Prisons, Surplus, Crisis, and Opposition in Globalizing California* (Berkeley: University of California Press, 2007); Elizabeth Hinton, *From the War on Poverty to the War on Crime: The Making of Mass Incarceration in America* (Cambridge, MA: Harvard University Press, 2016); Loïc Wacquant, "Deadly Symbiosis: When Ghetto and Prison Meet and Mesh," *Punishment and Society* 3, no. 1 (2001): 95–134.

2. Massey, *Categorically Unequal.*

3. David M. Frost et al., "Minority Stress, Activism, and Health in the Context of Economic Precarity: Results from a National Participatory Action Survey of Lesbian, Gay, Bisexual, Transgender, Queer, and Gender Nonconforming Youth," *American Journal of Community Psychology* 63, nos. 3–4 (2019): 511–26.

4. Kevin Leo Yabut Nadal, *Queering Law and Order: LGBTQ Communities and the Criminal Justice System* (Lanham, MD: Lexington Books, 2020).

5. Roberts, *Fatal Invention.*

6. Whitney K. Norris et al., "'You're Setting a Lot of People Up for Failure': What Formerly Incarcerated Women Would Tell Healthcare Decision Makers," *Health and Justice* 10, no. 4 (2022): 1–10.

7. Meda Chesney-Lind, "Imprisoning Women: The Unintended Victims of Mass Imprisonment," in *Invisible Punishment: The Collateral Consequences of Mass Imprisonment,* ed. Marc Mauer and Meda Chesney-Lind (New York: New Press, 2002), 79–89.

8. Beth Richie, "The Social Impact of Mass Incarceration on Women," in *Invisible Punishment: The Collateral Consequences of Mass Imprisonment,* ed. Marc Mauer and Meda Chesney-Lind (New York: New Press, 2002), 136–49.

9. Lisa Biggs, *The Healing Stage: Black Women, Incarceration, and the Art of Transformation* (Columbus: Ohio State Press, 2022).

10. Patricia Allard, "Crime, Punishment, and Economic Violence," in *Color of Violence: The Incite! Anthology,* ed. INCITE! Women of Color Against Violence (Durham, NC: Duke University Press, 2016), 157–63.

11. Alina Ball, "An Imperative Redefinition of 'Community': Incorporating Reentry Lawyers to Increase the Efficacy of Community Economic Development Initiatives," *UCLA Law Review* 55, no. 6 (2008): 1883–1908.

12. Michelle Alexander, *The New Jim Crow* (New York: New Press, 2010).

13. M. Belinda Tucker et al., "Imprisoning the Family: Incarceration in Black Los Angeles," in *Black Los Angeles: American Dreams and Racial*

Realities, ed. Darnell Hunt and Ana-Christina Ramon (New York: New York University Press, 2010), 168–87.

14. Alexandra Napatoff, *Punishment without Crime: How Our Massive Misdemeanor System Traps the Innocent and Makes America More Unequal* (New York: Basic Books, 2018).

15. Briggs, *Unlearning.*

16. Alexander, *New Jim Crow.*

17. Joan Petersilia, *When Prisoners Come Home: Parole and Prisoner Reentry* (New York: Oxford University Press, 2003).

18. Arneta Rogers, "How Police Brutality Harms Mothers: Linking Police Violence to the Reproductive Justice Movement," *Hastings Race and Poverty Law Journal* 12, no. 2 (Summer 2015): 205–34.

19. Ian A. Silver, Daniel C. Semenza, and Joseph L. Nedelec, "The Incarceration of Youths in an Adult Correctional Facility and Risk of Premature Death," *JAMA Network Open* 6, no. 7 (July 5, 2023): 1–10.

20. Elizabeth S. Barnert, "Confining Children in Adult Prisons and Premature Mortality: New Evidence to Inform Policy Action," *JAMA Network Open* 6, no. 7 (July 5, 2023), https://jamanetwork.com/journals/jamanetworkopen/fullarticle/2806844#:~:text=Their%20groundbreaking%20study%2C%20using%20national,ages%2018%2D39%20years)%20compared.

21. Monique Jindal et al., "Police Exposures and the Health and Well-Being of Black Youth in the U.S.: A Systematic Review," *JAMA Pediatrics* 176, no. 1 (2022): 78–88.

22. Rupa Marya and Raj Patel, *Inflamed: Deep Medicine and the Anatomy of Injustice* (New York: Farrar, Straus, and Giroux, 2021).

23. Marya and Patel, *Inflamed;* Michelle Jarman, "Race and Disability in U.S. Literature," in *The Cambridge Companion to Literature and Disability,* ed. Claire Barker and Stuart Murray (Cambridge: Cambridge University Press, 2018).

24. Julianna G. Alson et al., "Incorporating Measures of Structural Racism into Population Studies of Reproductive Health in the United States: A Narrative Review," *Health Equity* 5, no. 1 (2021): 49–58; Michael Massoglia and William Alex Pridemore, "Incarceration and Health," *Annual Review of Sociology* 41 (August 2015): 291–310; Christopher Wildeman and Hedwig Lee, "Women's Health in the Era of Mass Incarceration," *Annual Review of Sociology* 47 (2021): 543–65.

25. "Study Shows Racial Gaps in School Suspensions," *Louisiana Weekly,* September 20–26, 2010, 10.

26. US Department of Education, Office for Civil Rights, "Civil Rights Data Collection Data Snapshot: School Discipline," Issue Brief No. 1, March 2014, 1–24, https://civilrightsdata.ed.gov/assets/downloads/CRDC-School-Discipline-Snapshot.pdf.

27. African American Policy Forum, *Black Girls Matter: Pushed Out, Overpoliced, and Underprotected* (New York: Center for Intersectionality and Social Policy Studies, 2015).

28. Richie, "Social Impact."

29. Veronica Lerma, "Intersectional Criminalization: How Chicanas Experience and Navigate Criminalization through Interpersonal Relationships

with Latino Men and Boys," *Sociological Perspectives* 66, no. 2 (2022): 311–30.

30. Biggs, *Healing Stage.*

31. Allard, "Crime, Punishment."

32. Norris et al., "'You're Setting a Lot of People Up.'"

33. Geronimus et al., "Do US Black Women Experience."

34. International Women's Human Rights Clinic, "A Gendered Perspective on the Right to Housing in the United States," CUNY School of Law, November 30, 2009, www1.cuny.edu/mu/law/2009/11/30/a-gendered-perspective-on-the-right-to-housing-in-the-united-states/.

35. M. Stein and Galea, *Picture of Health.*

36. Hicks et al., *Still Running.*

37. Allen J. Fishbein and Patrick Woodall, *Women Are Prime Targets for Subprime Lending: Women Are Disproportionately Represented in High-Cost Mortgage Market,* Consumer Federation of America, December 2006, https://consumerfed.org/pdfs/WomenPrimeTargetsStudy120606.pdf.

38. Dorothy Roberts, *Torn Apart: How the Child Welfare System Destroys Black Families—and How Abolition Can Build a Safer World* (New York: Basic Books, 2022).

39. National Center on Family Homelessness, "Homeless Children: America's New Outcasts," fact sheet, National Center on Family Homelessness, accessed October 6, 2023, www.nn4youth.org/wp-content/uploads/A2Homeless Children.pdf.

40. Bess, Miller, and Meddipanah, "Effects of Housing Insecurity."

41. Roberts, *Torn Apart;* Richard P. Barth, "On Their Own: The Experiences of Youth after Foster Care," *Child and Adolescent Social Work* 7, no. 5 (October 1990): 419–40.

42. Roberts, *Torn Apart.*

43. Jill Maxwell, "Sexual Harassment at Home: Altering the Terms, Conditions, and Privileges of Rental Housing for Section 8 Recipients," *Wisconsin Women's Law Journal* 21 (2006): 223–61.

44. International Women's Human Rights Clinic, "Gendered Perspective."

45. Susan Saegert and Helene Clark, "Opening Doors: What a Right to Housing Means for Women," in *A Right to Housing: Foundation for a New Social Agenda,* ed. Rachel G. Bratt, Michael E. Stone, and Chester Hartman (Philadelphia: Temple University Press, 2006), 296–315.

46. Maxwell, "Sexual Harassment at Home."

47. Rigel Oliveri, "Sexual Harassment of Low Income Women by Landlords," *Cityscape* 21, no. 3 (2019): 261–84; Maxwell, "Sexual Harassment at Home"; Thomas Shellhamer et al. v Norman Lewallen and Jacqueline Lewallen, 770 F.2d 167 (6th Cir. 1985); United States of America v. John R. Koch, 352 F. Supp. 2d 970 (D. Neb. 2004).

48. Allard, "Crime, Punishment."

49. Alex F. Schwartz, *Housing Policy in the United States: An Introduction* (New York: Routledge, 2006).

50. American Civil Liberties Union, "ACLU Challenges Unlawful Housing Policy That Tears Families Apart," August 11, 2009, www.aclu.org/documents

/aclu-challenges-unlawful-housing-policy-tears-families-apart; Sharps v. The
Housing Authority of the City of Annapolis, Civil Case No. 02C09143799
(2009), www.aclu.org/cases/sharps-v-housing-authority-city-annapolis?document
=sharps-v-housing-authority-city-annapolis-complaint.

51. Todd Clear, *Imprisoning Communities: How Mass Incarceration Makes
Disadvantaged Neighborhoods Worse* (New York: Oxford University Press,
2007).

52. Ben-Moshe, *Decarcerating Disability.*

53. Nicholas L. Caverly, "Carceral Structures: Financialized Displacement
and Captivity in Detroit," *Anthropological Quarterly* 95, no. 2 (Spring 2022):
333–61.

54. Boen, "Criminal Justice Contacts."

55. Robert Fatureisi and Jack Leonard, "ID Errors Put Hundreds in L.A.
County Jails," *Los Angeles Times,* December 25, 2011, 1.

56. Rebecca Oyama, "Do Not (Re) Enter: The Rise of Criminal Background
Tenant Screening as a Violation of the Fair Housing Act," *Michigan Journal of
Race and Law* 15, no. 1 (Fall 2009): 181–222.

57. Oyama, "Do Not (Re) Enter."

58. Deborah L. McCoy and Jeffrey M. Vincent, "Housing and Education:
The Inextricable Link," in *Segregation: The Rising Costs for America,* ed. James
H. Carr and Nandinee K. Kutty, 125–50 (New York: Routledge, 2008).

59. Smirnova, *Prescription-to-Prison Pipeline.*

60. Gabriela Sandoval, "The Costs of Child Support," *Poverty and Race* 24,
no. 2 (March/April 2015): 1–2, 6.

61. Lynne Haney, *Prisons of Debt: The Afterlives of Incarcerated Fathers*
(Oakland: University of California Press, 2022).

62. G. Sandoval, "Costs of Child Support."

63. George L. Kelling and James Q. Wilson, "Broken Windows: The Police
and Neighborhood Safety," *The Atlantic,* March 1982, 29–38; For a critique of
broken windows policing, see Jordan T. Camp and Christina Heatherton, eds.,
Policing the Planet: Why the Policing Crisis Led to Black Lives Matter (New
York: Verso, 2016).

64. Napatoff, *Punishment without Crime.*

65. Massey, *Categorically Unequal;* Acevedo-Garcia and Osypuk, "Impacts
of Housing."

66. Napatoff, *Punishment without Crime,* 3.

67. Alexes Harris, *A Pound of Flesh: Monetary Sanctions as Punishment for
the Poor* (New York: Russell Sage Foundation, 2016).

68. American Friends Service Committee, "Our North Star: A Vision for
Community Safety beyond Prisons and Policing," *Quaker Action* 103, no. 2
(Fall 2022): 7–10.

69. David Helps, "'Neighborhood Nightmares': Drug Dens, Finance, and
the Political Economy of the Crack Crisis," *Journal of Urban History,* October
7, 2022, preprint, https://doi.org/10.1177/00961442221127278.

70. M. Stein and Galea, *Picture of Health.*

71. Jones, Squires, and Crump, "Relationship."

CHAPTER 6

1. Charlie Schlenker, "EEOC Finds State Farm Workers Discriminated Against on Basis of Race," WGLT, June 22, 2021, www.wglt.org/local-news /2021-06-19/eeoc-finds-state-farm-workers-discriminated-on-basis-of-race.

2. Campbell-Jackson v. State Farm Insurance, 1:21-cv-1044 (W.D. Mich., filed Dec. 9, 2021); Campbell-Jackson v. State Farm Insurance, 1:21-cv-1044 (W.D. Mich. Jul. 26, 2022).

3. Emily Flitter, "Where State Farm Sees 'a Lot of Fraud,' Black Customers See Discrimination," *New York Times*, March 18, 2022, www.nytimes.com/2022 /03/18/business/state-farm-fraud-black-customers.html.

4. Flitter, "Where State Farm Sees 'a Lot of Fraud.'"

5. Connectors Realty Grp. Corp. v. State Farm Fire & Cas. Co., 19 C 743 (N.D. Ill. Oct. 7, 2021).

6. Thomas Chan, "Service Quality and Unfair Racial Discrimination in Homeowners Insurance," *Journal of Risk and Insurance* 66, no. 1 (1999): 83–97; Benjamin Wiggins, *Calculating Race: Racial Discrimination in Risk Assessment* (New York: Oxford University Press, 2020).

7. Colin Gordon, *Mapping Decline: St. Louis and the Fate of American Cities* (Philadelphia: University of Pennsylvania Press, 2008); Karen Orren, *Corporate Power and Social Change* (Baltimore: Johns Hopkins University Press, 1974); J. Rios, *Black Lives;* Richard Rothstein, *The Color of Law: A Forgotten History of How Our Government Segregated America* (New York: Liveright, 2017).

8. Bench Ansfield, "The Crisis of Insurance and the Insuring of the Crisis: Riot Reinsurance and Redlining in the Aftermath of the 1960s Uprisings," *Journal of American History* 107, no. 4 (March 2021): 899–921.

9. Rothstein, *Color of Law*.

10. Caley Horan, *Insurance Era: Risk, Governance, and the Privatization of Security in Postwar America* (Chicago: University of Chicago Press, 2021).

11. Wiggins, *Calculating Race;* Rashida Richardson, "Racial Segregation and the Data-Driven Society: How Our Failure to Reckon with Root Causes Perpetuates Separate and Unequal Realities," *Berkeley Technology Law Journal* 36 (2021): 101–39.

12. Horan, *Insurance Era*.

13. Horan, *Insurance Era*.

14. Orren, *Corporate Power*.

15. Horan, *Insurance Era*.

16. Trafficante v. Metropolitan Life Ins., 409 U.S. 205 (1972).

17. Reskin, "Race Discrimination System."

18. Horan, *Insurance Era*.

19. Ansfield, "Crisis of Insurance."

20. Kahrl, *Black Tax*.

21. Jeff Larson et al., "How We Examined Racial Discrimination in Auto Insurance Prices," ProPublica, April 5, 2017, www.propublica.org/article /minority-neighborhoods-higher-car-insurance-premiums-methodology.

22. Amanda Nothaft and Patrick Cooney, "Building on Michigan's Auto Insurance Reform Law," M Poverty Solutions, December 1, 2021, 1–7, https://poverty.umich.edu/publications/building-on-michigans-auto-insurance-reform-law/.

23. Devin Fergus, *Land of the Fee: Hidden Costs and the Decline of the American Middle Class* (New York: Oxford University Press, 2018).

24. Nothaft and Cooney, "Building."

25. Gregory D. Squires, *Insurance Redlining: Disinvestment, Reinvestment, and the Evolving Role of Financial Institutions* (Lanham, MD: Rowman and Littlefield, 1997); Gregory D. Squires, "Racial Profiling, Insurance Style: Insurance Redlining and the Uneven Development of Metropolitan Areas," *Journal of Urban Affairs* 25, no. 4 (2003): 391–410.

26. Joe R. Feagin, *Racist America: Roots, Current Realities, and Future Reparations* (New York: Routledge, 2000).

27. Angel O. Torres, Robert Bullard, and Chad G. Johnson, "Closed Doors: Persistent Barriers to Fair Housing," in *Sprawl City: Race, Politics, and Planning in Atlanta*, ed. Robert Bullard, Glenn Johnson, and Angel O. Torres (Washington, DC: Island Press, 2000), 89–109.

28. Squires, *Insurance Redlining*.

29. C. Gordon, *Mapping Decline*.

30. Squires, "Racial Profiling, Insurance Style."

31. Ruqalijah Yearby, Brietta Clark, and José F. Figuroa, "Structural Racism in Historical and Modern U.S. Health Care Policy," *Health Affairs* 41, no. 2 (2022): 187–94.

32. Robert Vargas, *Uninsured in Chicago: How the Social Safety Net Leaves Latinos Behind* (New York: New York University Press, 2022).

33. David U. Himmelstein et al., "Prevalence and Risk Factors for Medical Debt and Subsequent Changes in Social Determinants of Health in the U.S.," *JAMA Network Open* 5, no. 9 (September 1, 2022): e2231898, https://doi.org/10.1001/jamanetworkopen.2022.31898.

34. M. Stein and Galea, *Picture of Health*.

35. Capital and Main, "Insured Americans Are Increasingly Putting Off Important Medical Treatments They Can't Afford," *Daily Kos*, July 30, 2023, www.dailykos.com/stories/2023/7/30/2183839/-Insured-Americans-are-increasingly-putting-off-important-medical-treatments-they-can-t-afford.

36. Emmanuella N. Asabor and Sten H. Vermund, "Conflicting Structural Racism in the Prevention and Control of Tuberculosis in the United States," *Clinical Infectious Diseases* 73, no. 9 (November 1, 2021): e3531-33555, https://doi.org/10.1093/cid/ciaa1763; Jonathan Metzl, *Dying of Whiteness: How the Politics of Racial Resentment Is Killing America's Heartland* (New York: Basic Books, 2020).

37. Yearby et al., "Structural Racism."

38. Jim Probasco, "The Insurance Industry Confronts Its Own Racism: The NAIC Tackles Racial Discrimination in the Insurance Sector," *Investopedia*, June 23, 2022, www.investopedia.com/race-and-insurance-5075141.

39. G. Himmelstein et al., "Hospitals That Serve."

40. Smirnova, *Prescription-to-Prison Pipeline*.

41. Michelle Saadi, *Claim It Yourself: The Accident Victim's Guide to Personal Injury Claims* (New York: Pharros Books, 1987).

42. R. Richardson, "Racial Segregation," 105.

43. Vargas, *Uninsured in Chicago.*

44. M. Stein and Galea, *Picture of Health.*

45. Julie Livingston and Andrew Ross, *Cars and Jails: Freedom Dreams, Debt and Carcerality* (New York: OR Books, 2022); Deb Gordon, "50% of Americans Carry Medical Debt, a Chronic New Condition for Millions," *Forbes Newsletter*, October 13, 2021, www.forbes.com/sites/debgordon/2021 /10/13/50-of-americans-now-carry-medical-debt-a-new-chronic-condition-for -millions/?sh=6a0c91915e5d.

46. D. Himmelstein et al., "Prevalence and Risk Factors."

47. Ehlers and Hinkson, "Introduction."

48. Bliss, "Meaning of Health Disparities," 108.

49. Vargas, *Uninsured in Chicago.*

50. Nadine Ehlers and Shiloh Krupar, "When Treating Patients Like Criminals Makes Sense: Medical Hot Spotting, Race, and Debt," in Ehlers and Hinkson, *Subprime Health*, 31–53.

51. Leslie R. Hinkson, "The High Cost of Having Hypertension While Black in America," in Ehlers and Hinkson, *Subprime Health*, 3–29.

52. Smirnova, *Prescription-to-Prison Pipeline.*

53. Smirnova, *Prescription-to-Prison Pipeline.*

54. Vargas, *Uninsured in Chicago,* 174.

55. Jessica T. Simes and Jacquelyn L. Jahn, "The Consequences of Medicaid Expansion under the Affordable Care Act for Police Arrests," *PLoS ONE* 17, no. 1 (January 2022): e0261512.

56. Lisa Rice and Deidre Swesnik, "Discriminatory Effects of Credit Scoring on Communities of Color," *Suffolk University Law Review* 46 (2013): 935–66.

57. James H. Carr, Michela Zonta, and Steven P. Hornburg, *State of Housing in Black America* (Latham, MD: National Association of Real Estate Brokers, 2022); Debby Goldberg and Lisa Rice. "The More Things Change, the More They Stay the Same: Race, Risk, and Access to Credit in a Changing Market," in *From Foreclosure to Fair Lending: Advocacy, Organizing, Occupy, and the Pursuit of Equitable Credit,* ed. Chester Hartman and Gregory D. Squires (New York: New Village Press, 2013), 21–40.

58. Kaya Naomi Williams, "Public, Safety, Risk," *Social Justice* 44, no. 1 (2017): 36–62; Benjamin, *Race after Technology.*

CHAPTER 7

1. Arthur C. Jones, *Wade in the Water: The Wisdom of the Spirituals* (Maryknoll, NY: Orbis Books, 2023).

2. Dan Walls et al., "Confronting Legacy Lead in Soils in the United States: Community-Engaged Researchers Doing Undone Science," *Environmental Science and Policy* 128 (2022): 165–74.

3. Doris Sommer, *The Work of Art in the World: Civic Agency and Public Humanities* (Durham, NC: Duke University Press, 2014).

4. Stephen Epstein, *Impure Science: AIDS, Activism, and the Politics of Knowledge* (Berkeley: University of California Press, 1998).

5. Ariana Ochoa Camacho et al., "El Poder y la Fuerza de la Pasión: Toward a Model of HIV/AIDS Education and Service Delivery from the Bottom Up," in *Emerging Perspectives in Health Education, Meaning, Culture, and Power*, ed. Heather M. Zoller and Mohan J. Dutta (New York: Routledge, 2008), 224–46.

6. Juana María Rodríguez, "Activism and Identity in the Ruins of Representation," in *AIDS and the Distribution of Crises*, ed. Jih-Fei Cheng, Alexandra Juhasz, and Nishant Shahani (Durham, NC: Duke University Press, 2020), 257–87.

7. Frost et al., "Minority Stress."

8. Rodríguez, "Activism and Identity," 262; Juana María Rodríguez, *Queer Latinidad: Identity Practices, Discursive Spaces* (New York: New York University Press, 2003), 80.

9. Adela Vásquez, "Finding a Home in Transgender Activism in San Francisco," in *Queer Brown Voices: Personal Narratives of Latina/o LGBTQ Activism*, ed. Uriel Quesada, Letitia Gomez, and Salvador Vidal-Ortiz (Austin: University of Texas Press, 2015), 212–20.

10. Rodríguez, "Activism and Identity."

11. Camacho et al., "Poder y la Fuerza."

12. Camacho et al., "Poder y la Fuerza."

13. Rodríguez, "Activism and Identity."

14. Camacho et al., "Poder y la Fuerza," 231.

15. Diana Taylor, *The Archive and the Repertoire: Performing Cultural Memory in the Americas* (Durham, NC: Duke University Press, 2003).

16. Zawadi Rucks-Ahidiana, "Theorizing Gentrification as a Process of Racial Capitalism," *City and Community* 21, no. 3 (September 2022): 173–92.

17. Waldron, *There's Something in the Water*; Ingrid R. G. Waldron, "The ENRICH Project: Blurring the Borders between Community and the Ivory Tower," *Kalfou* 5, no. 2 (Fall 2018): 394–405.

18. Louise Delisle and Ellen Sweeney, "Community Mobilization to Address Environmental Racism: The South End Environmental Injustice Society," *Kalfou* 5, no. 2 (Fall 2018): 313–18; Waldron, *There's Something in the Water*.

19. Waldron, *There's Something in the Water*.

20. Delisle and Sweeney, "Community Mobilization."

21. Robert Devet, "A Community of Widows: The Shelburne Dump and Environmental Racism," *Nova Scotia Advocate*, January 2, 2017.

22. Waldron, "ENRICH Project."

23. Delisle and Sweeney, "Community"; Waldron, *There's Something in the Water*; Waldron, "ENRICH Project."

24. Dorene Bernard, "Reconciliation and Environmental Racism in Mi'kma'ki," *Kalfou* 5, no. 2 (Fall 2018): 297–303.

25. Bernard, "Reconciliation and Environmental Racism."

26. Sadie Beaton, "The Sacred Moment: Learning, Responsibility, and Making Room," *Kalfou* 5, no. 2 (Fall 2018): 319–20.

27. Ashley E. Lucas, *Prison Theatre and the Global Crisis of Incarceration* (New York: Methuen, 2021).

28. Biggs, *Healing Stage.*

29. Daniel Rideau, Jerome Morgan, and Robert Jones, *Unbreakable Resolve: Triumphant Stories of 3 True Gentlemen* (Las Vegas, NV: Zen Magic, 2017); Students at the Center, *Go to Jail: Confronting a System of Oppression* (Aptos, CA: LMO Projects, 2021).

30. Daniel Rideau, Jerome Morgan, and Robert Jones, "Free-Dem Foundations and Unbreakable Resolve," University of Southern California lecture, author's notes, Los Angeles, February 6, 2020.

31. Jerome Morgan, "Education Is Improvisation: Improvisation Is Art," *Kalfou* 6, no. 2 (Fall 2019): 280–86.

32. Morgan, "Education Is Improvisation," 292.

33. Fair Housing Center of Western Michigan, *49507!* (Grand Rapids, MI: FHCWM, 2013).

34. Fair Housing Center of Western Michigan, *49507!*; Steelcase Foundation, "The 49507! Project," March 15, 2021, www.steelcasefoundation.org/the -49507-project/.

35. Environmental Health Coalition, "Our Work," accessed 2022, www .environmentalhealth.org/#.

36. Environmental Health Coalition, "Transit Is a Lifeline," *Toxinformer*, July 2023, 1–2.

37. Environmental Health Coalition, "Our Work."

38. Luke W. Cole and Sheila R. Foster, eds., *From the Ground Up: Environmental Racism and the Rise of the Environmental Justice Movement* (New York: New York University Press, 2001); Julie Sze, *Noxious New York: The Racial Politics of Urban Health and Environmental Justice* (Cambridge, MA: MIT Press, 2006); George Lipsitz, "Unexpected Affiliations: Environmental Justice and the New Social Movements," *Works and Days* 24, nos. 47–48 (February 2006): 25–44; Nelson, *Body and Soul*; Jenna M. Loyd, *Health Rights Are Civil Rights* (Minneapolis: University of Minnesota Press, 2014); Michael Mascarenhas, ed., *Lessons in Environmental Justice: From Civil Rights to Black Lives Matter and Idle No More* (Los Angeles: Sage Publications, 2021).

39. Árpád Skrabski, Maria Kopp, and Ichiro Kawachi, "Social Capital and Collective Efficacy in Hungary: Cross Sectional Associations with Middle Aged Female and Male Mortality Rates," *Journal of Epidemiology and Community Health* 58, no. 4 (2004): 340–45; Deborah A. Cohen et al., "Collective Efficacy and Obesity: The Potential Influence of Social Factors on Health," *Social Science and Medicine* 62, no. 3 (2006): 769–78; Emilie Phillips Smith et al., "Measuring Collective Efficacy among Children in Community-Based Afterschool Programs: Exploring Pathways to Prevention and Positive Youth Development," *American Journal of Community Psychology* 52, no. 12 (September 2013): 27–40; Rachel Tolbert Kimbro, Jeanne Brooks-Gunn, and Sara McLanahan, "Young Children in Urban Areas: Links among Neighborhood Characteristics, Weight Status, Outdoor Play, and Television Watching," *Social Science and Medicine* 72, no. 5 (2011): 668–76.

40. Jean Butel and Kathryn L. Braun, "The Role of Collective Efficacy in Reducing Health Disparities: A Systemic Review," *Family and Community Health* 42, no. 1 (2019): 8–19; Emma F. Thomas, Craig McGarty, and Kenneth

I. Mayor, "Aligning Identities, Emotions, and Beliefs to Create Commitment to Sustainable Social and Political Action," *Personality and Psychology Review* 13, no. 4 (2009): 194–218.

41. Krieger, *Epidemiology*.

CHAPTER 8

1. Cornel West, *Prophecy Deliverance! An Afro-American Revolutionary Christianity* (Philadelphia: Westminster Press, 1982).

2. Reese, *Black Food Geographies*.

3. Jesus Hernandez, *The Franklin Plan: Using Neighborhood-Based Energy Efficiency and Economic Development to Implement Sustainable Community Principles* (Sacramento, CA: Franklin Neighborhood Development Corporation and Franklin Boulevard Business Association, 2016).

4. Ryan N. Dennis, *Collective Creative Actions: Project Row Houses at 25* (Houston, TX: Project Row Houses, 2018), 78, https://projectrowhouses.org/project-row-houses-unveils-round-50-race-health-and-motherhood/.

5. Lipsitz, *How Racism Takes Place*.

6. National Fair Housing Alliance et al. v. Federal National Mortgage Association, Case No. 4:16-cv-06969-JSW (N.D. Cal.).

7. National Fair Housing Alliance, "National Fair Housing Alliance Awards $8.3 Million for 'Inclusive Communities Fund' Grants," press release, January 26, 2023, https://nationalfairhousing.org/national-fair-housing-alliance-awards-8-3-million-for-inclusive-communities-fund-grants/#:~:text=The%20grants%20allow%20for%20NFHA,been%20harmed%20by%20discriminatory%20practices; Charles C. Branas et al., "Citywide Cluster Randomized Trial to Restore Blighted Vacant Land and Its Effects on Violence, Crime, and Fear," *Proceedings of the National Academy of Sciences* 115, no. 12 (2018): 2946–51; Eugenia C. South et al., "Effect of Greening Vacant Land on Mental Health of Community-Dwelling Adults in a Cluster Randomized Trial," *JAMA Network Open* 1, no. 3 (2018): 3180298.

8. Rebecca Carter, *Prayers for the People: Homicide and Humanity in the Crescent City* (Chicago: University of Chicago Press, 2019).

9. Reese, *Black Food Geographies*.

10. Acta Non Verba, "Our Mission," accessed 2022, https://anvfarm.org/mission/.

11. Gregory D. Squires, ed., *The Fight for Fair Housing: Causes, Consequences, and Future Implications of the 1968 Federal Fair Housing Act* (New York: Routledge, 2018).

12. Robert W. Derlet and Mark Borden, "EPs Are the New Servants for Corporate America," *Emergency Medicine News* 44, no. 6 (June 2022): 5–6.

13. Baldwin, *In the Shadow*.

14. Patricia E. Tweet and Jessica W. Pardee, "Medical Gentrification and Transportation: Health Care Systems as Urban Redevelopers," *Sociological Spectrum* 43, no. 3 (2021): 229–54.

15. Lawrence T. Brown et al., "The Rise of Anchor Institutions and the Threat to Community Health: Protecting Community Wealth, Building Community Power," *Kalfou* 3, no. 1 (Spring 2016): 79–100.

16. Carr, Zonta, and Hornburg, *State of Housing.*

17. Clinical Problem Solvers, "Housing Is Health: Racism and Homelessness— Clinicians and Community Perspectives," episode 15, in *Anti-racism in Medicine* podcast series, https://clinicalproblemsolving.com/2022/04/05/episode-232-anti -racism-in-medicine-series-housing-is-health-racism-and-homelessness-clinician -community-perspectives/.

18. Clinical Problem Solvers, "Housing Is Health."

19. Colen, "Addressing Racial Disparities."

20. Kendra Liljenquist and Trumaini R. Coker, "Transferring Well-Child Care to Meet the Needs of Families at the Intersection of Racism and Poverty," *Academic Pediatrics* 21, no. 8S (November-December 2021): S102–S107.

21. Bovell-Ammon et al., "Housing Is Health."

22. Fan et al., "Housing Insecurity."

23. Robert Mark Silverman and Kelly L. Patterson, "The Four Horsemen of the Fair Housing Apocalypse: A Critique of Fair Housing Policy in the US," *Critical Sociology* 38, no. 1 (2011): 123–40; Elizabeth K. Julian, "The Duty to Affirmatively Further Fair Housing: A Legal as Well as a Policy Imperative," in *The Affordable Housing Reader,* 2nd ed., ed. Elizabeth J. Mueller and J. Rosie Tighe (New York: Routledge, 2022), 514–21.

24. Mehsra Baradaran and Darrick Hamilton, "Elizabeth Warren's New Housing Proposal Is Actually a Brilliant Plan to Close the Racial Wealth Gap," Popular Media 295, University of Georgia School of Law, Athens, GA, October 26, 2018, https://digitalcommons.law.uga.edu/cgi/viewcontent.cgi?article=1300& context=fac_pm; American Housing and Economic Mobility Act of 2021, S.1368, 117th Cong. (2021).

25. Antwan Jones, Gregory Squires, and Carolynn Nixon, "Ecological Associations between Inclusionary Zoning Policies and Cardiovascular Disease Risk Prevalence: An Observational Study," *Circulation: Cardiovascular Quality and Outcomes* 14, no. 9 (September 2021): 944-52.

26. S. White and Ojugbele, "Addressing Racial Disparities"; Kimberlé Crenshaw, "Twenty Years of Critical Race Theory: Looking Back to Move Forward," *Connecticut Law Review* 43, no. 5 (July 2011): 1253–1353.

27. Wendy Leo Moore, *Reproducing Racism: White Space, Elite Law Schools, and Racial Inequality* (Lanham, MD: Rowman and Littlefield, 2008); Eric Brown, *The Black Professional Middle Class: Race, Class, and Community in Post-Civil Rights Society* (New York: Routledge, 2014); Quinn Capers, Leon McDougle, and Daniel M. Clinchot, "Strategies for Achieving Diversity through Medical School Admissions," *Journal of Health Care for the Poor and Underserved* 29, no. 3 (February 2018): 9–18; S. White and Ojugbele, "Addressing Racial Disparities"; Johnson-Agbakwu et al., "Racism, COVID-19."

28. Melanie Tervalon and Jann Murray-Garcia, "Cultural Humility versus Cultural Competence: A Critical Distinction Defining Physician Training

Outcomes in Multicultural Education," *Journal of Health Care for the Poor and Underserved* 9, no. 2 (1998): 117–25.

29. S. White and Ojugbele, "Addressing Racial Disparities."

30. Ratcliff, *Social Determinants of Health;* Jenna M. Loyd, "Obamacare and Sovereign Debt: Race, Reparations, and the Haunting of Premature Death," in Ehlers and Hinkson, *Subprime Health,* 55–82.

31. Ehlers and Hinkson, "Introduction."

32. Montoya, *Making the Mexican Diabetic,* 90; James Ferguson, *The Antipolitics Machine: "Development," Depoliticization, and Bureaucratic Power in Lesotho* (Minneapolis: University of Minnesota Press, 1994).

33. Jennifer Tsai, "How Should Educators and Publishers Eliminate Racial Essentialism?," *AMA Journal of Ethics* 24, no. 3 (March 2022): 201–11.

34. Bailey, Feldman, and Bassett, "How Structural Racism Works"; Roberts, "Problem with Race-Based Medicine."

35. Leslie R. Hinkson, "The High Cost of Having Hypertension While Black in America," in Ehlers and Hinkson, *Subprime Health,* 3–29.

36. House, *Beyond Obamacare.*

37. Metzl and Hansen, "Structural Competency"; House, *Beyond Obamacare*; Lundy Braun and Barry Sanders, "Medical Education: Avoiding Racial Essentialism in Medical Science Curricula," *AMA Journal of Ethics* 19, no. 6 (June 2017): 518–27.

38. Metzl and Hansen, "Structural Competency"; Krieger, *Epidemiology.*

39. Nicole Franks et al., "The Time Is Now: Racism and the Responsibility of Emergency Medicine to Be Anti-racist," *Annals of Emergency Medicine* 78, no. 5 (November 2021): 577–86.

40. Bailey, Feldman, and Bassett, "How Structural Racism Works."

41. Ronald J. Thorpe Jr., Michelle Odden, and Lewis A. Lipsitz, "A Call to Action to Enhance Justice, Equity, Diversity, and Inclusion in the Journal of Gerontology Series A: Medical Sciences," *Journal of Gerontology Medical Sciences* 77, no. 1 (2021): 89–90.

42. S. White and Ojugbele, "Addressing Racial Disparities"; Ehlers and Krupar, "When Treating Patients."

43. Hinkson, "High Cost."

44. Cathleen J. Appelt et al., "Working Together for Health Equity: How a Multidisciplinary, Community Engaged Partnership Reframed Our Understandings of Pittsburgh's Maternal-Child Health Crisis," *Kalfou* 9, no. 1 (Spring 2022): 72–96.

45. Kevin Hazzard, *American Sirens: The Incredible Story of the Black Men Who Became America's First Paramedics* (New York: Hachette Books, 2022).

46. Joy Milligan, "Animus and Its Distortion of the Past," *Alabama Law Review* 74, no. 3 (2023): 728, 743.

47. Robert Schwemm, "The Limits of Litigation in Fulfilling the Fair Housing Act's Promise of Nondiscriminatory Home Loans," in *From Foreclosures to Fair Lending: Advocacy, Organizing, Occupy, and the Pursuit of Equitable Credit,* ed. Chester Hartman and Gregory D. Squires (New York: New Village Press, 2013), 229–48.

48. Kennedy v. City of Zanesville, No. 2:03-cv-1047, S.D. Ohio (2008); Committee Concerning Community Improvement et al. v. City of Modesto, CIV-F-04-6121 (2004).

49. George Lipsitz, "Fair Housing and Health: A Social Ecology Framework," in *Lessons in Environmental Justice: From Civil Rights to Black Lives Matter and Idle No More,* ed. Michael Mascarenhas (Los Angeles: Sage Publications, 2021), 184–98.

50. "Illinois City Will Pay $500,000 for Selectively Enforcing Building Codes against Latinos," *National Fair Housing Advocate* 10, no. 3 (September 2002); "Elgin Settles Complaints of Housing Discrimination," *Chicago Tribune,* August 20, 2002.

51. Michael P. Seng, "Restorative Justice: A Model of Conciliating Fair Housing Disputes," *Journal of Law in Society* 21, no. 2 (Winter 2021): 63–92.

52. National Fair Housing Alliance, "New Report Reveals Record Number of Housing Discrimination Complaints," press release, November 30, 2022, https://nationalfairhousing.org/new-report-reveals-record-number-of-housing-discrimination-complaints/#:~:text=The%20unprecedented%20number%20 of%2031%2C216,protections%20from%20the%20Trump%20administration.

53. Pooja S. Gehi and Gabriel Arkles, "Unraveling Injustice: Race and Class Impact of Medicaid Exclusions of Transition-Related Health Care for Transgender People," *Sexuality Research and Social Policy* 4, no. 4 (December 2007): 7–35.

54. American Friends Service Committee, "Our North Star."

55. Elizabeth S. Barnert et al., "Reimagining Children's Rights in the US," *JAMA Pediatrics* 176, no. 2 (2022): 1242–47.

56. Reskin, "Race Discrimination System."

57. Reskin, "Race Discrimination System"; Leah Gordon, *From Power to Prejudice: The Rise of Racial Individualism in Midcentury America* (Chicago: University of Chicago Press, 2015).

58. Breilh, *Critical Epidemiology.*

59. Reskin, "Race Discrimination System."

60. Sammi Schalk, *Black Disability Politics* (Durham, NC: Duke University Press, 2022), 150.

61. Quoted in James C. Scott, *Seeing Like a State: How Certain Schemes to Improve the Human Condition Have Failed* (New Haven, CT: Yale University Press, 1998), 322.

62. Hale, *Engaging Contradictions.*

63. Barbara Tomlinson, "Wicked Problems and Intersectionality Telephone," in *Antiracism, Inc.: Why the Way We Talk about Racial Justice Matters,* ed. Felice Blake, Paula Ioanide, and Alison Reed (Middletown, DE: punctum books, 2019), 161–87.

CHAPTER 9

1. King Jr., "Time to Break Silence," 243.

2. Robert W. Derlet, *Corporatizing American Health Care: How We Lost Our Health System* (Baltimore: Johns Hopkins University Press, 2021).

3. Bronwyn Davies and Sue Saltmarsh, "Gender Economies: Literacy and Gendered Production of Neoliberal Subjectivities," *Gender and Education* 19, no. 1 (2007): 1–20; Stuart Hall, "The Neoliberal Revolution," *Cultural Studies* 26, no. 6 (2011): 705–28.

4. Sommer, *Work of Art,* 89.

5. Metzl, *Dying of Whiteness.*

6. Pamela Illingworth and Wendy E. Parmet, *The Health of Newcomers: Immigration, Health Policy, and the Case for Global Solidarity* (New York: New York University Press, 2017).

7. Illingworth and Parmet, *Health of Newcomers,* 77.

8. Illingworth and Parmet, *Health of Newcomers.*

9. Camp and Heatherton, *Policing the Planet.*

10. Eve Garrow, "Banishing People to the Desert Does Not Solve Homelessness," ACLU of Southern California, February 22, 2021, www.aclusocal.org /en/news/banishing-people-desert-does-not-solve-homelessness.

11. Mapping Police Violence, "2021 Police Violence Report," 2022, https:// policeviolencereport.org/policeviolencereport2021.pdf.

12. Gehi and Arkles, "Unraveling Injustice."

13. Eugene T. Richardson et al., "Reparations for Black American Descendants of Persons Enslaved in the U.S. and Their Potential Impact on SARS-CoV-2 Transmission," *Social Science and Medicine* 276 (2021): 113741, https://doi .org/10.1016/j.socscimed.2021 113741.

14. Zachary Parolin and Emma K. Lee, "The Role of Poverty and Racial Discrimination in Exacerbating the Health Consequences of COVID-19," *Lancet Regional Health—Americas* 7 (March 2022): 1–9.

15. Briggs, *Unlearning,* 38.

16. Catherine MacKinnon, "Mackinnon J. Concurring with the Judgment," in *What Brown v. Board of Education Should Have Said,* ed. Jack M. Balkin (New York: New York University Press, 2002), 155.

17. American Public Health Association, "Advancing Racial Equity," 2022, www.apha.org/topics-and-issues/health-equity/racism-and-health/racism -declarations.

18. Max Jordan Nguemeni Tiako, Eugenia C. South, and Victor Ray, "Medical Schools as Racialized Organizations: How Race-Neutral Structures Sustain Racial Inequality in Medical Education—a Narrative Review," *Journal of General Internal Medicine* 37, no. 9 (July 2022): 2259–66.

19. Lundy Braun and Barry Saunders, "Medical Education: Avoiding Racial Essentialism in Medical Science Curricula," *AMA Journal of Ethics* 19, no. 6 (June 2017): 518–27.

20. Gbenga Ogedegbe, "Responsibility of Medical Journals in Addressing Racism in Health Care," *JAMA Network Open* 3, no. 8 (August 2020): 1–4.

21. Monica Casper, *Babylost: Racism, Survival, and the Quiet Poetics of Infant Mortality from A to Z* (New Brunswick, NJ: Rutgers University Press, 2022).

22. W. E. B. Du Bois, *The Philadelphia Negro: A Social Study* (Philadelphia: University of Pennsylvania Press, 1995).

23. Du Bois, *Philadelphia Negro,* 163.

Works Cited

Abelsohn, A. R., and M. Sanborn. "Lead and Children: Clinical Management for Family Physicians." *Canadian Family Physician / Medecin de Famille Canadien* 56, no. 6 (2010): 531–35.

Abraham, Heather R. "Appraisal Discrimination: Five Lessons for Litigators." *SMU Law Review* 76, no. 2 (2023): 205–62.

———. "Segregation Autopilot: How the Government Perpetuates Segregation and How to Stop It." *Iowa Law Review* 107 (2022): 1963–2025.

Acevedo-Garcia, Dolores. "Zip Code-Level Risk Factors for Tuberculosis: Neighborhood Environment and Residential Segregation in New Jersey, 1985–1992." *American Journal of Public Health* 91, no. 5 (2001): 734–41.

Acevedo-Garcia, Dolores, and Theresa L. Osypuk. "Impacts of Housing and Neighborhoods on Health: Pathways, Racial/Ethnic Disparities, and Policy Directions." In *Segregation: The Rising Costs for America,* edited by James H. Carr and Nandinee K. Kutty, 197–235. New York: Routledge, 2008.

African American Policy Forum. *Black Girls Matter: Pushed Out, Overpoliced and Underprotected.* New York: Center for Intersectionality and Social Policy Studies, 2015.

AFSCME. "Letter: Unions & Housing Advocates Continue to Call on UC to Divest from Blackstone and Instead Chart New Course on Affordable Housing." March 15, 2023. https://afscme3299.org/media/news/letter-unions -housing-advocates-continue-to-call-on-uc-to-divest-from-blackstone-and -instead-chart-new-course-on-affordable-housing/.

Aguilar, Sara, dir. and ed. International Institute for Critical Studies in Improvisation. *Stories of Impact: Improvisation and Convivencia in East L.A.* Video. Produced by IICSI and the Alliance for California Traditional Arts, 2021. https://improvisationinstitute.ca/document/stories-of-impact -improvisation-convivencia-in-east-la/.

Aiken, Charles S. "Race as a Factor in Municipal Underbounding." *Annals of the Association of American Geographers* 77, no. 4 (1987): 564–79.

AirNow. "Air Quality Index (AQI) Basics." Accessed October 14, 2023. www.airnow.gov/aqi/aqi-basics/.

Alexander, Michelle. *The New Jim Crow.* New York: New Press, 2010.

Allard, Patricia. "Crime, Punishment, and Economic Violence." In *Color of Violence: The Incite! Anthology,* edited by INCITE! Women of Color Against Violence, 157–63. Durham, NC: Duke University Press, 2016.

Alliance for California Traditional Arts. *Building Healthy Communities: Approaching Health Through Heritage and Culture in Boyle Heights.* Los Angeles: California Endowment, 2014.

Alliance of Californians for Community Empowerment. "Blackstone Comes to Collect: How America's Largest Landlord and Wall Street's Highest Paid CEO are Jacking Up Rents and Ramping Up Evictions." March 25, 2023. https://pestakeholder.org/reports/blackstone-comes-to-collect-how-americas-largest-landlord-and-wall-streets-highest-paid-ceo-are-jacking-up-rents-and-ramping-up-evictions/#:~:text=The%20Private%20Equity%20Stake-holder%20Project,highlights%20San%20Diego%20County%2C%20where.

Alson, Julianna G., Whitney R. Robinson, LaShawnDa Pittman, and Kerni M. Doll. "Incorporating Measures of Structural Racism into Population Studies of Reproductive Health in the United States: A Narrative Review." *Health Equity* 5, no. 1 (2021): 49–58.

American Civil Liberties Union. "ACLU Challenges Unlawful Housing Policy That Tears Families Apart." American Civil Liberties Union, August 11, 2009. www.aclu.org/documents/aclu-challenges-unlawful-housing-policy-tears-families-apart.

American Friends Service Committee. "Our North Star: A Vision for Community Safety beyond Prisons and Policing." *Quaker Action* 103, no. 2 (Fall 2022): 7–10.

American Public Health Association. "Advancing Racial Equity Webinar Series." 2022. https://www.apha.org/events-and-meetings/webinars/racial-equity.

Ansell, David. *The Death Gap: How Inequality Kills.* Chicago: University of Chicago Press, 2017.

Ansfield, Bench. "The Crisis of Insurance and the Insuring of the Crisis: Riot Reinsurance and Redlining in the Aftermath of the 1960s Uprisings." *Journal of American History* 107 (March 2021): 899–921.

Appelt, Cathleen J., Andrew T, Simpson, Jessica A. Devido, Sarah Greenwald, and Brittany Urban. "Working Together for Health Equity: How a Multidisciplinary, Community Engaged Partnership Reframed Our Understandings of Pittsburgh's Maternal-Child Health Crisis." *Kalfou* 9, no. 1 (Spring 2022): 72–96.

Asabor, Emmanuella N., and Sten H. Vermund. "Confronting Structural Racism in the Prevention and Control of Tuberculosis in the United States." *Clinical Infectious Diseases* 73, no. 9 (November 1, 2021): e-3531–e3535. https://doi.org/10.1093/cid/ciaa1763.

Atuahene, Bernadette. "'Our Taxes Are Too Damn High': Institutional Racism, Property Tax Assessments, and the Fair Housing Act." *Northwestern University Law Review*, no. 112 (2017–18): 1501–64.

———. "Predatory Cities." *California Law Review*, no. 108, no. 1 (2020): 107–82.

Atuahene, Bernadette, and Christopher Berry. "Taxed Out: Illegal Property Tax Assessments and the Epidemic of Tax Foreclosures in Detroit." *UC Irvine Law Review* 9, no. 4 (2019): 847–86.

Bailey, Zinzi D., Justin M. Feldman, and Mary T. Bassett. "How Structural Racism Works: Racist Policies as a Root Cause of U.S. Racial Health Inequities." *New England Journal of Medicine* 384, no. 8 (2021): 768–73.

Baker, Robert, and Matthew K. Wynia. "Living Histories of Structural Racism in Organize Medicine." *AMA Journal of Ethics* 23, no. 12 (2021): E995–E1003.

Baldwin, Davarian. *In the Shadow of the Ivory Tower: How Universities Are Plundering Our Cities*. New York: Bold Type Books, 2021.

Ball, Alina. "An Imperative Redefinition of 'Community': Incorporating Reentry Lawyers to Increase the Efficacy of Community Economic Development Initiatives" *UCLA Law Review* 55, no. 6 (2008): 1883–1908.

Baradaran, Mehsra, and Darrick Hamilton. "Elizabeth Warren's New Housing Proposal Is Actually a Brilliant Plan to Close the Racial Wealth Gap." *Popular Media* 295. University of Georgia School of Law, Athens, GA, October 26, 2018. https://digitalcommons.law.uga.edu/cgi/viewcontent.cgi?article=1300&context=fac_pm.

Barnert, Elizabeth S. "Confining Children in Adult Prisons and Premature Mortality—New Evidence to Inform Policy Action." *JAMA Network Open* 6, no. 7 (July 5, 2023), https://jamanetwork.com/journals/jamanetworkopen/fullarticle/2806844#:~:text=Their%20groundbreaking%20study%2C%20using%20national,ages%2018%2D39%20years)%20compared.

Barnert, Elizabeth S., Joseph Wright, Charlene Choi, Jonathan Todres, and Neal Halfon. "Reimagining Children's Rights in the US." *JAMA Pediatrics* 176, no. 2 (2022): 1242–47.

Barth, Richard P. "On Their Own: The Experiences of Youth after Foster Care." *Child and Adolescent Social Work* 7, no. 5 (October 1990): 419–40.

Bayor, Ronald, and Sandro Galea. "Public Health in the Precision-Medicine Era." In *Beyond Bioethics: Toward a New Biopolitics,* edited by Osagie K. Obasogie and Marcy Darnovsky, 267–70. Oakland: University of California Press, 2018.

Beaton, Sadie. "The Sacred Moment: Listening, Responsibility, and Making Room." *Kalfou* 5, no. 2 (Fall 2018): 319–320.

Benjamin, Ruha. *Race after Technology: Abolitionist Tools for the New Jim Code*. Medford, MA: Polity Press, 2019.

———. *Viral Justice: How We Grow the World We Want*. Princeton, NJ: Princeton University Press, 2022.

Ben-Moshe, Liat. *Decarcerating Disability: Deinstitutionalization and Prison Abolition*. Minneapolis: University of Minnesota Press, 2022.

Bernard, Dorene. "Reconciliation and Environmental Racism in Mi'kma'ki." *Kalfou* 5, no. 2 (Fall 2018): 297–303.

Bess, Kiana D., Alison Miller, and Roshanak Meddipanah. 2022. "The Effects of Housing Insecurity on Children's Health: A Scoping Review." *Health Promotion International* 38, no. 3 (2022): 1–11. https://doi.org/10.1093/heapro/daac006.

Biehl, João Guilherme. "The Activist State: Global Pharmaceuticals, AIDS, and Citizenship in Brazil." *Social Text* 22, no. 3 (2004): 105–32.

Biggs, Lisa. *The Healing Stage: Black Women, Incarceration, and the Art of Transformation.* Columbus: Ohio State University Press, 2022.

Bliss, Catherine. "The Meaning of Health Disparities." in *Subprime Health: Debt and Race in U.S. Medicine,* edited by Nadine Ehlers and Leslie R. Hinkson, 107–27. Minneapolis: University of Minnesota Press, 2017.

Boch, Akira, Betty Marin, and Quetzal Flores, directors. "Restorative Justice through Quilting—A Building Healthy Communities Story." YouTube, August 14, 2020. www.youtube.com/watch?v=zrm5 1DC7S4Y&feature=youtu.be.

Boen, Courtney E. "Criminal Justice Contacts and Psychophysiological Functioning in Early Adulthood Health Inequality in the Carceral State." *Journal of Health and Social Behavior* 61, no. 3 (2020): 290–306.

Boen, Courtney, Lisa A. Keister, and Nick Gratez. "Household Wealth and Child Body Mass Index: Patterns and Mechanisms." *RSF: The Russell Sage Foundation Journal of the Social Sciences* 7, no. 3 (2021): 80–100.

Bonam, Courtney M., Hilary B. Bergsieker, and Jennifer L. Erberhardt. "Polluting Black Space." *Journal of Experimental Psychology—General* 145, no. 11 (2016): 1561–82.

Bonam, Courtney M., Valerie J. Taylor, and Caitlyn Yantis. "Racialized Physical Space as Cultural Product." *Social and Personality Psychological Compass* 11, no. 9 (September 2017): 1–12.

Bovell-Ammon, Allison, Diane Yentel, Mike Koprowski, Chantelle Wilkinson, and Megan Sandel. "Housing Is Health: A Renewed Call for Federal Housing Investments in Affordable Housing for Families with Children." *Academic Pediatrics* 21, no. 1 (2021): 19–23.

Brambila, Andrea. "Appraisal Ethics Rule under Review after Federal Scrutiny." Inman, March 11, 2022. www.inman.com/2022/03/11/appraisal-ethics-rule-under-review-after-federal-scrutiny/.

Branas, Charles C., Eugenia South, Michelle C. Kondo, and John M. MacDonald. "Citywide Cluster Randomized Trial to Restore Blighted Vacant Land and Its Effects on Violence, Crime, and Fear." *Proceedings of the National Academy of Sciences* 115, no. 12 (2018): 2946–51.

Braun, Lundy, and Barry Saunders. "Medical Education: Avoiding Racial Essentialism in Medical Science Curricula." *AMA Journal of Ethics* 19, no. 6 (June 2017): 518–27.

Breilh, Jaime. *Critical Epidemiology and the People's Health.* New York: Oxford University Press, 2021.

Briggs, Charles L. *Unlearning: Rethinking Poetics, Pandemics, and the Politics of Knowledge.* Louisville: University Press of Colorado, 2021.

Briggs, Charles L., and Clara Mantini-Briggs. *Tell Me Why My Children Died: Rabies, Indigenous Knowledge, and Communicative Justice.* Durham, NC: Duke University Press, 2016.

Brown, Eric. *The Black Professional Middle Class: Race, Class, and Community in Post-Civil Rights Society.* New York: Routledge, 2014.

Brown, Lawrence T. *The Black Butterfly: The Harmful Politics of Race and Space in America.* Baltimore: Johns Hopkins University Press, 2021.

Brown, Lawrence T., Ashley Bachelder, Marisela B. Gomez, Alicia Sherrell, and Imani Bryan. "The Rise of Anchor Institutions and the Threat to Community Health: Protecting Community Wealth, Building Community Power." *Kalfou* 3, no. 1 (Spring 2016): 79–100.

Brown, Phil, Brian Mayer, Steven Zavetoski, Theo Luebke, Joshua Mandelbaum, Sabrina McCormick, and Mercedes Lyson. "The Health Politics of Asthma: Environmental Justice and Collective Illness Experience." In *Contested Illnesses: Citizens, Science, and Health Social Movements,* edited by Phil Brown, Rachel Morello-Frosch, Steven Zavetoski, and the Contested Illness Research Group, 108–22. Berkeley: University of California Press, 2012.

Brown, Stacy M. "DOJ Intervenes in Black Couple's Home Appraisal Lawsuit." *Minnesota Spokesman Recorder,* February 20, 2022.

Bullard, Robert. "Environmental Racism and the Environmental Justice Movement." in *Global Environmental Politics: From Person to Planet,* edited by Simon Nicholson and Paul Wagner, 238–45. New York: Routledge, 2014.

Bullard, Robert, and Beverly Wright, eds. *Race, Place, and Environmental Justice after Hurricane Katrina.* New York: Routledge, 2009.

Burgard, Sarah A., Kristin S. Seefeldt, and Sarah Zelner. "Housing Instability and Health: Findings from the Michigan Recession and Recovery Study." *Social Science and Medicine* 75, no. 12 (December 2012): 2215–24.

Burris, Alexandra. "Black Homeowner Had a White Friend Stand in for Third Appraisal. Her Home Value Doubled." *Indianapolis Star,* May 13, 2021.

Butel, Jean, and Kathryn L. Braun. "The Role of Collective Efficacy in Reducing Health Disparities: A Systematic Review." *Family and Community Health* 42, no. 1 (2019): 8–19.

Byrd, Jodi A. *Transit of Empire: Indigenous Critiques of Colonialism.* Minneapolis: University of Minnesota Press, 2015.

Cagney, Kathleen A., Christopher Browning, James Iveniuk, and Ned English. "The Onset of Depression during the Great Recession: Foreclosure and Older Adult Mental Health." *American Journal of Public Health* 104, no. 3 (March 2014): 498–505.

Camacho, Ariana Ochoa, Gust A. Yep, Prado Y. Gomez, and Elissa Velez. "El Poder y la Fuerza de la Pasión: Toward a Model of HIV/AIDS Education and Service Delivery from the 'Bottom Up.'" In *Emerging Perspectives in Health Education: Meaning, Culture, and Power,* edited by Heather M. Zoller and Mohan J. Dutta, 224–46. New York: Routledge, 2008.

Camp, Jordan T. *Incarcerating the Crisis: Freedom Struggles and the Rise of the Neoliberal State.* Oakland: University of California Press, 2016.

Camp, Jordan T., and Christina Heatherton, eds. *Policing the Planet: Why the Policing Crisis Led to Black Lives Matter.* New York: Verso, 2016.

Capers, Quinn, Leon McDougle and Daniel M. Clinchot. "Strategies for Achieving Diversity through Medical School Admissions." *Journal of Health Care for the Poor and Underserved* 29, no. 3 (February 2018): 9–18.

Capital and Main. "Insured Americans Are Increasingly Putting Off Important Medical Treatments They Can't Afford." *Daily Kos*, July 30, 2023. www .dailykos.com/stories/2023/7/30/2183839/-Insured-Americans-are -increasingly-putting-off-important-medical-treatments-they-can-t-afford.

Caraballo, César, Daisy S. Massey, Chima D. Ndumele, Trent Haywood, Shay-aan Kaleem, Terris King, Yuntian Liu, et al. "Excess Mortality and Years of Potential Life Lost among the Black Population in the US, 1999–2020." *JAMA* 329, no. 19 (May 16, 2023): 1625–1710.

Carmona, Tonantzin. "Understanding Latino Wealth to Address Disparities and Design Better Policies." Brookings, July 13, 2023. www.brookings.edu /articles/understanding-latino-wealth/.

Carr, James H., Michele Zonta, and Steven P. Hornburg. *State of Housing in Black America* Latham, MD: National Association of Real Estate Brokers, 2017.

Carter, Rebecca. *Prayers for the People: Homicide and Humanity in the Crescent City.* Chicago: University of Chicago Press, 2019.

Casper, Monica. *Babylost: Racism, Survival, and the Quiet Poetics of Infant Mortality, from A to Z.* New Brunswick, NJ: Rutgers University Press, 2022.

Caverly, Nicholas L. "Carceral Structures: Financialized Displacement and Captivity in Detroit." *Anthropological Quarterly* 95, no. 2 (Spring 2022): 333–61.

Center on the Developing Child. *Moving Upstream: Confronting Racism to Open Up Children's Potential.* Cambridge, MA: Center on the Developing Child, Harvard University, 2021.

Centers for Disease Control and Prevention. "A Century of U.S. Water Chlorination and Treatment: One of the Ten Greatest Public Health Achievements of the Twentieth Century." *Morbidity and Mortality Weekly Report* 48, no. 29 (1999): 621–29.

Chakraborty, Jayajit, and Paul A. Zandberger. "Children at Risk, Measuring Racial/Ethnic Disparities in Potential Exposure to Air Pollution at School and Home." *Journal of Epidemiology and Community Health* 61, no. 12 (December 2007): 1074–79.

Chan, Thomas S.F. "Service Quality and Unfair Racial Discrimination in Homeowners Insurance." *Journal of Risk and Insurance* 66, no. 1 (1999): 83–97.

Chan, Wayne, and Rodolfo Mendoza-Denton. "Status Based Recognition Sensitivity among Asian Americans: Implications for Psychological Distress." *Journal of Personality* 76, no. 5 (2008): 1317–46.

Chang, Lawrence, Amanda M. Stewart, Katherine Kester, Giselle Routhier, and Kenneth A. Michelson. "Emergency Department Use among Children in New York." *JAMA Pediatrics*, preprint April 10, 2023. https://jamanet-work.com/journals/jamapediatrics/article-abstract/2803663.

Charles, Camille Zubrinsky. 2006. *Won't You Be My Neighbor? Race, Class, and Residence in Los Angeles.* New York: Russell Sage Foundation.

Chesney-Lind, Meda. "Imprisoning Women: The Unintended Victims of Mass Imprisonment." In *Invisible Punishment: The Collateral Consequences of Mass Imprisonment,* edited by Marc Mauer and Meda Chesney-Lind, 79–89. New York: New Press, 2002.

Chetty, Raj, and Nathaniel Hendren. "The Impacts of Neighborhoods on Intergenerational Mobility I: Childhood Exposure Effects." *Quarterly Journal of Economics* 133, no. 3 (2018): 1107–62.

Chetty, Raj, Nathaniel Hendren, and Lawrence F. Katz. "The Effects of Exposure to Better Neighborhoods on Children: New Evidence from the Moving to Opportunity Experiment." *American Economic Review* 106, no. 4 (2016): 855–902.

Childhood Lead Poisoning Prevention Program (CLPPP). "2016 Data Report on Childhood Lead Testing and Elevated Levels: Michigan." Division of Environmental Health, Michigan Department of Health and Human Services. May 1, 2018, updated November 26, 2018. www.michigan.gov/-/media/Project/Websites/mileadsafe/Reports/2016_CLPPP_Annual_Report_5-1-18.pdf?rev=607b44316e234a4fbf41375bd80c1882.

Chisholm, N. Jamiyla. "American Medical Association Declares Racism a Public Health Threat." ColorLines, November 19, 2020. https://colorlines.com/article/american-medical-association-declares-racism-public-health-threat/.

Clear, Todd R. *Imprisoning Communities: How Mass Incarceration Makes Disadvantaged Neighborhoods Worse.* New York: Oxford University Press, 2007.

Clinical Problem Solvers. "Housing Is Health: Racism and Homelessness—Clinician and Community Perspectives." Episode 15, *Anti-racism in Medicine* podcast series, April 5, 2022. https://clinicalproblemsolving.com/2022/04/05/episode-232-anti-racism-in-medicine-series-housing-is-health-racism-and-homelessness-clinician-community-perspectives/.

Cobb, Ryon J., Courtney S. Thomas, Whitney N. Laster Pirtle, and William A. Darity Jr. "Self-Identified Race, Socially Assigned Skin Tone, and Adult Physiological Dysregulation: Assessing Multiple Dimensions of 'Race' in Health Disparities Research." *SSM—Population Health* 2 (2016): 595–602.

Cohen, Deborah A., Brian Karl Finch, Amy Bower, and Narayan Sastry. "Collective Efficacy and Obesity: The Potential Influence of Social Factors on Health." *Social Science and Medicine* 62, no. 3 (2006): 769–78.

Colburn, Gregg, and Clayton Page Aldern. *Homelessness Is a Housing Problem: How Structural Factors Explain U.S. Patterns.* Oakland: University of California Press, 2022.

Cole, Luke W., and Sheila R. Foster, eds. *From the Ground Up: Environmental Racism and the Rise of the Environmental Justice Movement.* New York: New York University Press, 2001.

Colen, Cynthia G. "Addressing Racial Disparities in Health Using Life Course Perspectives: Toward a Constructive Criticism." *Du Bois Review* 8, no. 1 (2011): 79–44.

Committee on Obstetric Practice. "Lead Screening during Pregnancy and Lactation." Committee Opinion No. 533, August 2012. www.acog.org/clinical/clinical-guidance/committee-opinion/articles/2012/08/lead-screening-during-pregnancy-and-lactation#:~:text=Committee%20on%20Obstetric%20Practice&text=Abstract%3A%20Prenatal%20lead%20exposure%20has,in%20both%20children%20and%20adults.

Connolly, Rachel, Jonah Lipsett, Manal Aboelata, Elva Yañez Jasneet Bains, and Michael Jerrett. "The Association of Green Space, Tree Canopy and

Parks with Life Expectancy in Neighborhoods in Los Angeles." *Environment International* 173 (March 2023): 107785.

Cooper, Anna Julia. *A Voice from the South: By a Black Woman of the South.* Facsimile ed. New York: Praeger, 1969.

Cooper, Richard S., Joan F. Kennelly, Ramon Durazo-Arvizu, Hyun-Jon Oh, George Kaplan, and John Lynch. "Relationship between Premature Mortality and Socioeconomic Factors in Black and White Populations of U.S. Metropolitan Areas." *Public Health Reports* 116, no. 5 (2001): 464–73.

Crane, Emma Shaw. "Lush Aftermath: Race, Labor, and Landscape in the Suburb." *Society and Space* 41, no. 2 (2023): 210–30.

Crenshaw, Kimberlé. "Demarginalizing the Intersection of Race and Sex: A Black Feminist Critique of Antidiscrimination Doctrine, Feminist Theory and Antiracist Politics." *University of Chicago Legal Forum* 14 (1989): 139–68.

———. "Mapping the Margins: Intersectionality, Identity Politics, and Violence against Women of Color." *Stanford Law Review* 43, no. 6 (1991): 1241–99.

———. "Twenty Years of Critical Race Theory: Looking Back to Move Forward." *Connecticut Law Review* 43, no. 5 (July 2011): 1253–1353.

Crist, Carolyn, and Lindsay Kalter. "JAMA Podcast on Racism in Medicine Generates Backlash." *The Hospitalist*, March 5, 2021. www.the-hospitalist.org/hospitalist/article/236777/diversity-medicine/jama-podcast-racism-medicine-faces-backlash.

Davies, Bronwyn, and Sue Saltmarsh. "Gender Economies: Literacy and the Gendered Production of Neoliberal Subjectivities." *Gender and Education* 19, no. 1 (2007): 1–20.

Delisle, Louise, and Ellen Sweeney. "Community Mobilization to Address Environmental Racism: The South End Environmental Injustice Society." *Kalfou* 5, no. 2 (Fall 2018): 313–18.

Dennis, Ryan N. *Collective Creative Actions: Project Row Houses at 25.* Houston, TX: Project Row Houses, 2018. https://projectrowhouses.org/project-row-houses-unveils-round-50-race-health-and-motherhood/.

Derlet, Robert W. *Corporatizing American Health Care: How We Lost Our Health System.* Baltimore: Johns Hopkins University Press, 2021.

Derlet, Robert W., and Mark Borden. "EPs Are the New Servants for Corporate America." *Emergency Medicine News* 44, no. 6 (June 2022): 5–6.

Desmond, Matthew. "Unaffordable America: Poverty, Housing, and Eviction." in *The Affordable Housing Reader,* 2nd ed., edited by Elizabeth J. Mueller and J. Rosie Tighe, 389–95. New York: Routledge, 2022.

Desmond, Matthew, and Rachel Tolbert Kimbro. "Eviction's Fallout: Housing, Hardship, and Health." *Social Forces* 94, no. 1 (2015): 295–324.

Devet, Robert. "A Community of Widows: The Shelburne Dump and Environmental Racism." *Nova Scotia Advocate*, January 2, 2017.

Dillon, Lindsey, and Julie Sze. "Police Power and Particulate Matters: Environmental Justice and the Spatialities of In/Securities in U.S. Cities." *English Language Notes* 54, no. 2 (Fall/Winter 2016): 13–23.

Dotson, Kristie. "Theorizing Jane Crow, Theorizing Unknowability." *Social Epistemology* 31, no. 5 (2017): 417–30.

Doucet-Battle, James. *Sweetness in the Blood: Race, Risk and Type 2 Diabetes.* Minneapolis: University of Minnesota Press, 2021.

Douglas, Gordon C. C. "Reclaiming Placemaking for an Alternative Politics of Legitimacy and Community in Homelessness." *International Journal of Politics, Culture, and Society* 36 (2023): 35–56.

Du Bois, W. E. B. *Black Reconstruction in America: 1860–1880.* New York: Free Press, 1998.

———. *The Philadelphia Negro: A Social Study.* Philadelphia: University of Pennsylvania Press, 1995.

Eberhardt, Jennifer L. *Biased: Uncovering the Hidden Prejudice That Shapes What We See, Think, and Do.* New York: Penguin, 2020.

Edelman, Benjamin, Michael Luca, and San Svirsky. "Racial Discrimination in the Sharing Economy: Evidence from a Field Experiment." *American Economic Journal: Applied Economics* 9, no. 2 (April 2017): 1–22.

Edwards, Earl J., and Pedro Noguera. "Seeing Our Most Vulnerable Homeless Students." In *Systemic Racism in America,* edited by Rashawn Ray and Hoda Mahmoudi, 112–38. New York: Routledge, 2022.

Edwards, Jonathan. "A Black Couple Says an Appraiser Lowballed Them. So, They 'Whitewashed' Their Home and Say the Value Shot Up." *Washington Post.* December 6, 2021.

Ehlers, Nadine, and Leslie R. Hinkson. "Introduction: Race-Based Medicine and the Specter of Debt." In *Subprime Health: Debt and Race in U.S. Medicine,* edited by Nadine Ehlers and Leslie R. Hinkson, vii–xxxi. Minneapolis: University of Minnesota Press, 2017.

———, eds. *Subprime Health: Debt and Race in U.S. Medicine.* Minneapolis: University of Minnesota Press, 2017.

Ehlers, Nadine, and Shiloh Krupar. "When Treating Patients Like Criminals Makes Sense: Medical Hot Spotting, Race, and Debt." In *Subprime Health: Debt and Race in U.S. Medicine,* edited by Nadine Ehlers and Leslie R. Hinkson, 31–53. Minneapolis: University of Minnesota Press, 2017.

Eisenberg, Alexa, Eric Seymour, Alex B. Hill, and Joshua Akers. "Toxic Structures: Speculation and Lead Exposure in Detroit's Single-Family Rental Market." *Health and Place* 64 (2020): 1–10.

"Elgin Settles Complaints of Housing Discrimination." *Chicago Tribune,* August 20, 2002.

Emerson, Michael, Karen J. Chai, and George Yancey. "Does Race Matter in Residential Segregation: Exploring the Preferences of White Americans." *American Sociological Review* 66, no. 6 (December 2001): 922–35.

Environmental Health Coalition. "Transit Is a Lifeline." *Toxinformer,* July 2023, 1–2.

Epstein, Steven. *Impure Science: AIDS Activism, and the Politics of Knowledge.* Berkeley: University of California Press, 1998.

Fair Housing Center of Western Michigan. *49507!* Grand Rapids, MI: FHCWM, 2013.

Fan, Qinjin, Danya E. Keene, Matthew Benegas, Sarah Gelhert, Laura M. Gottlieb, K. Robin Yabroff, and Craig E. Pollack. "Housing Insecurity among Patients with Cancer." *Journal of the National Cancer Institute* 114, no. 12 (September 21, 2022): 1584–92.

Farooqi Aijaz, M. Adamson, Fredrik Serenius, and Bruno Hägglöf. "Executive Functioning and Learning Skills of Adolescent Children Born at Fewer Than 26 Weeks of Gestation." *PLoS One* 11, no. 3 (2016). https:/doi.org/10.1371/journal.pone.0151819.

Fatureisi, Robert, and Jack Leonard. "ID Errors Put Hundreds in L.A. County Jails." *Los Angeles Times*, December 25, 2011, 1.

Fausto-Sterling, Anne. "Refashioning Race: DNA and the Politics of Health Care." *differences: A Journal of Feminist Cultural Studies* 15, no. 3 (2004): 1–37.

Feagin, Joe R. *Racist America: Roots, Current Realities, and Future Reparations*. New York: Routledge, 2000.

Fergus, Devin. *Land of the Fee: Hidden Costs and the Decline of the American Middle Class*. New York: Oxford University Press, 2018.

Ferguson, James. *The Anti-politics Machine: "Development," Depoliticization, and Bureaucratic Power in Lesotho*. Minneapolis: University of Minnesota Press, 1994.

Finnegan, Ryan. "The Growth and Shifting Spatial Distribution of Tent Encampments in Oakland, California." *Annals of the American Academy of Political and Social Science* 693, no. 1 (January 2021): 284–300.

Fishbein, Allen J., and Patrick Woodall. *Women Are Prime Targets for Subprime Lending: Women Are Disproportionately Represented in High-Cost Mortgage Market*. Consumer Federation of America, December 2006. https://consumerfed.org/pdfs/WomenPrimeTargetsStudy120606.pdf.

Flippen, Chenoa. "Unequal Returns to Housing Investments: A Study of Real Housing Appreciation among Black, White, and Hispanic Households." *Social Forces* 82, no. 4 (2006): 1523–55.

Flitter, Emily. "Where State Farm Sees 'a Lot of Fraud,' Black Customers See Discrimination." *New York Times*, March 18, 2022. www.nytimes.com/2022/03/18/business/state-farm-fraud-black-customers.html.

Franks, Nicole M., Katrina Gipson, Sheri-Ann Kaltiso, Anwar Osborne, and Sheryl L. Heron. "The Time Is Now: Racism and the Responsibility of Emergency Medicine to Be Anti-racist." *Annals of Emergency Medicine* 78, no. 5 (November 2021): 577–86.

Frost, David M., Michelle Fine, Maria Elena Torre, and Allison Cabana. "Minority Stress, Activism, and Health in the Context of Economic Precarity: Results from a National Participatory Action Survey of Lesbian, Gay, Bisexual, Transgender, Queer, and Gender Non-conforming Youth." *American Journal of Community Psychology* 63, nos. 3–4 (2019): 511–26.

Fullilove, Mindy Thompson. *Root Shock: How Tearing Up City Neighborhoods Hurts America and What We Can Do about It*. New York: Ballantine, 2016.

———. *Urban Alchemy*. New York: New Village Press, 2013.

Gabbay, Jonathan M., Amanda M. Stewart, and Ann Chen Wu. "Housing Instability and Homelessness: An Undertreated Pediatric Chronic Condition." *JAMA Pediatrics* 176, no. 11 (November 1, 2022): 1063–64. https://doi.org/10.1001/jamapediatrics.2022.3258.

Galarneau, Charlene. "Getting King's Words Right." *Journal of Health Care for the Poor and Underserved* 29 (2018): 5–8.

Garcia-Peña, Lorgia. *Translating Blackness: Latinx Colonialities in Global Perspective.* Durham, NC: Duke University Press, 2022.

Garner, Andrew S., and Jack P. Shonkoff. "Early Childhood Adversity, Toxic Stress, and the Role of the Pediatrician: Translating Developmental Science into Lifelong Health." *Pediatrics* 129, no. 1 (2012): e224–e231.

Garrow, Eve. "Banishing People to the Desert Does Not Solve Homelessness." ACLU of Southern California, February 22, 2021. www.aclusocal.org/en /news/banishing-people-desert-does-not-solve-homelessness.

Gee, Gilbert C., and Chandra L. Ford. "Structural Racism and Health Inequities: Old Issues, New Directions." *Du Bois Review* 8, no. 1 (2011): 115–32.

Gehi, Pooja S., and Gabriel Arkles. "Unraveling Injustice: Race and Class Impact of Medicaid Excursions of Transition-Related Health Care for Transgender People." *Sexuality Research and Social Policy* 4, no. 4 (December 2007): 7–35.

Geronimus, Arline T., Margaret T. Hicken, Jay A. Pearson, Sarah J. Seashols, Kelly L. Brown, and Tracey Dawson Cruz. "Do US Black Women Experience Stress-Related Accelerated Biological Aging? A Novel Theory and First Population-Based Test of Black-White Differences in Telomere Length." *Human Nature* 21 (2010): 19–38.

Gilmore, Ruth Wilson. "Forgotten Places and the Seeds of Grassroots Planning." In *Engaging Contradictions: Theory, Politics, and Methods of Activist Scholarship,* edited by Charles Hale, 31–61. Berkeley: University of California Press, 2008.

———. *Golden Gulag: Prisons, Surplus, Crisis, and Opposition in Globalizing California.* Berkeley: University of California Press, 2007.

Glick, Jennifer L., Alex Lopez, Miranda Pollock, and Katherine P. Theall. "Housing Insecurity and Intersecting Social Determinants of Health among Transgender People in the USA: A Targeted Ethnography." *International Journal of Transgenderism* 21, no. 3s (2020): 337–49.

Glotzer, Paige. *How The Suburbs Were Segregated: Developers and the Business of Exclusionary Housing, 1890–1960.* New York: Columbia University Press, 2020.

Golash-Boza, Tanya Maria. *Before Gentrification: The Creation of DC's Racial Wealth Gap.* Oakland: University of California Press, 2023.

Goldberg, Debby, and Lisa Rice. "The More Things Change, the More They Stay the Same: Race, Risk, and Access to Credit in a Changing Market." In *From Foreclosure to Fair Lending: Advocacy, Organizing, Occupy, and the Pursuit of Equitable Credit,* edited by Chester Hartman and Gregory D. Squires, 21–40. New York: New Village Press, 2013.

Goldstein, Bernard D. "The Precautionary Principle Also Applies to Public Health Actions." *American Journal of Public Health* 91, no. 9 (2001): 1358–61.

Gordon, Colin. *Mapping Decline: St. Louis and the Fate of American Cities.* Philadelphia: University of Pennsylvania Press, 2008.

Gordon, Deb. "50% of Americans Now Carry Medical Debt, a Chronic New Condition for Millions." *Forbes Newsletter*, October 13, 2021. www.forbes

.com/sites/debgordon/2021/10/13/50-of-americans-now-carry-medical-debt -a-new-chronic-condition-for-millions/?sh=e22328c5e5dd.

Gordon, Leah. *From Power to Prejudice: The Rise of Racial Individualism in Midcentury America.* Chicago: University of Chicago Press, 2015.

Grady, Sue C. "Racial Disparities in Low Birthweight and the Contribution of Residential Segregation: A Multilevel Analysis." *Social Science and Medicine* 63, no. 12 (2006): 3013–29.

Graetz, Nick, and Michael Esposito. "Historical Redlining and Contemporary Racial Disparities in Neighborhood Life Expectancy." *Social Forces* 102, no. 1 (2022): 1–22.

Gravlee, Clarence C. "How Race Becomes Biology: Embodiment of Social Inequality." *American Journal of Physical Anthropology* 139 (2008): 47–57.

Guzman, Pablo. "The Party." In *Boricuas: Influential Puerto Rican Writings: An Anthology,* edited by Robert Santiago, 52–59. New York: Ballantine Books, 1995.

Hale, Charles. *Engaging Contradictions: Theory, Politics, and Methods of Activist Scholarship.* Berkeley: University of California Press, 2008.

Hall, Stuart. "The Neoliberal Revolution." *Cultural Studies* 26, no. 6 (2011): 705–28.

Haney, Lynne. *Prisons of Debt: The Afterlives of Incarcerated Fathers.* Oakland: University of California Press, 2022.

Hanna-Attisha, Mona, Jenny LaChance, Richard Casey-Sadler, and Allison Champney Schnepp. "Elevated Blood Lead Levels in Children Associated with the Flint Drinking Water Crisis: A Spatial Analysis of Risk and Public Health Response." *American Journal of Public Health* 106, no. 2 (2016): 283–90. https://doi.org/10.2105/AJPH.2015.303003.

Harley, Earl H. "The Forgotten History of Defunct Black Medical Schools in the 19th and 20th Centuries and the Impact of the Flexner Report." *Journal of the National Medical Association* 98, no. 9 (2006): 1425–29.

Harris, Alexes. *A Pound of Flesh: Monetary Sanctions as Punishment for the Poor.* New York: Russell Sage Foundation, 2016.

Hartman, Chester, and Gregory D. Squires, eds. *From Foreclosure to Fair Lending: Advocacy, Organizing, Occupy, and the Pursuit of Equitable Credit.* New York: New Village Press, 2013.

———. *The Integration Debate: Competing Futures for American Cities.* New York: Routledge, 2010.

Hazzard, Kevin. *American Sirens: The Incredible Story of the Black Men Who Became America's First Paramedics.* New York: Hachette Books, 2022.

Helps, David. "'Neighborhood Nightmares': Drug Dens, Finance, and the Political Economy of the Crack Crisis." *Journal of Urban History,* October 7, 2022. Preprint. https://doi.org/10.1177/00961442221127278.

Henricks, Kasey, Chris D. Poulos, Iván Arenas, Ruben Ortiz, and Amanda E. Lewis. *475,106 Mistakes: When Tickets Are Issued under False Pretenses.* Chicago: University of Illinois, Chicago Institute for Research on Race and Public Policy, 2022.

Henry, Matthew. *Hydronarratives: Water, Environmental Justice and a Just Transition.* Lincoln: University of Nebraska Press, 2022.

Hepler, Laura. "A Black Couple 'Erased Themselves' from Their Home to See If the Appraised Value Would Go Up. It Did—by Nearly $500, 000." *San Francisco Chronicle*, December 5, 2021.

Hernandez, Jesus. *The Franklin Plan: Using Neighborhood-Based Energy Efficiency and Economic Development to Implement Sustainable Community Principles*. Sacramento, CA: Franklin Neighborhood Development Corporation and Franklin Boulevard Business Association, 2016.

Hernández, Kelly Lytle. *City of Inmates: Conquest, Rebellion, and the Rise of Human Caging in Los Angeles, 1771–1965*. Chapel Hill: University of North Carolina Press, 2017.

Hernández, Tanya Kateri. *Racial Innocence: Unmasking Latino Anti-Black Bias and the Struggle for Equality*. Boston: Beacon Press, 2022.

Hicks, Natasha, Fenaba Addo, Anne Price, and William Darity Jr. *Still Running up the Down Escalator: How Narratives Shape Our Understanding of Racial Wealth Inequality*. Durham, NC: Samuel DuBois Cook Center on Social Equality, 2021.

Highsmith, Andrew R. *Demolition Means Progress: Flint, Michigan, and the Fate of the American Metropolis*. Chicago: University of Chicago Press, 2015.

Himmelstein, David U., Samuel L. Dickman, Danny McCormick, David H. Bor, Adam Gaffney, and Steffie Woolhandler. "Prevalence and Risk Factors for Medical Debt and Subsequent Changes in Social Determinants of Health in the US." *JAMA Network Open* 5, no. 9 (September 16, 2022): 1–13. https://doi.org/10.1001/jamanetworkopen.20223 1898. l.

Himmelstein, Gracie, Joniqua N. Ceasar, and Kathryn E. W. Himmelstein. "Hospitals That Serve Many Black Patients Have Lower Revenues and Profits: Structural Racism in Hospital Financing." *Journal of General Internal Medicine* 38 (2023): 586–91.

Hinkson, Leslie R. "The High Cost of Having Hypertension While Black in America." in *Subprime Health: Debt and Race in U.S. Medicine,* edited by Nadine Ehlers and Leslie R. Hinkson, 3–29. Minneapolis: University of Minnesota Press, 2017.

Hinton, Elizabeth. *From the War on Poverty to the War on Crime: The Making of Mass Incarceration in America*. Cambridge, MA: Harvard University Press, 2016.

Hoffman, Jeremy S., Vivek Shandas, and Nicholas Pendleton. "The Effects of Historical Housing Policies on Resident Exposure to Intra-urban Heat: A Study of 108 US Urban Areas." *Climate* 8, no. 12 (2020): 1–15. https://doi.10.3390/cli8010012.

Horan, Caley. *Insurance Era: Risk, Governance, and the Privatization of Security in Postwar America*. Chicago: University of Chicago Press, 2021.

HoSang, Daniel Martinez. *A Wider Type of Freedom: How Struggles for Racial Justice Liberate Everyone*. Oakland: University of California Press, 2021.

House, James S. *Beyond Obamacare: Life, Death, and Social Policy*. New York: Russell Sage Foundation, 2015.

Howell, Junia, and Elizabeth Korver-Glenn. *Appraised: The Persistent Evaluation of White Neighborhoods as More Valuable Than Communities of

Color. St. Louis, MO: Weidenbaum Center on the Economy, Government, and Public Policy, 2022.

———. "Neighborhoods, Race, and the Twenty-First Century Housing Appraisal Industry." *Sociology of Race and Ethnicity* 4, no. 4 (2018): 473–90.

Howell, Junia, Ellen Whitehead, and Elizabeth Korver-Glenn. "Still Separate and Unequal: Persistent Racial Segregation and Inequality in Subsidized Housing." *Socius: Sociological Research for a Dynamic World* 9 (2023): 1–16.

Illingworth, Patricia, and Wendy E. Parmet. *The Health of Newcomers: Immigration, Health Policy, and the Case for Global Solidarity.* New York: New York University Press, 2017.

"Illinois City Will Pay $500,000 for Selectively Enforcing Building Codes against Latinos." *National Fair Housing Advocate* 10, no. 3 (September 2002).

Immergluck, Dan. "Old Wine in Private Equity Bottles? The Resurgence of Contract-for Deed Home Sales in US Urban Neighborhoods." *International Journal of Urban and Regional Research* 42, no. 4 (July 2018): 651–65.

———. *Red Hot City: Housing, Race, and Exclusion in Twenty-First Century Atlanta.* Oakland: University of California Press, 2022.

International Women's Human Rights Clinic. "A Gendered Perspective on the Right to Housing in the United States." CUNY School of Law, November 30, 2009. https://www1.cuny.edu/mu/law/2009/11/30/a-gendered-perspective-on -the-right-to-housing-in-the-united-states/.

Jackson, Sharon A., Roger T. Anderson, Norma J. Johnson, and Paul D. Sorlie. "The Relation of Residential Segregation to All-Cause Mortality: A Study in Black and White." *American Journal of Public Health* 90, no. 4 (2000): 615–17.

"Jacksonville Couple Says They Faced Discrimination in Home Appraisal Because of Wife's Race." ABC News, October 14, 2020.

Jamieson, Jeremy P., Katrina Koslov, Matthew K. Nock, and Wendy Berry Mendes. "Experiencing Discrimination Increases Risk Taking." *Psychological Science* 24 (2013): 131–39.

Jarman, Michelle. "Race and Disability in U.S. Literature." in *The Cambridge Companion to Literature and Disability,* edited by Clare Barker and Stuart Murray, 155–69. Cambridge: Cambridge University Press, 2018.

Jellyman, Timothy, and Nicholas Spencer. "Residential Mobility in Childhood and Health Outcomes: A Systematic Review." *Journal of Epidemiology and Community Health* 62, no. 7 (July 2008): 584–92.

Jha, Ashish K., E. John Orav, and Zhonghe Li, and Arnold M. Epstein. "Concentration and Quality of Hospitals That Care for Elderly Black Patients." *Archives of Internal Medicine* 167, no. 11 (2007): 1177–82.

Jindal, Monique, Kamila B. Mistry, Maria Trent, Ashlyn McRae, and Rachel L. J. Thornton. "Police Exposures and the Health and Well-Being of Black Youth in the U.S.: A Systematic Review." *JAMA Pediatrics* 176, no. 1 (2022): 78–88.

Johnson, Portia, Patricia Markham Risica, Kim M. Gans, Ursee Kirtiania, and Shiriki K. Kumanyika. "Association of Perceived Racial Discrimination with Eating Behaviors and Obesity among Participants in the *Sister Talk* Study."

Journal of the National Black Nurses Association 23, no. 1 (July 2012): 34–40.

Johnson, Walter. *The Broken Heart of America: St. Louis and the Violent History of the United States.* New York: Basic Books, 2020.

———. "What Do We Mean When We Say 'Structural Racism'?" *Kalfou* 3, no. 1 (Spring 2016): 36–62.

Johnson-Agbakwu, Crista E., Nyima S. Ali, Corrina M. Oxford, Shana Wingo, Emily Manin, and Dean V. Coonrod. "Racism, COVID-19, and Health Equity in the USA: A Call to Action." *Journal of Racial and Ethnic Health Disparities* no. 9 (2022): 52–58.

Johnston, Jill E., and Andrea Hricko. "Industrial Lead Poisoning in Los Angeles: Anatomy of a Public Health Failure." *Environmental Justice* 10, no. 5 (2017): 162–67.

Jones, Antwan, Gregory D. Squires, and Sarah Crump. "The Relationship between Inclusionary Zoning Policies and Population Health." *Housing and Society* 49, no. 1 (2022): 38–57.

Jones, Antwan, Gregory D. Squires, and Carolynn Nixon. "Ecological Associations between Inclusionary Zoning Policies and Cardiovascular Disease Risk Prevalence: An Observational Study." *Circulation: Cardiovascular Quality and Outcomes* 14, no. 9 (September 2021): 944–52.

Jones, Arthur C. *Wade in the Water: The Wisdom of the Spirituals.* Maryknoll, NY: Orbis Books, 2023.

Jones, Camara Phyllis. "Invited Commentary: 'Race,' Racism and the Practice of Epidemiology." *American Journal of Epidemiology* 154, no. 4 (2001): 299–304.

Julian, Elizabeth K. "The Duty to Affirmatively Further Fair Housing: A Legal as Well as a Policy Imperative." in *The Affordable Housing Reader,* 2nd ed., edited by Elizabeth J. Mueller and J. Rosie Tighe, 514–21. New York: Routledge, 2022.

Jung, Moon-kie. *Beneath the Surface of White Supremacy: Denaturalizing U.S. Racisms Past and Present.* Stanford, CA: Stanford University Press, 2015.

Kahrl, Andrew W. *The Black Tax: 150 Years of Theft, Exploitation, and Dispossession in America.* Chicago: University of Chicago Press, 2024.

———. "Capitalizing on the Urban Fiscal Crisis: Predatory Tax Buyers in 1970s Chicago." *Journal of Urban History* 44, no. 3 (2018): 382–401.

———. "From Commons to Capital: The Creative Destruction of Coastal Real Estate, Environments, and Communities in the U.S. South." *Transatlantica* no. 2 (2020): 1–16.

———. "Investing in Distress: Tax Delinquency and Predatory Tax Buying in Urban America." *Critical Sociology* 43, no. 2 (2017): 199–219.

Kamin, Debra. "Black Homeowners Face Discrimination in Appraisals." *New York Times,* August 27, 2020.

Katz, Yarden. *Artificial Whiteness: Politics and Ideology in Artificial Intelligence.* New York: Columbia University Press, 2020.

Kelling, George L., and James Q. Wilson. "Broken Windows: The Police and Neighborhood Safety." *The Atlantic,* March 1982, 29–38.

Kendi, Sadiqa, and Michelle Macy. "The Injury Equity Framework: Establishing a Unified Approach for Addressing Inequalities." *New England Journal of Medicine* 388 (2023): 774–76.

Kiel, Paul, and Annie Waldman. "The Color of Debt: How Collection Suits Squeeze Black Neighborhoods." ProPublica, October 8, 2015. www.propublica.org/article/debt-collection-lawsuits-squeeze-black-neighborhoods.

Kimbro, Rachel Tolbert, Jeanne Brooks-Gunn, and Sara McLanahan. "Young Children in Urban Areas: Links among Neighborhood Characteristics, Weight Status, Outdoor Play, and Television Watching." *Social Science and Medicine* 72, no. 5 (2011): 668–76.

King, Martin Luther, Jr. "A Time to Break Silence." In *A Testament of Hope: The Essential Writings and Speeches of Martin Luther King, Jr.*, edited by James M. Washington, 231–44. New York: Harper Collins, 1986.

Kinney, Rebecca. "America's Great Comeback Story: The White Possessive in Detroit Tourism." *American Quarterly* 70, no. 4 (December 2018): 777–806.

Klinenberg, Eric. *Heat Wave: A Social Autopsy of Disaster in Chicago*. Chicago: University of Chicago Press, 2015.

Koplan, Carol, and Anna Chard. "Adverse Early Life Experiences as a Social Determinant of Mental Health." *Psychiatric Annals* 44, no. 1 (2014): 39–45.

Korver-Glenn, Elizabeth. *Race Brokers: Housing Markets and Segregation in 21st Century Urban America*. New York: Oxford University Press, 2021.

Krieger, Nancy. "Discrimination and Health Inequities." In *Social Epidemiology*, edited by Lisa F. Berkman and Ichiro Kawachi, 36–75. New York: Oxford University Press, 2000.

———. "Discrimination and Health Inequities." *International Journal of Health Services* 44, no. 4 (2014): 643–710.

———. "Embodiment: A Conceptual Glossary for Epidemiology." *Journal for Epidemiology and Community Health* 59 (2005): 350–55.

———. *Epidemiology and the People's Health: Theory and Context*. New York: Oxford University Press, 2011.

Labban, Muhieddine, Chang-Rong Chen, Nicola Frego, David-Dan Nguyen, Stuart R. Lipsitz, Amanda J. Reich, Timothy Rebbeck, et al. "Disparities in Travel-Related Barriers to Accessing Health Care from the 2017 National Household Travel Survey." *JAMA Network Open* 6, no. 7 (2023): 1–14.

Lang, Robert E., and Rebecca H. Sohmer. "Legacy of the Housing Act of 1949: The Past, Present, and Future of Federal Housing and Urban Policy." *Housing Policy Debate* 11, no. 2 (2000): 291–98.

Larson, Jeff, Julia Angwin, Lauren Kirchner, and Surva Mattu for ProPublica, and Dina Haner, Michael Saccucci, Keith Newsom-Stewart, Andrew Cohen and Martin Roman for Consumer Reports. "How We Examined Racial Discrimination in Auto Insurance Prices." ProPublica, April 5, 2017. www.propublica.org/article/minority-neighborhoods-higher-car-insurance-premiums-methodology.

La Veist, Thomas A. "Racial Segregation and Longevity among African Americans: An Individual-Level Analysis." *Health Services Research* 38, no. 6, part 2 (2003): 1719–34.

Leibel, Sydney, Bob Geng, Wanda Phipatanakul, Euyhyun Lee, and Phyllis Hartigan. "Screening Social Determinants of Health in a Multidisciplinary Severe Asthma Clinic Program." *Pediatric Quality and Safety* 5, no. 5 (2020): 1–6.

Lerma, Veronica. "Intersectional Criminalization: How Chicanas Experience and Navigate Criminalization through Interpersonal Relationships with Latino Men and Boys." *Sociological Perspectives* 66, no. 2 (2022): 311–30.

Lewis, Tené T., Allison E. Aiello, Sue Leurgans, Jeremiah Kelly, and Lisa Barnes. "Self-Reported Experiences of Everyday Discrimination Are Associated with Elevated C-reactive Protein Levels in Older African-American Adults." *Brain, Behavior, and Immunity* 24 (2010): 438–43.

Liljenquist, Kendra, and Trumaini R. Coker. "Transferring Well-Child Care to Meet the Needs of Families at the Intersection of Racism and Poverty." *Academic Pediatrics* 21, no. 8S (November-December 2021): S102–S107.

Linde, Sebastian, Rebekah J. Walker, Jennifer A. Campbell, and Leonard E. Egede. "Historic Residential Redlining and Present-Day Social Determinants of Health, Home Evictions, and Food Insecurity within US Neighborhoods." *Journal of General Internal Medicine* 38 (2023): 3321–28. https://doi.org/10.1007/s11606-023-08258-5.

Lindsay, Gordon B., Ray M. Merrill, and Riley J. Hedin. "The Contribution of Public Health and Improved Social Conditions to Increased Life Expectancy: An Analysis of Public Awareness." *Journal of Community Medicine and Health Education* 4, no. 5 (2014): 1–5.

Lipsitz, George. "Fair Housing and Health: A Social Ecology Framework." in *Lessons in Environmental Justice: From Civil Rights to Black Lives Matter and Idle No More,* edited by Michael Mascarenhas, 184–98. Thousand Oaks, CA: Sage Publications, 2021.

———. *How Racism Takes Place.* Philadelphia: Temple University Press, 2011.

———. *The Possessive Investment in Whiteness: How White People Profit from Identity Politics.* 20th anniversary ed. Philadelphia: Temple University Press, 2018.

———. "Unexpected Affiliations: Environmental Justice and the New Social Movements." *Works and Days* 24, nos. 47–48 (February 2006): 25–44.

Lipsitz, George, and Alliance for California Traditional Arts. *Saludarte: Building Health Equity on the Bedrock of Traditional Arts and Culture.* Los Angeles: Alliance for California Traditional Arts, 2020.

Livingston, Julie, and Andrew Ross. *Cars and Jails: Freedom Dreams, Debt and Carcerality.* New York: OR Books, 2022.

Loyd, Jenna M. *Health Rights Are Civil Rights.* Minneapolis: University of Minnesota Press, 2014.

———. "Obamacare and Sovereign Debt: Race, Reparations, and the Haunting of Premature Death." In *Subprime Health: Debt and Race in U.S. Medicine,* edited by Nadine Ehlers and Leslie R. Hinkson, 55–82. Minneapolis: University of Minnesota Press, 2017.

Lucas, Ashley E. *Prison Theatre and the Global Crisis of Incarceration.* New York: Methuen, 2021.

Lynch, Emile E., Lorraine Halinka Malcoe, Sarah E. Laurent, Jason Richardson, Bruce C. Mitchell, and Helen C.S. Meier. "The Legacy of Structural

Racism: Associations between Historic Redlining, Current Mortgage Lending, and Health." *Population Health* 14 (June 2021): 1–10.

Lyons, Christopher J., Maria B. Velez, and Xuanying Chen. "Inheriting the Grade: HOLC 'Redlining' Maps and Contemporary Neighborhood Crime." *Socius: Sociological Research for a Dynamic World* 9 (2023): 1–19.

MacDonald, Christine. "Detroit Kids' Lead Poisoning Rates Higher Than Flint." *Detroit News*, November 14, 2017. www.detroitnews.com/story /news/local/detroit-city/2017/11/14/lead-poisoning-children-detroit /107683688/.

MacKinnon, Catherine. "MacKinnon J., Concurring with the Judgment." In *What "Brown v. Board of Education" Should Have Said*, edited by Jack M. Balkin, 143–57. New York: NYU Press, 2002.

Mapping Police Violence. "2021 Police Violence Report." 2022. https://police-violencereport.org/policeviolencereport2021.pdf.

Markowitz, Gerald, and David Rosner. *Lead Wars: The Politics of Science and the Fate of American's Children*. Berkeley: University of California Press, 2013.

Marya, Rupa, and Raj Patel. *Inflamed: Deep Medicine and the Anatomy of Injustice*. New York: Farrar, Straus, and Giroux, 2021.

Mascarenhas, Michael, ed. *Lessons in Environmental Justice: From Civil Rights to Black Lives Matter and Idle No More*. Los Angeles: Sage Publications, 2021.

Massey, Douglas S. 2007. *Categorically Unequal: The American Stratification System*. New York: Russell Sage Foundation.

Massoglia, Michael, and William Alex Pridemore. "Incarceration and Health." *Annual Review of Sociology* 41 (August 2015): 291–310.

Matsuda, Mari. *Where Is Your Body? And Other Essays on Race, Gender, and the Law*. Boston: Beacon Press, 1997.

Matthew, Dayna Bowen. *Just Health: Treating Structural Racism to Heal America*. New York: New York University Press, 2022.

Maxwell, Jill. "Sexual Harassment at Home: Altering the Terms, Conditions and Privileges of Rental Housing for Section 8 Recipients." *Wisconsin Women's Law Journal* 21 (2006): 223–61.

May, Lucy. "This Black Family's Home Appraisal Grew by $92,000 after They Removed All Signs of Their Race." WCPO Cincinnati, August 19, 2021. www .wcpo.com/news/our-community/this-black-familys-home-appraisal-grew -by-92-000-after-they-removed-all-signs-of-their-race.

McArdle, Nancy, and Dolores Acevedo-Garcia. "Consequences of Segregation for Children's Opportunity and Well-Being." In *The Affordable Housing Reader*, 2nd ed., edited by Elizabeth J. Mueller and J. Rosie Tighe, 113–22. New York: Routledge, 2017.

McClure, Elizabeth, Linda Feinstein, Evette Cordoba, Christian Douglas, Michael Emch, Whitney Robinson, Sandra Galea, et al. "The Legacy of Redlining in the Effect of Foreclosure on Detroit's Residents' Self-Rated Health." *Health and Place* 55 (2019): 9–19.

McCoy, Deborah L., and Jeffrey M. Vincent. "Housing and Education: The Inextricable Link." In *Segregation: The Rising Costs for America*, edited by James H. Carr and Nandinee K. Kutty, 125–50. New York: Routledge, 2008.

Menendian, Stephen, and Richard Rothstein. "The Kerner Commission and Housing Policy: The Road Not Taken: Housing and Criminal Justice 50 Years after the Kerner Commission Report." With Nirali Beri. In *The Affordable Housing Reader*, 2nd ed., edited by Elizabeth J. Mueller and J. Rosie Tighe, 41–51. New York: Routledge, 2019.

Metzl, Jonathan M. *Dying of Whiteness: How the Politics of Racial Resentment Is Killing America's Heartland.* New York: Basic Books, 2020.

———. *The Protest Psychosis: How Schizophrenia Became a Black Disease.* Boston: Beacon Press, 2009.

Metzl, Jonathan M., and Helena Hansen. "Structural Competency: Theorizing a New Medical Engagement with Stigma and Inequality." *Social Science Medicine* 106 (2014): 126–33.

Milligan, Joy. "Animus and Its Distortion of the Past." *Alabama Law Review* 74, no. 3 (2023): 725–53.

Mirowsky, John, and Catherine Ross. *Social Causes of Psychological Distress.* New Brunswick, NJ: Aldine Transaction, 2012.

Mlynaryk, Nicole. "Cancer Patients Facing Housing Instability Show Greater Risk of Mortality." *UC San Diego Today*, September 16, 2022. https://today.ucsd.edu/story/cancer-patients-facing-housing-instability-show-greater-risk-of-mortality.

Mock, Brentin. "Federal Legislation Could Tackle the Racial Gap in Home Appraisals." Bloomberg.com, March 1, 2022. www.bloomberg.com/news/articles/2022-03-01/bill-would-address-racial-bias-in-appraised-home-values.

Molina, Natalia. *Fit to Be Citizens? Public Health and Race in Los Angeles, 1879–1939.* Berkeley: University of California Press, 2006.

Montoya, Michael J. *Making the Mexican Diabetic: Race, Science, and the Genetics of Inequality.* Berkeley: University of California Press, 2011.

Moody, Heather, Joe T. Darden, and Bruce Wm. Pigozzi. "The Relationship of Neighborhood Socioeconomic Differences and Racial Residential Segregation in Childhood Blood Levels in Metropolitan Detroit." *Journal of Urban Health* 93, no. 5 (2016): 820–39.

Moody, Heather, Linda Elaine Easley, and Melissa Sissen. "Water Shutoffs during Covid-19 and Black Lives: Case Study Detroit." *Environmental Justice* 15, no. 5 (2022): 313–18.

Moody, Heather A., and Sue C. Grady. "Lead Emissions and Population Vulnerability in the Detroit Metropolitan Area, 2006–2013: Impact of Pollution, Housing Age and Neighborhood Racial Isolation and Poverty on Blood Lead in Children." *International Journal of Environmental Research and Public Health* 14, no. 12 (2017): 1445.

———. "Lead Emissions and Population Vulnerability in the Detroit (Michigan, USA) Metropolitan Area, 2006–2013: A Spatial and Temporal Analysis." *International Journal of Environmental Research and Public Health* 18, no. 5 (2021): 2747.

Moore, Wendy Leo. *Reproducing Racism: White Space, Elite Law Schools, and Racial Inequality.* Lanham, MD: Rowman and Littlefield, 2008.

Morales, Iris. "Palante, Siempre Palante." In *The Puerto Rican Movement: Voices from the Diaspora,* edited by Andres Torres and Jose E. Velasquez, 210–27. Philadelphia: Temple University Press, 1998.

Morello-Frosch, Rachel, Manuel Pastor, and James Sadd. "Environmental Justice and the Precautionary Principle: Air Toxics Exposures and Health Risks among School Children in Los Angeles." In *Contested Illnesses: Citizens, Science, and Health Social Movements,* edited by Phil Brown, Rachel Morello-Frosch, Steven Zavetoski, and the Contested Illnesses Research Group, 64–76. Berkeley: University of California Press, 2012.

Morgan, Jerome. "Education Is Improvisation: Improvisation Is Art." *Kalfou* 6, no. 2 (Fall 2019): 280–86.

Morrison, Toni. "Home." In *The House That Race Built: Black Americans, U.S. Terrain,* edited by Wahneema Lubiano, 3–12. New York: Pantheon Books, 1997.

Mueller, Alexandra R., and Utpal Dutta. "Brownfields and Children under 18 in Detroit." *Journal of Civil Engineering and Architecture* 15 (2021): 17–27.

Mueller, Elizabeth J., and J. Rosie Tighe, eds. *The Affordable Housing Reader.* 2nd ed. New York: Routledge, 2022.

Murakawa, Naomi. "The Origins of the Carceral Crisis: Racial Order as 'Law and Order' in Postwar American Politics." In *Race and American Political Development,* edited by Joseph Lowndes, Julie Novkov, and Dorian T. Warren, chap. 10. New York: Routledge, 2008.

Murry, Velma McBride, P. Adama Brown, Gene H. Brody, Carolyn E, Cutrona, and Ronald Simons. "Racial Discrimination as a Moderator of the Links among Stress, Maternal Psychological Functioning and Family Relationships." *Journal of Marriage and Family* 63, no. 4 (2001): 915–26.

Nadal, Kevin Leo Yabut. *Queering Law and Order: LGBTQ Communities and the Criminal Justice System.* Lanham, MD: Lexington Books, 2020.

Napatoff, Alexandra. *Punishment without Crime: How Our Massive Misdemeanor System Traps the Innocent and Makes America More Unequal.* New York: Basic Books, 2018.

Nardone, Anthony, Joey Chiang, and Jason Coburn. "Historic Redlining and Urban Health Today in U.S. Cities." *Environmental Justice* 13, no. 4 (2020): 109–19.

National Center on Family Homelessness. "Homeless Children: America's New Outcasts." Fact sheet, National Center on Family Homelessness, accessed October 6, 2023. www.nn4youth.org/wp-content/uploads/A2Homeless Children.pdf.

Neavling, Steve. "Lead Poisoning Endangers Generations of Detroit Children with No End in Sight." *Metro Times,* November 18, 2020. www.metrotimes .com/news/lead-poisoning-endangers-generations-of-detroit-children-with -no-end-in-sight-25809555.

Neff, Kristin Jones. "How the Austin Family's Historic Marin City Pole Home Became at the Center of a Legal Fight against Discriminatory Housing Practices." *Marin* magazine, January 21, 2022.

Nelson, Alondra. *Body and Soul: The Black Panther Party and the Fight against Medical Discrimination.* Minneapolis: University of Minnesota Press, 2013.

Nesper, Larry. *The Walleye War: The Struggle for Ojibwe Spearfishing and Treaty Rights*. Lincoln: University of Nebraska Press, 2002.

Nishida, Akemi. *Just Care: Messy Entanglements of Disability, Dependency, and Desire*. Philadelphia: Temple University Press, 2022.

Norris, Whitney K., M. Kathryn Allison, Marley F. Fradley, and Melissa Zielinski. "'You're Setting a Lot of People Up for Failure': What Formerly Incarcerated Women Would Tell Healthcare Decision Makers." *Health and Justice* 10, no. 4 (2022): 1–10.

Nothaft, Amanda, and Patrick Cooney. "Building on Michigan's Auto Insurance Reform Law." M Poverty Solutions, December 2021, 1–7. https://poverty.umich.edu/publications/building-on-michigans-auto-insurance-reform-law/.

Ogedegbe, Gbenga. "Responsibility of Medical Journals in Addressing Racism in Health Care." *JAMA Network Open* 3, no. 8 (August 20, 2020): 1–4.

Oliveri, Rigel. "Sexual Harassment of Low Income Women by Landlords." *Cityscape* 21, no. 3 (2019): 261–84.

Opportunity360. *Report for Census Tract: 2042*. Opportunity360 Measurement Report. Enterprise Community Partners, n.d., accessed December 11, 2019, enterprisecommunity.org/opportunity360, no longer accessible at website.

Orren, Karen. *Corporate Power and Social Change*. Baltimore: Johns Hopkins University Press, 1974.

Ostfield-Johns, Sharon, Elena Aragona, and Louis Hart. "Removing Race from Hyperbilirubinemia Guidelines Is Not Enough." *JAMA Pediatrics* 176, no. 12 (2022): 1163–64.

Oyama, Rebecca. "Do Not (Re)Enter: The Rise of Criminal Background Tenant Screening as a Violation of the Fair Housing Act." *Michigan Journal of Race and Law* 15, no. 1 (Fall 2009): 181–222.

Pacewicz, Josh, and John N. Robinson III. "Pocketbook Policing: How Race Shapes Municipal Reliance on Punitive Fines and Fees in the Chicago Suburbs." *Socio-Economic Review* 19, no. 3 (2021): 975–1003.

Park, K-Sue. "How Did Redlining Make Money?" Just Money, September 25, 2023, 1–5.https://justmoney.org/k-sue-park-how-did-redlining-make-money/.

Parolin, Zachary, and Emma K. Lee. "The Role of Poverty and Racial Discrimination in Exacerbating the Health Consequences of Covid-19." *Lancet Regional Health—Americas* 7 (March 2022): 1–9.

Parr, Josh. "Young Laotian Women Build a Bridge in Richmond." *Shades of Power* 1, no. 4 (1999): 1–4.

Paschal, Olivia. "'This Is the Red Cross. Do You Have Food?'" *The Atlantic*, October 4, 2018, 1–13.

Perry, Andre, Jonathan Rothwell, and David Harshbarger. *The Devaluation of Assets in Black Neighborhoods: The Case of Residential Property*. Washington, DC: Metropolitan Policy Program, Brookings Institution, 2018.

Petersilia, Joan. *When Prisoners Come Home: Parole and Prisoner Reentry*. New York: Oxford University Press, 2003.

Pollack, Craig Evan, Laken C. Roberts, Roger D. Peng, Pete Simbolic, David Judy, Susan Balcer-Whaley, Torie Grant, et al. "Association of a Housing

Mobility Program with Childhood Asthma Symptoms and Exacerbations." *JAMA* 329, no. 19 (May 16, 2023): 1671–81.

Pollock, Anne. *Medicating Race.* Durham, NC: Duke University Press, 2012.

Powell, Richard, and Jeremy Porter. "Redlining, Concentrated Disadvantage, and Crime: The Effects of Discriminatory Government Policies on Urban Violent Crime." *American Journal of Criminal Justice* 48 (August 2022): 1132–56. https://doi.org/10.1007/s12103-022-09688-3.

Probasco, Jim. "The Insurance Industry Confronts Its Own Racism: The NAIC Tackles Racial Discrimination in the Insurance Sector." Investopedia, February 22, 2022.

Pulido, Laura. *Environmentalism and Economic Justice: Two Chicano Struggles in the Southwest.* Tucson: University of Arizona Press, 1996.

Purifoy, Danielle, and Louise Seamster. "Creative Extraction: Black Towns in White Space." *Environment and Planning D: Society and Space* 39, no. 1 (2021): 47–66.

Rahman, Md Mostafijur, Rob McConnell, Hannah Schlaerth, Joseph Ko, Sam Silva, Frederick W. Lurmann, Lawrence Palinkas, et al. "The Effects of Coexposure to Extremes of Heat and Particulate Air Pollution on Mortality in California: Implications for Climate Change." *American Journal of Respiratory and Critical Care Medicine* 206, no. 9 (2022): 1117–27.

Ralph, Laurence. "Becoming Aggrieved: An Alternative Framework of Care in Black Chicago." *RSF: The Russell Sage Foundation Journal of the Social Sciences* 1, no. 2 (November 2015): 31–41.

Ratcliff, Kathryn Strother. *The Social Determinants of Health: Looking Upstream.* Cambridge: Polity Press, 2017.

Rector, Josiah. *Toxic Debt: An Environmental Justice History of Detroit.* Chapel Hill: University of North Carolina Press, 2022.

Reece, Jason. "Confronting the Legacy of 'Separate but Equal': Can the History of Race, Real Estate, and Discrimination Engage and Inform Contemporary Policy." *RSF: The Russell Sage Foundation Journal of the Social Sciences* 7, no. 1 (2021): 110–33.

Reese, Ashanté M. *Black Food Geographies: Race, Self-Reliance, and Food Access in Washington, D.C.* Chapel Hill: University of North Carolina Press, 2019.

Reskin, Barbara. "The Race Discrimination System." *Annual Review of Sociology* 38 (2012): 17–35.

Rice, Lisa, and Deidre Swesnik. "Discriminatory Effects of Credit Scoring on Communities of Color." *Suffolk University Law Review* 46 (2013): 935–66.

Richardson, Eugene T., Momin M. Malik, William A. Darity, Jr., A. Kirsten Mullen, Michelle E, Morse, Maya Malik, Aletha Maybank et al. "Reparations for Black American Descendants of Persons Enslaved in the U.S. and Their Potential Impact on SARS-CoV-2 Transmission." *Social Science and Medicine* 276 (2021): 113741. https://doi.org/10.1016/j.socscimed.2021.113741.

Richardson, Rashida. "Racial Segregation and the Data-Driven Society: How Our Failure to Reckon with Root Causes Perpetuates Separate and Unequal Realities." *Berkeley Technology Law Journal* 36 (2021): 101–39.

Richardson, Sarah S. "Race and IQ in the Postgenomic Age: The Microcephaly Case." *Biosocieties* 6, no. 4 (2011): 420–46.

Richie, Beth. "The Social Impact of Mass Incarceration on Women." In *Invisible Punishment: The Collateral Consequences of Mass Imprisonment,* edited by Marc Mauer and Meda Chesney-Lind, 136–49. New York: New Press, 2002.

Richmond, Caroline. "Obituary: Lester Breslow." *The Lancet* 380 (July 21, 2012): 212.

Rideau, Daniel, Jerome Morgan, and Robert Jones. *Unbreakable Resolve: Triumphant Stories of 3 True Gentlemen.* Las Vegas, NV: Zen Magic, 2017.

Rios, Jodi. *Black Lives and Spatial Matters: Policing Blackness and Practicing Freedom in Suburban St. Louis.* Ithaca, NY: Cornell University Press, 2020.

———. "Flesh in the Street." *Kalfou* 3, no. 2 (Spring 2016): 63–78.

Rios, Sarah. "Valley Fever: Environmental Racism and Health Justice." PhD diss., University of California, Santa Barbara, 2018.

Roberts, Dorothy. *Fatal Invention: How Science, Politics, and Big Business Recreate Race in the Twenty-First Century.* New York: New Press, 2012.

———. "The Problem with Race-Based Medicine." In *Beyond Bioethics: Toward a New Biopolitics,* edited by Osagie K. Obasogie and Marcy Darnovsky, 410–14. Oakland: University of California Press, 2018.

———. *Torn Apart: How the Child Welfare System Destroys Black Families—and How Abolition Can Build a Safer World.* New York: Basic Books, 2022.

Robinson, Cedric J. *Black Marxism: The Making of the Black Radical Tradition.* Chapel Hill: University of North Carolina Press, 2000.

Robinson, John III. "Making Markets on the Margins: Housing Finance Agencies and the Racial Politics of Credit Expansion." *American Journal of Sociology* 125, no. 4 (2020): 974–1029.

Rodríguez, Juana María. "Activism and Identity in the Ruins of Representation." In *AIDS and the Distribution of Crises,* edited by Jih-Fei Cheng, Alexandra Juhasz, and Nishant Shahani. Durham, NC: Duke University Press, 2020.

———. *Queer Latinidad: Identity Practices, Discursive Spaces.* New York: New York University Press, 2003.

Rogers, Arneta. "How Police Brutality Harms Mothers: Linking Police Violence to the Reproductive Justice Movement." *Hastings Race and Poverty Law Journal* 12, no. 2 (Summer 2015): 205–34.

Rogers, Richard G., Robert A. Hummer, Elizabeth M. Lawrence, Trent Davidson, and Samuel Fishman. "Dying Young in the United States: What's Driving High Death Rates among Americans under Age 25 and What Can Be Done?" *Population Bulletin* 76, no. 2 (January 19, 2023): 1–4.

Rose, Tricia. *Black Noise: Rap Music and Black Culture in Contemporary America.* Hanover, NH: Wesleyan University Press, 1994.

———. *Metaracism: How Systemic Racism Devastates Black Lives—and How We Break Free.* New York: Basic Books, 2024.

Rothstein, Richard. *The Color of Law: A Forgotten History of How Our Government Segregated America.* New York: Liveright, 2017.

Rouse, Carolyn Moxley. *Uncertain Suffering: Racial Health Disparities and Sickle Cell Disease.* Berkeley: University of California Press, 2009.

Royal, Dr. Erroll L. *Traces of Places and Faces of African Americans From the New Bern Community.* Las Vegas, NV: Independently Published, 2022.

Rucks-Ahidiana, Zawadi. "Theorizing Gentrification as a Process of Racial Capitalism." *City and Community* 21, no. 3 (September 2022): 173–92.

Ruffins, Ranger. "The Answer Really Lies in the Community: Exploring Inequity in Resilience Planning through Community Voices: A Study of Post-Florence New Bern, North Carolina." MA thesis, University of North Carolina-Chapel Hill, 2020.

Rupa, Marya, and Raj Patel. *Inflamed: Deep Medicine and the Anatomy of Injustice.* New York: Farrar, Straus, and Giroux, 2021.

Saadi, Michelle. *Claim It Yourself: The Accident Victim's Guide to Personal Injury Claims.* New York: Pharos Books, 1987.

Saegert, Susan, and Helene Clark. "Opening Doors: What a Right to Housing Means for Women." in *A Right to Housing: Foundation for a New Social Agenda,* edited by Rachel G. Bratt, Michael E. Stone, and Chester Hartman, 296–315. Philadelphia: Temple University Press, 2006.

Sampson, Robert J., and Alix S. Winter. "The Racial Ecology of Lead Poisoning: Toxic Inequality in Chicago Neighborhoods, 1995–2013." *Du Bois Review* 13, no. 2 (2016): 261–84.

Sandel, Megan, Richard Sheward, Stephanie Ettinger de Cuba, Sharon Coleman, Deborah Frank, Mariana Chilton, Maureen Black, et al. "Unstable Housing and Caregiver and Child Health in Renter Families." *Pediatrics* 141, no. 2 (2018): 1–10.

Sanders-Phillips, Kathy, Beverlyn Settles-Reeves, Doren Walker, and Janeese Brownlow. "Social Inequality and Racial Discrimination: Risk Factors for Health Disparities in Children of Color." *Pediatrics* 124, no. 3 (2009): S176–S186.

Sandoval, Chela. *Methodology of the Oppressed.* Minneapolis: University of Minnesota Press, 2000.

Sandoval, Gabriela. "The Costs of Child Support." *Poverty and Race* 24, no. 2 (March/April 2015): 1–2, 6.

Satcher, David, Gregory E. Fryer Jr., Jessica McCann, Adewale Troutman, Steven H. Woolf, and George Rust. "What If We Were Equal? A Comparison of the Black-White Mortality Gap in 1960 and 2000." *Health Affairs* 24, no. 2 (March 2005): 459–64.

Schalk, Sami. *Black Disability Politics.* Durham, NC: Duke University Press, 2022.

Schindler, Anne. 2020. "Jacksonville Couple Sees Home Appraisal Jump 40 Percent After They Remove All Traces of 'Blackness.'" FirstCoast News, August 25. www.firstcoastnews.com/article/news/local/jacksonville-couple-sees-home-appraisal-jump-40-percent-after-they-remove-all-traces-of-blackness/77-c3087e8c-0c65-4fb9-8319-da82f5c0ea20#:~.

Schlenker, Charlie. "EEOC Finds State Farm Workers Discriminated Against on Basis of Race." WGLT, June 22, 2021. www.wglt.org/local-news/2021-06-19/eeoc-finds-state-farm-workers-discriminated-on-basis-of-race.

Schmit, K. M., Z. Wansaula, R. Pratt, S. F. Price, and A. J. Langer. "Tuberculosis—United States." *Morbidity and Mortality Weekly Report*, no. 66 (2017): 289–94.

Schwartz, Alex F. *Housing Policy in the United States: An Introduction.* New York: Routledge, 2006.

Schwemm, Robert. "The Limits of Litigation in Fulfilling the Fair Housing Act's Promise of Nondiscriminatory Home Loans." in *From Foreclosure to Fair Lending: Advocacy, Organization, Occupy, and the Pursuit of Equitable Credit,* edited by Chester Hartman and Gregory D. Squires, 229–48. New York: New Village Press, 2013.

Scott, James C. *Seeing Like a State: How Certain Schemes to Improve the Human Condition Have Failed.* New Haven, CT: Yale University Press, 1998.

Seamster, Louise. "When Democracy Disappears: Emergency Management in Benton Harbor." *Du Bois Review* 15, no. 2 (2018): 295–322.

Seng, Michael P. "Restorative Justice: A Model of Conciliating Fair Housing Disputes." *Journal of Law in Society* 21, no. 2 (Winter 2021): 63–92.

Shah, Bindi. *Laotian Daughters: Working toward Community, Belonging, and Environmental Justice.* Philadelphia: Temple University Press, 2011.

Shah, Nayan. *Contagious Divides: Epidemics and Race in San Francisco's Chinatown.* Berkeley: University of California Press, 2001.

Shapiro, Thomas M. *The Hidden Cost of Being African American: How Wealth Perpetuates Inequality.* New York: Oxford University Press, 2004.

Sharkey, Patrick. *Stuck in Place: Urban Neighborhoods and the End of Progress toward Racial Equality.* Chicago: University of Chicago Press, 2013.

Silver, Ian A., Daniel C. Semenza, and Joseph L. Nedelec. "Incarceration of Youths in an Adult Correctional Facility and Risk of Premature Death." *JAMA Network Open* 6, no. 7 (July 5, 2023): 1–10.

Silverman, Robert Mark, and Kelly L. Patterson. "The Four Horsemen of the Fair Housing Apocalypse: A Critique of Fair Housing Policy in the US." *Critical Sociology* 38, no. 1 (2011): 123–40.

Simes, Jessica T., and Jaquelyn L. Jahn. "The Consequences of Medicaid Expansion under the Affordable Care Act for Police Arrests." *PLoS One* 17, no. 1 (January 2022): e0261512.

Skrabski, Árpád, Maria Kopp, and Ichiro Kawachi. "Social Capital and Collective Efficacy in Hungary: Cross Sectional Associations with Middle Aged Female and Male Mortality Rates." *Journal of Epidemiology and Community Health* 58, no. 4 (2004): 340–45.

Smirnova, Michelle. *The Prescription-to-Prison Pipeline: The Medicalization and Criminalization of Pain.* Durham, NC: Duke University Press, 2023.

Smith, Emilie Phillips, D. Wayne Osgood, Linda Caldwell, Kathryn Hines, and Daniel F. Perkins. "Measuring Collective Efficacy among Children in Community-Based Afterschool Programs: Exploring Pathways to Prevention and Positive Youth Development." *American Journal of Community Psychology* 52, nos. 1–2 (September 2013): 27–40.

Smith, Shanna L., and Cathy Cloud. "Welcome to the Neighborhood? The Persistence of Discrimination and Segregation." In *The Integration Debate:*

Competing Futures for American Cities, edited by Chester Hartman and Gregory D. Squires. New York: Routledge, 2010.

Sommer, Doris. *The Work of Art in the World: Civic Agency and Public Humanities.* Durham, NC: Duke University Press, 2014.

South, Eugenia C., Bernadette C. Hohl, Michelle C. Kondo, John M. MacDonald, and Charles C. Branas. "Effect of Greening Vacant Land on Mental Health of Community-Dwelling Adults: A Cluster Randomized Trial." *JAMA Network Open* 1, no. 3 (2018): 3180298.

Squires, Gregory D., ed. *The Fight for Fair Housing: Causes, Consequences, and Future Implications of the 1968 Federal Fair Housing Act.* New York: Routledge, 2018.

———. *Insurance Redlining: Disinvestment, Reinvestment, and the Evolving Role of Financial Institutions.* Lanham, MD: Rowman and Littlefield, 1997.

———. "Racial Profiling, Insurance Style: Insurance Redlining and the Uneven Development of Metropolitan Areas." *Journal of Urban Affairs* 25, no. 4 (2003): 391–410.

Squires, Gregory D., and Charis E. Kubrin. *Privileged Places: Race, Residence, and the Structure of Opportunity.* Boulder, CO: Lynne Rienner, 2006.

Starbuck, Amanda, and Ronald White. *Living in the Shadow of Danger: Poverty, Race and Unequal Chemical Facility Hazards.* Washington, DC: Center for Effective Government, 2016.

Steelcase Foundation. "The 49507 Project." March 15, 2021. www.steelcase foundation.org/the-49507-project/.

Stein, Emma. "Detroit Overtaxed Homeowners $600m, Years Later, Advocates Still Seeking Reparations." *Detroit Free Press,* January 22, 2022.

Stein, Michael, and Sandro Galea. *The Picture of Health.* Washington, DC: APHA Press, 2022.

Stein, Samuel. *Capital City: Gentrification and the Real Estate State.* New York: Verso, 2019.

Stern, Alexandra. *Eugenic Nation: Faults and Frontiers of Breeding in Modern America.* Berkeley: University of California Press, 2015.

Strand, Palma Joy, and Nicholas A. Mirkay. "Racialized Tax Inequity: Wealth, Racism, and the U.S. System of Taxation." *Northwestern Journal of Law and Social Policy* 15, no. 3 (Spring 2020): 267–304.

Stretesky, Paul B. "The Distribution of Air Lead Levels across U.S. Counties: Implications for the Production of Racial Inequality." *Sociological Spectrum* 23, no. 1 (2003): 91–118.

Strohschein, Lisa, and Rose Weitz. *The Sociology of Health, Illness, and Health Care in Canada.* Toronto: Nelson Education, 2013.

Students at the Center. *Go to Jail: Confronting a System of Oppression.* Aptos, CA: LMO Projects, 2021.

"Study Shows Racial Gaps in School Suspensions." *Louisiana Weekly,* September 20–26, 2010, 10.

Subramanian, S.V., Dolores Acevedo-Garcia, and Theresa Osypuk. "Racial Residential Segregation and Geographic Heterogeneity in Black/White Disparity in Poor Self-Rated Health in the U.S.: A Multilevel Statistical Analysis." *Social Science and Medicine* 60, no. 8 (2005): 1667–79.

Sze, Julie. *Environmental Justice in a Moment of Danger.* Oakland: University of California Press, 2020.

———. *Noxious New York: The Racial Politics of Urban Health and Environmental Justice.* Cambridge: MIT Press, 2006.

Tadiar, Neferti. "Domestic Bodies of the Philippines." *Sojourn* 12, no. 2 (1997): 153–91.

———. "Manila's New Metropolitan Form." *differences* 5, no. 3 (Fall 1993): 154–78.

Taylor, Diana. *The Archive and the Repertoire: Performing Cultural Memory in the Americas.* Durham, NC: Duke University Press, 2003.

Taylor, Dorceta E. *Toxic Communities: Environmental Racism, Industrial Pollution, and Residential Mobility.* New York: New York University Press, 2014.

Tervalon, Melanie, and Jann Murray-Garcia. "Cultural Humility versus Cultural Competence: A Critical Distinction Defining Physician Training Outcomes in Multicultural Education." *Journal of Health Care for the Poor and Underserved* 9, no. 2 (1998): 117–25.

Thiele, Bret. "The Human Right to Adequate Housing: A Tool for Promoting and Protecting Individual and Community Health." *American Journal of Public Health* 92, no. 5 (May 2002): 712–15.

Thomas, Emma F., Craig McGarty, and Kenneth I. Mavor. "Aligning Identities, Emotions, and Beliefs to Create Commitment to Sustainable Social and Political Action." *Personality and Psychology Review* 13, no. 4 (2009): 194–218.

Thorpe, Ronald J., Jr., Michelle Odden, and Lewis A. Lipsitz. "A Call to Action to Enhance Justice, Equity, Diversity, and the Inclusion in the Journal of Gerontology Series A: Medical Sciences." *Journal of Gerontology Medical Sciences* 77, no. 1 (2021): 89–90.

Tiako, Max Jordan Nguemeni, Victor Ray, and Eugenia South. "Medical Schools as Racialized Organizations: How Race-Neutral Structures Sustain Racial Inequality in Medical Education—a Narrative Review." *Journal of General Internal Medicine* 37, no. 9 (July 2022): 2259–66.

Tomlinson, Barbara. *Undermining Intersectionality: The Perils of Powerblind Feminism.* Philadelphia: Temple University Press, 2019.

———."Wicked Problems and Intersectionality Telephone." in *Antiracism Inc.: Why the Way We Talk about Racial Justice Matters,* edited by Felice Blake, Paula Ioanide, and Alison Reed, 161–87. Middletown, DE. punctum books, 2019.

Torres, Angel O., Robert D. Bullard, and Chad G. Johnson. "Closed Doors: Persistent Barriers to Fair Housing." In *Sprawl City: Race, Politics, and Planning in Atlanta,* edited by Robert Bullard, Glenn Johnson, and Angel Torres, 89–109. Washington, DC: Island Press, 2000.

Tsai, Jennifer. "How Should Educators and Publishers Eliminate Racial Essentialism?" *AMA Journal of Ethics* 24, no. 3 (March 2022): 201–11.

Tucker, M. Belinda, Neva Pemberton, Mary Weaver, Gwendelyn Rivera, and Carrie Petrucci. "Imprisoning the Family: Incarceration in Black Los

Angeles." In *Black Los Angeles: American Dreams and Racial Realities*, edited by Darnell Hunt and Ana-Christina Ramon, 168–87. New York: New York University Press, 2010.

Turner, Margery A., Rob Santos, Diane K. Levy, Doug Wissoker, Claudia Aranda, and Rob Pitingolo. *Housing Discrimination against Racial and Ethnic Minorities 2012*. Washington, DC: US Department of Housing and Urban Development, Office of Policy Development and Research, 2013.

Tweet, Patricia E., and Jessica W. Pardee. "Medical Gentrification and Transportation: Health Care Systems as Urban Redevelopers." *Sociological Spectrum* 43, no. 3 (2021): 229–54.

US Department of Education Office for Civil Rights. "Civil Rights Data Collection Data Snapshot: School Discipline." Issue Brief No. 1, March 2014. https://civilrightsdata.ed.gov/assets/downloads/CRDC-School-Discipline-Snapshot.pdf.

Van Dyke, Miriam E., Viola Vaccarino, Sandra B. Dunbar, Priscilla Pemu, Gary H. Gibbons, Arshed A. Quyyumi, and Tené Lewis. *Psychoneuroendocrinology* 82 (2017): 9–16.

Vargas, Robert. *Uninsured in Chicago: How the Social Safety Net Leaves Latinos Behind*. New York: New York University Press, 2022.

Vázquez, Adela. "Finding a Home in Transgender Activism in San Francisco." in *Queer Brown Voices: Personal Narratives of Latina/o LGBTQ Activism*, edited by Uriel Quesada, Letitia Gomez, and Salvador Vidal-Ortiz, 212–20. Austin: University of Texas Press, 2015.

Verdery, Katherine. *What Was Socialism and What Comes Next?* Princeton, NJ: Princeton University Press, 1996.

Villarosa, Linda. *Under the Skin: The Hidden Toll of Racism on American Lives and on the Health of Our Nation*. New York: Doubleday, 2022.

Voelkel, J., D. Hellman, R. Sakuma, and Y. Shandas. "Assessing Vulnerability to Urban Heat: A Study of Disproportionate Heat Exposure and Access to Refuge by Socio-Demographic Status in Portland, Oregon." *International Journal of Environmental Research and Public Health* 15 (2018): 640. https://doi.10.3390/ijerph15040640.

Wacquant, Loïc. "Deadly Symbiosis: When Ghetto and Prison Meet and Mesh." *Punishment and Society* 3, no. 1 (2001): 95–134.

Waitzkin, Howard. *Medicine and Public Health at the End of Empire*. New York: Routledge, 2016.

Wakefield, Sarah E.L., and Jamie Baxter. "Linking Health Inequality and Environmental Justice: Articulating a Precautionary Framework for Research and Action." *Environmental Justice* 3, no. 3 (September 2010): 95–102.

Waldron, Ingrid R.G. "The ENRICH Project: Blurring the Borders between Community and the Ivory Tower." *Kalfou* 5, no. 2 (Fall 2018): 394–405.

———. *There's Something in the Water: Environmental Racism in Indigenous and Black Communities*. Winnipeg: Fernwood, 2018.

Walls, Dan, Abby Kinchy, Tal Margalit, Monica D. Ramírez, and Salvatore Engel-Di Mauro. "Confronting Legacy Lead in Soils in the United States: Community-Engaged Researchers Doing Undone Science." *Environmental Science and Policy* 128 (2022): 165–74.

Wang, Kyungsoon. "Housing Instability and Socioeconomic Disparities in Health: Evidence from the U.S. Economic Recession." *Journal of Racial and Ethnic Health Disparities* 9, no. 6 (2022): 2451–67.

———. "Neighborhood Foreclosures and Health Disparities in the U.S. Cities." *Cities* 97 (2020): 1–14.

Washington, Harriet A. *Medical Apartheid: The Dark History of Medical Experimentation on Black Americans from Colonial Times to the Present.* New York: Anchor Books, 2006.

———. *A Terrible Thing to Waste: Environmental Racism and Its Assault on the American Mind.* New York: Little Brown Spark, 2019.

WeCount! *The Human Landscape: Wages and Working Conditions of Plant Nursery Workers in South Miami-Dade County.* Homestead, FL: WeCount!, 2018. https://drive.google.com/file/d/1G-C_X0FQ7kkg-C9qha95pgz_x8t8s-gRv/view?pli=1.

West, Cornel. *Prophesy Deliverance! An Afro-American Revolutionary Christianity.* Philadelphia: Westminster Press, 1982.

Whaley, Rick, and Walter Bresette. *Walleye Warriors: An Effective Alliance against Racism and for the Earth.* Philadelphia: New Society, 1994.

White, Monica. *Freedom Farmers: Agricultural Resistance and the Black Freedom Movement.* Chapel Hill: University of North Carolina Press, 2019.

White, Stephanie, and Olutosin Ojugbele. "Addressing Racial Disparities in Medical Education." *Curriculum in Context* 6, no. 2 (July 2019): 1–6.

Wiggins, Benjamin. *Calculating Race: Racial Discrimination in Risk Assessment.* New York: Oxford University Press, 2020.

Wildeman, Christopher, and Hedwig Lee. "Women's Health in the Era of Mass Incarceration." *Annual Review of Sociology* 47 (2021): 543–65.

Wilkinson, Richard, and Kate Pickett. *The Spirit Level: Why More Equal Societies Almost Always Do Better.* London: Allen Lane, 2009.

Williams, David R., and Chiquita Collins. "Racial Segregation: A Fundamental Cause of Racial Disparities in Health." *Public Health Reports* 116, no. 5 (2001): 404–16.

Williams, David R., Jourdyn A. Lawrence, and Brigette Davis. "Racism and Health: Evidence and Needed Research." *Annual Review of Public Health* 40 (2019): 105–25.

Williams, Kaya Naomi. "Public, Safety, Risk." *Social Justice* 44, no. 1 (2017): 36–62.

Wilson, Bev. "Urban Heat Management and the Legacy of Redlining." *Journal of the American Planning Association* 88, no. 4 (2020): 443–57.

Wilson, Neal J. "Building Equity by Eliminating Lead Poisoning: Prospects for a Green New Deal." Working Paper No. 131, Global Institute for Sustainable Prosperity, August 2021. www.global-isp.org/wp-content/uploads/WP-131.pdf.

Woolf, Steven, Robert E. Johnson, George Fryer Jr., George Rust, and David Satcher. "The Health Impact of Resolving Racial Disparities: An Analysis of U.S. Mortality Data." *American Journal of Public Health* 98, suppl. 1 (September 2008): S26-S28.

Yap, Maureen, Morgan Williams, Lisa Rice, Scott Chang, Peter Christensen, and Stephen M. Dane. *Identifying Bias and Barriers, Promoting Equity: An Analysis of the U.S. PAP Standards and Appraiser Qualifications Criteria*. Washington, DC: National Fair Housing Alliance, 2022.

Yearby, Ruqalijah, Brietta Clark, and José F. Figuroa. "Structural Racism in Historical and Modern U.S. Health Care Policy." *Health Affairs* 41, no. 2 (2022): 187–94.

Index

abandoned dwellings and places, 22, 31, 34, 95, 136, 188–91

Abraham, Heather R., 45–47

Acta Non Verba project, 190

addiction, 154–155

adolescence, 39, 41, 122, 204

adverse early life experiences, 39–41

affirmatively furthering fair housing, 45–47, 59, 121–22, 146, 152

AIDS, 42, 85, 163–69, 173

Affordable Care Act, 155, 220

Africa, 72–73, 85, 161–62, 174

African American Policy Forum, 8, 126

African Canadian, 169–71

alcohol and drug use, 40, 126

algorithms, 3, 16, 151–52

Alliance for California Traditional Arts, 8, 49–52, 178–81

American Academy of Pediatrics, 22, 74, 129, 201

American Association of Medical Colleges, 225

American Friends Service Committee, 135–36, 210

American Housing and Economic Mobility Act, 199

American Medical Association, 69–77

American Public Health Association, 2, 225

anemia, 40, 79, 80

Angola Penitentiary (Louisiana), 175–76

appraisal discrimination, 93–106;

assumptions about demand, 98; comparison model, 98; demographics of profession, 98; effect on Black neighborhoods, 100; effect on Latinx neighborhoods, 100; hiding Black identity from appraisers, 96–98; psychological experiments, 117–18

Army Corps of Engineers, 108

arson, 147

artivistas, 9, 178–81

arts-based mobilizations for health and housing justice, 161–85

Asian American: Asian American Immigrant Women Advocates, 9; Asian Pacific Environmental Network, 79–80; birth rate, 41; breast cancer rate, 80; categorization as high risk group, 74; health mobilization, 79–80; houseless children in New York, 61; Grand Rapids, Michigan, 182; place-related health problems, 63; Richmond, California, 79–80; term, 13, 89; youth in high-opportunity neighborhoods, 60

asthma: among houseless children, 37, 61, 129; associated with lead poisoning, 30; Black/white disparities, 66; childhood incidence in Detroit, 34; childhood incidence in New York City, 37; death rate among Black children, 37, 62; declines in morbidity because of voucher-supported childhood moves to

AMERICAN CROSSROADS

Edited by Earl Lewis, George Lipsitz, George Sánchez, Dana Takagi, Laura Briggs, and Nikhil Pal Singh

Founded in 1893,
UNIVERSITY OF CALIFORNIA PRESS
publishes bold, progressive books and journals
on topics in the arts, humanities, social sciences,
and natural sciences—with a focus on social
justice issues—that inspire thought and action
among readers worldwide.

The UC PRESS FOUNDATION
raises funds to uphold the press's vital role
as an independent, nonprofit publisher, and
receives philanthropic support from a wide
range of individuals and institutions—and from
committed readers like you. To learn more, visit
ucpress.edu/supportus.